Inside Macintosh®
Volume II

Addison-Wesley Publishing Company, Inc.
Reading, Massachusetts   Menlo Park, California   New York
Don Mills, Ontario   Wokingham, England   Amsterdam   Bonn
Sidney   Singapore   Tokyo   Madrid   San Juan   Paris
Seoul   Milan   Mexico City   Taipei

© Apple Computer, Inc., 1985
20525 Mariani Avenue
Cupertino, CA 95014
(408) 996-1010

Apple, the Apple logo, LaserWriter, Lisa, Macintosh, the Macintosh logo, and MacWorks are registered trademarks of Apple Computer, Inc.

MacDraw, MacPaint, and MacWrite are registered trademarks of Claris Corporation.

Simultaneously published in the United States and Canada.

Written by Caroline Rose with Bradley Hacker, Robert Anders, Katie Withey, Mark Metzler, Steve Chernicoff, Chris Espinosa, Andy Averill, Brent Davis, and Brian Howard, assisted by Sandy Tompkins-Leffler and Louella Pizzuti. Special thanks to Cary Clark and Scott Knaster.

This book was produced using the Apple Macintosh computer and the LaserWriter printer.

ISBN 0-201-17732-3
14 15 16 17 18 19 20 - MU - 9594939291
Fourteenth printing, October 1991

Inside Macintosh
Volume II

Contents

PREFACE

ABOUT INSIDE MACINTOSH

Inside Macintosh is a three-volume set of manuals that tells you what you need to know to write software for the Apple® Macintosh™ 128K, 512K, or XL (or a Lisa® running MacWorks™ XL). Although directed mainly toward programmers writing standard Macintosh applications, *Inside Macintosh* also contains the information needed to write simple utility programs, desk accessories, device drivers, or any other Macintosh software. It includes:

■ the user interface guidelines for applications on the Macintosh

■ a complete description of the routines available for your program to call (both those built into the Macintosh and others on disk), along with related concepts and background information

■ a description of the Macintosh 128K and 512K hardware

It does *not* include information about:

■ Programming in general.

■ Getting started as a developer. For this, write to:

> Developer Relations
> Mail Stop 27-S
> Apple Computer, Inc.
> 20525 Mariani Avenue
> Cupertino, CA 95014

■ Any specific development system, except where indicated. You'll need to have additional documentation for the development system you're using.

■ The Standard Apple Numeric Environment (SANE), which your program can access to perform extended-precision floating-point arithmetic and transcendental functions. This environment is described in the *Apple Numerics Manual*.

You should already be familiar with the basic information that's in *Macintosh*, the owner's guide, and have some experience using a standard Macintosh application (such as MacWrite™).

The Language

The routines you'll need to call are written in assembly language, but (with a few exceptions) they're also accessible from high-level languages, such as Pascal on the Lisa Workshop development system. *Inside Macintosh* documents the Lisa Pascal interfaces to the routines and the symbolic names defined for assembly-language programmers using the Lisa Workshop; if you're using a different development system, its documentation should tell you how to apply the information presented here to that system.

Inside Macintosh is intended to serve the needs of both high-level language and assembly-language programmers. Every routine is shown in its Pascal form (if it has one), but assembly-language programmers are told how they can access the routines. Information of interest only to assembly-language programmers is isolated and labeled so that other programmers can conveniently skip it.

Familiarity with Lisa Pascal (or a similar high-level language) is recommended for all readers, since it's used for most examples. Lisa Pascal is described in the documentation for the Lisa Pascal Workshop.

What's in Each Volume

Inside Macintosh consists of three volumes. Volume I begins with the following information of general interest:

- a "road map" to the software and the rest of the documentation

- the user interface guidelines

- an introduction to memory management (the least you need to know, with a complete discussion following in Volume II)

- some general information for assembly-language programmers

It then describes the various parts of the **User Interface Toolbox**, the software in ROM that helps you implement the standard Macintosh user interface in your application. This is followed by descriptions of other, RAM-based software that's similar in function to the User Interface Toolbox. (The software overview in the Road Map chapter gives further details.)

Volume II describes the **Operating System**, the software in ROM that does basic tasks such as input and output, memory management, and interrupt handling. As in Volume I, some functionally similar RAM-based software is then described.

Volume III discusses your program's interface with the Finder and then describes the Macintosh 128K and 512K hardware. A comprehensive summary of all the software is provided, followed by some useful appendices and a glossary of all terms defined in *Inside Macintosh*.

Version Numbers

This edition of *Inside Macintosh* describes the following versions of the software:

- version 105 of the ROM in the Macintosh 128K or 512K

- version 112 of the ROM image installed by MacWorks in the Macintosh XL

- version 1.1 of the Lisa Pascal interfaces and the assembly-language definitions

Some of the RAM-based software is read from the file named System (usually kept in the System Folder). This manual describes the software in the System file whose creation date is May 2, 1984.

A HORSE OF A DIFFERENT COLOR

On an innovative system like the Macintosh, programs don't look quite the way they do on other systems. For example, instead of carrying out a sequence of steps in a predetermined order, your program is driven primarily by user actions (such as clicking and typing) whose order cannot be predicted.

You'll probably find that many of your preconceptions about how to write applications don't apply here. Because of this, and because of the sheer volume of information in *Inside Macintosh*, it's essential that you read the Road Map chapter. It will help you get oriented and figure out where to go next.

THE STRUCTURE OF A TYPICAL CHAPTER

Most chapters of *Inside Macintosh* have the same structure, as described below. Reading through this now will save you a lot of time and effort later on. It contains important hints on how to find what you're looking for within this vast amount of technical documentation.

Every chapter begins with a very brief description of its subject and a list of what you should already know before reading that chapter. Then there's a section called, for example, "About the Window Manager", which gives you more information about the subject, telling you what you can do with it in general, elaborating on related user interface guidelines, and introducing terminology that will be used in the chapter. This is followed by a series of sections describing important related concepts and background information; unless they're noted to be for advanced programmers only, you'll have to read them in order to understand how to use the routines described later.

Before the routine descriptions themselves, there's a section called, for example, "Using the Window Manager". It introduces you to the routines, telling you how they fit into the general flow of an application program and, most important, giving you an idea of which ones you'll need to use. Often you'll need only a few routines out of many to do basic operations; by reading this section, you can save yourself the trouble of learning routines you'll never use.

Then, for the details about the routines, read on to the next section. It gives the calling sequence for each routine and describes all the parameters, effects, side effects, and so on.

Following the routine descriptions, there may be some sections that won't be of interest to all readers. Usually these contain information about advanced techniques, or behind the scenes details for the curious.

For review and quick reference, each chapter ends with a summary of the subject matter, including the entire Pascal interface and a separate section for assembly-language programmers.

CONVENTIONS

The following notations are used in *Inside Macintosh* to draw your attention to particular items of information:

Note: A note that may be interesting or useful

Warning: A point you need to be cautious about

Assembly-language note: A note of interest to assembly-language programmers only

[Not in ROM]

Routines marked with this notation are not part of the Macintosh ROM. Depending on how the interfaces have been set up on the development system you're using, these routines may or may not be available. They're available to users of Lisa Pascal; other users should check the documentation for their development system for more information. (For related information of interest to assembly-language programmers, see chapter 4 of Volume I.)

1 THE MEMORY MANAGER

ABOUT THIS CHAPTER

This chapter describes the Memory Manager, the part of the Macintosh Operating System that controls the dynamic allocation of memory space in the heap.

ABOUT THE MEMORY MANAGER

Using the Memory Manager, your program can maintain one or more independent areas of heap memory (called **heap zones**) and use them to allocate blocks of memory of any desired size. Unlike stack space, which is always allocated and released in strict LIFO (last-in-first-out) order, blocks in the heap can be allocated and released in any order, according to your program's needs. So instead of growing and shrinking in an orderly way like the stack, the heap tends to become fragmented into a patchwork of allocated and free blocks, as shown in Figure 1. The Memory Manager does all the necessary "housekeeping" to keep track of the blocks as it allocates and releases them.

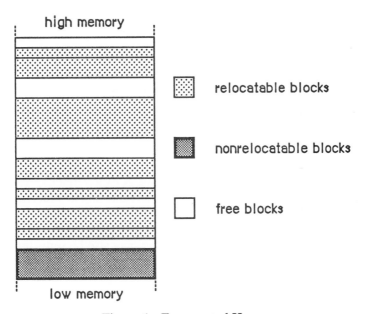

Figure 1. Fragmented Heap

The Memory Manager always maintains at least two heap zones: a **system heap zone** that's used by the Operating System and an **application heap zone** that's used by the Toolbox and your application program. The system heap zone is initialized to a fixed size when the system starts up; typically this size is 16.75K bytes on a Macintosh 128K, and 48K on a Macintosh 512K or XL.

Note: The initial size of the system heap zone is determined by the system startup information stored on a volume; for more information, see the section "Data Organization on Volumes" in chapter 4. The default initial size of this zone depends on the memory size of the machine and may be different in future versions of the Macintosh.

Objects in the system heap zone remain allocated even when one application terminates and another starts up. In contrast, the application heap zone is automatically reinitialized at the start of each new application program, and the contents of any previous application zone are lost.

Assembly-language note: If desired, you can prevent the application heap zone from being reinitialized when an application starts up; see the discussion of the Chain procedure in chapter 2 for details.

The initial size of the application zone is 6K bytes, but it can grow as needed. Your program can create additional heap zones if it chooses, either by subdividing this original application zone or by allocating space on the stack for more heap zones.

Note: In this chapter, unless otherwise stated, the term "application heap zone" (or "application zone") always refers to the original application heap zone provided by the system, before any subdivision.

Your program's code typically resides in the application zone, in space reserved for it at the request of the Segment Loader. Similarly, the Resource Manager requests space in the application zone to hold resources it has read into memory from a resource file. Toolbox routines that create new entities of various kinds, such as NewWindow, NewControl, and NewMenu, also call the Memory Manager to allocate the space they need.

At any given time, there's one **current heap zone**, to which most Memory Manager operations implicitly apply. You can control which heap zone is current by calling a Memory Manager procedure. Whenever the system needs to access its own (system) heap zone, it saves the setting of the current heap zone and restores it later.

Space within a heap zone is divided into contiguous pieces called **blocks**. The blocks in a zone fill it completely: Every byte in the zone is part of exactly one block, which may be either **allocated** (reserved for use) or **free** (available for allocation). Each block has a **block header** for the Memory Manager's own use, followed by the block's **contents**, the area available for use by your application or the system (see Figure 2). There may also be some unused bytes at the end of the block, beyond the end of the contents. A block can be of any size, limited only by the size of the heap zone itself.

Assembly-language note: Blocks are always aligned on even word boundaries, so you can access them with word (.W) and long-word (.L) instructions.

An allocated block may be **relocatable** or **nonrelocatable**. Relocatable blocks can be moved around within the heap zone to create space for other blocks; nonrelocatable blocks can never be moved. These are permanent properties of a block. If relocatable, a block may be **locked** or **unlocked**; if unlocked, it may be **purgeable** or **unpurgeable**. These attributes can be set and changed as necessary. Locking a relocatable block prevents it from being moved. Making a block purgeable allows the Memory Manager to remove it from the heap zone, if necessary, to

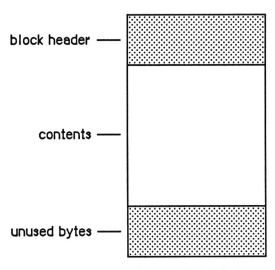

Figure 2. A Block

make room for another block. (Purging of blocks is discussed further below under "How Heap Space Is Allocated".) A newly allocated relocatable block is initially unlocked and unpurgeable.

Relocatable blocks are moved only by the Memory Manager, and only at well-defined, predictable times. In particular, only the routines listed in Appendix B can cause blocks to move, and these routines can never be called from within an interrupt. If your program doesn't call these routines, you can rely on blocks not being moved.

POINTERS AND HANDLES

Relocatable and nonrelocatable blocks are referred to in different ways: nonrelocatable blocks by pointers, relocatable blocks by handles. When the Memory Manager allocates a new block, it returns a pointer or handle to the contents of the block (not to the block's header) depending on whether the block is nonrelocatable (Figure 3) or relocatable (Figure 4).

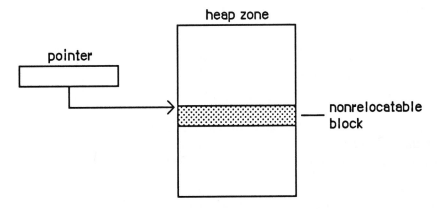

Figure 3. A Pointer to a Nonrelocatable Block

A pointer to a nonrelocatable block never changes, since the block itself can't move. A pointer to a relocatable block can change, however, since the block can move. For this reason, the Memory Manager maintains a single nonrelocatable **master pointer** to each relocatable block. The master pointer is created at the same time as the block and set to point to it. When you allocate a relocatable block, the Memory Manager returns a pointer to the master pointer, called a **handle** to the block (see Figure 4). If the Memory Manager later has to move the block, it has only to update the master pointer to point to the block's new location.

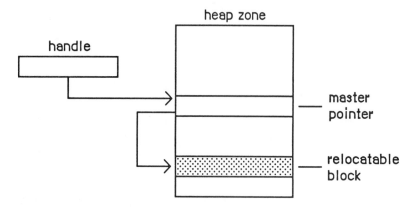

Figure 4. A Handle to a Relocatable Block

HOW HEAP SPACE IS ALLOCATED

The Memory Manager allocates space for relocatable blocks according to a "first fit" strategy. It looks for a free block of at least the requested size, scanning forward from the end of the last block allocated and "wrapping around" from the top of the zone to the bottom if necessary. As soon as it finds a free block big enough, it allocates the requested number of bytes from that block.

If a single free block can't be found that's big enough, the Memory Manager will try to create the needed space by **compacting** the heap zone: moving allocated blocks together in order to collect the free space into a single larger block. Only relocatable, unlocked blocks are moved. The compaction continues until either a free block of at least the requested size has been created or the entire heap zone has been compacted. Figure 5 illustrates what happens when the entire heap must be compacted to create a large enough free block.

Nonrelocatable blocks (and relocatable ones that are temporarily locked) interfere with the compaction process by forming immovable "islands" in the heap. This can prevent free blocks from being collected together and lead to fragmentation of the available free space, as shown in Figure 6. (Notice that the Memory Manager will never move a relocatable block around a nonrelocatable block.) To minimize this problem, the Memory Manager tries to keep all the nonrelocatable blocks together at the bottom of the heap zone. When you allocate a nonrelocatable block, the Memory Manager will try to make room for the new block near the bottom of the zone, by moving other blocks upward, expanding the zone, or purging blocks from it (see below).

Warning: To avoid heap fragmentation, use relocatable instead of nonrelocatable blocks.

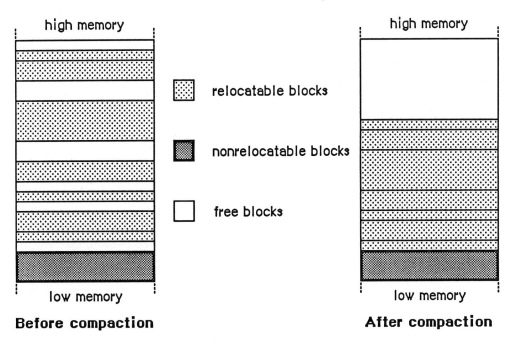

Figure 5. Heap Compaction

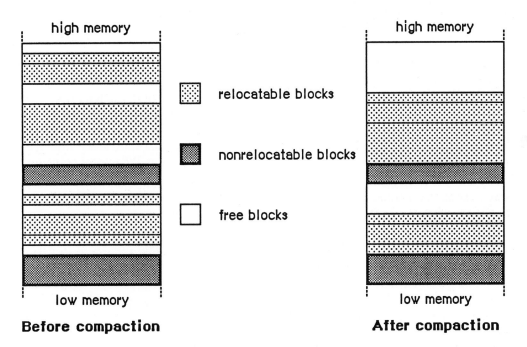

Figure 6. Fragmentation of Free Space

If the Memory Manager can't satisfy the allocation request after compacting the entire heap zone, it next tries expanding the zone by the requested number of bytes (rounded up to the nearest 1K bytes). Only the original application zone can be expanded, and only up to a certain limit (discussed more fully under "The Stack and the Heap"). If any other zone is current, or if the application zone has already reached or exceeded its limit, this step is skipped.

Next the Memory Manager tries to free space by **purging** blocks from the zone. Only relocatable blocks can be purged, and then only if they're explicitly marked as unlocked and purgeable. Purging a block removes it from its heap zone and frees the space it occupies. The space occupied by the block's master pointer itself remains allocated, but the master pointer is set to NIL. Any handles to the block now point to a NIL master pointer, and are said to be **empty**. If your program later needs to refer to the purged block, it must detect that the handle has become empty and ask the Memory Manager to **reallocate** the block. This operation updates the master pointer (see Figure 7).

> **Warning:** Reallocating a block recovers only its space, not its contents (which were lost when the block was purged). It's up to your program to reconstitute the block's contents.

Finally, if all else fails, the Memory Manager calls the **grow zone function**, if any, for the current heap zone. This is an optional routine that an application can provide to take any last-ditch measures to try to "grow" the zone by freeing some space in it. The grow zone function can try to create additional free space by purging blocks that were previously marked unpurgeable, unlocking previously locked blocks, and so on. The Memory Manager will call the grow zone function repeatedly, compacting the heap again after each call, until either it finds the space it's looking for or the grow zone function has exhausted all possibilities. In the latter case, the Memory Manager will finally give up and report that it's unable to satisfy the allocation request.

> **Note:** The Memory Manager moves a block by copying the entire block to a new location; it won't "slide" a block up or down in memory. If there isn't free space at least as large as the block, the block is effectively not relocatable.

Dereferencing a Handle

Accessing a block by double indirection, through its handle instead of through its master pointer, requires an extra memory reference. For efficiency, you may sometimes want to **dereference** the handle—that is, make a copy of the block's master pointer, and then use that pointer to access the block by single indirection. But *be careful!* Any operation that allocates space from the heap may cause the underlying block to be moved or purged. In that event, the master pointer itself will be correctly updated, but your copy of it will be left dangling.

One way to avoid this common type of program bug is to lock the block before dereferencing its handle. For example:

```
VAR  aPointer: Ptr;
     aHandle: Handle;
     . . .

aHandle := NewHandle(...);     {create relocatable block}
. . .
HLock(aHandle);                {lock before dereferencing}
aPointer := aHandle^;          {dereference handle}
WHILE ... DO
  BEGIN
  ...aPointer^...              {use simple pointer}
  END;
HUnlock(aHandle)               {unlock block when finished}
```

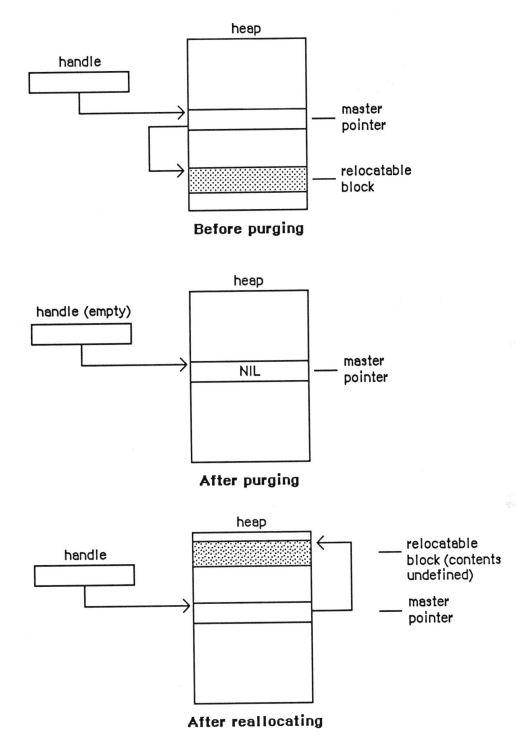

Figure 7. Purging and Reallocating a Block

Assembly-language note: To dereference a handle in assembly language, just copy the master pointer into an address register and use it to access the block by single indirection.

Remember, however, that when you lock a block it becomes an "island" in the heap that may interfere with compaction and cause free space to become fragmented. It's recommended that you use this technique only in parts of your program where efficiency is critical, such as inside tight inner loops that are executed many times (and that don't allocate other blocks).

Warning: Don't forget to unlock the block again when you're through with the dereferenced handle.

Instead of locking the block, you can update your copy of the master pointer after any "dangerous" operation (one that can invalidate the pointer by moving or purging the block it points to). For a complete list of all routines that may move or purge blocks, see Appendix B.

The Lisa Pascal compiler frequently dereferences handles during its normal operation. You should take care to write code that will protect you when the compiler dereferences handles in the following cases:

- Use of the WITH statement with a handle, such as

```
WITH aHandle^^ DO ...
```

- Assigning the result of a function that can move or purge blocks (or of any function in a package or another segment) to a field in a record referred to by a handle, such as

```
aHandle^^.field := NewHandle(...)
```

A problem may arise because the compiler generates code that dereferences the handle before calling NewHandle—and NewHandle may move the block containing the field.

- Passing an argument of more than four bytes referred to by a handle, to a routine that can move or purge a block or to any routine in a package or another segment. For example:

```
TEUpdate(hTE^^.viewRect,hTE)
```

or

```
DrawString(theControl^^.contrlTitle)
```

You can avoid having the compiler generate and use dangling pointers by locking a block before you use its handle in the above situations. Or you can use temporary variables, as in the following:

```
temp := NewHandle(...);
aHandle^^.field := temp
```

THE STACK AND THE HEAP

The LIFO nature of the stack makes it particularly convenient for memory allocation connected with the activation and deactivation of routines (procedures and functions). Each time a routine is called, space is allocated for a **stack frame**. The stack frame holds the routine's parameters, local variables, and return address. Upon exit from the routine, the stack frame is released, restoring the stack to the same state it was in when the routine was called.

In Lisa Pascal, all stack management is done by the compiler. When you call a routine, the compiler generates code to reserve space if necessary for a function result, place the parameter values and return link on the stack, and jump to the routine. The routine can then allocate space on the stack for its own local variables.

Before returning, the routine releases the stack space occupied by its local variables, return link, and parameters. If the routine is a function, it leave its result on the stack for the calling program.

The application heap zone and the stack share the same area in memory, growing toward each other from opposite ends (see Figure 8). Naturally it would be disastrous for either to grow so far that it collides with the other. To help prevent such collisions, the Memory Manager enforces a limit on how far the application heap zone can grow toward the stack. Your program can set this **application heap limit** to control the allotment of available space between the stack and the heap.

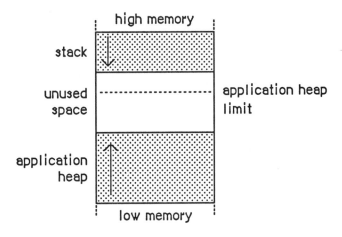

Figure 8. The Stack and the Heap

The application heap limit marks the boundary between the space available for the application heap zone and the space reserved exclusively for the stack. At the start of each application program, the limit is initialized to allow 8K bytes for the stack. Depending on your program's needs, you can adjust the limit to allow more heap space at the expense of the stack or vice versa.

Assembly-language note: The global variables DefltStack and MinStack contain the default and minimum sizes of the stack, respectively.

Notice that the limit applies only to expansion of the *heap*; it has no effect on how far the *stack* can expand. Athough the heap can never expand beyond the limit into space reserved for the stack, there's nothing to prevent the stack from crossing the limit. It's up to you to set the limit low enough to allow for the maximum stack depth your program will ever need.

Note: Regardless of the limit setting, the application zone is never allowed to grow to within 1K of the current end of the stack. This gives a little extra protection in case the stack is approaching the boundary or has crossed over onto the heap's side, and allows some safety margin for the stack to expand even further.

To help detect collisions between the stack and the heap, a "stack sniffer" routine is run sixty times a second, during the Macintosh's vertical retrace interrupt. This routine compares the current ends of the stack and the heap and invokes the System Error Handler in case of a collision.

The stack sniffer can't prevent collisions, it can only detect them after the fact: A lot of computation can take place in a sixtieth of a second. In fact, the stack can easily expand into the heap, overwrite it, and then shrink back again before the next activation of the stack sniffer, escaping detection completely. The stack sniffer is useful mainly during software development; the alert box the System Error Handler displays can be confusing to your program's end user. Its purpose is to warn you, the programmer, that your program's stack and heap are colliding, so that you can adjust the heap limit to correct the problem before the user ever encounters it.

GENERAL-PURPOSE DATA TYPES

The Memory Manager includes a number of type definitions for general-purpose use. The types listed below are explained in chapter 3 of Volume I.

```
TYPE   SignedByte = -128..127;
       Byte       = 0..255;
       Ptr        = ^SignedByte;
       Handle     = ^Ptr;

       Str255       = STRING[255];
       StringPtr    = ^Str255;
       StringHandle = ^StringPtr;

       ProcPtr = Ptr;

       Fixed = LONGINT;
```

For specifying the sizes of blocks in the heap, the Memory Manager defines a special type called Size:

```
TYPE Size = LONGINT;
```

All Memory Manager routines that deal with block sizes expect parameters of type Size or return them as results.

MEMORY ORGANIZATION

This section discusses the organization of memory in the Macintosh 128K, 512K, and XL.

Note: The information presented in this section may be different in future versions of Macintosh system software.

The organization of the Macintosh 128K and 512K RAM is shown in Figure 9. The variable names listed on the right in the figure refer to global variables for use by assembly-language programmers.

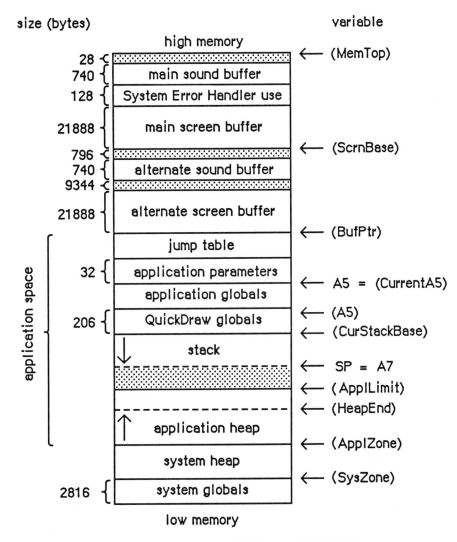

Figure 9. Macintosh 128K and 512K RAM

Assembly-language note: The global variables, shown in parentheses, contain the addresses of the indicated areas. Names identified as marking the end of an area actually refer to the address *following* the last byte in that area.

The lowest 2816 bytes are used for system globals. Immediately following this are the system heap and the **application space**, which is memory available for dynamic allocation by applications. Most of the application space is shared between the stack and the application heap, with the heap growing forward from the bottom of the space and the stack growing backward from the top. The remainder of the application space is occupied by QuickDraw global variables, the application's global variables, the application parameters, and the jump table. The **application parameters** are 32 bytes of memory located above the application globals; they're reserved for use by the system. The first application parameter is the address of the first QuickDraw global variable (thePort). The jump table is explained in chapter 2.

Note: Some development systems may place the QuickDraw global variables in a different location, but the first application parameter will always point to them.

Assembly-language note: The location pointed to by register A5 will always point to the first QuickDraw global variable.

At (almost) the very end of memory are the main sound buffer, used by the Sound Driver to control the sounds emitted by the built-in speaker and by the Disk Driver to control disk motor speed, and the main screen buffer, which holds the bit image to be displayed on the Macintosh screen. The area between the main screen and sound buffers is used by the System Error Handler.

There are alternate screen and sound buffers for special applications. If you use either or both of these, the memory available for use by your application is reduced accordingly. The Segment Loader provides routines for specifying that an alternate screen or sound buffer will be used.

Note: The alternate screen and sound buffers may not be supported in future versions of the Macintosh. The main and alternate sound buffers, as well as the alternate screen buffer, are not supported on the Macintosh XL.

The memory organization of a Macintosh XL is shown in Figure 10.

MEMORY MANAGER DATA STRUCTURES

This section discusses the internal data structures of the Memory Manager. You don't need to know this information if you're just using the Memory Manager routinely to allocate and release blocks of memory from the application heap zone.

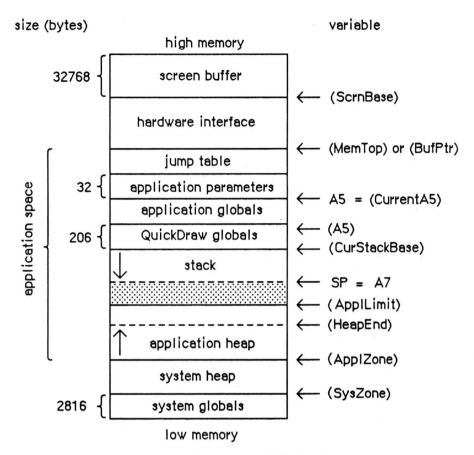

Figure 10. Macintosh XL RAM

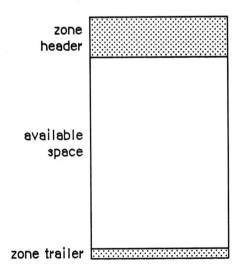

Figure 11. Structure of a Heap Zone

Structure of Heap Zones

Each heap zone begins with a 52-byte **zone header** and ends with a 12-byte **zone trailer** (see Figure 11). The header contains all the information the Memory Manager needs about that heap zone; the trailer is just a minimum-size free block (described in the next section) placed at the end of the zone as a marker. All the remaining space between the header and trailer is available for allocation.

In Pascal, a heap zone is defined as a **zone record** of type Zone. It's always referred to with a **zone pointer** of type THz ("the heap zone"):

```
TYPE  THz = ^Zone;
      Zone = RECORD
                bkLim:       Ptr;       {zone trailer block}
                purgePtr:    Ptr;       {used internally}
                hFstFree:    Ptr;       {first free master pointer}
                zcbFree:     LONGINT;   {number of free bytes}
                gzProc:      ProcPtr;   {grow zone function}
                moreMast:    INTEGER;   {master pointers to allocate}
                flags:       INTEGER;   {used internally}
                cntRel:      INTEGER;   {not used}
                maxRel:      INTEGER;   {not used}
                cntNRel:     INTEGER;   {not used}
                maxNRel:     INTEGER;   {not used}
                cntEmpty:    INTEGER;   {not used}
                cntHandles:  INTEGER;   {not used}
                minCBFree:   LONGINT;   {not used}
                purgeProc:   ProcPtr;   {purge warning procedure}
                sparePtr:    Ptr;       {used internally}
                allocPtr:    Ptr;       {used internally}
                heapData:    INTEGER    {first usable byte in zone}
             END;
```

> **Warning:** The fields of the zone header are for the Memory Manager's own internal use. You can examine the contents of the zone's fields, but in general it doesn't make sense for your program to try to change them. The few exceptions are noted below in the discussions of the specific fields.

BkLim is a pointer to the zone's trailer block. Since the trailer is the last block in the zone, bkLim is a pointer to the byte *following* the last byte of usable space in the zone.

HFstFree is a pointer to the first free master pointer in the zone. Instead of just allocating space for one master pointer each time a relocatable block is created, the Memory Manager "preallocates" several master pointers at a time; as a group they form a nonrelocatable block. The moreMast field of the zone record tells the Memory Manager how many master pointers at a time to preallocate for this zone.

> **Note:** Master pointers are allocated 32 at a time for the system heap zone and 64 at a time for the application zone; this may be different on future versions of the Macintosh.

All master pointers that are allocated but not currently in use are linked together into a list beginning in the hFstFree field. When you allocate a new relocatable block, the Memory

Manager removes the first available master pointer from this list, sets it to point to the new block, and returns its address to you as a handle to the block. (If the list is empty, it allocates a fresh block of moreMast master pointers.) When you release a relocatable block, its master pointer isn't released, but is linked onto the beginning of the list to be reused. Thus the amount of space devoted to master pointers can increase, but can never decrease until the zone is reinitialized.

The zcbFree field always contains the number of free bytes remaining in the zone. As blocks are allocated and released, the Memory Manager adjusts zcbFree accordingly. This number represents an upper limit on the size of block you can allocate from this heap zone.

> **Warning:** It may not actually be possible to allocate a block as big as zcbFree bytes. Because nonrelocatable and locked blocks can't be moved, it isn't always possible to collect all the free space into a single block by compaction.

The gzProc field is a pointer to the grow zone function. You can supply a pointer to your own grow zone function when you create a new heap zone and can change it at any time.

> **Warning:** Don't store directly into the gzProc field; if you want to supply your own grow zone function, you must do so with a procedure call (InitZone or SetGrowZone).

PurgeProc is a pointer to the zone's **purge warning procedure,** or NIL if there is none. The Memory Manager will call this procedure before it purges a block from the zone.

> **Warning:** Whenever you call the Resource Manager with SetResPurge(TRUE), it installs its own purge warning procedure, overriding any purge warning procedure you've specified to the Memory Manager; for further details, see chapter 5 of Volume I.

The last field of a zone record, heapData, is a dummy field marking the bottom of the zone's usable memory space. HeapData nominally contains an integer, but this integer has no significance in itself—it's just the first two bytes in the block header of the first block in the zone. The purpose of the heapData field is to give you a way of locating the effective bottom of the zone. For example, if myZone is a zone pointer, then

```
@(myZone^.heapData)
```

is a pointer to the first usable byte in the zone, just as

```
myZone^.bkLim
```

is a pointer to the byte following the last usable byte in the zone.

Structure of Blocks

Every block in a heap zone, whether allocated or free, has a block header that the Memory Manager uses to find its way around in the zone. Block headers are completely transparent to your program. All pointers and handles to allocated blocks point to the beginning of the block's contents, following the end of the header. Similarly, all block sizes seen by your program refer to the block's **logical size** (the number of bytes in its contents) rather than its **physical size** (the number of bytes it actually occupies in memory, including the header and any unused bytes at the end of the block).

Since your program shouldn't normally have to deal with block headers directly, there's no Pascal record type defining their structure. A block header consists of eight bytes, as shown in Figure 12.

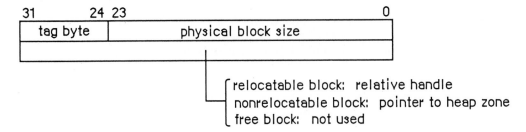

Figure 12. Block Header

The first byte of the block header is the tag byte, discussed below. The next three bytes contain the block's physical size in bytes. Adding this number to the block's address gives the address of the next block in the zone.

The contents of the second long word (four bytes) in the block header depend on the type of block. For relocatable blocks, it contains the block's **relative handle**: a pointer to the block's master pointer, expressed as an offset relative to the start of the heap zone rather than as an absolute memory address. Adding the relative handle to the zone pointer produces a true handle for this block. For nonrelocatable blocks, the second long word of the header is just a pointer to the block's zone. For free blocks, these four bytes are unused.

The structure of a tag byte is shown in Figure 13.

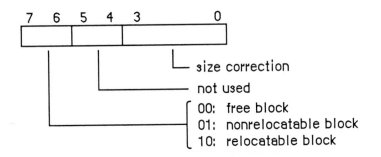

Figure 13. Tag Byte

Assembly-language note: You can use the global constants tyBkFree, tyBkNRel, and tyBkRel to test whether the value of the tag byte indicates a free, nonrelocatable, or relocatable block, respectively.

The "size correction" in the tag byte of a block header is the number of unused bytes at the end of the block, beyond the end of the block's contents. It's equal to the difference between the block's logical and physical sizes, excluding the eight bytes of overhead for the block header:

physicalSize = logicalSize + sizeCorrection + 8

There are two reasons why a block may contain such unused bytes:

■ The Memory Manager allocates space only in even numbers of bytes. If the block's logical size is odd, an extra, unused byte is added at the end to keep the physical size even.

■ The minimum number of bytes in a block is 12. This minimum applies to all blocks, free as well as allocated. If allocating the required number of bytes from a free block would leave a fragment of fewer than 12 free bytes, the leftover bytes are included unused at the end of the newly allocated block instead of being returned to free storage.

Structure of Master Pointers

The master pointer to a relocatable block has the structure shown in Figure 14. The low-order three bytes of the long word contain the address of the block's contents. The high-order byte contains some flag bits that specify the block's current status. Bit 7 of this byte is the **lock bit** (1 if the block is locked, 0 if it's unlocked); bit 6 is the **purge bit** (1 if the block is purgeable, 0 if it's unpurgeable). Bit 5 is used by the Resource Manager to identify blocks containing resource information; such blocks are marked by a 1 in this bit.

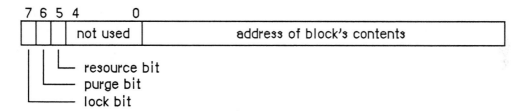

Figure 14. Structure of a Master Pointer

Warning: Note that the flag bits in the high-order byte have numerical significance in any operation performed on a master pointer. For example, the lock bit is also the sign bit.

Assembly-language note: You can use the mask in the global variable Lo3Bytes to determine the value of the low-order three bytes of a master pointer. To determine the value of bits 5, 6, and 7, you can use the global constants resourc, purge, and lock, respectively.

USING THE MEMORY MANAGER

There's ordinarily no need to initialize the Memory Manager before using it. The system heap zone is automatically initialized each time the system starts up, and the application heap zone each time an application program starts up. In the unlikely event that you need to reinitialize the application zone while your program is running, you can call InitApplZone.

When your application starts up, it should allocate the memory it requires in the most space-efficient manner possible, ensuring that most of the nonrelocatable blocks it will need are packed together at the bottom of the heap. The main segment of your program should call the

MaxApplZone procedure, which expands the application heap zone to its limit. Then call the procedure MoreMasters repeatedly to allocate as many blocks of master pointers as your application and any desk accessories will need. Next initialize QuickDraw and the Window Manager (if you're going to use it).

To allocate a new relocatable block, use NewHandle; for a nonrelocatable block, use NewPtr. These functions return a handle or a pointer, as the case may be, to the newly allocated block. To release a block when you're finished with it, use DisposHandle or DisposPtr.

You can also change the size of an already allocated block with SetHandleSize or SetPtrSize, and find out its current size with GetHandleSize or GetPtrSize. Use HLock and HUnlock to lock and unlock relocatable blocks. Before locking a relocatable block, call MoveHHi.

> **Note:** If you lock a relocatable block, unlock it at the earliest possible opportunity. Before allocating a block that you know will be locked for long periods of time, call ResrvMem to make room for the block as near as possible to the bottom of the zone.

In some situations it may be desirable to determine the handle that points to a given master pointer. To do this you can call the RecoverHandle function. For example, a relocatable block of code might want to find out the handle that refers to it, so it can lock itself down in the heap.

Ordinarily, you shouldn't have to worry about compacting the heap or purging blocks from it; the Memory Manager automatically takes care of this for you. You can control which blocks are purgeable with HPurge and HNoPurge. If for some reason you want to compact or purge the heap explicitly, you can do so with CompactMem or PurgeMem. To explicitly purge a specific block, use EmptyHandle.

> **Warning:** Before attempting to access any purgeable block, you must check its handle to make sure the block is still allocated. If the handle is empty, then the block has been purged; before accessing it, you have to reallocate it by calling ReallocHandle, and then recreate its contents. (If it's a resource block, just call the Resource Manager procedure LoadResource; it checks the handle and reads the resource into memory if it's not already in memory.)

You can find out how much free space is left in a heap zone by calling FreeMem (to get the total number of free bytes) or MaxMem (to get the size of the largest single free block and the maximum amount by which the zone can grow). Beware: MaxMem compacts the entire zone and purges all purgeable blocks. To determine the current application heap limit, use GetApplLimit; to limit the growth of the application zone, use SetApplLimit. To install a grow zone function to help the Memory Manager allocate space in a zone, use SetGrowZone.

You can create additional heap zones for your program's own use, either within the original application zone or in the stack, with InitZone. If you do maintain more than one heap zone, you can find out which zone is current at any given time with GetZone and switch from one to another with SetZone. Almost all Memory Manager operations implicitly apply to the current heap zone. To refer to the system heap zone or the (original) application heap zone, use the Memory Manager function SystemZone or ApplicZone. To find out which zone a particular block resides in, use HandleZone (if the block is relocatable) or PtrZone (if it's nonrelocatable).

> **Warning:** Be sure, when calling routines that access blocks, that the zone in which the block is located is the current zone.

Note: Most applications will just use the original application heap zone and never have to worry about which zone is current.

After calling any Memory Manager routine, you can determine whether it was successfully completed or failed, by calling MemError.

Warning: Code that will be executed via an interrupt must not make any calls to the Memory Manager, directly or indirectly, and can't depend on handles to unlocked blocks being valid.

MEMORY MANAGER ROUTINES

In addition to their normal results, many Memory Manager routines yield a result code that you can examine by calling the MemError function. The description of each routine includes a list of all result codes it may yield.

Assembly-language note: When called from assembly language, not all Memory Manager routines return a result code. Those that do always leave it as a word-length quantity in the low-order word of register D0 on return from the trap. However, some routines leave something else there instead; see the descriptions of individual routines for details. Just before returning, the trap dispatcher tests the low-order word of D0 with a TST.W instruction, so that on return from the trap the condition codes reflect the status of the result code, if any.

The stack-based interface routines called from Pascal always yield a result code. If the underlying trap doesn't return one, the interface routine "manufactures" a result code of noErr and stores it where it can later be accessed with MemError.

Assembly-language note: You can specify that some Memory Manager routines apply to the system heap zone instead of the current zone by setting bit 10 of the routine trap word. If you're using the Lisa Workshop Assembler, you do this by supplying the word SYS (uppercase) as the second argument to the routine macro:

```
_FreeMem ,SYS
```

If you want a block of memory to be cleared to zeroes when it's allocated by a NewPtr or NewHandle call, set bit 9 of the routine trap word. You can do this by supplying the word CLEAR (uppercase) as the second argument to the routine macro:

```
_NewHandle ,CLEAR
```

You can combine SYS and CLEAR in the same macro call, but SYS must come first:

```
_NewHandle ,SYS,CLEAR
```

The description of each routine lists whether SYS or CLEAR is applicable. (The syntax shown above and in the routine descriptions applies to the Lisa Workshop Assembler; programmers using another development system should consult its documentation for the proper syntax.)

Initialization and Allocation

PROCEDURE InitApplZone;

Trap macro	_InitApplZone
On exit	D0: result code (word)

InitApplZone initializes the application heap zone and makes it the current zone. The contents of any previous application zone are lost; all previously existing blocks in that zone are discarded. The zone's grow zone function is set to NIL. InitApplZone is called by the Segment Loader when starting up an application; you shouldn't normally need to call it.

> **Warning:** Reinitializing the application zone from within a running program is tricky, since the program's code itself normally resides in the application zone. To do it safely, the code containing the InitApplZone call cannot be in the application zone.

Result codes   noErr   No error

PROCEDURE SetApplBase (startPtr: Ptr);

Trap macro	_SetAppBase
On entry	A0: startPtr (pointer)
On exit	D0: result code (word)

SetApplBase changes the starting address of the application heap zone to the address designated by startPtr, and then calls InitApplZone. SetApplBase is normally called only by the system itself; you should never need to call this procedure.

Since the application heap zone begins immediately following the end of the system zone, changing its starting address has the effect of changing the size of the system zone. The system zone can be made larger, but never smaller; if startPtr points to an address lower than the current end of the system zone, it's ignored and the application zone's starting address is left unchanged.

> **Warning:** Like InitApplZone, SetApplBase is a tricky operation, because the program's code itself normally resides in the application heap zone. To do it safely, the code containing the SetApplBase call cannot be in the application zone.

Result codes   noErr   No error

```
PROCEDURE InitZone (pGrowZone: ProcPtr; cMoreMasters: INTEGER;
        limitPtr,startPtr: Ptr);
```

Trap macro	_InitZone		
On entry	A0:	pointer to parameter block	
Parameter block			
	0	startPtr	pointer
	4	limitPtr	pointer
	8	cMoreMasters	word
	10	pGrowZone	pointer
On exit	D0:	result code (word)	

InitZone creates a new heap zone, initializes its header and trailer, and makes it the current zone. The startPtr parameter is a pointer to the first byte of the new zone; limitPtr points to the first byte beyond the end of the zone. The new zone will occupy memory addresses from ORD(startPtr) through ORD(limitPtr)–1.

CMoreMasters tells how many master pointers should be allocated at a time for the new zone. This number of master pointers are created initially; should more be needed later, they'll be added in increments of this same number.

The pGrowZone parameter is a pointer to the grow zone function for the new zone, if any. If you're not defining a grow zone function for this zone, pass NIL.

The new zone includes a 52-byte header and a 12-byte trailer, so its actual usable space runs from ORD(startPtr)+52 through ORD(limitPtr)–13. In addition, there's an eight-byte header for the master pointer block, as well as four bytes for each master pointer, within this usable area. Thus the total available space in the zone, in bytes, is initially

$$ORD(limitPtr) - ORD(startPtr) - 64 - (8 + (4*cMoreMasters))$$

This number must not be less than 0. Note that the amount of available space in the zone will decrease as more master pointers are allocated.

Result codes	noErr	No error

```
FUNCTION GetApplLimit : Ptr;   [Not in ROM]
```

GetApplLimit returns the current application heap limit. It can be used in conjunction with SetApplLimit, described below, to determine and then change the application heap limit.

Assembly-language note: The global variable ApplLimit contains the current application heap limit.

```
PROCEDURE SetApplLimit (zoneLimit: Ptr);
```

Trap macro	_SetApplLimit
On entry	A0: zoneLimit (pointer)
On exit	D0: result code (word)

SetApplLimit sets the application heap limit, beyond which the application heap can't be expanded. The actual expansion isn't under your program's control, but is done automatically by the Memory Manager when necessary to satisfy allocation requests. Only the original application zone can be expanded.

ZoneLimit is a pointer to a byte in memory beyond which the zone will not be allowed to grow. The zone can grow to include the byte *preceding* zoneLimit in memory, but no farther. If the zone already extends beyond the specified limit it won't be cut back, but it will be prevented from growing any more.

Warning: Notice that zoneLimit is *not* a byte count. To limit the application zone to a particular size (say 8K bytes), you have to write something like

```
SetApplLimit(Ptr(ApplicZone)+8192)
```

The Memory Manager function ApplicZone is explained below.

Assembly-language note: You can just store the new application heap limit in the global variable ApplLimit.

Result codes	noErr	No error
	memFullErr	Not enough room in heap zone

```
PROCEDURE MaxApplZone;    [Not in ROM]
```

MaxApplZone expands the application heap zone to the application heap limit without purging any blocks currently in the zone. If the zone already extends to the limit, it won't be changed.

Assembly-language note: To expand the application heap zone to the application heap limit from assembly language, call this Pascal procedure from your program.

Result codes	noErr	No error

```
PROCEDURE MoreMasters;
```

Trap macro	_MoreMasters

MoreMasters allocates another block of master pointers in the current heap zone. This procedure is usually called very early in an application.

Result codes	noErr	No error
	memFullErr	Not enough room in heap zone

Heap Zone Access

```
FUNCTION GetZone : THz;
```

Trap macro	_GetZone
On exit	A0: function result (pointer)
	D0: result code (word)

GetZone returns a pointer to the current heap zone.

> **Assembly-language note:** The global variable TheZone contains a pointer to the current heap zone.

Result codes	noErr	No error

```
PROCEDURE SetZone (hz: THz);
```

Trap macro	_SetZone
On entry	A0: hz (pointer)
On exit	D0: result code (word)

SetZone sets the current heap zone to the zone pointed to by hz.

> **Assembly-language note:** You can set the current heap zone by storing a pointer to it in the global variable TheZone.

Result codes	noErr	No error

```
FUNCTION SystemZone : THz;    [Not in ROM]
```

SystemZone returns a pointer to the system heap zone.

Assembly-language note: The global variable SysZone contains a pointer to the system heap zone.

```
FUNCTION ApplicZone : THz;    [Not in ROM]
```

ApplicZone returns a pointer to the original application heap zone.

Assembly-language note: The global variable ApplZone contains a pointer to the original application heap zone.

Allocating and Releasing Relocatable Blocks

```
FUNCTION NewHandle (logicalSize: Size) : Handle;
```

Trap macro	_NewHandle	
	_NewHandle ,SYS	(applies to system heap)
	_NewHandle ,CLEAR	(clears allocated block)
	_NewHandle ,SYS,CLEAR	(applies to system heap and clears allocated block)
On entry	D0: logicalSize (long word)	
On exit	A0: function result (handle)	
	D0: result code (word)	

NewHandle attempts to allocate a new relocatable block of logicalSize bytes from the current heap zone and then return a handle to it. The new block will be unlocked and unpurgeable. If logicalSize bytes can't be allocated, NewHandle returns NIL.

NewHandle will pursue all available avenues to create a free block of the requested size, including compacting the heap zone, increasing its size, purging blocks from it, and calling its grow zone function, if any.

Result codes	noErr	No error
	memFullErr	Not enough room in heap zone

```
PROCEDURE DisposHandle (h: Handle);
```

Trap macro	_DisposHandle
On entry	A0: h (handle)
On exit	D0: result code (word)

DisposHandle releases the memory occupied by the relocatable block whose handle is h.

Warning: After a call to DisposHandle, all handles to the released block become invalid and should not be used again. Any subsequent calls to DisposHandle using an invalid handle will damage the master pointer list.

Result codes	noErr	No error
	memWZErr	Attempt to operate on a free block

```
FUNCTION GetHandleSize (h: Handle) : Size;
```

Trap macro	_GetHandleSize
On entry	A0: h (handle)
On exit	D0: if >= 0, function result (long word)
	if < 0, result code (word)

GetHandleSize returns the logical size, in bytes, of the relocatable block whose handle is h. In case of an error, GetHandleSize returns 0.

Assembly-language note: Recall that the trap dispatcher sets the condition codes before returning from a trap by testing the low-order word of register D0 with a TST.W instruction. Since the block size returned in D0 by _GetHandleSize is a full 32-bit long word, the word-length test sets the condition codes incorrectly in this case. To branch on the contents of D0, use your own TST.L instruction on return from the trap to test the full 32 bits of the register.

Result codes	noErr	No error [Pascal only]
	nilHandleErr	NIL master pointer
	memWZErr	Attempt to operate on a free block

```
PROCEDURE SetHandleSize (h: Handle; newSize: Size);
```

Trap macro	_SetHandleSize
On entry	A0: h (handle)
	D0: newSize (long word)
On exit	D0: result code (word)

SetHandleSize changes the logical size of the relocatable block whose handle is h to newSize bytes.

Note: Be prepared for an attempt to increase the size of a locked block to fail, since there may be a block above it that's either nonrelocatable or locked.

Result codes	noErr	No error
	memFullErr	Not enough room in heap zone
	nilHandleErr	NIL master pointer
	memWZErr	Attempt to operate on a free block

```
FUNCTION HandleZone (h: Handle) : THz;
```

Trap macro	_HandleZone
On entry	A0: h (handle)
On exit	A0: function result (pointer)
	D0: result code (word)

HandleZone returns a pointer to the heap zone containing the relocatable block whose handle is h. In case of an error, the result returned by HandleZone is undefined and should be ignored.

Warning: If handle h is empty (points to a NIL master pointer), HandleZone returns a pointer to the current heap zone.

Result codes	noErr	No error
	memWZErr	Attempt to operate on a free block

```
FUNCTION RecoverHandle (p: Ptr) : Handle;
```

Trap macro	_RecoverHandle _RecoverHandle ,SYS (applies to system heap)
On entry	A0: p (pointer)
On exit	A0: function result (handle) D0: unchanged

RecoverHandle returns a handle to the relocatable block pointed to by p.

Assembly-language note: The trap _RecoverHandle doesn't return a result code in register D0; the previous contents of D0 are preserved unchanged.

Result codes   noErr   No error [Pascal only]

```
PROCEDURE ReallocHandle (h: Handle; logicalSize: Size);
```

Trap macro	_ReallocHandle
On entry	A0: h (handle) D0: logicalSize (long word)
On exit	D0: result code (word)

ReallocHandle allocates a new relocatable block with a logical size of logicalSize bytes. It then updates handle h by setting its master pointer to point to the new block. The main use of this procedure is to reallocate space for a block that has been purged. Normally h is an empty handle, but it need not be: If it points to an existing block, that block is released before the new block is created.

In case of an error, no new block is allocated and handle h is left unchanged.

Result codes	noErr	No error
	memFullErr	Not enough room in heap zone
	memWZErr	Attempt to operate on a free block
	memPurErr	Attempt to purge a locked block

Allocating and Releasing Nonrelocatable Blocks

```
FUNCTION NewPtr (logicalSize: Size) : Ptr;
```

Trap macro	_NewPtr	
	_NewPtr ,SYS	(applies to system heap)
	_NewPtr ,CLEAR	(clears allocated block)
	_NewPtr ,SYS,CLEAR	(applies to system heap and clears allocated block)
On entry	D0: logicalSize (long word)	
On exit	A0: function result (pointer)	
	D0: result code (word)	

NewPtr attempts to allocate a new nonrelocatable block of logicalSize bytes from the current heap zone and then return a pointer to it. If logicalSize bytes can't be allocated, NewPtr returns NIL.

NewPtr will pursue all available avenues to create a free block of the requested size at the lowest possible location in the heap zone, including compacting the heap zone, increasing its size, purging blocks from it, and calling its grow zone function, if any.

Result codes	noErr	No error
	memFullErr	Not enough room in heap zone

```
PROCEDURE DisposPtr (p: Ptr);
```

Trap macro	_DisposPtr
On entry	A0: p (pointer)
On exit	D0: result code (word)

DisposPtr releases the memory occupied by the nonrelocatable block pointed to by p.

Warning: After a call to DisposPtr, all pointers to the released block become invalid and should not be used again. Any subsequent calls to DisposPtr using an invalid pointer will damage the master pointer list.

Result codes	noErr	No error
	memWZErr	Attempt to operate on a free block

```
FUNCTION GetPtrSize (p: Ptr) : Size;
```

Trap macro	_GetPtrSize
On entry	A0: p (pointer)
On exit	D0: if >= 0, function result (long word)
	if < 0, result code (word)

GetPtrSize returns the logical size, in bytes, of the nonrelocatable block pointed to by p. In case of an error, GetPtrSize returns 0.

Assembly-language note: Recall that the trap dispatcher sets the condition codes before returning from a trap by testing the low-order word of register D0 with a TST.W instruction. Since the block size returned in D0 by _GetPtrSize is a full 32-bit long word, the word-length test sets the condition codes incorrectly in this case. To branch on the contents of D0, use your own TST.L instruction on return from the trap to test the full 32 bits of the register.

Result codes	noErr	No error [Pascal only]
	memWZErr	Attempt to operate on a free block

```
PROCEDURE SetPtrSize (p: Ptr; newSize: Size);
```

Trap macro	_SetPtrSize
On entry	A0: p (pointer)
	D0: newSize (long word)
On exit	D0: result code (word)

SetPtrSize changes the logical size of the nonrelocatable block pointed to by p to newSize bytes.

Result codes	noErr	No error
	memFullErr	Not enough room in heap zone
	memWZErr	Attempt to operate on a free block

```
FUNCTION PtrZone (p: Ptr) : THz;
```

Trap macro	_PtrZone
On entry	A0: p (pointer)
On exit	A0: function result (pointer)
	D0: result code (word)

PtrZone returns a pointer to the heap zone containing the nonrelocatable block pointed to by p. In case of an error, the result returned by PtrZone is undefined and should be ignored.

Result codes	noErr	No error
	memWZErr	Attempt to operate on a free block

Freeing Space in the Heap

```
FUNCTION FreeMem : LONGINT;
```

Trap macro	_FreeMem
	_FreeMem ,SYS (applies to system heap)
On exit	D0: function result (long word)

FreeMem returns the total amount of free space in the current heap zone, in bytes. Note that it usually isn't possible to allocate a block of this size, because of fragmentation due to nonrelocatable or locked blocks.

Result codes	noErr	No error [Pascal only]

```
FUNCTION MaxMem (VAR grow: Size) : Size;
```

Trap macro	_MaxMem
	_MaxMem ,SYS (applies to system heap)
On exit	D0: function result (long word)
	A0: grow (long word)

MaxMem compacts the current heap zone and purges all purgeable blocks from the zone. It returns as its result the size in bytes of the largest contiguous free block in the zone after the compaction. If the current zone is the original application heap zone, the grow parameter is set to the maximum number of bytes by which the zone can grow. For any other heap zone, grow is set to 0. MaxMem doesn't actually expand the zone or call its grow zone function.

Result codes   noErr   No error [Pascal only]

```
FUNCTION CompactMem (cbNeeded: Size) : Size;
```

Trap macro	_CompactMem
	_CompactMem ,SYS (applies to system heap)
On entry	D0: cbNeeded (long word)
On exit	D0: function result (long word)

CompactMem compacts the current heap zone by moving relocatable blocks down and collecting free space together until a contiguous block of at least cbNeeded free bytes is found or the entire zone is compacted; it doesn't purge any purgeable blocks. CompactMem returns the size in bytes of the largest contiguous free block remaining. Note that it doesn't actually allocate the block.

Result codes   noErr   No error [Pascal only]

```
PROCEDURE ResrvMem (cbNeeded: Size);
```

Trap macro	_ResrvMem
	_ResrvMem ,SYS (applies to system heap)
On entry	D0: cbNeeded (long word)
On exit	D0: result code (word)

ResrvMem creates free space for a block of cbNeeded contiguous bytes at the lowest possible position in the current heap zone. It will try every available means to place the block as close as possible to the bottom of the zone, including moving other blocks upward, expanding the zone, or purging blocks from it. Note that ResrvMem doesn't actually allocate the block.

Note: When you allocate a relocatable block that you know will be locked for long periods of time, call ResrvMem first. This reserves space for the block near the bottom of the heap zone, where it will interfere with compaction as little as possible. It isn't necessary to call ResrvMem for a nonrelocatable block; NewPtr calls it automatically. It's also called automatically when locked resources are read into memory.

| Result codes | noErr | No error |
| | memFullErr | Not enough room in heap zone |

```
PROCEDURE PurgeMem (cbNeeded: Size);
```

Trap macro	_PurgeMem	
	_PurgeMem ,SYS	(applies to system heap)
On entry	D0: cbNeeded (long word)	
On exit	D0: result code (word)	

PurgeMem sequentially purges blocks from the current heap zone until a contiguous block of at least cbNeeded free bytes is created or the entire zone is purged; it doesn't compact the heap zone. Only relocatable, unlocked, purgeable blocks can be purged. Note that PurgeMem doesn't actually allocate the block.

Result codes	noErr	No error
	memFullErr	Not enough room in heap zone

```
PROCEDURE EmptyHandle (h: Handle);
```

Trap macro	_EmptyHandle
On entry	A0: h (handle)
On exit	A0: h (handle)
	D0: result code (word)

EmptyHandle purges the relocatable block whose handle is h from its heap zone and sets its master pointer to NIL (making it an empty handle). If h is already empty, EmptyHandle does nothing.

Note: Since the space occupied by the block's master pointer itself remains allocated, all handles pointing to it remain valid but empty. When you later reallocate space for the block with ReallocHandle, the master pointer will be updated, causing all existing handles to access the new block correctly.

The block whose handle is h must be unlocked, but need not be purgeable.

Result codes	noErr	No error
	memWZErr	Attempt to operate on a free block
	memPurErr	Attempt to purge a locked block

Properties of Relocatable Blocks

PROCEDURE HLock (h: Handle);

Trap macro	_HLock
On entry	A0: h (handle)
On exit	D0: result code (word)

HLock locks a relocatable block, preventing it from being moved within its heap zone. If the block is already locked, HLock does nothing.

> **Warning:** To prevent heap fragmentation, you should always call MoveHHi before locking a relocatable block.

Result codes	noErr	No error
	nilHandleErr	NIL master pointer
	memWZErr	Attempt to operate on a free block

PROCEDURE HUnlock (h: Handle);

Trap macro	_HUnlock
On entry	A0: h (handle)
On exit	D0: result code (word)

HUnlock unlocks a relocatable block, allowing it to be moved within its heap zone. If the block is already unlocked, HUnlock does nothing.

Result codes	noErr	No error
	nilHandleErr	NIL master pointer
	memWZErr	Attempt to operate on a free block

PROCEDURE HPurge (h: Handle);

Trap macro	_HPurge
On entry	A0: h (handle)
On exit	D0: result code (word)

HPurge marks a relocatable block as purgeable. If the block is already purgeable, HPurge does nothing.

Note: If you call HPurge on a locked block, it won't unlock the block, but it will mark the block as purgeable. If you later call HUnlock, the block will be subject to purging.

Result codes	noErr	No error
	nilHandleErr	NIL master pointer
	memWZErr	Attempt to operate on a free block

```
PROCEDURE HNoPurge (h: Handle);
```

Trap macro	_HNoPurge
On entry	A0: h (handle)
On exit	D0: result code (word)

HNoPurge marks a relocatable block as unpurgeable. If the block is already unpurgeable, HNoPurge does nothing.

Result codes	noErr	No error
	nilHandleErr	NIL master pointer
	memWZErr	Attempt to operate on a free block

Grow Zone Operations

```
PROCEDURE SetGrowZone (growZone: ProcPtr);
```

Trap macro	_SetGrowZone
On entry	A0: growZone (pointer)
On exit	D0: result code (word)

SetGrowZone sets the current heap zone's grow zone function as designated by the growZone parameter. A NIL parameter value removes any grow zone function the zone may previously have had.

Note: If your program presses the limits of the available heap space, it's a good idea to have a grow zone function of some sort. At the very least, the grow zone function should take some graceful action—such as displaying an alert box with the message "Out of memory"—instead of just failing unpredictably.

If it has failed to create a block of the needed size after compacting the zone, increasing its size (in the case of the original application zone), and purging blocks from it, the Memory Manager calls the grow zone function as a last resort.

The grow zone function should be of the form

```
FUNCTION MyGrowZone (cbNeeded: Size) : LONGINT;
```

The cbNeeded parameter gives the physical size of the needed block in bytes, *including the block header*. The grow zone function should attempt to create a free block of at least this size. It should return a nonzero number if it's able to allocate some memory, or 0 if it's not able to allocate any.

If the grow zone function returns 0, the Memory Manager will give up trying to allocate the needed block and will signal failure with the result code memFullErr. Otherwise it will compact the heap zone and try again to allocate the block. If still unsuccessful, it will continue to call the grow zone function repeatedly, compacting the zone again after each call, until it either succeeds in allocating the needed block or receives a zero result and gives up.

The usual way for the grow zone function to free more space is to call EmptyHandle to purge blocks that were previously marked unpurgeable. Another possibility is to unlock blocks that were previously locked

> **Note:** Although just unlocking blocks doesn't actually free any additional space in the zone, the grow zone function should still return a nonzero result in this case. This signals the Memory Manager to compact the heap and try again to allocate the needed block.

> **Warning:** Depending on the circumstances in which the grow zone function is called, there may be a particular block within the heap zone that must not be moved. For this reason, it's essential that your grow zone function call the function GZSaveHnd (see below).

> Result codes   noErr   No error

```
FUNCTION GZSaveHnd : Handle;    [Not in ROM]
```

GZSaveHnd returns a handle to a relocatable block that must not be moved by the grow zone function, or NIL if there is no such block. Your grow zone function must be sure to call GZSaveHnd; if a handle is returned, it must ensure that this block is *not* moved.

> **Assembly-language note:** You can find the same handle in the global variable GZRootHnd.

Miscellaneous Routines

```
PROCEDURE BlockMove (sourcePtr,destPtr: Ptr; byteCount: Size);
```

Trap macro	_BlockMove
On entry	A0: sourcePtr (pointer)
	A1: destPtr (pointer)
	D0: byteCount (long word)
On exit	D0: result code (word)

BlockMove moves a block of byteCount consecutive bytes from the address designated by sourcePtr to that designated by destPtr. No pointers are updated. BlockMove works correctly even if the source and destination blocks overlap.

Result codes	noErr	No error

```
FUNCTION TopMem : Ptr;   [Not in ROM]
```

On a Macintosh 128K or 512K, TopMem returns a pointer to the end of RAM; on the Macintosh XL, it returns a pointer to the end of the memory available for use by the application.

Assembly-language note: This value is stored in the global variable MemTop.

```
PROCEDURE MoveHHi (h: Handle);   [Not in ROM]
```

MoveHHi moves the relocatable block whose handle is h toward the top of the current heap zone, until the block hits either a nonrelocatable block, a locked relocatable block, or the last block in the current heap zone. By calling MoveHHi before you lock a relocatable block, you can avoid fragmentation of the heap, as well as make room for future pointers as low in the heap as possible.

Result codes	noErr	No error
	nilHandleErr	NIL master pointer
	memLockedErr	Block is locked

```
FUNCTION MemError : OSErr;   [Not in ROM]
```

MemError returns the result code produced by the last Memory Manager routine called directly by your program. (OSErr is an Operating System Utility data type declared as INTEGER.)

Assemby-language note: To get a routine's result code from assembly language, look in register D0 on return from the routine (except for certain routines as noted).

CREATING A HEAP ZONE ON THE STACK

The following code is an example of how advanced programmers can get the space for a new heap zone from the stack:

```
CONST zoneSize = 2048;
VAR   zoneArea: PACKED ARRAY[1..zoneSize] OF SignedByte;
      stackZone: THz;
      limit: Ptr;
      . . .


stackZone := @zoneArea;
limit := POINTER(ORD(stackZone)+zoneSize);
InitZone(NIL,16,limit,@zoneArea)
```

The heap zone created by this method will be usable until the routine containing this code is completed (because its variables will then be released).

Assembly-language note: Here's how you might do the same thing in assembly language:

```
zoneSize   .EQU    2048
           . . .
           MOVE.L  SP,A2              ;save stack pointer for limit
           SUB.W   #zoneSize,SP       ;make room on stack
           MOVE.L  SP,A1              ;save stack pointer for start
           MOVE.L  A1,stackZone       ;store as zone pointer


           SUB.W   #14,SP             ;allocate space on stack
           CLR.L   pGrowZone(SP)      ;NIL grow zone function
           MOVE.W  #16,cMoreMasters(SP) ;16 master pointers
           MOVE.L  A2,limitPtr(SP)    ;pointer to zone trailer
           MOVE.L  A1,startPtr(SP)    ;pointer to first byte
                                      ; of zone


           MOVE.L  SP,A0              ;point to argument block
           _InitZone                  ;create zone 1
           ADD.W   #14,SP             ;pop arguments off stack
           . . .
```

SUMMARY OF THE MEMORY MANAGER

Constants

```
CONST { Result codes }

    memFullErr    = -108;    {not enough room in heap zone}
    memLockedErr  = -117;    {block is locked}
    memPurErr     = -112;    {attempt to purge a locked block}
    memWZErr      = -111;    {attempt to operate on a free block}
    nilHandleErr  = -109;    {NIL master pointer}
    noErr         =   0;     {no error}
```

Data Types

```
TYPE SignedByte = -128..127;
     Byte          = 0..255;
     Ptr           = ^SignedByte;
     Handle        = ^Ptr;

     Str255        = STRING[255];
     StringPtr     = ^Str255;
     StringHandle  = ^StringPtr;

     ProcPtr = Ptr;

     Fixed = LONGINT;

     Size = LONGINT;

     THz  = ^Zone;
     Zone = RECORD
                bkLim:       Ptr;        {zone trailer block}
                purgePtr:    Ptr;        {used internally}
                hFstFree:    Ptr;        {first free master pointer}
                zcbFree:     LONGINT;    {number of free bytes}
                gzProc:      ProcPtr;    {grow zone function}
                moreMast:    INTEGER;    {master pointers to allocate}
                flags:       INTEGER;    {used internally}
                cntRel:      INTEGER;    {not used}
                maxRel:      INTEGER;    {not used}
                cntNRel:     INTEGER;    {not used}
                maxNRel:     INTEGER;    {not used}
                cntEmpty:    INTEGER;    {not used}
                cntHandles:  INTEGER;    {not used}
                minCBFree:   LONGINT;    {not used}
                purgeProc:   ProcPtr;    {purge warning procedure}
                sparePtr:    Ptr;        {used internally}
                allocPtr:    Ptr;        {used internally}
                heapData:    INTEGER     {first usable byte in zone}
            END;
```

Routines

Initialization and Allocation

```
PROCEDURE InitApplZone;
PROCEDURE SetApplBase    (startPtr: Ptr);
PROCEDURE InitZone       (pGrowZone: ProcPtr; cMoreMasters: INTEGER;
                          limitPtr,startPtr: Ptr);
FUNCTION  GetApplLimit : Ptr;   [Not in ROM]
PROCEDURE SetApplLimit   (zoneLimit: Ptr);
PROCEDURE MaxApplZone;   [Not in ROM]
PROCEDURE MoreMasters;
```

Heap Zone Access

```
FUNCTION  GetZone :    THz;
PROCEDURE SetZone     (hz: THz);
FUNCTION  SystemZone : THz;   [Not in ROM]
FUNCTION  ApplicZone : THz;   [Not in ROM]
```

Allocating and Releasing Relocatable Blocks

```
FUNCTION  NewHandle      (logicalSize: Size) : Handle;
PROCEDURE DisposHandle   (h: Handle);
FUNCTION  GetHandleSize  (h: Handle) : Size;
PROCEDURE SetHandleSize  (h: Handle; newSize: Size);
FUNCTION  HandleZone     (h: Handle) : THz;
FUNCTION  RecoverHandle  (p: Ptr) : Handle;
PROCEDURE ReallocHandle  (h: Handle; logicalSize: Size);
```

Allocating and Releasing Nonrelocatable Blocks

```
FUNCTION  NewPtr     (logicalSize: Size) : Ptr;
PROCEDURE DisposPtr  (p: Ptr);
FUNCTION  GetPtrSize (p: Ptr) : Size;
PROCEDURE SetPtrSize (p: Ptr; newSize: Size);
FUNCTION  PtrZone    (p: Ptr) : THz;
```

Freeing Space in the Heap

```
FUNCTION  FreeMem :    LONGINT;
FUNCTION  MaxMem      (VAR grow: Size) : Size;
FUNCTION  CompactMem  (cbNeeded: Size) : Size;
PROCEDURE ResrvMem    (cbNeeded: Size);
PROCEDURE PurgeMem    (cbNeeded: Size);
PROCEDURE EmptyHandle (h: Handle);
```

Properties of Relocatable Blocks

```
PROCEDURE HLock      (h: Handle);
PROCEDURE HUnlock    (h: Handle);
PROCEDURE HPurge     (h: Handle);
PROCEDURE HNoPurge   (h: Handle);
```

Grow Zone Operations

```
PROCEDURE SetGrowZone  (growZone: ProcPtr);
FUNCTION  GZSaveHnd :   Handle;   [Not in ROM]
```

Miscellaneous Routines

```
PROCEDURE BlockMove   (sourcePtr,destPtr: Ptr; byteCount: Size);
FUNCTION  TopMem :     Ptr;   [Not in ROM]
PROCEDURE MoveHHi     (h: Handle);   [Not in ROM]
FUNCTION  MemError :   OSErr;   [Not in ROM]
```

Grow Zone Function

```
FUNCTION MyGrowZone (cbNeeded: Size) : LONGINT;
```

Assembly-Language Information

Constants

```
; Values for tag byte of a block header

tyBkFree      .EQU     0      ;free block
tyBkNRel      .EQU     1      ;nonrelocatable block
tyBkRel       .EQU     2      ;relocatable block

; Flags for the high-order byte of a master pointer

lock          .EQU     7      ;lock bit
purge         .EQU     6      ;purge bit
resourc       .EQU     5      ;resource bit

; Result codes

memFullErr    .EQU    -108    ;not enough room in heap zone
memLockedErr  .EQU    -117    ;block is locked
memPurErr     .EQU    -112    ;attempt to purge a locked block
memWZErr      .EQU    -111    ;attempt to operate on a free block
nilHandleErr  .EQU    -109    ;NIL master pointer
noErr         .EQU     0      ;no error
```

Zone Record Data Structure

bkLim	Pointer to zone trailer block
hFstFree	Pointer to first free master pointer
zcbFree	Number of free bytes (long)
gzProc	Address of grow zone function
mAllocCnt	Master pointers to allocate (word)
purgeProc	Address of purge warning procedure
heapData	First usable byte in zone

Block Header Data Structure

tagBC	Tag byte and physical block size (long)
handle	Relocatable block: relative handle
	Nonrelocatable block: zone pointer
blkData	First byte of block contents

Parameter Block Structure for InitZone

startPtr	Pointer to first byte in zone
limitPtr	Pointer to first byte beyond end of zone
cMoreMasters	Number of master pointers for zone (word)
pGrowZone	Address of grow zone function

Routines

Trap macro	On entry	On exit
_InitApplZone		D0: result code (word)
_SetApplBase	A0: startPtr (ptr)	D0: result code (word)

_InitZone	A0: ptr to parameter block
	    0 startPtr (ptr)
	    4 limitPtr (ptr)
	    8 cMoreMasters (word)
	  10 pGrowZone (ptr)
		D0: result code (word)

_SetApplLimit	A0: zoneLimit (ptr)	D0: result code (word)
_MoreMasters		
_GetZone		A0: function result (ptr) D0: result code (word)
_SetZone	A0: hz (ptr)	D0: result code (word)
_NewHandle	D0: logicalSize (long)	A0: function result (handle) D0: result code (word)
_DisposHandle	A0: h (handle)	D0: result code (word)

Trap macro	On entry	On exit
_GetHandleSize	A0: h (handle)	D0: if >=0, function result (long) if <0, result code (word)
_SetHandleSize	A0: h (handle) D0: newSize (long)	D0: result code (word)
_HandleZone	A0: h (handle)	A0: function result (ptr) D0: result code (word)
_RecoverHandle	A0: p (ptr)	A0: function result (handle) D0: unchanged
_ReallocHandle	A0: h (handle) D0: logicalSize (long)	D0: result code (word)
_NewPtr	D0: logicalSize (long)	A0: function result (ptr) D0: result code (word)
_DisposPtr	A0: p (ptr)	D0: result code (word)
_GetPtrSize	A0: p (ptr)	D0: if >=0, function result (long) if <0, result code (word)
_SetPtrSize	A0: p (ptr) D0: newSize (long)	D0: result code (word)
_PtrZone	A0: p (ptr)	A0: function result (ptr) D0: result code (word)
_FreeMem		D0: function result (long)
_MaxMem		D0: function result (long) A0: grow (long)
_CompactMem	D0: cbNeeded (long)	D0: function result (long)
_ResrvMem	D0: cbNeeded (long)	D0: result code (word)
_PurgeMem	D0: cbNeeded (long)	D0: result code (word)
_EmptyHandle	A0: h (handle)	A0: h (handle) D0: result code (word)
_HLock	A0: h (handle)	D0: result code (word)
_HUnlock	A0: h (handle)	D0: result code (word)
_HPurge	A0: h (handle)	D0: result code (word)
_HNoPurge	A0: h (handle)	D0: result code (word)
_SetGrowZone	A0: growZone (ptr)	D0: result code (word)
_BlockMove	A0: sourcePtr (ptr) A1: destPtr (ptr) D0: byteCount (long)	D0: result code (word)

Variables

DefltStack	Default space allotment for stack (long)
MinStack	Minimum space allotment for stack (long)
MemTop	Address of end of RAM (on Macintosh XL, end of RAM available to applications)
ScrnBase	Address of main screen buffer
BufPtr	Address of end of jump table
CurrentA5	Address of boundary between application globals and application parameters
CurStackBase	Address of base of stack; start of application globals
ApplLimit	Application heap limit
HeapEnd	Address of end of application heap zone
ApplZone	Address of application heap zone
SysZone	Address of system heap zone
TheZone	Address of current heap zone
GZRootHnd	Handle to relocatable block not to be moved by grow zone function

2   THE SEGMENT LOADER

2 Segment Loader

2 Segment Loader

ABOUT THIS CHAPTER

This chapter describes the Segment Loader, the part of the Macintosh Operating System that lets you divide your application into several parts and have only some of them in memory at a time. The Segment Loader also provides routines for accessing information about documents that the user has selected to be opened or printed.

You should already be familiar with:

- the basic concepts behind the Resource Manager

- the Memory Manager

ABOUT THE SEGMENT LOADER

The Segment Loader allows you to divide the code of your application into several parts or **segments**. The Finder starts up an application by calling a Segment Loader routine that loads in the **main segment** (the one containing the main program). Other segments are loaded in automatically when they're needed. Your application can call the Segment Loader to have these segments removed from memory when they're no longer needed.

The Segment Loader enables you to have programs larger than 32K bytes, the maximum size of a single segment. Also, any code that isn't executed often (such as code for printing) needn't occupy memory when it isn't being used, but can instead be in a separate segment that's "swapped in" when needed.

This mechanism may remind you of the resources of an application, which the Resource Manager reads into memory when necessary. An application's segments are in fact themselves stored as resources; their resource type is 'CODE'. A "loaded" segment has been read into memory by the Resource Manager and locked (so that it's neither relocatable nor purgeable). When a segment is unloaded, it's made relocatable and purgeable.

Every segment has a name. If you do nothing about dividing your program into segments, it will consist only of the main segment. Dividing your program into segments means specifying in your source file the beginning of each segment by name. The names are for your use only; they're not kept around after linking.

FINDER INFORMATION

When the Finder starts up your application, it passes along a list of documents selected by the user to be printed or opened, if any. This information is called the **Finder information**; its structure is shown in Figure 1.

It's up to your application to access the Finder information and open or print the documents selected by the user.

The message in the first word of the Finder information indicates whether the documents are to be opened (0) or printed (1), and the count following it indicates the number of documents (0 if none). The rest of the Finder information specifies each of the selected documents by volume

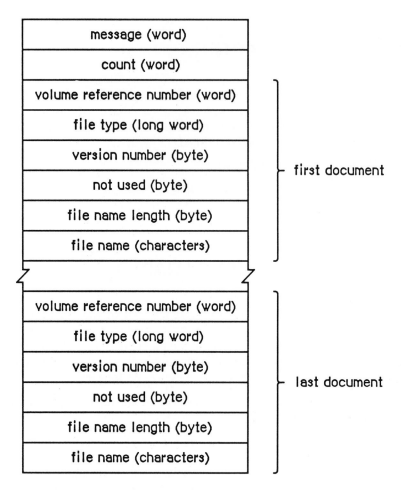

Figure 1. Finder Information

reference number, file type, version number, and file name; these terms are explained in chapter 4 of Volume II and chapter 1 of Volume III. File names are padded to an even number of bytes if necessary.

Your application should start up with an empty untitled document on the desktop if there are no documents listed in the Finder information. If one or more documents are to be opened, your application should go through each document one at a time, and determine whether it can be opened. If it can be opened, you should do so, and then check the next document in the list (unless you've opened your maximum number of documents, in which case you should ignore the rest). If your application doesn't recognize a document's file type (which can happen if the user selected your application along with another application's document), you may want to open the document anyway and check its internal structure to see if it's a compatible type. Display an alert box including the name of each document that can't be opened.

If one or more documents are to be printed, your application should go through each document in the list and determine whether it can be printed. If any documents can be printed, the application should display the standard Print dialog box and then print each document—preferably without doing its entire startup sequence. For example, it may not be necessary to show the menu bar or the document window. If the document can't be printed, ignore it; it may be intended for another application.

USING THE SEGMENT LOADER

When your application starts up, you should determine whether any documents were selected to be printed or opened by it. First call CountAppFiles, which returns the number of selected documents and indicates whether they're to be printed or opened. If the number of selected documents is 0, open an empty untitled document in the normal manner. Otherwise, call GetAppFiles once for each selected document. GetAppFiles returns information about each document, including its file type. Based on the file type, your application can decide how to treat the document, as described in the preceding section. For each document that your application opens or prints, call ClrAppFiles, which indicates to the Finder that you've processed it.

To unload a segment when it's no longer needed, call UnloadSeg. If you don't want to keep track of when each particular segment should be unloaded, you can call UnloadSeg for every segment in your application at the end of your main event loop. This isn't harmful, since the segments aren't purged unless necessary.

Note: The main segment is always loaded and locked.

Warning: A segment should never unload the segment that called it, because the return addresses on the stack would refer to code that may be moved or purged.

Another procedure, GetAppParms, lets you get information about your application such as its name and the reference number for its resource file. The Segment Loader also provides the ExitToShell procedure—a way for an application to quit and return the user to the Finder.

Finally, there are three advanced routines that can be called only from assembly language: Chain, Launch, and LoadSeg. Chain starts up another application without disturbing the application heap. Thus the current application can let another application take over while still keeping its data around in the heap. Launch is called by the Finder to start up an application; it's like Chain but doesn't retain the application heap. LoadSeg is called indirectly (via the jump table, as described later) to load segments when necessary—that is, whenever a routine in an unloaded segment is invoked.

SEGMENT LOADER ROUTINES

Assembly-language note: Instead of using CountAppFiles, GetAppFiles, and ClrAppFiles, assembly-language programmers can access the Finder information via the global variable AppParmHandle, which contains a handle to the Finder information. Parse the Finder information as shown in Figure 1 above. For each document that your application opens or prints, set the file type in the Finder information to 0.

```
PROCEDURE CountAppFiles (VAR message: INTEGER; VAR count:
          INTEGER);   [Not in ROM]
```

CountAppFiles deciphers the Finder information passed to your application, and returns information about the documents that were selected when your application started up. It returns the number of selected documents in the count parameter, and a number in the message parameter that indicates whether the documents are to opened or printed:

```
CONST appOpen  = 0;   {open the document(s)}
      appPrint = 1;   {print the document(s)}
```

```
PROCEDURE GetAppFiles (index: INTEGER; VAR theFile: AppFile);
          [Not in ROM]
```

GetAppFiles returns information about a document that was selected when your application started up (as listed in the Finder information). The index parameter indicates the file for which information should be returned; it must be between 1 and the number returned by CountAppFiles, inclusive. The information is returned in the following data structure:

```
TYPE AppFile = RECORD
                  vRefNum: INTEGER; {volume reference number}
                  fType:   OSType;  {file type}
                  versNum: INTEGER; {version number}
                  fName:   Str255   {file name}
               END;
```

```
PROCEDURE ClrAppFiles (index: INTEGER);   [Not in ROM]
```

ClrAppFiles changes the Finder information passed to your application about the specified file such that the Finder knows you've processed the file. The index parameter must be between 1 and the number returned by CountAppFiles. You should call ClrAppFiles for every document your application opens or prints, so that the information returned by CountAppFiles and GetAppFiles is always correct. (ClrAppFiles sets the file type in the Finder information to 0.)

```
PROCEDURE GetAppParms (VAR apName: Str255; VAR apRefNum: INTEGER;
          VAR apParam: Handle);
```

GetAppParms returns information about the current application. It returns the application name in apName and the reference number for the application's resource file in apRefNum. A handle to the Finder information is returned in apParam, but the Finder information is more easily accessed with the GetAppFiles call.

Assembly-language note: Assembly-language programmers can instead get the application name, reference number, and handle to the Finder information directly from the global variables CurApName, CurApRefNum, and AppParmHandle.

Note: If you simply want the application's resource file reference number, you can call the Resource Manager function CurResFile when the application starts up.

```
PROCEDURE UnloadSeg (routineAddr: Ptr);
```

UnloadSeg unloads a segment, making it relocatable and purgeable; routineAddr is the address of any externally referenced routine in the segment. The segment won't actually be purged until the memory it occupies is needed. If the segment is purged, the Segment Loader will reload it the next time one of the routines in it is called.

> **Note:** UnloadSeg will work only if called from outside the segment to be unloaded.

```
PROCEDURE ExitToShell;
```

ExitToShell provides an exit from an application by starting up the Finder (after releasing the entire application heap).

Assembly-language note: ExitToShell actually launches the application whose name is stored in the global variable FinderName.

Advanced Routines

The routines below are provided for advanced programmers; they can be called only from assembly language.

Chain procedure

Trap macro   _Chain

On entry   (A0): pointer to application's file name (preceded by length byte)
                    4(A0): configuration of sound and screen buffers (word)

Chain starts up an application without doing anything to the application heap, so the current application can let another application take over while still keeping its data around in the heap.

Chain also configures memory for the sound and screen buffers. The value you pass in 4(A0) determines which sound and screen buffers are allocated:

- If you pass 0 in 4(A0), you get the main sound and screen buffers; in this case, you have the largest amount of memory available to your application.

- Any positive value in 4(A0) causes the alternate sound buffer and main screen buffer to be allocated.

- Any negative value in 4(A0) causes the alternate sound buffer and alternate screen buffer to be allocated.

The memory map in chapter 1 shows the locations of the screen and sound buffers.

Warning: The sound buffers and alternate screen buffer are not supported on the Macintosh XL, and the alternate sound and screen buffers may not be supported in future versions of the Macintosh.

Note: You can get the most recent value passed in 4(A0) to the Chain procedure from the global variable CurPageOption.

Chain closes the resource file for any previous application and opens the resource file for the application being started; call DetachResource for any resources that you still wish to access.

Launch procedure

Trap macro	_Launch
On entry	(A0): pointer to application's file name (preceded by length byte)
	4(A0): configuration of sound and screen buffers (word)

Launch is called by the Finder to start up an application and will rarely need to be called by an application itself. It's the same as the Chain procedure (described above) except that it frees the storage occupied by the application heap and restores the heap to its original size.

Note: Launch preserves a special handle in the application heap which is used for preserving the desk scrap between applications; see chapter 15 of Volume I for details.

LoadSeg procedure

Trap macro	_LoadSeg
On entry	stack: segment number (word)

LoadSeg is called indirectly via the jump table (as described in the following section) when the application calls a routine in an unloaded segment. It loads the segment having the given segment number, which was assigned by the Linker. If the segment isn't in memory, LoadSeg calls the Resource Manager to read it in. It changes the jump table entries for all the routines in the segment from the "unloaded" to the "loaded" state and then invokes the routine that was called.

Note: Since LoadSeg is called via the jump table, there isn't any need for you to call it yourself.

THE JUMP TABLE

This section describes how the Segment Loader works internally, and is included here for advanced programmers; you don't have to know about this to be able to use the common Segment Loader routines.

The loading and unloading of segments is implemented through the application's **jump table**. The jump table contains one eight-byte entry for every externally referenced routine in every segment; all the entries for a particular segment are stored contiguously. The location of the jump table is shown in chapter 1.

When the Linker encounters a call to a routine in another segment, it creates a jump table entry for the routine (see Figure 2). The jump table refers to segments by segment numbers assigned by the Linker. If the segment is loaded, the jump table entry contains code that jumps to the routine. If the segment isn't loaded, the entry contains code that loads the segment.

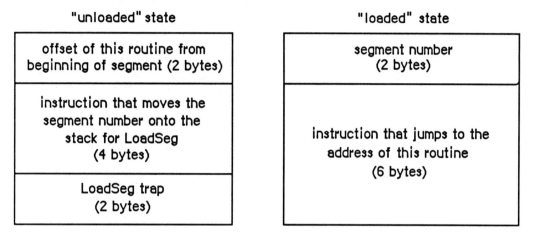

Figure 2. Format of a Jump Table Entry

When a segment is unloaded, all its jump table entries are in the "unloaded" state. When a call to a routine in an unloaded segment is made, the code in the last six bytes of its jump table entry is executed. This code calls LoadSeg, which loads the segment into memory, transforms all of its jump table entries to the "loaded" state, and invokes the routine by executing the instruction in the last six bytes of the jump table entry. Subsequent calls to the routine also execute this instruction. If UnloadSeg is called to unload the segment, it restores the jump table entries to their "unloaded" state. Notice that whether the segment is loaded or unloaded, the last six bytes of the jump table entry are executed; the effect depends on the state of the entry at the time.

To be able to set all the jump table entries for a segment to a particular state, LoadSeg and UnloadSeg need to know exactly where in the jump table all the entries are located. They get this information from the segment header, four bytes at the beginning of the segment which contain the following:

Number of bytes	Contents
2 bytes	Offset of the first routine's entry from the beginning of the jump table
2 bytes	Number of entries for this segment

When an application starts up, its jump table is read in from segment 0 (which is the 'CODE' resource with an ID of 0). This is a special segment created by the Linker for every executable file. It contains the following:

Number of bytes	Contents
4 bytes	"Above A5" size; size in bytes from location pointed to by A5 to upper end of application space
4 bytes	"Below A5" size; size in bytes of application globals plus QuickDraw globals
4 bytes	Length of jump table in bytes
4 bytes	Offset to jump table from location pointed to by A5
n bytes	Jump table

Note: For all applications, the offset to the jump table from the location pointed to by A5 is 32, and the "above A5" size is 32 plus the length of the jump table.

The Segment Loader then executes the first entry in the jump table, which loads the main segment ('CODE' resource 1) and starts the application.

Assembly-language note: The offset to the jump table from the location pointed to by A5 is stored in the global variable CurJTOffset.

SUMMARY OF THE SEGMENT LOADER

Constants

```
CONST { Message returned by CountAppleFiles }

    appOpen  = 0;   {open the document(s)}
    appPrint = 1;   {print the document(s)}
```

Data Types

```
TYPE AppFile = RECORD
                 vRefNum: INTEGER; {volume reference number}
                 fType:   OSType;  {file type}
                 versNum: INTEGER; {version number}
                 fName:   Str255   {file name}
               END;
```

Routines

```
PROCEDURE CountAppFiles (VAR message: INTEGER; VAR count: INTEGER);   [Not
                            in ROM]
PROCEDURE GetAppFiles   (index: INTEGER; VAR theFile: AppFile);   [Not in
                            ROM]
PROCEDURE ClrAppFiles   (index: INTEGER);   [Not in ROM]
PROCEDURE GetAppParms   (VAR apName: Str255; VAR apRefNum: INTEGER; VAR
                            apParam: Handle);
PROCEDURE UnloadSeg     (routineAddr: Ptr);
PROCEDURE ExitToShell;
```

Assembly-Language Information

Advanced Routines

Trap macro	On entry
_Chain	(A0): pointer to application's file name (preceded by length byte)
	4(A0): configuration of sound and screen buffers (word)
_Launch	(A0): pointer to application's file name (preceded by length byte)
	4(A0): configuration of sound and screen buffers (word)
_LoadSeg	stack: segment number (word)

Variables

AppParmHandle	Handle to Finder information
CurApName	Name of current application (length byte followed by up to 31 characters)
CurApRefNum	Reference number of current application's resource file (word)
CurPageOption	Sound/screen buffer configuration passed to Chain or Launch (word)
CurJTOffset	Offset to jump table from location pointed to by A5 (word)
FinderName	Name of the Finder (length byte followed by up to 15 characters)

3 THE OPERATING SYSTEM EVENT MANAGER

3 OS Event

ABOUT THIS CHAPTER

This chapter describes the Operating System Event Manager, the part of the Operating System that reports low-level user actions such as mouse-button presses and keystrokes. Usually your application will find out about events by calling the Toolbox Event Manager, which calls the Operating System Event Manager for you, but in some situations you'll need to call the Operating System Event Manager directly.

> **Note:** All references to "the Event Manager" in this chapter refer to the Operating System Event Manager.

You should already be familiar with the Toolbox Event Manager.

> **Note:** Constants and data types defined in the Operating System Event Manager are presented in detail in the Toolbox Event Manager chapter (chapter 8 of Volume I), since they're necessary for using that part of the Toolbox. They're also listed in the summary of this chapter.

ABOUT THE OPERATING SYSTEM EVENT MANAGER

The Event Manager is the part of the Operating System that detects low-level, hardware-related events: mouse, keyboard, disk-inserted, device driver, and network events. It stores information about these events in the event queue and provides routines that access the queue (analogous to GetNextEvent and EventAvail in the Toolbox Event Manager). It also allows your application to post its own events into the event queue. Like the Toolbox Event Manager, the Operating System Event Manager returns a null event if it has no other events to report.

The Toolbox Event Manager calls the Operating System Event Manager to retrieve events from the event queue; in addition, it reports activate and update events, which aren't kept in the queue. It's extremely unusual for an application not to have to know about activate and update events, so usually you'll call the Toolbox Event Manager to get events.

The Operating System Event Manager also lets you:

- remove events from the event queue
- set the system event mask, to control which types of events get posted into the queue

USING THE OPERATING SYSTEM EVENT MANAGER

If you're using application-defined events in your program, you'll need to call the Operating System Event Manager function PostEvent to post them into the event queue. This function is sometimes also useful for reposting events that you've removed from the event queue with GetNextEvent.

In some situations you may want to remove from the event queue some or all events of a certain type or types. You can do this with the procedure FlushEvents. A common use of FlushEvents is to get rid of any stray events left over from before your application started up.

You'll probably never call the other Operating System Event Manager routines: GetOSEvent, which gets an event from the event queue, removing it from the queue in the process; OSEventAvail, for looking at an event without dequeueing it; and SetEventMask, which changes the setting of the system event mask.

OPERATING SYSTEM EVENT MANAGER ROUTINES

Posting and Removing Events

```
FUNCTION PostEvent (eventCode: INTEGER; eventMsg: LONGINT) :
          OSErr;
```

Trap macro	_PostEvent
On entry	A0: eventCode (word)
	D0: eventMsg (long word)
On exit	D0: result code (word)

PostEvent places in the event queue an event of the type designated by eventCode, with the event message specified by eventMsg and with the current time, mouse location, and state of the modifier keys and mouse button. It returns a result code (of type OSErr, defined as INTEGER in the Operating System Utilities) equal to one of the following predefined constants:

```
CONST noErr    = 0;   {no error (event posted)}
      evtNotEnb = 1;   {event type not designated in system event mask}
```

Warning: Be very careful when posting any events other than your own application-defined events into the queue; attempting to post an activate or update event, for example, will interfere with the internal operation of the Toolbox Event Manager, since such events aren't normally placed in the queue at all.

Warning: If you use PostEvent to repost an event, remember that the event time, location, and state of the modifier keys and mouse button will all be changed from their values when the event was originally posted, possibly altering the meaning of the event.

```
PROCEDURE FlushEvents (eventMask,stopMask: INTEGER);
```

Trap macro	_FlushEvents
On entry	D0: low-order word: eventMask
	high-order word: stopMask
On exit	D0: 0 or event code (word)

FlushEvents removes events from the event queue as specified by the given event masks. It removes all events of the type or types specified by eventMask, up to but not including the first event of any type specified by stopMask; if the event queue doesn't contain any events of the types specified by eventMask, it does nothing. To remove all events specified by eventMask, use a stopMask value of 0.

At the beginning of your application, it's usually a good idea to call FlushEvents(everyEvent,0) to empty the event queue of any stray events that may have been left lying around, such as unprocessed keystrokes typed to the Finder.

Assembly-language note: On exit from this routine, D0 contains 0 if all events were removed from the queue or, if not, an event code specifying the type of event that caused the removal process to stop.

Accessing Events

```
FUNCTION GetOSEvent (eventMask: INTEGER; VAR theEvent:
        EventRecord) : BOOLEAN;
```

Trap macro	_GetOSEvent
On entry	A0: pointer to event record theEvent
	D0: eventMask (word)
On exit	D0: 0 if non-null event returned, or –1 if null event returned (byte)

GetOSEvent returns the next available event of a specified type or types and removes it from the event queue. The event is returned as the value of the parameter theEvent. The eventMask parameter specifies which event types are of interest. GetOSEvent will return the next available event of any type designated by the mask. If no event of any of the designated types is available, GetOSEvent returns a null event and a function result of FALSE; otherwise it returns TRUE.

Note: Unlike the Toolbox Event Manager function GetNextEvent, GetOSEvent doesn't call the Desk Manager to see whether the system wants to intercept and respond to the event; nor does it perform GetNextEvent's processing of the alarm and Command-Shift-number combinations.

```
FUNCTION OSEventAvail (eventMask: INTEGER; VAR theEvent:
            EventRecord) : BOOLEAN;
```

Trap macro	_OSEventAvail
On entry	A0: pointer to event record theEvent
	D0: eventMask (word)
On exit	D0: 0 if non-null event returned, or −1 if null event returned (byte)

OSEventAvail works exactly the same as GetOSEvent (above) except that it doesn't remove the event from the event queue.

Note: An event returned by OSEventAvail will not be accessible later if in the meantime the queue becomes full and the event is discarded from it; since the events discarded are always the oldest ones in the queue, however, this will happen only in an unusually busy environment.

Setting the System Event Mask

```
PROCEDURE SetEventMask (theMask: INTEGER);   [Not in ROM]
```

SetEventMask sets the system event mask to the specified event mask. The Operating System Event Manager will post only those event types that correspond to bits set in the mask. (As usual, it will not post activate and update events, which are generated by the Window Manager and not stored in the event queue.) The system event mask is initially set to post all except key-up events.

Warning: Because desk accessories may rely on receiving certain types of events, your application shouldn't set the system event mask to prevent any additional types (besides key-up) from being posted. You should use SetEventMask only to enable key-up events in the unusual case that your application needs to respond to them.

Assembly-language note: The system event mask is available to assembly-language programmers in the global variable SysEvtMask.

STRUCTURE OF THE EVENT QUEUE

The event queue is a standard Macintosh Operating System queue, as described in chapter 13. Most programmers will never need to access the event queue directly; some advanced programmers, though, may need to do so for special purposes.

Each entry in the event queue contains information about an event:

```
TYPE EvQEl = RECORD
                qLink:           QElemPtr;    {next queue entry}
                qType:           INTEGER;     {queue type}
                evtQWhat:        INTEGER;     {event code}
                evtQMessage:     LONGINT;     {event message}
                evtQWhen:        LONGINT;     {ticks since startup}
                evtQWhere:       Point;       {mouse location}
                evtQModifiers:   INTEGER      {modifier flags}
            END;
```

QLink points to the next entry in the queue, and qType indicates the queue type, which must be ORD(evType). The remaining five fields of the event queue entry contain exactly the same information about the event as do the fields of the event record for that event; see chapter 8 of Volume I for a detailed description of the contents of these fields.

You can get a pointer to the header of the event queue by calling the Operating System Event Manager function GetEvQHdr.

```
FUNCTION GetEvQHdr : QHdrPtr;    [Not in ROM]
```

GetEvQHdr returns a pointer to the header of the event queue.

Assembly-language note: The global variable EventQueue contains the header of the event queue.

SUMMARY OF THE OPERATING SYSTEM EVENT MANAGER

Constants

```
CONST { Event codes }

    nullEvent    = 0;    {null}
    mouseDown    = 1;    {mouse-down}
    mouseUp      = 2;    {mouse-up}
    keyDown      = 3;    {key-down}
    keyUp        = 4;    {key-up}
    autoKey      = 5;    {auto-key}
    updateEvt    = 6;    {update; Toolbox only}
    diskEvt      = 7;    {disk-inserted}
    activateEvt  = 8;    {activate; Toolbox only}
    networkEvt   = 10;   {network}
    driverEvt    = 11;   {device driver}
    app1Evt      = 12;   {application-defined}
    app2Evt      = 13;   {application-defined}
    app3Evt      = 14;   {application-defined}
    app4Evt      = 15;   {application-defined}

    { Masks for keyboard event message }

    charCodeMask = $000000FF;    {character code}
    keyCodeMask  = $0000FF00;    {key code}

    { Masks for forming event mask }

    mDownMask    = 2;       {mouse-down}
    mUpMask      = 4;       {mouse-up}
    keyDownMask  = 8;       {key-down}
    keyUpMask    = 16;      {key-up}
    autoKeyMask  = 32;      {auto-key}
    updateMask   = 64;      {update}
    diskMask     = 128;     {disk-inserted}
    activMask    = 256;     {activate}
    networkMask  = 1024;    {network}
    driverMask   = 2048;    {device driver}
    app1Mask     = 4096;    {application-defined}
    app2Mask     = 8192;    {application-defined}
    app3Mask     = 16384;   {application-defined}
    app4Mask     = -32768;  {application-defined}
    everyEvent   = -1;      {all event types}
```

```
{ Modifier flags in event record }

activeFlag = 1;        {set if window being activated}
btnState   = 128;      {set if mouse button up}
cmdKey     = 256;      {set if Command key down}
shiftKey   = 512;      {set if Shift key down}
alphaLock  = 1024;     {set if Caps Lock key down}
optionKey  = 2048;     {set if Option key down}

{ Result codes returned by PostEvent }

noErr     = 0;   {no error (event posted)}
evtNotEnb = 1;   {event type not designated in system event mask}
```

Data Types

```
TYPE EventRecord =  RECORD
                       what:       INTEGER;    {event code}
                       message:    LONGINT;    {event message}
                       when:       LONGINT;    {ticks since startup}
                       where:      Point;      {mouse location}
                       modifiers:  INTEGER     {modifier flags}
                    END;

     EvQEl = RECORD
                qLink:          QElemPtr;   {next queue entry}
                qType:          INTEGER;    {queue type}
                evtQWhat:       INTEGER;    {event code}
                evtQMessage:    LONGINT;    {event message}
                evtQWhen:       LONGINT;    {ticks since startup}
                evtQWhere:      Point;      {mouse location}
                evtQModifiers:  INTEGER     {modifier flags}
             END;
```

Routines

Posting and Removing Events

```
FUNCTION  PostEvent   (eventCode: INTEGER; eventMsg: LONGINT) : OSErr;
PROCEDURE FlushEvents (eventMask,stopMask: INTEGER);
```

Accessing Events

```
FUNCTION GetOSEvent    (eventMask: INTEGER; VAR theEvent: EventRecord) :
                        BOOLEAN;
FUNCTION OSEventAvail  (eventMask: INTEGER; VAR theEvent: EventRecord) :
                        BOOLEAN;
```

Setting the System Event Mask

PROCEDURE SetEventMask (theMask: INTEGER);   [Not in ROM]

Directly Accessing the Event Queue

FUNCTION GetEvQHdr : QHdrPtr;   [Not in ROM]

Assembly-Language Information

Constants

```
; Event codes

nullEvt          .EQU     0      ;null
mButDwnEvt       .EQU     1      ;mouse-down
mButUpEvt        .EQU     2      ;mouse-up
keyDwnEvt        .EQU     3      ;key-down
keyUpEvt         .EQU     4      ;key-up
autoKeyEvt       .EQU     5      ;auto-key
updatEvt         .EQU     6      ;update; Toolbox only
diskInsertEvt    .EQU     7      ;disk-inserted
activateEvt      .EQU     8      ;activate; Toolbox only
networkEvt       .EQU     10     ;network
ioDrvrEvt        .EQU     11     ;device driver
app1Evt          .EQU     12     ;application-defined
app2Evt          .EQU     13     ;application-defined
app3Evt          .EQU     14     ;application-defined
app4Evt          .EQU     15     ;application-defined


; Modifier flags in event record

activeFlag       .EQU     0      ;set if window being activated
btnState         .EQU     2      ;set if mouse button up
cmdKey           .EQU     3      ;set if Command key down
shiftKey         .EQU     4      ;set if Shift key down
alphaLock        .EQU     5      ;set if Caps Lock key down
optionKey        .EQU     6      ;set if Option key down


; Result codes returned by PostEvent

noErr            .EQU     0      ;no error (event posted)
evtNotEnb        .EQU     1      ;event type not designated in system
                                 ; event mask
```

Event Record Data Structure

evtNum	Event code (word)
evtMessage	Event message (long)
evtTicks	Ticks since startup (long)
evtMouse	Mouse location (point; long)
evtMeta	State of modifier keys (byte)
evtMBut	State of mouse button (byte)
evtBlkSize	Size in bytes of event record

Event Queue Entry Data Structure

qLink	Pointer to next queue entry
qType	Queue type (word)
evtQWhat	Event code (word)
evtQMessage	Event message (long)
evtQWhen	Ticks since startup (long)
evtQWhere	Mouse location (point; long)
evtQMeta	State of modifier keys (byte)
evtQMBut	State of mouse button (byte)
evtQBlkSize	Size in bytes of event queue entry

Routines

Trap macro	On entry	On exit
_PostEvent	A0: eventCode (word) D0: eventMsg (long)	D0: result code (word)
_FlushEvents	D0: low word: eventMask high word: stopMask	D0: 0 or event code (word)
_GetOSEvent and _OSEventAvail	A0: ptr to event record theEvent D0: eventMask (word)	D0: 0 if non-null event, −1 if null event (byte)

Variables

SysEvtMask	System event mask (word)
EventQueue	Event queue header (10 bytes)

4 THE FILE MANAGER

4 File Manager

ABOUT THIS CHAPTER

This chapter describes the File Manager, the part of the Operating System that controls the exchange of information between a Macintosh application and files. The File Manager allows you to create and access any number of files containing whatever information you choose.

ABOUT THE FILE MANAGER

The File Manager is the part of the Operating System that handles communication between an application and files on block devices such as disk drives. (Block devices are discussed in chapter 6.) Files are a principal means by which data is stored and transmitted on the Macintosh. A **file** is a named, ordered sequence of bytes. The File Manager contains routines used to read from and write to files.

Volumes

A **volume** is a piece of storage medium, such as a disk, formatted to contain files. A volume can be an entire disk or only part of a disk. The 400K-byte 3 1/2-inch Macintosh disk is one volume.

> **Note:** Specialized memory devices other than disks can also contain volumes, but the information in this chapter applies only to volumes on disk.

You identify a volume by its **volume name**, which consists of any sequence of 1 to 27 printing characters. When passed to a routine, volume names must always be followed by a colon (:) to distinguish them from other names. You can use uppercase and lowercase letters when naming volumes, but the File Manager ignores case when comparing names (it doesn't ignore diacritical marks).

> **Note:** The colon after a volume name should be used only when calling File Manager routines; it should never be seen by the user.

A volume contains descriptive information about itself, including its name and a **file directory** that lists information about files contained on the volume; it also contains files. The files are contained in **allocation blocks**, which are areas of volume space occupying multiples of 512 bytes.

A volume can be mounted or unmounted. A volume becomes **mounted** when it's in a disk drive and the File Manager reads descriptive information about the volume into memory. Once mounted, a volume may remain in a drive or be ejected. Only mounted volumes are known to the File Manager, and an application can access information on mounted volumes only. A volume becomes **unmounted** when the File Manager releases the memory used to store the descriptive information. Your application should unmount a volume when it's finished with the volume, or when it needs the memory occupied by the volume.

The File Manager assigns each mounted volume a **volume reference number** that you can use instead of its volume name to refer to it. Every mounted volume is also assigned a **volume buffer**, which is temporary storage space in the heap used when reading or writing information on the volume. The number of volumes that may be mounted at any time is limited only by the number of drives attached and available memory.

A mounted volume can be on-line or off-line. A mounted volume is **on-line** as long as the volume buffer and all the descriptive information read from the volume when it was mounted remain in memory (about 1K to 1.5K bytes); it becomes **off-line** when all but 94 bytes of descriptive information are released. You can access information on on-line volumes immediately, but off-line volumes must be placed on-line before their information can be accessed. An application should place a volume off-line whenever it needs most of the memory the volume occupies. When an application ejects a volume from a drive, the File Manager automatically places the volume off-line.

To prevent unauthorized writing to a volume, volumes can be **locked**. Locking a volume involves either setting a software flag on the volume or changing some part of the volume physically (for example, sliding a tab from one position to another on a disk). Locking a volume ensures that none of the data on the volume can be changed.

Accessing Volumes

You can access a mounted volume via its volume name or volume reference number. On-line volumes in disk drives can also be accessed via the **drive number** of the drive on which the volume is mounted (the internal drive is number 1, the external drive is number 2, and any additional drives connected to the Macintosh will have larger numbers). When accessing a mounted volume, you should always use the volume name or volume reference number, rather than a drive number, because the volume may have been ejected or placed off-line. Whenever possible, use the volume reference number (to avoid confusion between volumes with the same name).

One volume is always the **default volume**. Whenever you call a routine to access a volume but don't specify which volume, the default volume is accessed. Initially, the volume used to start up the application is the default volume, but an application can designate any mounted volume as the default volume.

Whenever the File Manager needs to access a mounted volume that's been ejected from its drive, the dialog box shown in Figure 1 is displayed, and the File Manager waits until the user inserts the disk named volName into a drive.

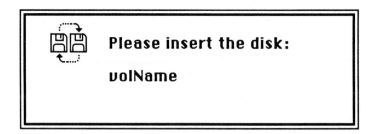

Figure 1. Disk-Switch Dialog

Note: This dialog is actually a system error alert, as described in chapter 12.

Files

A file is a finite sequence of numbered bytes. Any byte or group of bytes in the sequence can be accessed individually. A file is identified by its **file name** and **version number**. A file name consists of any sequence of 1 to 255 printing characters, excluding colons (:). You can use uppercase and lowercase letters when naming files, but the File Manager ignores case when comparing names (it doesn't ignore diacritical marks). The version number is any number from 0 to 255, and is used by the File Manager to distinguish between different files with the same name. A byte within a file is identified by its position within the ordered sequence.

> **Warning:** Your application should constrain file names to fewer than 64 characters, because the Finder will generate an error if given a longer name. You should always assign files a version number of 0, because the Resource Manager, Segment Loader, and Standard File Package won't operate on files with nonzero version numbers, and the Finder ignores version numbers.

There are two parts or **forks** to a file: the **data fork** and the **resource fork**. Normally the resource fork of an application file contains the resources used by the application, such as menus, fonts, and icons, and also the application code itself. The data fork can contain anything an application wants to store there. Information stored in resource forks should always be accessed via the Resource Manager. Information in data forks can only be accessed via the File Manager. For simplicity, "file" will be used instead of "data fork" in this chapter.

The size of a file is limited only by the size of the volume it's on. Each byte is numbered: The first byte is byte 0. You can read bytes from and write bytes to a file either singly or in sequences of unlimited length. Each read or write operation can start anywhere in the file, regardless of where the last operation began or ended. Figure 2 shows the structure of a file.

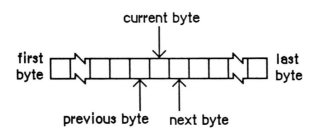

Figure 2. A File

A file's maximum size is defined by its **physical end-of-file**, which is 1 greater than the number of the last byte in its last allocation block (see Figure 3). The physical end-of-file is equivalent to the maximum number of bytes the file can contain. A file's actual size is defined by its **logical end-of-file**, which is 1 greater than the number of the last byte in the file. The logical end-of-file is equivalent to the actual number of bytes in the file, since the first byte is byte number 0. The physical end-of-file is always greater than the logical end-of-file. For example, an empty file (one with 0 bytes) in a 1K-byte allocation block has a logical end-of-file of 0 and a physical end-of-file of 1024. A file with 50 bytes has a logical end-of-file of 50 and a physical end-of-file of 1024.

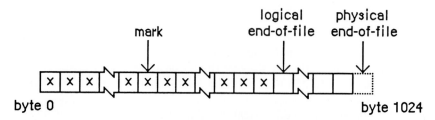

mark   logical end-of-file   physical end-of-file

byte 0   byte 1024

Figure 3. End-of-File and Mark

The current position marker, or **mark**, is the number of the next byte that will be read or written. The value of the mark can't exceed the value of the logical end-of-file. The mark automatically moves forward one byte for every byte read from or written to the file. If, during a write operation, the mark meets the logical end-of-file, both are moved forward one position for every additional byte written to the file. Figure 4 shows the movement of the mark and logical end-of-file.

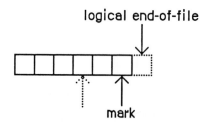

logical end-of-file

mark

Beginning position

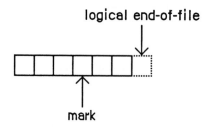

logical end-of-file

mark

After reading two bytes

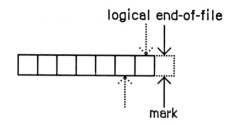

logical end-of-file

mark

After writing two bytes

Figure 4. Movement of Mark and Logical End-of-File

If, during a write operation, the mark must move past the physical end-of-file, another allocation block is added to the file—the physical end-of-file is placed one byte beyond the end of the new allocation block, and the mark and logical end-of-file are placed at the first byte of the new allocation block.

An application can move the logical end-of-file to anywhere from the beginning of the file to the physical end-of-file (the mark is adjusted accordingly). If the logical end-of-file is moved to a position more than one allocation block short of the current physical end-of-file, the unneeded allocation block will be deleted from the file. The mark can be placed anywhere from the first byte in the file to the logical end-of-file.

Accessing Files

A file can be **open** or **closed**. An application can perform only certain operations, such as reading and writing, on open files; other operations, such as deleting, can be performed only on closed files.

To open a file, you must identify the file and the volume containing it. When a file is opened, the File Manager creates an **access path**, a description of the route to be followed when accessing the file. The access path specifies the volume on which the file is located (by volume reference number, drive number, or volume name) and the location of the file on the volume. Every access path is assigned a unique **path reference number** (a number greater than 0) that's used to refer to it. You should always refer to a file via its path reference number, to avoid confusion between files with the same name.

A file can have one access path open for writing or for both reading and writing, and one or more access paths for reading only; there cannot be more than one access path that writes to a file. Each access path is separate from all other access paths to the file. A maximum of 12 access paths can be open at one time. Each access path can move its own mark and read at the position it indicates. All access paths to the same file share common logical and physical end-of-file markers.

The File Manager reads descriptive information about a newly opened file from its volume and stores it in memory. For example, each file has **open permission** information, which indicates whether data can only be read from it, or both read from and written to it. Each access path contains **read/write permission** information that specifies whether data is allowed to be read from the file, written to the file, both read and written, or whatever the file's open permission allows. If an application wants to write data to a file, both types of permission information must allow writing; if either type allows reading only, then no data can be written.

When an application requests that data be read from a file, the File Manager reads the data from the file and transfers it to the application's **data buffer**. Any part of the data that can be transferred in entire 512-byte blocks is transferred directly. Any part of the data composed of fewer than 512 bytes is also read from the file in one 512-byte block, but placed in temporary storage space in memory. Then, only the bytes containing the requested data are transferred to the application.

When an application writes data to a file, the File Manager transfers the data from the application's data buffer and writes it to the file. Any part of the data that can be transferred in entire 512-byte blocks is written directly. Any part of the data composed of fewer than 512 bytes is placed in temporary storage space in memory until 512 bytes have accumulated; then the entire block is written all at once.

Normally the temporary space in memory used for all reading and writing is the volume buffer, but an application can specify that an **access path buffer** be used instead for a particular access path (see Figure 5).

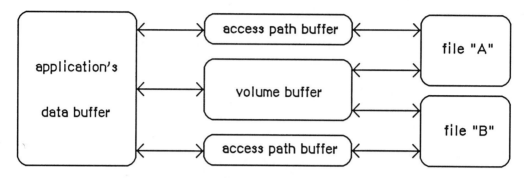

Figure 5. Buffers For Transferring Data

Warning: You must lock any access path buffers of files in relocatable blocks, so their location doesn't change while the file is open.

Your application can **lock** a file to prevent unauthorized writing to it. Locking a file ensures that none of the data in it can be changed. This is distinct from the user-accessible lock maintained by the Finder, which won't let you rename or delete a locked file, but will let you change the data contained in the file.

Note: Advanced programmers: The File Manager can also read a continuous stream of characters or a line of characters. In the first case, you ask the File Manager to read a specific number of bytes: When that many have been read or when the mark has reached the logical end-of-file, the read operation terminates. In the second case, called **newline mode**, the read will terminate when either of the above conditions is met or when a specified character, the **newline character**, is read. The newline character is usually Return (ASCII code $0D), but can be any character. Information about newline mode is associated with each access path to a file, and can differ from one access path to another.

FILE INFORMATION USED BY THE FINDER

A file directory on a volume lists information about all the files on the volume. The information used by the Finder is contained in a data structure of type FInfo:

```
TYPE FInfo = RECORD
            fdType:     OSType;    {file type}
            fdCreator:  OSType;    {file's creator}
            fdFlags:    INTEGER;   {flags}
            fdLocation: Point;     {file's location}
            fdFldr:     INTEGER    {file's window}
          END;
```

Normally an application need only set the file type and creator when a file is created, and the Finder will manipulate the other fields. (File type and creator are discussed in chapter 1 of Volume III.)

FdFlags indicates whether the file's icon is invisible, whether the file has a bundle, and other characteristics used internally by the Finder:

Bit	Meaning
13	Set if file has a bundle
14	Set if file's icon is invisible

Masks for these two bits are available as predefined constants:

```
CONST fHasBundle = 8192;    {set if file has a bundle}
      fInvisible = 16384;   {set if file's icon is invisible}
```

For more information about bundles, see chapter 1 of Volume III.

The last two fields indicate where the file's icon will appear if the icon is visible. FdLocation contains the location of the file's icon in its window, given in the local coordinate system of the window. It's used by the Finder to position the icon; when creating a file you should set it to 0 and let the Finder position the icon for you. FdFldr indicates the window in which the file's icon will appear, and may contain one of the following values:

```
CONST fTrash   = -3;  {file is in Trash window}
      fDesktop = -2;  {file is on desktop}
      fDisk    =  0;  {file is in disk window}
```

If fdFldr contains a positive number, the file's icon will appear in a folder; the numbers that identify folders are assigned by the Finder. You can also get the folder number of an existing file, and place additional files in that same folder.

USING THE FILE MANAGER

You can call File Manager routines via three different methods: high-level Pascal calls, low-level Pascal calls, and assembly language. The high-level Pascal calls are designed for Pascal programmers interested in using the File Manager in a simple manner; they provide adequate file I/O and don't require much special knowledge to use. The low-level Pascal and assembly-language calls are designed for advanced Pascal programmers and assembly-language programmers interested in using the File Manager to its fullest capacity; they require some special knowledge to be used most effectively.

Information for all programmers follows here. The next two sections contain special information for high-level Pascal programmers and for low-level Pascal and assembly-language programmers.

Note: The names used to refer to File Manager routines here are actually the assembly-language macro names for the low-level routines, but the Pascal routine names are very similar.

The File Manager is automatically initialized each time the system starts up.

To create a new, empty file, call Create. Create allows you to set some of the information stored on the volume about the file.

To open a file, call Open. The File Manager creates an access path and returns a path reference number that you'll use every time you want to refer to it. Before you open a file, you may want to call the Standard File Package, which presents the standard interface through which the user can specify the file to be opened. The Standard File Package will return the name of the file, the volume reference number of the volume containing the file, and additional information. (If the user inserts an unmounted volume into a drive, the Standard File Package will automatically call the Disk Initialization Package to attempt to mount it.)

After opening a file, you can transfer data from it to an application's data buffer with Read, and send data from an application's data buffer to the file with Write. You can't use Write on a file whose open permission only allows reading, or on a file on a locked volume.

You can specify the byte position of the mark before calling Read or Write by calling SetFPos. GetFPos returns the byte position of the mark.

Once you've completed whatever reading and writing you want to do, call Close to close the file. Close writes the contents of the file's access path buffer to the volume and deletes the access path. You can remove a closed file (both forks) from a volume by calling Delete.

To protect against power loss or unexpected disk ejection, you should periodically call FlushVol (probably after each time you close a file), which writes the contents of the volume buffer and all access path buffers (if any) to the volume and updates the descriptive information contained on the volume.

Whenever your application is finished with a disk, or the user chooses Eject from a menu, call Eject. Eject calls FlushVol, places the volume off-line, and then physically ejects the volume from its drive.

The preceding paragraphs covered the simplest File Manager routines. The remainder of this section describes the less commonly used routines, some of which are available only to advanced programmers.

Applications will normally use the Resource Manager to open resource forks and change the information contained within, but programmers writing unusual applications (such as a disk-copying utility) might want to use the File Manager to open resource forks. This is done by calling OpenRF. As with Open, the File Manager creates an access path and returns a path reference number that you'll use every time you want to refer to this resource fork.

When the Toolbox Event Manager function GetNextEvent receives a disk-inserted event, it calls the Desk Manager function SystemEvent. SystemEvent calls the File Manager function MountVol, which attempts to mount the volume on the disk. GetNextEvent then returns the disk-inserted event: The low-order word of the event message contains the number of the drive, and the high-order word contains the result code of the attempted mounting. If the result code indicates that an error occurred, you'll need to call the Disk Initialization Package to allow the user to initialize or eject the volume.

Note: Applications that rely on the Operating System Event Manager function GetOSEvent to learn about events (and don't call GetNextEvent) must explicitly call MountVol to mount volumes.

After a volume has been mounted, your application can call GetVolInfo, which will return the name of the volume, the amount of unused space on the volume, and a volume reference number that you can use to refer to that volume.

To minimize the amount of memory used by mounted volumes, an application can unmount or place off-line any volumes that aren't currently being used. To unmount a volume, call UnmountVol, which flushes a volume (by calling FlushVol) and releases all of the memory used for it (about 1 to 1.5K bytes). To place a volume off-line, call OffLine, which flushes a volume and releases all of the memory used for it except for 94 bytes of descriptive information about the volume. Off-line volumes are placed on-line by the File Manager as needed, but your application must remount any unmounted volumes it wants to access. The File Manager itself may place volumes off-line during its normal operation.

If you would like all File Manager calls to apply to one volume, you can specify that volume as the default. You can use SetVol to set the default volume to any mounted volume, and GetVol to learn the name and volume reference number of the default volume.

Normally, volume initialization and naming is handled by the Standard File Package, which calls the Disk Initialization Package. If you want to initialize a volume explicitly or erase all files from a volume, you can call the Disk Initialization Package directly. When you want to change the name of a volume, call the File Manager function Rename.

Whenever a disk has been reconstructed in an attempt to salvage lost files (because its directory or other file-access information has been destroyed), the logical end-of-file of each file will probably be equal to each physical end-of-file, regardless of where the actual logical end-of-file is. The first time an application attempts to read from a file on a reconstructed volume, it will blindly pass the correct logical end-of-file and read misinformation until it reaches the new, incorrect logical end-of-file. To prevent this from happening, an application should always maintain an independent record of the logical end-of-file of each file it uses. To determine the File Manager's conception of the length of a file, or find out how many bytes have yet to be read from it, call GetEOF, which returns the logical end-of-file. You can change the length of a file by calling SetEOF.

Allocation blocks are automatically added to and deleted from a file as necessary. If this happens to a number of files alternately, each of the files will be contained in allocation blocks scattered throughout the volume, which increases the time required to access those files. To prevent such fragmentation of files, you can allocate a number of contiguous allocation blocks to an open file by calling Allocate.

Instead of calling FlushVol, an unusual application might call FlushFile. FlushFile forces the contents of a file's volume buffer and access path buffer (if any) to be written to its volume. FlushFile doesn't update the descriptive information contained on the volume, so the volume information won't be correct until you call FlushVol.

To get information about a file stored on a volume (such as its name and creation date), call GetFileInfo. You can change this information by calling SetFileInfo. Changing the name or version number of a file is accomplished by calling Rename or SetFilType, respectively; they have a similar effect, since both the file name and version number are needed to identify a file. You can lock or unlock a file by calling SetFilLock or RstFilLock, respectively. Given a path reference number, you can get the volume reference number of the volume containing that file by calling GetVRefNum.

4 File Manager

HIGH-LEVEL FILE MANAGER ROUTINES

This section describes all the high-level Pascal routines of the File Manager. For information on calling the low-level Pascal and assembly-language routines, see the next section.

When accessing a volume other than the default volume, you must identify it by its volume name, its volume reference number, or the drive number of its drive. The parameter names used in identifying a volume are volName, vRefNum, and drvNum. VRefNum and drvNum are both integers. VolName is a pointer, of type StringPtr, to a volume name.

> **Note:** VolName is declared as type StringPtr instead of type STRING to allow you to pass NIL in routines where the parameter is optional.

The File Manager determines which volume to access by using one of the following:

1. VolName. (If volName points to a zero-length name, an error is returned.)

2. If volName is NIL or points to an improper volume name, then vRefNum or drvNum (only one is given per routine).

3. If vRefNum or drvNum is 0, the default volume. (If there isn't a default volume, an error is returned.)

> **Warning:** Before you pass a parameter of type StringPtr to a File Manager routine, be sure that memory has been allocated for the variable. For example, the following statements will ensure that memory is allocated for the variable myStr:

```
VAR   myStr: Str255;
      . . .

result := GetVol(@myStr,myRefNum)
```

When accessing a closed file on a volume, you must identify the volume by the method given above, and identify the file by its name in the fileName parameter. (The high-level File Manager routines will work only with files having a version number of 0.) FileName can contain either the file name alone or the file name prefixed by a volume name.

> **Note:** Although fileName can include both the volume name and the file name, applications shouldn't encourage users to prefix a file name with a volume name.

You can't specify an access path buffer when calling high-level Pascal routines. All access paths open on a volume will share the volume buffer, causing a slight increase in the amount of time required to access files.

All high-level File Manager routines return an integer result code of type OSErr as their function result. Each routine description lists all of the applicable result codes, along with a short description of what the result code means. Lengthier explanations of all the result codes can be found in the summary at the end of this chapter.

Accessing Volumes

```
FUNCTION GetVInfo (drvNum: INTEGER; volName: StringPtr; VAR
        vRefNum: INTEGER; VAR freeBytes: LONGINT) : OSErr;
        [Not in ROM]
```

GetVInfo returns the name, reference number, and available space (in bytes), in volName, vRefNum, and freeBytes, for the volume in the drive specified by drvNum.

Result codes	noErr	No error
	nsvErr	No default volume
	paramErr	Bad drive number

```
FUNCTION GetVRefNum (pathRefNum: INTEGER; VAR vRefNum: INTEGER) :
        OSErr;   [Not in ROM]
```

Given a path reference number in pathRefNum, GetVRefNum returns the volume reference number in vRefNum.

Result codes	noErr	No error
	rfNumErr	Bad reference number

```
FUNCTION GetVol (volName: StringPtr; VAR vRefNum: INTEGER) :
        OSErr;   [Not in ROM]
```

GetVol returns the name of the default volume in volName and its volume reference number in vRefNum.

Result codes	noErr	No error
	nsvErr	No such volume

```
FUNCTION SetVol (volName: StringPtr; vRefNum: INTEGER) : OSErr;
        [Not in ROM]
```

SetVol sets the default volume to the mounted volume specified by volName or vRefNum.

Result codes	noErr	No error
	bdNamErr	Bad volume name
	nsvErr	No such volume
	paramErr	No default volume

```
FUNCTION FlushVol (volName: StringPtr; vRefNum: INTEGER) : OSErr;
        [Not in ROM]
```

On the volume specified by volName or vRefNum, FlushVol writes the contents of the associated volume buffer and descriptive information about the volume (if they've changed since the last time FlushVol was called).

Result codes   noErr   No error

	bdNamErr	Bad volume name
	extFSErr	External file system
	ioErr	I/O error
	nsDrvErr	No such drive
	nsvErr	No such volume
	paramErr	No default volume

```
FUNCTION UnmountVol (volName: StringPtr; vRefNum: INTEGER) :
          OSErr;   [Not in ROM]
```

UnmountVol unmounts the volume specified by volName or vRefNum, by calling FlushVol to flush the volume buffer, closing all open files on the volume, and releasing the memory used for the volume.

> **Warning:** Don't unmount the startup volume.

Result codes		
	noErr	No error
	bdNamErr	Bad volume name
	extFSErr	External file system
	ioErr	I/O error
	nsDrvErr	No such drive
	nsvErr	No such volume
	paramErr	No default volume

```
FUNCTION Eject (volName: StringPtr; vRefNum: INTEGER) : OSErr;
          [Not in ROM]
```

Eject flushes the volume specified by volName or vRefNum, places it off-line, and then ejects the volume.

Result codes		
	noErr	No error
	bdNamErr	Bad volume name
	extFSErr	External file system
	ioErr	I/O error
	nsDrvErr	No such drive
	nsvErr	No such volume
	paramErr	No default volume

Accessing Files

```
FUNCTION Create (fileName: Str255; vRefNum: INTEGER; creator:
          OSType; fileType: OSType) : OSErr;   [Not in ROM]
```

Create creates a new file (both forks) with the specified name, file type, and creator, on the specified volume. (File type and creator are discussed in chapter 1 of Volume III.) The new file is unlocked and empty. The date and time of its creation and last modification are set to the current date and time.

Result codes	noErr	No error
	bdNamErr	Bad file name
	dupFNErr	Duplicate file name and version
	dirFulErr	File directory full
	extFSErr	External file system
	ioErr	I/O error
	nsvErr	No such volume
	vLckdErr	Software volume lock
	wPrErr	Hardware volume lock

```
FUNCTION FSOpen (fileName: Str255; vRefNum: INTEGER; VAR refNum:
        INTEGER) : OSErr;   [Not in ROM]
```

FSOpen creates an access path to the file having the name fileName on the volume specified by vRefNum. A path reference number is returned in refNum. The access path's read/write permission is set to whatever the file's open permission allows.

Result codes	noErr	No error
	bdNamErr	Bad file name
	extFSErr	External file system
	fnfErr	File not found
	ioErr	I/O error
	nsvErr	No such volume
	opWrErr	File already open for writing
	tmfoErr	Too many files open

```
FUNCTION OpenRF (fileName: Str255; vRefNum: INTEGER; VAR refNum:
        INTEGER) : OSErr;   [Not in ROM]
```

OpenRF is similar to FSOpen; the only difference is that OpenRF opens the resource fork of the specified file rather than the data fork. A path reference number is returned in refNum. The access path's read/write permission is set to whatever the file's open permission allows.

Note: Normally you should access a file's resource fork through the routines of the Resource Manager rather than the File Manager. OpenRF doesn't read the resource map into memory; it's really only useful for block-level operations such as copying files.

Result codes	noErr	No error
	bdNamErr	Bad file name
	extFSErr	External file system
	fnfErr	File not found
	ioErr	I/O error
	nsvErr	No such volume
	opWrErr	File already open for writing
	tmfoErr	Too many files open

```
FUNCTION FSRead (refNum: INTEGER; VAR count: LONGINT; buffPtr:
        Ptr) : OSErr;   [Not in ROM]
```

FSRead attempts to read the number of bytes specified by the count parameter from the open file whose access path is specified by refNum, and transfer them to the data buffer pointed to by buffPtr. The read operation begins at the current mark, so you might want to precede this with a call to SetFPos. If you try to read past the logical end-of-file, FSRead moves the mark to the end-of-file and returns eofErr as its function result. After the read is completed, the number of bytes actually read is returned in the count parameter.

Result codes		
	noErr	No error
	eofErr	End-of-file
	extFSErr	External file system
	fnOpnErr	File not open
	ioErr	I/O error
	paramErr	Negative count
	rfNumErr	Bad reference number

```
FUNCTION FSWrite (refNum: INTEGER; VAR count: LONGINT; buffPtr:
        Ptr) : OSErr;   [Not in ROM]
```

FSWrite takes the number of bytes specified by the count parameter from the buffer pointed to by buffPtr and attempts to write them to the open file whose access path is specified by refNum. The write operation begins at the current mark, so you might want to precede this with a call to SetFPos. After the write is completed, the number of bytes actually written is returned in the count parameter.

Result codes		
	noErr	No error
	dskFulErr	Disk full
	fLckdErr	File locked
	fnOpnErr	File not open
	ioErr	I/O error
	paramErr	Negative count
	rfNumErr	Bad reference number
	vLckdErr	Software volume lock
	wPrErr	Hardware volume lock
	wrPermErr	Read/write permission doesn't allow writing

```
FUNCTION GetFPos (refNum: INTEGER; VAR filePos: LONGINT) : OSErr;
        [Not in ROM]
```

GetFPos returns, in filePos, the mark of the open file whose access path is specified by refNum.

Result codes		
	noErr	No error
	extFSErr	External file system
	fnOpnErr	File not open
	ioErr	I/O error
	rfNumErr	Bad reference number

```
FUNCTION SetFPos (refNum: INTEGER; posMode: INTEGER; posOff:
           LONGINT) : OSErr;   [Not in ROM]
```

SetFPos sets the mark of the open file whose access path is specified by refNum, to the position specified by posMode and posOff. PosMode indicates how to position the mark; it must contain one of the following values:

```
CONST fsAtMark    = 0;   {at current mark}
      fsFromStart = 1;   {offset relative to beginning of file}
      fsFromLEOF  = 2;   {offset relative to logical end-of-file}
      fsFromMark  = 3;   {offset relative to current mark}
```

PosOff specifies the byte offset (either positive or negative), relative to the position specified by posMode, where the mark should be set (except when posMode is equal to fsAtMark, in which case posOff is ignored). If you try to set the mark past the logical end-of-file, SetFPos moves the mark to the end-of-file and returns eofErr as its function result.

Result codes	noErr	No error
	eofErr	End-of-file
	extFSErr	External file system
	fnOpnErr	File not open
	ioErr	I/O error
	posErr	Attempt to position before start of file
	rfNumErr	Bad reference number

```
FUNCTION GetEOF (refNum: INTEGER; VAR logEOF: LONGINT) : OSErr;
          [Not in ROM]
```

GetEOF returns, in logEOF, the logical end-of-file of the open file whose access path is specified by refNum.

Result codes	noErr	No error
	extFSErr	External file system
	fnOpnErr	File not open
	ioErr	I/O error
	rfNumErr	Bad reference number

```
FUNCTION SetEOF (refNum: INTEGER; logEOF: LONGINT) : OSErr;   [Not in
          ROM]
```

SetEOF sets the logical end-of-file of the open file whose access path is specified by refNum, to the position specified by logEOF. If you attempt to set the logical end-of-file beyond the physical end-of-file, the physical end-of-file is set to one byte beyond the end of the next free allocation block; if there isn't enough space on the volume, no change is made, and SetEOF returns dskFulErr as its function result. If logEOF is 0, all space occupied by the file on the volume is released.

Result codes   noErr   No error

	noErr	No error
	dskFulErr	Disk full
	extFSErr	External file system
	fLckdErr	File locked
	fnOpnErr	File not open
	ioErr	I/O error
	rfNumErr	Bad reference number
	vLckdErr	Software volume lock
	wPrErr	Hardware volume lock
	wrPermErr	Read/write permission doesn't allow writing

```
FUNCTION Allocate (refNum: INTEGER; VAR count: LONGINT) : OSErr;
     [Not in ROM]
```

Allocate adds the number of bytes specified by the count parameter to the open file whose access path is specified by refNum, and sets the physical end-of-file to one byte beyond the last block allocated. The number of bytes actually allocated is rounded up to the nearest multiple of the allocation block size, and returned in the count parameter. If there isn't enough empty space on the volume to satisfy the allocation request, Allocate allocates the rest of the space on the volume and returns dskFulErr as its function result.

Result codes	noErr	No error
	dskFulErr	Disk full
	fLckdErr	File locked
	fnOpnErr	File not open
	ioErr	I/O error
	rfNumErr	Bad reference number
	vLckdErr	Software volume lock
	wPrErr	Hardware volume lock
	wrPermErr	Read/write permission doesn't allow writing

```
FUNCTION FSClose (refNum: INTEGER) : OSErr;   [Not in ROM]
```

FSClose removes the access path specified by refNum, writes the contents of the volume buffer to the volume, and updates the file's entry in the file directory.

Note: Some information stored on the volume won't be correct until FlushVol is called.

Result codes	noErr	No error
	extFSErr	External file system
	fnfErr	File not found
	fnOpnErr	File not open
	ioErr	I/O error
	nsvErr	No such volume
	rfNumErr	Bad reference number

Changing Information About Files

All of the routines described in this section affect both forks of the file, and don't require the file to be open.

```
FUNCTION GetFInfo (fileName: Str255; vRefNum: INTEGER; VAR
        fndrInfo: FInfo) : OSErr;   [Not in ROM]
```

For the file having the name fileName on the specified volume, GetFInfo returns information used by the Finder in fndrInfo (see the section "File Information Used by the Finder").

Result codes	noErr	No error
	bdNamErr	Bad file name
	extFSErr	External file system
	fnfErr	File not found
	ioErr	I/O error
	nsvErr	No such volume
	paramErr	No default volume

```
FUNCTION SetFInfo (fileName: Str255; vRefNum: INTEGER; fndrInfo:
        FInfo) : OSErr;   [Not in ROM]
```

For the file having the name fileName on the specified volume, SetFInfo sets information used by the Finder to fndrInfo (see the section "File Information Used by the Finder").

Result codes	noErr	No error
	extFSErr	External file system
	fLckd Err	File locked
	fnfErr	File not found
	ioErr	I/O error
	nsvErr	No such volume
	vLckdErr	Software volume lock
	wPrErr	Hardware volume lock

```
FUNCTION SetFLock (fileName: Str255; vRefNum: INTEGER) : OSErr;
        [Not in ROM]
```

SetFLock locks the file having the name fileName on the specified volume. Access paths currently in use aren't affected.

Note: This lock is controlled by your application, and is distinct from the user-accessible lock maintained by the Finder.

4 File Manager

Result codes	noErr	No error
	extFSErr	External file system
	fnfErr	File not found
	ioErr	I/O error
	nsvErr	No such volume
	vLckdErr	Software volume lock
	wPrErr	Hardware volume lock

```
FUNCTION RstFLock (fileName: Str255; vRefNum: INTEGER) : OSErr;
        [Not in ROM]
```

RstFLock unlocks the file having the name fileName on the specified volume. Access paths currently in use aren't affected.

Result codes	noErr	No error
	extFSErr	External file system
	fnfErr	File not found
	ioErr	I/O error
	nsvErr	No such volume
	vLckdErr	Software volume lock
	wPrErr	Hardware volume lock

```
FUNCTION Rename (oldName: Str255; vRefNum: INTEGER; newName:
        Str255) : OSErr;   [Not in ROM]
```

Given a file name in oldName, Rename changes the name of the file to newName. Access paths currently in use aren't affected. Given a volume name in oldName or a volume reference number in vRefNum, Rename changes the name of the specified volume to newName.

Warning: If you're renaming a volume, be sure that oldName ends with a colon, or Rename will consider it a file name.

Result codes	noErr	No error
	bdNamErr	Bad file name
	dirFulErr	Directory full
	dupFNErr	Duplicate file name
	extFSErr	External file system
	fLckdErr	File locked
	fnfErr	File not found
	fsRnErr	Problem during rename
	ioErr	I/O error
	nsvErr	No such volume
	paramErr	No default volume
	vLckdErr	Software volume lock
	wPrErr	Hardware volume lock

```
FUNCTION FSDelete (fileName: Str255; vRefNum: INTEGER) : OSErr;
         [Not in ROM]
```

FSDelete removes the closed file having the name fileName from the specified volume.

>   **Note:** This function will delete *both* forks of the file.

Result codes		
	noErr	No error
	bdNamErr	Bad file name
	extFSErr	External file system
	fBsyErr	File busy
	fLckdErr	File locked
	fnfErr	File not found
	ioErr	I/O error
	nsvErr	No such volume
	vLckdErr	Software volume lock
	wPrErr	Hardware volume lock

LOW-LEVEL FILE MANAGER ROUTINES

This section contains information for programmers using the low-level Pascal or assembly-language routines of the File Manager, and describes them in detail.

Most low-level File Manager routines can be executed either **synchronously** (meaning that the application can't continue until the routine is completed) or **asynchronously** (meaning that the application is free to perform other tasks while the routine is executing). Some cannot be executed asynchronously, because they use the Memory Manager to allocate and release memory.

When an application calls a File Manager routine asynchronously, an **I/O request** is placed in the **file I/O queue,** and control returns to the calling program—possibly even before the actual I/O is completed. Requests are taken from the queue one at a time, and processed; meanwhile, the calling program is free to work on other things.

The calling program may specify a **completion routine** to be executed at the end of an asynchronous operation.

At any time, you can clear all queued File Manager calls except the current one by using the InitQueue procedure. InitQueue is especially useful when an error occurs and you no longer want queued calls to be executed.

Routine parameters passed by an application to the File Manager and returned by the File Manager to an application are contained in a **parameter block,** which is a data structure in the heap or stack. Most low-level calls to the File Manager are of the form

```
FUNCTION PBCallName (paramBlock: ParmBlkPtr; async: BOOLEAN) : OSErr;
```

PBCallName is the name of the routine. ParamBlock points to the parameter block containing the parameters for the routine. If async is TRUE, the call is executed asynchronously; otherwise the call is executed synchronously. The routine returns an integer result code of type OSErr. Each routine description lists all of the applicable result codes, along with a short description of what the result code means. Lengthier explanations of all the result codes can be found in the summary at the end of this chapter.

Assembly-language note: When you call a File Manager routine, A0 must point to a parameter block containing the parameters for the routine. If you want the routine to be executed asynchronously, set bit 10 of the routine trap word. You can do this by supplying the word ASYNC as the second argument to the routine macro. For example:

```
_Read    ,ASYNC
```

You can set or test bit 10 of a trap word by using the global constant asyncTrpBit. (The syntax shown above applies to the Lisa Workshop Assembler; programmers using another development system should consult its documentation for the proper syntax.)

All routines except InitQueue return a result code in D0.

Routine Parameters

There are three different kinds of parameter blocks you'll pass to File Manager routines. Each kind is used with a particular set of routine calls: I/O routines, file information routines, and volume information routines.

The lengthy, variable-length data structure of a parameter block is given below. The Device Manager and File Manager use this same data structure, but only the parts relevant to the File Manager are discussed here. Each kind of parameter block contains eight fields of standard information and nine to 16 fields of additional information:

```
TYPE ParamBlkType  = (ioParam,fileParam,volumeParam,cntrlParam);

ParamBlockRec = RECORD
                 qLink:       QElemPtr;     {next queue entry}
                 qType:       INTEGER;      {queue type}
                 ioTrap:      INTEGER;      {routine trap}
                 ioCmdAddr:   Ptr;          {routine address}
                 ioCompletion: ProcPtr;     {completion routine}
                 ioResult:    OSErr;        {result code}
                 ioNamePtr:   StringPtr;    {volume or file name}
                 ioVRefNum:   INTEGER;      {volume reference or }
                                            { drive number}
                 CASE ParamBlkType OF
                  ioParam:
                   . . .  {I/O routine parameters}
                  fileParam:
                   . . .  {file information routine parameters}
                  volumeParam:
                   . . .  {volume information routine parameters}
                  cntrlParam:
                   . . .  {used by the Device Manager}
                END;

    ParmBlkPtr = ^ParamBlockRec;
```

The first four fields in each parameter block are handled entirely by the File Manager, and most programmers needn't be concerned with them; programmers who are interested in them should see the section "Data Structures in Memory".

IOCompletion contains a pointer to a completion routine to be executed at the end of an asynchronous call; it should be NIL for asynchronous calls with no completion routine, and is automatically set to NIL for all synchronous calls.

> **Warning:** Completion routines are executed at the interrupt level and must preserve all registers other than A0, A1, and D0–D2. Your completion routine must not make any calls to the Memory Manager, directly or indirectly, and can't depend on handles to unlocked blocks being valid. If it uses application globals, it must also ensure that register A5 contains the address of the boundary between the application globals and the application parameters; for details, see SetUpA5 and RestoreA5 in chapter 13.

> **Assembly-language note:** When your completion routine is called, register A0 points to the parameter block of the asynchronous call and register D0 contains the result code.

Routines that are executed asynchronously return control to the calling program with the result code noErr as soon as the call is placed in the file I/O queue. This isn't an indication of successful call completion, but simply indicates that the call was successfully queued. To determine when the call is actually completed, you can poll the ioResult field; this field is set to 1 when the call is made, and receives the actual result code upon completion of the call. Completion routines are executed after the result code is placed in ioResult.

IONamePtr points to either a volume name or a file name (which can be prefixed by a volume name).

> **Note:** Although ioNamePtr can include both the volume name and the file name, applications shouldn't encourage users to prefix a file name with a volume name.

IOVRefNum contains either the reference number of a volume or the drive number of a drive containing a volume.

For routines that access volumes, the File Manager determines which volume to access by using one of the following:

1. IONamePtr, a pointer to the volume name (which must be followed by a colon).
2. If ioNamePtr is NIL, or points to an improper volume name, then ioVRefNum. (If ioVRefNum is negative, it's a volume reference number; if positive, it's a drive number.)
3. If ioVRefNum is 0, the default volume. (If there isn't a default volume, an error is returned.)

For routines that access closed files, the File Manager determines which file to access by using ioNamePtr, a pointer to the name of the file (and possibly also of the volume).

- If the string pointed to by ioNamePtr doesn't include the volume name, the File Manager uses steps 2 and 3 above to determine the volume.

- If ioNamePtr is NIL or points to an improper file name, an error is returned.

I/O Parameters

When you call one of the I/O routines, you'll use these nine additional fields after the standard eight fields in the parameter block:

```
ioParam:
  (ioRefNum:    INTEGER;       {path reference number}
   ioVersNum:   SignedByte;    {version number}
   ioPermssn:   SignedByte;    {read/write permission}
   ioMisc:      Ptr;           {miscellaneous}
   ioBuffer:    Ptr;           {data buffer}
   ioReqCount:  LONGINT;       {requested number of bytes}
   ioActCount:  LONGINT;       {actual number of bytes}
   ioPosMode:   INTEGER;       {positioning mode and newline character}
   ioPosOffset: LONGINT);      {positioning offset}
```

For routines that access open files, the File Manager determines which file to access by using the path reference number in ioRefNum. IOVersNum is the file's version number, normally 0. IOPermssn requests permission to read or write via an access path, and must contain one of the following values:

```
CONST fsCurPerm   = 0;   {whatever is currently allowed}
      fsRdPerm    = 1;   {request to read only}
      fsWrPerm    = 2;   {request to write only}
      fsRdWrPerm  = 3;   {request to read and write}
```

This request is compared with the open permission of the file. If the open permission doesn't allow I/O as requested, a result code indicating the error is returned.

The content of ioMisc depends on the routine called. It contains either a new logical end-of-file, a new version number, a pointer to an access path buffer, or a pointer to a new volume or file name. Since ioMisc is of type Ptr, you'll need to perform type coercion to correctly interpret the value of ioMisc when it contains an end-of-file (a LONGINT) or version number (a SignedByte).

IOBuffer points to a data buffer into which data is written by Read calls and from which data is read by Write calls. IOReqCount specifies the requested number of bytes to be read, written, or allocated. IOActCount contains the number of bytes actually read, written, or allocated.

IOPosMode and ioPosOffset contain positioning information used for Read, Write, and SetFPos calls. IOPosMode contains the positioning mode; bits 0 and 1 indicate how to position the mark, and you can use the following predefined constants to set or test their value:

```
CONST fsAtMark     = 0;   {at current mark}
      fsFromStart  = 1;   {offset relative to beginning of file}
      fsFromLEOF   = 2;   {offset relative to logical end-of-file}
      fsFromMark   = 3;   {offset relative to current mark}
```

IOPosOffset specifies the byte offset (either positive or negative), relative to the position specified by the positioning mode, where the operation will be performed (except when the positioning mode is fsAtMark, in which case ioPosOffset is ignored).

To have the File Manager verify that all data written to a volume exactly matches the data in memory, make a Read call right after the Write call. The parameters for a read-verify operation are the same as for a standard Read call, except that the following constant must be added to the positioning mode:

```
CONST rdVerify = 64;   {read-verify mode}
```

The result code ioErr is returned if any of the data doesn't match.

> **Note:** Advanced programmers: Bit 7 of ioPosMode is the newline flag; it's set if read operations should terminate at a newline character. The ASCII code of the newline character is specified in the high-order byte of ioPosMode. If the newline flag is set, the data will be read one byte at a time until the newline character is encountered, ioReqCount bytes have been read, or the end-of-file is reached. If the newline flag is clear, the data will be read one byte at a time until ioReqCount bytes have been read or the end-of-file is reached.

File Information Parameters

Some File Manager routines, including GetFileInfo and SetFileInfo, use the following 16 additional fields after the standard eight fields in the parameter block:

```
fileParam:
(ioFRefNum:    INTEGER;      {path reference number}
 ioFVersNum:   SignedByte;   {version number}
 filler1:      SignedByte;   {not used}
 ioFDirIndex:  INTEGER;      {sequence number of file}
 ioFlAttrib:   SignedByte;   {file attributes}
 ioFlVersNum:  SignedByte;   {version number}
 ioFlFndrInfo: FInfo;        {information used by the Finder}
 ioFlNum:      LONGINT;      {file number}
 ioFlStBlk:    INTEGER;      {first allocation block of data fork}
 ioFlLgLen:    LONGINT;      {logical end-of-file of data fork}
 ioFlPyLen:    LONGINT;      {physical end-of-file of data fork}
 ioFlRStBlk:   INTEGER;      {first allocation block of resource fork}
 ioFlRLgLen:   LONGINT;      {logical end-of-file of resource fork}
 ioFlRPyLen:   LONGINT;      {physical end-of-file of resource fork}
 ioFlCrDat:    LONGINT;      {date and time of creation}
 ioFlMdDat:    LONGINT);     {date and time of last modification}
```

IOFDirIndex contains the sequence number of the file, and can be used as a way of indexing all the files on a volume. IOFlNum is a unique number assigned to a file; most programmers needn't be concerned with file numbers, but those interested can read the section "Data Organization on Volumes".

> **Note:** IOFDirIndex maintains the sequence numbers without gaps, so you can use it as a way of indexing all the files on a volume.

IOFlAttrib contains the following file attributes:

Bit   Meaning
0   Set if file is locked

IOFlStBlk and ioFlRStBlk contain 0 if the file's data or resource fork is empty, respectively. The date and time in the ioFlCrDat and ioFlMdDat fields are specified in seconds since midnight, January 1, 1904.

Volume Information Parameters

When you call GetVolInfo, you'll use the following 14 additional fields:

```
volumeParam:
 (filler2:        LONGINT;      {not used}
  ioVolIndex:     INTEGER;      {volume index}
  ioVCrDate:      LONGINT;      {date and time of initialization}
  ioVLsBkUp:      LONGINT;      {date and time of last backup}
  ioVAtrb:        INTEGER;      {bit 15=1 if volume locked}
  ioVNmFls:       INTEGER;      {number of files in directory}
  ioVDirSt:       INTEGER;      {first block of directory}
  ioVBlLn:        INTEGER;      {length of directory in blocks}
  ioVNmAlBlks:    INTEGER;      {number of allocation blocks}
  ioVAlBlkSiz:    LONGINT;      {size of allocation blocks}
  ioVClpSiz:      LONGINT;      {number of bytes to allocate}
  ioAlBlSt:       INTEGER;      {first block in volume block map}
  ioVNxtFNum:     LONGINT;      {next unused file number}
  ioVFrBlk:       INTEGER);     {number of unused allocation blocks}
```

IOVolIndex contains the **volume index**, another method of referring to a volume; the first volume mounted has an index of 1, and so on.

> **Note:** IOVolIndex maintains the volume numbers sequentially (without gaps), so you can use it as a way of indexing all mounted volumes.

Most programmers needn't be concerned with the parameters providing information about file directories and block maps (such as ioVNmFls), but interested programmers can read the section "Data Organization on Volumes".

Routine Descriptions

This section describes the procedures and functions. Each routine description includes the low-level Pascal form of the call and the routine's assembly-language macro. A list of the fields in the parameter block affected by the call is also given.

Assembly-language note: The field names given in these descriptions are those of the ParamBlockRec data type; see the summary at the end of this chapter for the names of the corresponding assembly-language offsets. (The names for some offsets differ from their Pascal equivalents, and in certain cases more than one name for the same offset is provided.)

The number next to each parameter name indicates the byte offset of the parameter from the start of the parameter block pointed to by register A0; only assembly-language programmers need be concerned with it. An arrow next to each parameter name indicates whether it's an input, output, or input/output parameter:

Arrow **Meaning**
→ Parameter is passed to the routine

← Parameter is returned by the routine

↔ Parameter is passed to and returned by the routine

Initializing the File I/O Queue

```
PROCEDURE FInitQueue;
```

Trap macro   _InitQueue

FInitQueue clears all queued File Manager calls except the current one.

Accessing Volumes

To get the volume reference number of a volume, given the path reference number of a file on that volume, both Pascal and assembly-language programmers should call the high-level File Manager function GetVRefNum.

```
FUNCTION PBMountVol (paramBlock: ParmBlkPtr) : OSErr;
```

Trap macro   _MountVol

Parameter block

←	16	ioResult	word
↔	22	ioVRefNum	word

PBMountVol mounts the volume in the drive specified by ioVRefNum, and returns a volume reference number in ioVRefNum. If there are no volumes already mounted, this volume becomes the default volume. PBMountVol is always executed synchronously.

Result codes		
	noErr	No error
	badMDBErr	Bad master directory block
	extFSErr	External file system
	ioErr	I/O error
	memFullErr	Not enough room in heap zone
	noMacDskErr	Not a Macintosh disk
	nsDrvErr	No such drive
	paramErr	Bad drive number
	volOnLinErr	Volume already on-line

```
FUNCTION PBGetVInfo (paramBlock: ParmBlkPtr; async: BOOLEAN) :
         OSErr;
```

Trap macro   _GetVolInfo

Parameter block

→	12	ioCompletion	pointer
←	16	ioResult	word
↔	18	ioNamePtr	pointer
↔	22	ioVRefNum	word
→	28	ioVolIndex	word
←	30	ioVCrDate	long word
←	34	ioVLsBkUp	long word
←	38	ioVAtrb	word
←	40	ioVNmFls	word
←	42	ioVDirSt	word
←	44	ioVBlLn	word
←	46	ioVNmAlBlks	word
←	48	ioVAlBlkSiz	long word
←	52	ioVClpSiz	long word
←	56	ioAlBlSt	word
←	58	ioVNxtFNum	long word
←	62	ioVFrBlk	word

PBGetVInfo returns information about the specified volume. If ioVolIndex is positive, the File Manager attempts to use it to find the volume; for instance, if ioVolIndex is 2, the File Manager will attempt to access the second mounted volume. If ioVolIndex is negative, the File Manager uses ioNamePtr and ioVRefNum in the standard way to determine which volume. If ioVolIndex is 0, the File Manager attempts to access the volume by using ioVRefNum only. The volume reference number is returned in ioVRefNum, and the volume name is returned in ioNamePtr (unless ioNamePtr is NIL).

Result codes	noErr	No error
	nsvErr	No such volume
	paramErr	No default volume

```
FUNCTION PBGetVol (paramBlock: ParmBlkPtr; async: BOOLEAN) :
         OSErr;
```

Trap macro   _GetVol

Parameter block

→	12	ioCompletion	pointer
←	16	ioResult	word
←	18	ioNamePtr	pointer
←	22	ioVRefNum	word

PBGetVol returns the name of the default volume in ioNamePtr (unless ioNamePtr is NIL) and its volume reference number in ioVRefNum.

Result codes   noErr   No error
                          nsvErr   No default volume

```
FUNCTION PBSetVol (paramBlock: ParmBlkPtr; async: BOOLEAN) :
        OSErr;
```

Trap macro   _SetVol

Parameter block

→	12	ioCompletion	pointer
←	16	ioResult	word
→	18	ioNamePtr	pointer
→	22	ioVRefNum	word

PBSetVol sets the default volume to the mounted volume specified by ioNamePtr or ioVRefNum.

Result codes	noErr	No error
	bdNamErr	Bad volume name
	nsvErr	No such volume
	paramErr	No default volume

```
FUNCTION PBFlushVol (paramBlock: ParmBlkPtr; async: BOOLEAN) :
        OSErr;
```

Trap macro   _FlushVol

Parameter block

→	12	ioCompletion	pointer
←	16	ioResult	word
→	18	ioNamePtr	pointer
→	22	ioVRefNum	word

On the volume specified by ioNamePtr or ioVRefNum, PBFlushVol writes descriptive information about the volume, the contents of the associated volume buffer, and all access path buffers for the volume (if they've changed since the last time PBFlushVol was called). The date and time of the last modification to the volume are set to the current date and time.

Result codes	noErr	No error
	bdNamErr	Bad volume name
	extFSErr	External file system
	ioErr	I/O error
	nsDrvErr	No such drive
	nsvErr	No such volume
	paramErr	No default volume

```
FUNCTION PBUnmountVol (paramBlock: ParmBlkPtr) : OSErr;
```

Trap macro   _UnmountVol

Parameter block

←	16	ioResult	word
→	18	ioNamePtr	pointer
→	22	ioVRefNum	word

PBUnmountVol unmounts the volume specified by ioNamePtr or ioVRefNum, by calling PBFlushVol to flush the volume, closing all open files on the volume, and releasing the memory used for the volume. PBUnmountVol is always executed synchronously.

Warning: Don't unmount the startup volume.

Result codes	noErr	No error
	bdNamErr	Bad volume name
	extFSErr	External file system
	ioErr	I/O error
	nsDrvErr	No such drive
	nsvErr	No such volume
	paramErr	No default volume

```
FUNCTION PBOffLine (paramBlock: ParmBlkPtr) : OSErr;
```

Trap macro   _OffLine

Parameter block

→	12	ioCompletion	pointer
←	16	ioResult	word
→	18	ioNamePtr	pointer
→	22	ioVRefNum	word

PBOffLine places off-line the volume specified by ioNamePtr or ioVRefNum, by calling PBFlushVol to flush the volume, and releasing all the memory used for the volume except for 94 bytes of descriptive information. PBOffLine is always executed synchronously.

Result codes	noErr	No error
	bdNamErr	Bad volume name
	extFSErr	External file system
	ioErr	I/O error
	nsDrvErr	No such drive
	nsvErr	No such volume
	paramErr	No default volume

```
FUNCTION PBEject (paramBlock: ParmBlkPtr) : OSErr;
```

Trap macro   _Eject

Parameter block

→	12	ioCompletion	pointer
←	16	ioResult	word
→	18	ioNamePtr	pointer
→	22	ioVRefNum	word

PBEject flushes the volume specified by ioNamePtr or ioVRefNum, places it off-line, and then ejects the volume.

Assembly-language note: You may invoke the macro _Eject asynchronously; the first part of the call is executed synchronously, and the actual ejection is executed asynchronously.

Result codes   noErr   No error
                 bdNamErr   Bad volume name
                 extFSErr   External file system
                 ioErr   I/O error
                 nsDrvErr   No such drive
                 nsvErr   No such volume
                 paramErr   No default volume

Accessing Files

```
FUNCTION PBCreate (paramBlock: ParmBlkPtr; async: BOOLEAN) :
          OSErr;
```

Trap macro   _Create

Parameter block

→	12	ioCompletion	pointer
←	16	ioResult	word
→	18	ioNamePtr	pointer
→	22	ioVRefNum	word
→	26	ioFVersNum	byte

PBCreate creates a new file (both forks) having the name ioNamePtr and the version number ioFVersNum, on the volume specified by ioVRefNum. The new file is unlocked and empty. The date and time of its creation and last modification are set to the current date and time. If the file created isn't temporary (that is, if it will exist after the application terminates), the application should call PBSetFInfo (after PBCreate) to fill in the information needed by the Finder.

Assembly-language note: If a desk accessory creates a file, it should always create it on the system startup volume (and not on the default volume) by passing the reference number of the system startup volume in ioVRefNum. The volume reference number can be obtained by calling the high-level File Manager function GetVRefNum with the reference number of the system resource file, which is stored in the global variable SysMap.

Result codes	noErr	No error
	bdNamErr	Bad file name
	dupFNErr	Duplicate file name and version
	dirFulErr	File directory full
	extFSErr	External file system
	ioErr	I/O error
	nsvErr	No such volume
	vLckdErr	Software volume lock
	wPrErr	Hardware volume lock

```
FUNCTION PBOpen (paramBlock: ParmBlkPtr; async: BOOLEAN) : OSErr;
```

Trap macro   _Open

Parameter block

→	12	ioCompletion	pointer
←	16	ioResult	word
→	18	ioNamePtr	pointer
→	22	ioVRefNum	word
←	24	ioRefNum	word
→	26	ioVersNum	byte
→	27	ioPermssn	byte
→	28	ioMisc	pointer

PBOpen creates an access path to the file having the name ioNamePtr and the version number ioVersNum, on the volume specified by ioVRefNum. A path reference number is returned in ioRefNum.

IOMisc either points to a 524-byte portion of memory to be used as the access path's buffer, or is NIL if you want the volume buffer to be used instead.

   Warning: All access paths to a single file that's opened multiple times should share the same buffer so that they will read and write the same data.

IOPermssn specifies the path's read/write permission. A path can be opened for writing even if it accesses a file on a locked volume, and an error won't be returned until a PBWrite, PBSetEOF, or PBAllocate call is made.

If you attempt to open a locked file for writing, PBOpen will return permErr as its function result. If you attempt to open a file for writing and it already has an access path that allows writing, PBOpen will return the reference number of the existing access path in ioRefNum and opWrErr as its function result.

Result codes	noErr	No error
	bdNamErr	Bad file name
	extFSErr	External file system
	fnfErr	File not found
	ioErr	I/O error
	nsvErr	No such volume
	opWrErr	File already open for writing
	permErr	Attempt to open locked file for writing
	tmfoErr	Too many files open

```
FUNCTION PBOpenRF (paramBlock: ParmBlkPtr; async: BOOLEAN) :
        OSErr;
```

Trap macro	_OpenRF

Parameter block

→	12	ioCompletion	pointer
←	16	ioResult	word
→	18	ioNamePtr	pointer
→	22	ioVRefNum	word
←	24	ioRefNum	word
→	26	ioVersNum	byte
→	27	ioPermssn	byte
→	28	ioMisc	pointer

PBOpenRF is identical to PBOpen, except that it opens the file's resource fork instead of its data fork.

Note: Normally you should access a file's resource fork through the routines of the Resource Manager rather than the File Manager. PBOpenRF doesn't read the resource map into memory; it's really only useful for block-level operations such as copying files.

Result codes	noErr	No error
	bdNamErr	Bad file name
	extFSErr	External file system
	fnfErr	File not found
	ioErr	I/O error
	nsvErr	No such volume
	opWrErr	File already open for writing
	permErr	Attempt to open locked file for writing
	tmfoErr	Too many files open

```
FUNCTION PBRead (paramBlock: ParmBlkPtr; async: BOOLEAN) : OSErr;
```

Trap macro   _Read

Parameter block

→	12	ioCompletion	pointer
←	16	ioResult	word
→	24	ioRefNum	word
→	32	ioBuffer	pointer
→	36	ioReqCount	long word
←	40	ioActCount	long word
→	44	ioPosMode	word
↔	46	ioPosOffset	long word

PBRead attempts to read ioReqCount bytes from the open file whose access path is specified by ioRefNum, and transfer them to the data buffer pointed to by ioBuffer. The position of the mark is specified by ioPosMode and ioPosOffset. If you try to read past the logical end-of-file, PBRead moves the mark to the end-of-file and returns eofErr as its function result. After the read is completed, the mark is returned in ioPosOffset and the number of bytes actually read is returned in ioActCount.

Result codes	noErr	No error
	eofErr	End-of-file
	extFSErr	External file system
	fnOpnErr	File not open
	ioErr	I/O error
	paramErr	Negative ioReqCount
	rfNumErr	Bad reference number

```
FUNCTION PBWrite (paramBlock: ParmBlkPtr; async: BOOLEAN) : OSErr;
```

Trap macro   _Write

Parameter block

→	12	ioCompletion	pointer
←	16	ioResult	word
→	24	ioRefNum	word
→	32	ioBuffer	pointer
→	36	ioReqCount	long word
←	40	ioActCount	long word
→	44	ioPosMode	word
↔	46	ioPosOffset	long word

PBWrite takes ioReqCount bytes from the buffer pointed to by ioBuffer and attempts to write them to the open file whose access path is specified by ioRefNum. The position of the mark is specified by ioPosMode and ioPosOffset. After the write is completed, the mark is returned in ioPosOffset and the number of bytes actually written is returned in ioActCount.

Result codes   noErr   No error
                             dskFulErr   Disk full
                             fLckdErr   File locked
                             fnOpnErr   File not open
                             ioErr   I/O error

	noErr	No error
	dskFulErr	Disk full
	fLckdErr	File locked
	fnOpnErr	File not open
	ioErr	I/O error
	paramErr	Negative ioReqCount
	posErr	Attempt to position before start of file
	rfNumErr	Bad reference number
	vLckdErr	Software volume lock
	wPrErr	Hardware volume lock
	wrPermErr	Read/write permission doesn't allow writing

```
FUNCTION PBGetFPos (paramBlock: ParmBlkPtr; async: BOOLEAN) :
        OSErr;
```

Trap macro   _GetFPos

Parameter block

→	12	ioCompletion	pointer
←	16	ioResult	word
→	24	ioRefNum	word
←	36	ioReqCount	long word
←	40	ioActCount	long word
←	44	ioPosMode	word
←	46	ioPosOffset	long word

PBGetFPos returns, in ioPosOffset, the mark of the open file whose access path is specified by ioRefNum. It sets ioReqCount, ioActCount, and ioPosMode to 0.

Result codes	noErr	No error
	extFSErr	External file system
	fnOpnErr	File not open
	gfpErr	Error during GetFPos
	ioErr	I/O error
	rfNumErr	Bad reference number

```
FUNCTION PBSetFPos (paramBlock: ParmBlkPtr; async: BOOLEAN) :
        OSErr;
```

Trap macro   _SetFPos

Parameter block

→	12	ioCompletion	pointer
←	16	ioResult	word
→	24	ioRefNum	word
→	44	ioPosMode	word
↔	46	ioPosOffset	long word

PBSetFPos sets the mark of the open file whose access path is specified by ioRefNum, to the position specified by ioPosMode and ioPosOffset. The position at which the mark is actually set is returned in ioPosOffset. If you try to set the mark past the logical end-of-file, PBSetFPos moves the mark to the end-of-file and returns eofErr as its function result.

Result codes	noErr	No error
	eofErr	End-of-file
	extFSErr	External file system
	fnOpnErr	File not open
	ioErr	I/O error
	posErr	Attempt to position before start of file
	rfNumErr	Bad reference number

FUNCTION PBGetEOF (paramBlock: ParmBlkPtr; async: BOOLEAN) :
        OSErr;

Trap macro   _GetEOF

Parameter block

→	12	ioCompletion	pointer
←	16	ioResult	word
→	24	ioRefNum	word
←	28	ioMisc	long word

PBGetEOF returns, in ioMisc, the logical end-of-file of the open file whose access path is specified by ioRefNum.

Result codes	noErr	No error
	extFSErr	External file system
	fnOpnErr	File not open
	ioErr	I/O error
	rfNumErr	Bad reference number

FUNCTION PBSetEOF (paramBlock: ParmBlkPtr; async: BOOLEAN) :
        OSErr;

Trap macro   _SetEOF

Parameter block

→	12	ioCompletion	pointer
←	16	ioResult	word
→	24	ioRefNum	word
→	28	ioMisc	long word

PBSetEOF sets the logical end-of-file of the open file whose access path is specified by ioRefNum, to ioMisc. If you attempt to set the logical end-of-file beyond the physical end-of-file, the physical end-of-file is set to one byte beyond the end of the next free allocation block; if there isn't enough space on the volume, no change is made, and PBSetEOF returns dskFulErr as its function result. If ioMisc is 0, all space occupied by the file on the volume is released.

Result codes   noErr   No error
     dskFulErr   Disk full
     extFSErr   External file system
     fLckdErr   File locked
     fnOpnErr   File not open
     ioErr   I/O error
     rfNumErr   Bad reference number
     vLckdErr   Software volume lock
     wPrErr   Hardware volume lock
     wrPermErr   Read/write permission doesn't allow writing

```
FUNCTION PBAllocate (paramBlock: ParmBlkPtr; async: BOOLEAN) :
        OSErr;
```

Trap macro   _Allocate

Parameter block

→	12	ioCompletion	pointer
←	16	ioResult	word
→	24	ioRefNum	word
→	36	ioReqCount	long word
←	40	ioActCount	long word

PBAllocate adds ioReqCount bytes to the open file whose access path is specified by ioRefNum, and sets the physical end-of-file to one byte beyond the last block allocated. The number of bytes actually allocated is rounded up to the nearest multiple of the allocation block size, and returned in ioActCount. If there isn't enough empty space on the volume to satisfy the allocation request, PBAllocate allocates the rest of the space on the volume and returns dskFulErr as its function result.

Result codes   noErr   No error
     dskFulErr   Disk full
     fLckdErr   File locked
     fnOpnErr   File not open
     ioErr   I/O error
     rfNumErr   Bad reference number
     vLckdErr   Software volume lock
     wPrErr   Hardware volume lock
     wrPermErr   Read/write permission doesn't allow writing

4 File Manager

```
FUNCTION PBFlushFile (paramBlock: ParmBlkPtr; async: BOOLEAN) :
         OSErr;
```

Trap macro   _FlushFile

Parameter block

→	12	ioCompletion	pointer
←	16	ioResult	word
→	24	ioRefNum	word

PBFlushFile writes the contents of the access path buffer indicated by ioRefNum to the volume, and updates the file's entry in the file directory.

Warning: Some information stored on the volume won't be correct until PBFlushVol is called.

Result codes

noErr	No error
extFSErr	External file system
fnfErr	File not found
fnOpnErr	File not open
ioErr	I/O error
nsvErr	No such volume
rfNumErr	Bad reference number

```
FUNCTION PBClose (paramBlock: ParmBlkPtr; async: BOOLEAN) :
         OSErr;
```

Trap macro   _Close

Parameter block

→	12	ioCompletion	pointer
←	16	ioResult	word
→	24	ioRefNum	word

PBClose writes the contents of the access path buffer specified by ioRefNum to the volume and removes the access path.

Warning: Some information stored on the volume won't be correct until PBFlushVol is called.

Result codes

noErr	No error
extFSErr	External file system
fnfErr	File not found
fnOpnErr	File not open
ioErr	I/O error
nsvErr	No such volume
rfNumErr	Bad reference number

Changing Information About Files

All of the routines described in this section affect both forks of a file, and don't require the file to be open.

```
FUNCTION PBGetFInfo (paramBlock: ParmBlkPtr; async: BOOLEAN) :
         OSErr;
```

Trap macro   _GetFileInfo

Parameter block

→	12	ioCompletion	pointer
←	16	ioResult	word
↔	18	ioNamePtr	pointer
→	22	ioVRefNum	word
←	24	ioFRefNum	word
→	26	ioFVersNum	byte
→	28	ioFDirIndex	word
←	30	ioFlAttrib	byte
←	31	ioFlVersNum	byte
←	32	ioFlFndrInfo	16 bytes
←	48	ioFlNum	long word
←	52	ioFlStBlk	word
←	54	ioFlLgLen	long word
←	58	ioFlPyLen	long word
←	62	ioFlRStBlk	word
←	64	ioFlRLgLen	long word
←	68	ioFlRPyLen	long word
←	72	ioFlCrDat	long word
←	76	ioFlMdDat	long word

PBGetFInfo returns information about the specified file. If ioFDirIndex is positive, the File Manager returns information about the file whose sequence number is ioFDirIndex on the volume specified by ioVRefNum (see the section "Data Organization on Volumes" if you're interested in using this method). If ioFDirIndex is negative or 0, the File Manager returns information about the file having the name ioNamePtr and the version number ioFVersNum, on the volume specified by ioFVRefNum. If the file is open, the reference number of the first access path found is returned in ioFRefNum, and the name of the file is returned in ioNamePtr (unless ioNamePtr is NIL).

Result codes	noErr	No error
	bdNamErr	Bad file name
	extFSErr	External file system
	fnfErr	File not found
	ioErr	I/O error
	nsvErr	No such volume
	paramErr	No default volume

```
FUNCTION PBSetFInfo (paramBlock: ParmBlkPtr; async: BOOLEAN) :
         OSErr;
```

Trap macro   _SetFileInfo

Parameter block

→	12	ioCompletion	pointer
←	16	ioResult	word
→	18	ioNamePtr	pointer
→	22	ioVRefNum	word
→	26	ioFVersNum	byte
→	32	ioFlFndrInfo	16 bytes
→	72	ioFlCrDat	long word
→	76	ioFlMdDat	long word

PBSetFInfo sets information (including the date and time of creation and modification, and information needed by the Finder) about the file having the name ioNamePtr and the version number ioFVersNum, on the volume specified by ioVRefNum. You should call PBGetFInfo just before PBSetFInfo, so the current information is present in the parameter block.

Result codes	noErr	No error
	bdNamErr	Bad file name
	extFSErr	External file system
	fLckdErr	File locked
	fnfErr	File not found
	ioErr	I/O error
	nsvErr	No such volume
	vLckdErr	Software volume lock
	wPrErr	Hardware volume lock

```
FUNCTION PBSetFLock (paramBlock: ParmBlkPtr; async: BOOLEAN) :
         OSErr;
```

Trap macro   _SetFilLock

Parameter block

→	12	ioCompletion	pointer
←	16	ioResult	word
→	18	ioNamePtr	pointer
→	22	ioVRefNum	word
→	26	ioFVersNum	byte

PBSetFLock locks the file having the name ioNamePtr and the version number ioFVersNum on the volume specified by ioVRefNum. Access paths currently in use aren't affected.

Note: This lock is controlled by your application, and is distinct from the user-accessible lock maintained by the Finder.

Result codes   noErr   No error

extFSErr	External file system
fnfErr	File not found
ioErr	I/O error
nsvErr	No such volume
vLckdErr	Software volume lock
wPrErr	Hardware volume lock

```
FUNCTION PBRstFLock (paramBlock: ParmBlkPtr; async: BOOLEAN) :
          OSErr;
```

Trap macro   _RstFilLock

Parameter block

→	12	ioCompletion	pointer
←	16	ioResult	word
→	18	ioNamePtr	pointer
→	22	ioVRefNum	word
→	26	ioFVersNum	byte

PBRstFLock unlocks the file having the name ioNamePtr and the version number ioFVersNum on the volume specified by ioVRefNum. Access paths currently in use aren't affected.

Result codes   noErr   No error

extFSErr	External file system
fnfErr	File not found
ioErr	I/O error
nsvErr	No such volume
vLckdErr	Software volume lock
wPrErr	Hardware volume lock

```
FUNCTION PBSetFVers (paramBlock: ParmBlkPtr; async: BOOLEAN) :
          OSErr;
```

Trap macro   _SetFilType

Parameter block

→	12	ioCompletion	pointer
←	16	ioResult	word
→	18	ioNamePtr	pointer
→	22	ioVRefNum	word
→	26	ioVersNum	byte
→	28	ioMisc	byte

PBSetFVers changes the version number of the file having the name ioNamePtr and version number ioVersNum, on the volume specified by ioVRefNum, to the version number stored in the high-order byte of ioMisc. Access paths currently in use aren't affected.

Warning: The Resource Manager, the Segment Loader, and the Standard File Package operate only on files with version number 0; changing the version number of a file to a nonzero number will prevent them from operating on it.

Result codes   noErr   No error
                bdNamErr   Bad file name
                dupFNErr   Duplicate file name and version
                extFSErr   External file system
                fLckdErr   File locked
                fnfErr   File not found
                nsvErr   No such volume
                ioErr   I/O error
                paramErr   No default volume
                vLckdErr   Software volume lock
                wPrErr   Hardware volume lock

```
FUNCTION PBRename (paramBlock: ParmBlkPtr; async: BOOLEAN) :
          OSErr;
```

Trap macro   _Rename

Parameter block

→	12	ioCompletion	pointer
←	16	ioResult	word
→	18	ioNamePtr	pointer
→	22	ioVRefNum	word
→	26	ioVersNum	byte
→	28	ioMisc	pointer

Given a file name in ioNamePtr and a version number in ioVersNum, PBRename changes the name of the file to the name specified by ioMisc. Access paths currently in use aren't affected. Given a volume name in ioNamePtr or a volume reference number in ioVRefNum, it changes the name of the volume to the name specified by ioMisc.

Warning: If you're renaming a volume, be sure that the volume name given in ioNamePtr ends with a colon, or Rename will consider it a file name.

Result codes   noErr   No error
                bdNamErr   Bad file name
                dirFulErr File directory full
                dupFNErr   Duplicate file name and version
                extFSErr   External file system
                fLckdErr   File locked
                fnfErr   File not found
                fsRnErr   Problem during rename
                ioErr   I/O error
                nsvErr   No such volume
                paramErr   No default volume
                vLckdErr   Software volume lock
                wPrErr   Hardware volume lock

```
FUNCTION PBDelete (paramBlock: ParmBlkPtr; async: BOOLEAN) :
        OSErr;
```

Trap macro   _Delete

Parameter block

→	12	ioCompletion	pointer
←	16	ioResult	word
→	18	ioNamePtr	pointer
→	22	ioVRefNum	word
→	26	ioFVersNum	byte

PBDelete removes the closed file having the name ioNamePtr and the version number ioFVersNum, from the volume specified by ioVRefNum.

Note: This function will delete *both* forks of the file.

Result codes	noErr	No error
	bdNamErr	Bad file name
	extFSErr	External file system
	fBsyErr	File busy
	fLckdErr	File locked
	fnfErr	File not found
	nsvErr	No such volume
	ioErr	I/O error
	vLckdErr	Software volume lock
	wPrErr	Hardware volume lock

DATA ORGANIZATION ON VOLUMES

This section explains how information is organized on volumes. Most of the information is accessible only through assembly language, but some advanced Pascal programmers may be interested.

The File Manager communicates with device drivers that read and write data via block-level requests to devices containing Macintosh-initialized volumes. (Macintosh-initialized volumes are volumes initialized by the Disk Initialization Package.) The actual type of volume and device is unimportant to the File Manager; the only requirements are that the volume was initialized by the Disk Initialization Package and that the device driver is able to communicate via block-level requests.

The 3 1/2-inch built-in and optional external drives are accessed via the Disk Driver. If you want to use the File Manager to access files on Macintosh-initialized volumes on other types of devices, you must write a device driver that can read and write data via block-level requests to the device on which the volume will be mounted. If you want to access files on volumes not initialized by the Macintosh, you must write your own external file system (see the section "Using an External File System").

The information on all block-formatted volumes is organized in **logical blocks** and allocation blocks. Logical blocks contain a number of bytes of standard information (512 bytes on Macintosh-initialized volumes), and an additional number of bytes of information specific to the

Disk Driver (12 bytes on Macintosh-initialized volumes; for details, see chapter 7). Allocation blocks are composed of any integral number of logical blocks, and are simply a means of grouping logical blocks together in more convenient parcels.

The remainder of this section applies only to Macintosh-initialized volumes; the information may be different in future versions of Macintosh system software. Other volumes must be accessed via an external file system, and the information on them must be organized by an external initializing program.

A Macintosh-initialized volume contains **system startup information** in logical blocks 0 and 1 (see Figure 6) that's read in at system startup. This information consists of certain configurable system parameters, such as the capacity of the event queue, the initial size of the system heap, and the number of open files allowed. The development system you're using may include a utility program for modifying the system startup blocks on a volume.

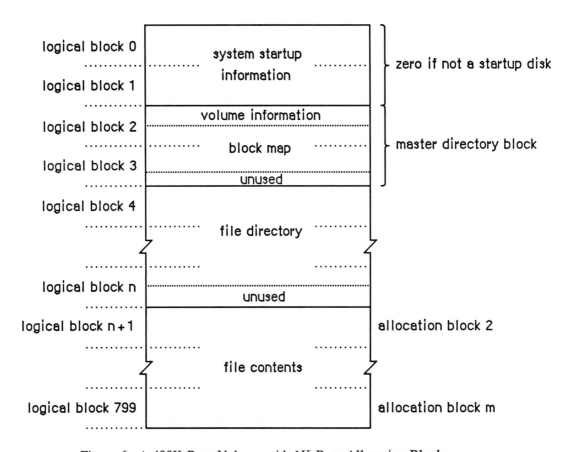

Figure 6. A 400K-Byte Volume with 1K-Byte Allocation Blocks

Logical block 2 of the volume begins the **master directory block**. The master directory block contains **volume information** and the volume allocation block map, which records whether each block on the volume is unused or what part of a file it contains data from.

The master directory "block" always occupies two blocks—the Disk Initialization Package varies the allocation block size as necessary to achieve this constraint.

In the next logical block following the block map begins the file directory, which contains descriptions and locations of all the files on the volume. The rest of the logical blocks on the volume contain files or garbage (such as parts of deleted files). The exact format of the volume information, volume allocation block map, and file directory is explained in the following sections.

Volume Information

The volume information is contained in the first 64 bytes of the master directory block (see Figure 7). This information is written on the volume when it's initialized, and modified thereafter by the File Manager.

byte		
0	drSigWord (word)	always $D2D7
2	drCrDate (long word)	date and time of initialization
6	drLsBkUp (long word)	date and time of last backup
10	drAtrb (word)	volume attributes
12	drNmFls (word)	number of files in directory
14	drDirSt (word)	first block of directory
16	drBlLen (word)	length of directory in blocks
18	drNmAlBlks (word)	number of allocation blocks on volume
20	drAlBlkSiz (long word)	size of allocation blocks
24	drClpSiz (long word)	number of bytes to allocate
28	drAlBlSt (word)	first allocation block in block map
30	drNxtFNum (long word)	next unused file number
34	drFreeBks (word)	number of unused allocation blocks
36	drVN (byte)	length of volume name
37	drVN + 1 (bytes)	characters of volume name

Figure 7. Volume Information

DrAtrb contains the **volume attributes**, as follows:

Bit   Meaning
  7   Set if volume is locked by hardware
 15   Set if volume is locked by software

DrClpSiz contains the minimum number of bytes to allocate each time the Allocate function is called, to minimize fragmentation of files; it's always a multiple of the allocation block size. DrNxtFNum contains the next unused file number (see the "File Directory" section below for an explanation of file numbers).

Warning: The format of the volume information may be different in future versions of Macintosh system software.

Volume Allocation Block Map

The volume allocation block map represents every allocation block on the volume with a 12-bit entry indicating whether the block is unused or allocated to a file. It begins in the master directory block at the byte following the volume information, and continues for as many logical blocks as needed.

The first entry in the block map is for block number 2; the block map doesn't contain entries for the system startup blocks. Each entry specifies whether the block is unused, whether it's the last block in the file, or which allocation block is next in the file:

Entry	Meaning
0	Block is unused
1	Block is the last block of the file
2 to 4095	Number of next block in the file

For instance, assume that there's one file on the volume, stored in allocation blocks 8, 11, 12, and 17; the first 16 entries of the block map would read

0 0 0 0 0 0 11 0 0 12 17 0 0 0 0 1

The first allocation block on a volume typically follows the file directory. It's numbered 2 because of the special meaning of numbers 0 and 1.

Note: As explained below, it's possible to begin the allocation blocks immediately following the master directory block and place the file directory somewhere within the allocation blocks. In this case, the allocation blocks occupied by the file directory must be marked with $FFF's in the allocation block map.

File Directory

The file directory contains an entry for each file. Each entry lists information about one file on the volume, including its name and location. Each file is listed by its own unique **file number,** which the File Manager uses to distinguish it from other files on the volume.

A file directory entry contains 51 bytes plus one byte for each character in the file name. If the file names average 20 characters, a directory can hold seven file entries per logical block. Entries are always an integral number of words and don't cross logical block boundaries. The length of a file directory depends on the maximum number of files the volume can contain; for example, on a 400K-byte volume the file directory occupies 12 logical blocks.

The file directory conventionally follows the block map and precedes the allocation blocks, but a volume-initializing program could actually place the file directory anywhere within the allocation blocks as long as the blocks occupied by the file directory are marked with $FFF's in the block map.

The format of a file directory entry is shown in Figure 8.

byte 0	flFlags (byte)	bit 7 = 1 if entry used; bit 0 = 1 if file locked
1	flTyp (byte)	version number
2	flUsrWds (16 bytes)	information used by the Finder
18	flFlNum (long word)	file number
22	flStBlk (word)	first allocation block of data fork
24	flLgLen (long word)	logical end-of-file of data fork
28	flPyLen (long word)	physical end-of-file of data fork
32	flRStBlk (word)	first allocation block of resource fork
34	flRLgLen (long word)	logical end-of-file of resource fork
38	flRPyLen (long word)	physical end-of-file of resource fork
42	flCrDat (long word)	date and time of creation
46	flMdDat (long word)	date and time of last modification
50	flNam (byte)	length of file name
51	flNam + 1 (bytes)	characters of file name

Figure 8. A File Directory Entry

FlStBlk and flRStBlk are 0 if the data or resource fork doesn't exist. FlCrDat and flMdDat are given in seconds since midnight, January 1, 1904.

Each time a new file is created, an entry for the new file is placed in the file directory. Each time a file is deleted, its entry in the file directory is cleared, and all blocks used by that file on the volume are released.

Warning: The format of the file directory may be different in future versions of Macintosh system software.

DATA STRUCTURES IN MEMORY

This section describes the memory data structures used by the File Manager and any external file system that accesses files on Macintosh-initialized volumes. Some of this data is accessible only through assembly language.

The data structures in memory used by the File Manager and all external file systems include:

- the file I/O queue, listing all asynchronous routines awaiting execution (including the currently executing routine, if any)

- the volume-control-block queue, listing information about each mounted volume

- copies of volume allocation block maps (one for each on-line volume)

- the file-control-block buffer, listing information about each access path

- volume buffers (one for each on-line volume)

- optional access path buffers (one for each access path)

- the drive queue, listing information about each drive connected to the Macintosh

The File I/O Queue

The file I/O queue is a standard Operating System queue (described in chapter 13) that contains parameter blocks for all asynchronous routines awaiting execution. Each time a routine is called, an entry is placed in the queue; each time a routine is completed, its entry is removed from the queue.

Each entry in the file I/O queue consists of a parameter block for the routine that was called. Most of the fields of this parameter block contain information needed by the specific File Manager routines; these fields are explained above in the section "Low-Level File Manager Routines". The first four fields of the parameter block, shown below, are used by the File Manager in processing the I/O requests in the queue.

```
TYPE ParamBlockRec =  RECORD
                 qLink:      QElemPtr;  {next queue entry}
                 qType:      INTEGER;   {queue type}
                 ioTrap:     INTEGER;   {routine trap}
                 ioCmdAddr:  Ptr;       {routine address}
                   . . .                {rest of block}
               END;
```

QLink points to the next entry in the queue, and qType indicates the queue type, which must always be ORD(ioQType). IOTrap and ioCmdAddr contain the trap word and address of the File Manager routine that was called.

You can get a pointer to the header of the file I/O queue by calling the File Manager function GetFSQHdr.

```
FUNCTION GetFSQHdr : QHdrPtr;    [Not in ROM]
```

GetFSQHdr returns a pointer to the header of the file I/O queue.

Assembly-language note: The global variable FSQHdr contains the header of the file I/O queue.

Volume Control Blocks

Each time a volume is mounted, its volume information is read from it and is used to build a new **volume control block** in the **volume-control-block queue** (unless an ejected or off-line volume is being remounted). A copy of the volume allocation block map is also read from the volume and placed in the system heap, and a volume buffer is created in the system heap.

The volume-control-block queue is a standard Operating System queue that's maintained in the system heap. It contains a volume control block for each mounted volume. A volume control block is a 94-byte nonrelocatable block that contains volume-specific information, including the first 64 bytes of the master directory block (bytes 8-71 of the volume control block match bytes 0-63 of the volume information). It has the following structure:

```
TYPE VCB =
    RECORD
        qLink:      QElemPtr;    {next queue entry}
        qType:      INTEGER;     {queue type}
        vcbFlags:   INTEGER;     {bit 15=1 if dirty}
        vcbSigWord: INTEGER;     {always $D2D7}
        vcbCrDate:  LONGINT;     {date and time of initialization}
        vcbLsBkUp:  LONGINT;     {date and time of last backup}
        vcbAtrb:    INTEGER;     {volume attributes}
        vcbNmFls:   INTEGER;     {number of files in directory}
        vcbDirSt:   INTEGER;     {first block of directory}
        vcbBlLn:    INTEGER;     {length of directory in blocks}
        vcbNmBlks:  INTEGER;     {number of allocation blocks}
        vcbAlBlkSiz: LONGINT;    {size of allocation blocks}
        vcbClpSiz:  LONGINT;     {number of bytes to allocate}
        vcbAlBlSt:  INTEGER;     {first allocation block in block map}
        vcbNxtFNum: LONGINT;     {next unused file number}
        vcbFreeBks: INTEGER;     {number of unused allocation blocks}
        vcbVN:      STRING[27];  {volume name}
        vcbDrvNum:  INTEGER;     {drive number}
        vcbDRefNum: INTEGER;     {driver reference number}
        vcbFSID:    INTEGER;     {file-system identifier}
        vcbVRefNum: INTEGER;     {volume reference number}
        vcbMAdr:    Ptr;         {pointer to block map}
        vcbBufAdr:  Ptr;         {pointer to volume buffer}
        vcbMLen:    INTEGER;     {number of bytes in block map}
        vcbDirIndex: INTEGER;    {used internally}
        vcbDirBlk:  INTEGER      {used internally}
    END;
```

QLink points to the next entry in the queue, and qType indicates the queue type, which must always be ORD(fsQType). Bit 15 of vcbFlags is set if the volume information has been changed by a routine call since the volume was last affected by a FlushVol call. VCBAtrb contains the volume attributes, as follows:

Bit	Meaning
0-2	Set if inconsistencies were found between the volume information and the file directory when the volume was mounted
6	Set if volume is busy (one or more files are open)
7	Set if volume is locked by hardware
15	Set if volume is locked by software

VCBDirSt contains the number of the first logical block of the file directory; vcbNmBlks, the number of allocation blocks on the volume; vcbAlBlSt, the number of the first logical block in the block map; and vcbFreeBks, the number of unused allocation blocks on the volume.

VCBDrvNum contains the drive number of the drive on which the volume is mounted; vcbDRefNum contains the driver reference number of the driver used to access the volume. When a mounted volume is placed off-line, vcbDrvNum is cleared. When a volume is ejected, vcbDrvNum is cleared and vcbDRefNum is set to the negative of vcbDrvNum (becoming a positive number). VCBFSID identifies the file system handling the volume; it's 0 for volumes handled by the File Manager, and nonzero for volumes handled by other file systems.

When a volume is placed off-line, its buffer and block map are released. When a volume is unmounted, its volume control block is removed from the volume-control-block queue.

You can get a pointer to the header of the volume-control-block queue by calling the File Manager function GetVCBQHdr.

```
FUNCTION GetVCBQHdr : QHdrPtr;    [Not in ROM]
```

GetVCBQHdr returns a pointer to the header of the volume-control-block queue.

Assembly-language note: The global variable VCBQHdr contains the header of the volume-control-block queue. The default volume's volume control block is pointed to by the global variable DefVCBPtr.

File Control Blocks

Each time a file is opened, the file's directory entry is used to build a **file control block** in the **file-control-block buffer**, which contains information about all access paths. Each open fork of a file requires one access path. Two access paths are used for the system and application resource files (whose resource forks are always open); this leaves a capacity of up to 10 file control blocks on a Macintosh 128K, and up to 46 file control blocks on the Macintosh 512K and XL.

Note: The size of the file-control-block buffer is determined by the system startup information stored on a volume.

The file-control-block buffer is a nonrelocatable block in the system heap; the first word contains the length of the buffer. You can refer to the file-control-block buffer by using the global variable FCBSPtr, which points to the length word. Each file control block contains 30 bytes of information about an access path (Figure 9).

byte		
byte 0	fcbFlNum (long word)	file number
4	fcbMdRByt (byte)	flags
5	fcbTypByt (byte)	version number
6	fcbSBlk (word)	first allocation block of file
8	fcbEOF (long word)	logical end-of-file
12	fcbPLen (long word)	physical end-of-file
16	fcbCrPs (long word)	mark
20	fcbVPtr (pointer)	pointer to volume control block
24	fcbBfAdr (pointer)	pointer to access path buffer
28	fcbFlPos (word)	for internal use of File Manager

Figure 9. A File Control Block

Warning: The size and structure of a file control block may be different in future versions of Macintosh system software.

Bit 7 of fcbMdRByt is set if the file has been changed since it was last flushed; bit 1 is set if the entry describes a resource fork; bit 0 is set if data can be written to the file.

The Drive Queue

Disk drives connected to the Macintosh are opened when the system starts up, and information describing each is placed in the **drive queue**. This is a standard Operating System queue, and each entry in it has the following structure:

```
TYPE DrvQEl = RECORD
            qLink:     QElemPtr;  {next queue entry}
            qType:     INTEGER;   {queue type}
            dQDrive:   INTEGER;   {drive number}
            dQRefNum:  INTEGER;   {driver reference number}
            dQFSID:    INTEGER;   {file-system identifier}
            dQDrvSize: INTEGER    {number of logical blocks}
          END;
```

QLink points to the next entry in the queue, and qType indicates the queue type, which must always be ORD(drvQType). DQDrive contains the drive number of the drive on which the volume is mounted; dQRefNum contains the driver reference number of the driver controlling the device on which the volume is mounted. DQFSID identifies the file system handling the volume in the drive; it's 0 for volumes handled by the File Manager, and nonzero for volumes handled by other file systems. If the volume isn't a 3 1/2-inch disk, dQDrvSize contains the number of 512-byte blocks on the volume mounted in this drive; if the volume is a 3 1/2-inch disk, this field isn't used. Four bytes of flags precede each drive queue entry; they're accessible only from assembly language.

Assembly-language note: These bytes contain the following:

Byte	Contents
0	Bit 7=1 if volume is locked
1	0 if no disk in drive; 1 or 2 if disk in drive; 8 if nonejectable disk in drive; $FC-$FF if disk was ejected within last 1.5 seconds
2	Used internally during system startup
3	Bit 7=0 if disk is single-sided

You can get a pointer to the header of the drive queue by calling the File Manager function GetDrvQHdr.

```
FUNCTION GetDrvQHdr : QHdrPtr;    [Not in ROM]
```

GetDrvQHdr returns a pointer to the header of the drive queue.

Assembly-language note: The global variable DrvQHdr contains the header of the drive queue.

The drive queue can support any number of drives, limited only by memory space.

USING AN EXTERNAL FILE SYSTEM

The File Manager is used to access files on Macintosh-initialized volumes. If you want to access files on other volumes, you must write your own external file system and volume-initializing program. After the external file system has been written, it must be used in conjunction with the File Manager as described in this section.

Before any File Manager routines are called, you must place the memory location of the external file system in the global variable ToExtFS, and link the drive(s) accessed by your file system into the drive queue. As each volume is mounted, you must create your own volume control block for each mounted volume and link each one into the volume-control-block queue. As each access path is opened, you must create your own file control block and add it to the file-control-block buffer.

All SetVol, GetVol, and GetVolInfo calls then can be handled by the File Manager via the volume-control-block queue and drive queue; external file systems needn't support these calls.

When the application calls any other File Manager routine accessing a volume, the File Manager passes control to the address contained in ToExtFS (if ToExtFS is 0, the File Manager returns directly to the application with the result code extFSErr). The external file system must then use the information in the file I/O queue to handle the call as it wishes, set the result code, and return control to the File Manager. Control is passed to an external file system for the following specific routine calls:

- for MountVol if the drive queue entry for the requested drive has a nonzero file-system identifier

- for Create, Open, OpenRF, GetFileInfo, SetFileInfo, SetFilLock, RstFilLock, SetFilType, Rename, Delete, FlushVol, Eject, OffLine, and UnmountVol, if the volume control block for the requested file or volume has a nonzero file-system identifier

- for Close, Read, Write, Allocate, GetEOF, SetEOF, GetFPos, SetFPos, and FlushFile, if the file control block for the requested file points to a volume control block with a nonzero file-system identifier

4 File Manager

SUMMARY OF THE FILE MANAGER

Constants

```
CONST { Flags in file information used by the Finder }

        fHasBundle =  8192; {set if file has a bundle}
        fInvisible = 16384; {set if file's icon is invisible}
        fTrash     = -3;    {file is in Trash window}
        fDesktop   = -2;    {file is on desktop}
        fDisk      =  0;    {file is in disk window}

        { Values for requesting read/write access }

        fsCurPerm  = 0;  {whatever is currently allowed}
        fsRdPerm   = 1;  {request to read only}
        fsWrPerm   = 2;  {request to write only}
        fsRdWrPerm = 3;  {request to read and write}

        { Positioning modes }

        fsAtMark    = 0;  {at current mark}
        fsFromStart = 1;  {offset relative to beginning of file}
        fsFromLEOF  = 2;  {offset relative to logical end-of-file}
        fsFromMark  = 3;  {offset relative to current mark}
        rdVerify    = 64; {add to above for read-verify}
```

Data Types

```
TYPE FInfo = RECORD
                fdType:     OSType;  {file type}
                fdCreator:  OSType;  {file's creator}
                fdFlags:    INTEGER; {flags}
                fdLocation: Point;   {file's location}
                fdFldr:     INTEGER  {file's window}
             END;

     ParamBlkType  = (ioParam,fileParam,volumeParam,cntrlParam);

     ParmBlkPtr    = ^ParamBlockRec;
     ParamBlockRec = RECORD
        qLink:        QElemPtr;  {next queue entry}
        qType:        INTEGER;   {queue type}
        ioTrap:       INTEGER;   {routine trap}
        ioCmdAddr:    Ptr;       {routine address}
        ioCompletion: ProcPtr;   {completion routine}
        ioResult:     OSErr;     {result code}
        ioNamePtr:    StringPtr; {volume or file name}
        ioVRefNum:    INTEGER;   {volume reference or drive number}
```

```
CASE ParamBlkType OF
  ioParam:
   (ioRefNum:       INTEGER;      {path reference number}
    ioVersNum:      SignedByte;   {version number}
    ioPermssn:      SignedByte;   {read/write permission}
    ioMisc:         Ptr;          {miscellaneous}
    ioBuffer:       Ptr;          {data buffer}
    ioReqCount:     LONGINT;      {requested number of bytes}
    ioActCount:     LONGINT;      {actual number of bytes}
    ioPosMode:      INTEGER;      {positioning mode and newline character}
    ioPosOffset:    LONGINT);     {positioning offset}
  fileParam:
   (ioFRefNum:      INTEGER;      {path reference number}
    ioFVersNum:     SignedByte;   {version number}
    filler1:        SignedByte;   {not used}
    ioFDirIndex:    INTEGER;      {sequence number of file}
    ioFlAttrib:     SignedByte;   {file attributes}
    ioFlVersNum:    SignedByte    {version number}
    ioFlFndrInfo:   FInfo;        {information used by the Finder}
    ioFlNum:        LONGINT;      {file number}
    ioFlStBlk:      INTEGER;      {first allocation block of data fork}
    ioFlLgLen:      LONGINT;      {logical end-of-file of data fork}
    ioFlPyLen:      LONGINT;      {physical end-of-file of data fork}
    ioFlRStBlk:     INTEGER;      {first allocation block of resource }
                                  { fork}
    ioFlRLgLen:     LONGINT;      {logical end-of-file of resource fork}
    ioFlRPyLen:     LONGINT;      {physical end-of-file of resource }
                                  { fork}
    ioFlCrDat:      LONGINT;      {date and time of creation}
    ioFlMdDat:      LONGINT);     {date and time of last modification}
  volumeParam:
   (filler2:        LONGINT;      {not used}
    ioVolIndex:     INTEGER;      {volume index}
    ioVCrDate:      LONGINT;      {date and time of initialization}
    ioVLsBkUp:      LONGINT;      {date and time of last backup}
    ioVAtrb:        INTEGER;      {bit 15=1 if volume locked}
    ioVNmFls:       INTEGER;      {number of files in directory}
    ioVDirSt:       INTEGER;      {first block of directory}
    ioVBlLn:        INTEGER;      {length of directory in blocks}
    ioVNmAlBlks:    INTEGER;      {number of allocation blocks}
    ioVAlBlkSiz:    LONGINT;      {size of allocation blocks}
    ioVClpSiz:      LONGINT;      {number of bytes to allocate}
    ioAlBlSt:       INTEGER;      {first allocation block in block map}
    ioVNxtFNum:     LONGINT;      {next unused file number}
    ioVFrBlk:       INTEGER);     {number of unused allocation blocks}
  cntrlParam:
    . . .  {used by Device Manager}
  END;
```

```
VCB = RECORD
        qLink:         QElemPtr;   {next queue entry}
        qType:         INTEGER;    {queue type}
        vcbFlags:      INTEGER;    {bit 15=1 if dirty}
        vcbSigWord:    INTEGER;    {always $D2D7}
        vcbCrDate:     LONGINT;    {date and time of initialization}
        vcbLsBkUp:     LONGINT;    {date and time of last backup}
        vcbAtrb:       INTEGER;    {volume attributes}
        vcbNmFls:      INTEGER;    {number of files in directory}
        vcbDirSt:      INTEGER;    {first block of directory}
        vcbBlLn:       INTEGER;    {length of directory in blocks}
        vcbNmBlks:     INTEGER;    {number of allocation blocks}
        vcbAlBlkSiz:   LONGINT;    {size of allocation blocks}
        vcbClpSiz:     LONGINT;    {number of bytes to allocate}
        vcbAlBlSt:     INTEGER;    {first allocation block in block map}
        vcbNxtFNum:    LONGINT;    {next unused file number}
        vcbFreeBks:    INTEGER;    {number of unused allocation blocks}
        vcbVN:         STRING[27]; {volume name}
        vcbDrvNum      INTEGER;    {drive number}
        vcbDRefNum:    INTEGER;    {driver reference number}
        vcbFSID:       INTEGER;    {file-system identifier}
        vcbVRefNum:    INTEGER;    {volume reference number}
        vcbMAdr:       Ptr;        {pointer to block map}
        vcbBufAdr:     Ptr;        {pointer to volume buffer}
        vcbMLen:       INTEGER;    {number of bytes in block map}
        vcbDirIndex:   INTEGER;    {used internally}
        vcbDirBlk:     INTEGER     {used internally}
      END;

DrvQEl = RECORD
        qLink:         QElemPtr;   {next queue entry}
        qType:         INTEGER;    {queue type}
        dQDrive:       INTEGER;    {drive number}
        dQRefNum:      INTEGER;    {driver reference number}
        dQFSID:        INTEGER;    {file-system identifier}
        dQDrvSize:     INTEGER     {number of logical blocks}
      END;
```

High-Level Routines [Not in ROM]

Accessing Volumes

```
FUNCTION GetVInfo     (drvNum: INTEGER; volName: StringPtr; VAR vRefNum:
                       INTEGER; VAR freeBytes: LONGINT) : OSErr;
FUNCTION GetVRefNum   (pathRefNum: INTEGER; VAR vRefNum: INTEGER) : OSErr;
FUNCTION GetVol       (volName: StringPtr; VAR vRefNum: INTEGER) : OSErr;
FUNCTION SetVol       (volName: StringPtr; vRefNum: INTEGER) : OSErr;
FUNCTION FlushVol     (volName: StringPtr; vRefNum: INTEGER) : OSErr;
FUNCTION UnmountVol   (volName: StringPtr; vRefNum: INTEGER) : OSErr;
FUNCTION Eject        (volName: StringPtr; vRefNum: INTEGER) : OSErr;
```

Accessing Files

```
FUNCTION Create     (fileName: Str255; vRefNum: INTEGER; creator: OSType;
                     fileType: OSType) : OSErr;
FUNCTION FSOpen     (fileName: Str255; vRefNum: INTEGER; VAR refNum:
                     INTEGER) : OSErr;
FUNCTION OpenRF     (fileName: Str255; vRefNum: INTEGER; VAR refNum:
                     INTEGER) : OSErr;
FUNCTION FSRead     (refNum: INTEGER; VAR count: LONGINT; buffPtr: Ptr) :
                     OSErr;
FUNCTION FSWrite    (refNum: INTEGER; VAR count: LONGINT; buffPtr: Ptr) :
                     OSErr;
FUNCTION GetFPos    (refNum: INTEGER; VAR filePos: LONGINT) : OSErr;
FUNCTION SetFPos    (refNum: INTEGER; posMode: INTEGER; posOff: LONGINT) :
                     OSErr;
FUNCTION GetEOF     (refNum: INTEGER; VAR logEOF: LONGINT) : OSErr;
FUNCTION SetEOF     (refNum: INTEGER; logEOF: LONGINT) : OSErr;
FUNCTION Allocate   (refNum: INTEGER; VAR count: LONGINT) : OSErr;
FUNCTION FSClose    (refNum: INTEGER) : OSErr;
```

Changing Information About Files

```
FUNCTION GetFInfo (fileName: Str255; vRefNum: INTEGER; VAR fndrInfo:
                   FInfo) : OSErr;
FUNCTION SetFInfo (fileName: Str255; vRefNum: INTEGER; fndrInfo: FInfo):
                   OSErr;
FUNCTION SetFLock (fileName: Str255; vRefNum: INTEGER) : OSErr;
FUNCTION RstFLock (fileName: Str255; vRefNum: INTEGER) : OSErr;
FUNCTION Rename   (oldName: Str255; vRefNum: INTEGER; newName: Str255) :
                   OSErr;
FUNCTION FSDelete (fileName: Str255; vRefNum: INTEGER) : OSErr;
```

Low-Level Routines

Initializing the File I/O Queue

```
PROCEDURE FInitQueue;
```

Accessing Volumes

```
FUNCTION PBMountVol (paramBlock: ParmBlkPtr) : OSErr;
    ←   16    ioResult          word
    ↔   22    ioVRefNum         word
```

```
FUNCTION PBGetVInfo (paramBlock: ParmBlkPtr; async: BOOLEAN) : OSErr;
    →   12      ioCompletion        pointer
    ←   16      ioResult            word
    ↔   18      ioNamePtr           pointer
    ↔   22      ioVRefNum           word
    →   28      ioVolIndex          word
    ←   30      ioVCrDate           long word
    ←   34      ioVLsBkUp           long word
    ←   38      ioVAtrb             word
    ←   40      ioVNmFls            word
    ←   42      ioVDirSt            word
    ←   44      ioVBlLn             word
    ←   46      ioVNmAlBlks         word
    ←   48      ioVAlBlkSiz         long word
    ←   52      ioVClpSiz           long word
    ←   56      ioAlBlSt            word
    ←   58      ioVNxtFNum          long word
    ←   62      ioVFrBlk            word


FUNCTION PBGetVol (paramBlock: ParmBlkPtr; async: BOOLEAN) : OSErr;
    →   12      ioCompletion        pointer
    ←   16      ioResult            word
    ←   18      ioNamePtr           pointer
    ←   22      ioVRefNum           word


FUNCTION PBSetVol (paramBlock: ParmBlkPtr; async: BOOLEAN) : OSErr;
    →   12      ioCompletion        pointer
    ←   16      ioResult            word
    →   18      ioNamePtr           pointer
    →   22      ioVRefNum           word


FUNCTION PBFlushVol (paramBlock: ParmBlkPtr; async: BOOLEAN) : OSErr;
    →   12      ioCompletion        pointer
    ←   16      ioResult            word
    →   18      ioNamePtr           pointer
    →   22      ioVRefNum           word


FUNCTION PBUnmountVol (paramBlock: ParmBlkPtr) : OSErr;
    ←   16      ioResult            word
    →   18      ioNamePtr           pointer
    →   22      ibVRefNum           word


FUNCTION PBOffLine (paramBlock: ParmBlkPtr) : OSErr;
    →   12      ioCompletion        pointer
    ←   16      ioResult            word
    →   18      ioNamePtr           pointer
    →   22      ioVRefNum           word
```

```
FUNCTION PBEject (paramBlock: ParmBlkPtr) : OSErr;
    →   12      ioCompletion        pointer
    ←   16      ioResult            word
    →   18      ioNamePt            pointer
    →   22      ioVRefNum           word
```

Accessing Files

```
FUNCTION PBCreate (paramBlock: ParmBlkPtr; async: BOOLEAN) : OSErr;
    →   12      ioCompletion        pointer
    ←   16      ioResult            word
    →   18      ioNamePtr           pointer
    →   22      ioVRefNum           word
    →   26      ioFVersNum          byte
```

```
FUNCTION PBOpen (paramBlock: ParmBlkPtr; async: BOOLEAN) : OSErr;
    →   12      ioCompletion        pointer
    ←   16      ioResult            word
    →   18      ioNamePtr           pointer
    →   22      ioVRefNum           word
    ←   24      ioRefNum            word
    →   26      ioVersNum           byte
    →   27      ioPermssn           byte
    →   28      ioMisc              pointer
```

```
FUNCTION PBOpenRF (paramBlock: ParmBlkPtr; async: BOOLEAN) : OSErr;
    →   12      ioCompletion        pointer
    ←   16      ioResult            word
    →   18      ioNamePtr           pointer
    →   22      ioVRefNum           word
    ←   24      ioRefNum            word
    →   26      ioVersNum           byte
    →   27      ioPermssn           byte
    →   28      ioMisc              pointer
```

```
FUNCTION PBRead (paramBlock: ParmBlkPtr; async: BOOLEAN) : OSErr;
    →   12      ioCompletion        pointer
    ←   16      ioResult            word
    →   24      ioRefNum            word
    →   32      ioBuffer            pointer
    →   36      ioReqCount          long word
    ←   40      ioActCount          long word
    →   44      ioPosMode           word
    ↔   46      ioPosOffset         long word
```

4 File Manager

```
FUNCTION PBWrite (paramBlock: ParmBlkPtr; async: BOOLEAN) : OSErr;
    →   12      ioCompletion        pointer
    ←   16      ioResult            word
    →   24      ioRefNum            word
    →   32      ioBuffer            pointer
    →   36      ioReqCount          long word
    ←   40      ioActCount          long word
    →   44      ioPosMode           word
    ↔   46      ioPosOffset         long word


FUNCTION PBGetFPos (paramBlock: ParmBlkPtr; async: BOOLEAN) : OSErr;
    →   12      ioCompletion        pointer
    ←   16      ioResult            word
    →   24      ioRefNum            word
    ←   36      ioReqCount          long word
    ←   40      ioActCount          long word
    ←   44      ioPosMode           word
    ←   46      ioPosOffset         long word


FUNCTION PBSetFPos (paramBlock: ParmBlkPtr; async: BOOLEAN) : OSErr;
    →   12      ioCompletion        pointer
    ←   16      ioResult            word
    →   24      ioRefNum            word
    →   44      ioPosMode           word
    ↔   46      ioPosOffset         long word


FUNCTION PBGetEOF (paramBlock: ParmBlkPtr; async: BOOLEAN) : OSErr;
    →   12      ioCompletion        pointer
    ←   16      ioResult            word
    →   24      ioRefNum            word
    ←   28      ioMisc              long word


FUNCTION PBSetEOF (paramBlock: ParmBlkPtr; async: BOOLEAN) : OSErr;
    →   12      ioCompletion        pointer
    ←   16      ioResult            word
    →   24      ioRefNum            word
    →   28      ioMisc              long word


FUNCTION PBAllocate (paramBlock: ParmBlkPtr; async: BOOLEAN) : OSErr;
    →   12      ioCompletion        pointer
    ←   16      ioResult            word
    →   24      ioRefNum            word
    →   36      ioReqCount          long word
    ←   40      ioActCount          long word


FUNCTION PBFlushFile (paramBlock: ParmBlkPtr; async: BOOLEAN) : OSErr;
    →   12      ioCompletion        pointer
    ←   16      ioResult            word
    →   24      ioRefNum            word
```

```
FUNCTION PBClose (paramBlock: ParmBlkPtr; async: BOOLEAN) : OSErr;
```
→	12	ioCompletion	pointer
←	16	ioResult	word
→	24	ioRefNum	word

Changing Information About Files

```
FUNCTION PBGetFInfo (paramBlock: ParmBlkPtr; async: BOOLEAN) : OSErr;
```
→	12	ioCompletion	pointer
←	16	ioResult	word
↔	18	ioNamePtr	pointer
→	22	ioVRefNum	word
←	24	ioFRefNum	word
→	26	ioFVersNum	byte
→	28	ioFDirIndex	word
←	30	ioFlAttrib	byte
←	31	ioFlVersNum	byte
←	32	ioFlFndrInfo	16 bytes
←	48	ioFlNum	long word
←	52	ioFlStBlk	word
←	54	ioFlLgLen	long word
←	58	ioFlPyLen	long word
←	62	ioFlRStBlk	word
←	64	ioFlRLgLen	long word
←	68	ioFlRPyLen	long word
←	72	ioFlCrDat	long word
←	76	ioFlMdDat	long word

```
FUNCTION PBSetFInfo (paramBlock: ParmBlkPtr; async: BOOLEAN) : OSErr;
```
→	12	ioCompletion	pointer
←	16	ioResult	word
→	18	ioNamePtr	pointer
→	22	ioVRefNum	word
→	26	ioFVersNum	byte
→	32	ioFlFndrInfo	16 bytes
→	72	ioFlCrDat	long word
→	76	ioFlMdDat	long word

```
FUNCTION PBSetFLock (paramBlock: ParmBlkPtr; async: BOOLEAN) : OSErr;
```
→	12	ioCompletion	pointer
←	16	ioResult	word
→	18	ioNamePtr	pointer
→	22	ioVRefNum	word
→	26	ioFVersNum	byte

```
FUNCTION PBRstFLock (paramBlock: ParmBlkPtr; async: BOOLEAN) : OSErr;
```
→	12	ioCompletion	pointer
←	16	ioResult	word
→	18	ioNamePtr	pointer
→	22	ioVRefNum	word
→	26	ioFVersNum	byte

```
FUNCTION PBSetFVers (paramBlock: ParmBlkPtr; async: BOOLEAN) : OSErr;
    →   12      ioCompletion      pointer
    ←   16      ioResult          word
    →   18      ioNamePtr         pointer
    →   22      ioVRefNum         word
    →   26      ioVersNum         byte
    →   28      ioMisc            byte

FUNCTION PBRename (paramBlock: ParmBlkPtr; async: BOOLEAN) : OSErr;
    →   12      ioCompletion      pointer
    ←   16      ioResult          word
    →   18      ioNamePtr         pointer
    →   22      ioVRefNum         word
    →   26      ioVersNum         byte
    →   28      ioMisc            pointer

FUNCTION PBDelete (paramBlock: ParmBlkPtr; async: BOOLEAN) : OSErr;
    →   12      ioCompletion      pointer
    ←   16      ioResult          word
    →   18      ioNamePtr         pointer
    →   22      ioVRefNum         word
    →   26      ioFVersNum        byte
```

Accessing Queues [Not in ROM]

```
FUNCTION GetFSQHdr  : QHdrPtr;
FUNCTION GetVCBQHdr : QHdrPtr;
FUNCTION GetDrvQHdr : QHdrPtr;
```

Result Codes

Name	Value	Meaning
badMDBErr	−60	Master directory block is bad; must reinitialize volume
bdNamErr	−37	Bad file name or volume name (perhaps zero-length)
dirFulErr	−33	File directory full
dskFulErr	−34	All allocation blocks on the volume are full
dupFNErr	−48	A file with the specified name and version number already exists
eofErr	−39	Logical end-of-file reached during read operation
extFSErr	−58	External file system; file-system identifier is nonzero, or path reference number is greater than 1024
fBsyErr	−47	One or more files are open
fLckdErr	−45	File locked
fnfErr	−43	File not found
fnOpnErr	−38	File not open

Name	Value	Meaning
fsRnErr	−59	Problem during rename
gfpErr	−52	Error during GetFPos
ioErr	−36	I/O error
memFullErr	−108	Not enough room in heap zone
noErr	0	No error
noMacDskErr	−57	Volume lacks Macintosh-format directory
nsDrvErr	−56	Specified drive number doesn't match any number in the drive queue
nsvErr	−35	Specified volume doesn't exist
opWrErr	−49	The read/write permission of only one access path to a file can allow writing
paramErr	−50	Parameters don't specify an existing volume, and there's no default volume
permErr	−54	Attempt to open locked file for writing
posErr	−40	Attempt to position before start of file
rfNumErr	−51	Reference number specifies nonexistent access path
tmfoErr	−42	Too many files open
volOffLinErr	−53	Volume not on-line
volOnLinErr	−55	Specified volume is already mounted and on-line
vLckdErr	−46	Volume is locked by a software flag
wrPermErr	−61	Read/write permission doesn't allow writing
wPrErr	−44	Volume is locked by a hardware setting

Assembly-Language Information

Constants

```
; Flags in file information used by the Finder

fHasBundle      .EQU      13      ;set if file has a bundle
fInvisible      .EQU      14      ;set if file's icon is invisible

; Flags in trap words

asnycTrpBit     .EQU      10      ;set for an asynchronous call
noQueueBit      .EQU       9      ;set for immediate execution
```

```
; Values for requesting read/write access

fsCurPerm       .EQU    0       ;whatever is currently allowed
fsRdPerm        .EQU    1       ;request to read only
fsWrPerm        .EQU    2       ;request to write only
fsRdWrPerm      .EQU    3       ;request to read and write

; Positioning modes

fsAtMark        .EQU    0       ;at current mark
fsFromStart     .EQU    1       ;offset relative to beginning of file
fsFromLEOF      .EQU    2       ;offset relative to logical end-of-file
fsFromMark      .EQU    3       ;offset relative to current mark
rdVerify        .EQU    64      ;add to above for read-verify
```

Structure of File Information Used by the Finder

fdType	File type (long)
fdCreator	File's creator (long)
fdFlags	Flags (word)
fdLocation	File's location (point; long)
fdFldr	File's window (word)

Standard Parameter Block Data Structure

qLink	Pointer to next queue entry
qType	Queue type (word)
ioTrap	Routine trap (word)
ioCmdAddr	Routine address
ioCompletion	Address of completion routine
ioResult	Result code (word)
ioFileName	Pointer to file name (preceded by length byte)
ioVNPtr	Pointer to volume name (preceded by length byte)
ioVRefNum	Volume reference number (word)
ioDrvNum	Drive number (word)

I/O Parameter Block Data Structure

ioRefNum	Path reference number (word)
ioFileType	Version number (byte)
ioPermssn	Read/write permission (byte)
ioNewName	Pointer to new file or volume name for Rename
ioLEOF	Logical end-of-file for SetEOF (long)
ioOwnBuf	Pointer to access path buffer
ioNewType	New version number for SetFilType (byte)
ioBuffer	Pointer to data buffer
ioReqCount	Requested number of bytes (long)
ioActCount	Actual number of bytes (long)
ioPosMode	Positioning mode and newline character (word)

ioPosOffset   Positioning offset (long)
ioQElSize   Size in bytes of I/O parameter block

Structure of File Information Parameter Block

ioRefNum	Path reference number (word)
ioFileType	Version number (byte)
ioFDirIndex	Sequence number of file (word)
ioFlAttrib	File attributes (byte)
ioFFlType	Version number (byte)
ioFlUsrWds	Information used by the Finder (16 bytes)
ioFFlNum	File number (long)
ioFlStBlk	First allocation block of data fork (word)
ioFlLgLen	Logical end-of-file of data fork (long)
ioFlPyLen	Physical end-of-file of data fork (long)
ioFlRStBlk	First allocation block of resource fork (word)
ioFlRLgLen	Logical end-of-file of resource fork (long)
ioFlRPyLen	Physical end-of-file of resource fork (long)
ioFlCrDat	Date and time of creation (long)
ioFlMdDat	Date and time of last modification (long)
ioFQElSize	Size in bytes of file information parameter block

Structure of Volume Information Parameter Block

ioVolIndex	Volume index (word)
ioVCrDate	Date and time of initialization (long)
ioVLsBkUp	Date and time of last backup (long)
ioVAtrb	Volume attributes (word)
ioVNmFls	Number of files in directory (word)
ioVDirSt	First block of directory (word)
ioVBlLn	Length of directory in blocks (word)
ioVNmAlBlks	Number of allocation blocks on volume (word)
ioVAlBlkSiz	Size of allocation blocks (long)
ioVClpSiz	Number of bytes to allocate (long)
ioAlBlSt	First allocation block in block map (word)
ioVNxtFNum	Next unused file number (long)
ioVFrBlk	Number of unused allocation blocks (word)
ioVQElSize	Size in bytes of volume information parameter block

Volume Information Data Structure

drSigWord	Always $D2D7 (word)
drCrDate	Date and time of initialization (long)
drLsBkUp	Date and time of last backup (long)
drAtrb	Volume attributes (word)
drNmFls	Number of files in directory (word)
drDirSt	First block of directory (word)
drBlLn	Length of directory in blocks (word)
drNmAlBlks	Number of allocation blocks on volume (word)
drAlBlkSiz	Size of allocation blocks (long)

4 File Manager

drClpSiz   Number of bytes to allocate (long)
drAlBlSt   First allocation block in block map (word)
drNxtFNum   Next unused file number (long)
drFreeBks   Number of unused allocation blocks (word)
drVN   Volume name preceded by length byte (28 bytes)

File Directory Entry Data Structure

flFlags   Bit 7=1 if entry used; bit 0=1 if file locked (byte)
flTyp   Version number (byte)
flUsrWds   Information used by the Finder (16 bytes)
flFlNum   File number (long)
flStBlk   First allocation block of data fork (word)
flLgLen   Logical end-of-file of data fork (long)
flPyLen   Physical end-of-file of data fork (long)
flRStBlk   First allocation block of resource fork (word)
flRLgLen   Logical end-of-file of resource fork (long)
flRPyLen   Physical end-of-file of resource fork (long)
flCrDat   Date and time file of creation (long)
flMdDat   Date and time of last modification (long)
flNam   File name preceded by length byte

Volume Control Block Data Structure

qLink   Pointer to next queue entry
qType   Queue type (word)
vcbFlags   Bit 15=1 if volume control block is dirty (word)
vcbSigWord   Always $D2D7 (word)
vcbCrDate   Date and time of initialization (word)
vcbLsBkUp   Date and time of last backup (long)
vcbAtrb   Volume attributes (word)
vcbNmFls   Number of files in directory (word)
vcbDirSt   First block of directory (word)
vcbBlLn   Length of directory in blocks (word)
vcbNmBlks   Number of allocation blocks on volume (word)
vcbAlBlkSiz   Size of allocation blocks (long)
vcbClpSiz   Number of bytes to allocate (long)
vcbAlBlSt   First allocation block in block map (word)
vcbNxtFNum   Next unused file number (long)
vcbFreeBks   Number of unused allocation blocks (word)
vcbVN   Volume name preceded by length byte (28 bytes)
vcbDrvNum   Drive number of drive in which volume is mounted (word)
vcbDRefNum   Driver reference number of driver for drive in which volume is mounted (word)
vcbFSID   File-system identifier (word)
vcbVRefNum   Volume reference number (word)
vcbMAdr   Pointer to volume block map
vcbBufAdr   Pointer to volume buffer
vcbMLen   Number of bytes in volume block map (word)

File Control Block Data Structure

fcbFlNum	File number (long)
fcbMdRByt	Flags (byte)
fcbTypByt	Version number (byte)
fcbSBlk	First allocation block of file (word)
fcbEOF	Logical end-of-file (long)
fcbPLen	Physical end-of-file (long)
fcbCrPs	Mark (long)
fcbVPtr	Pointer to volume control block (long)
fcbBfAdr	Pointer to access path buffer (long)

Drive Queue Entry Data Structure

qLink	Pointer to next queue entry
qType	Queue type (word)
dQDrive	Drive number (word)
dQRefNum	Driver reference number (word)
dQFSID	File-system identifier (word)
dQDrvSize	Number of logical blocks (word)

Macro Names

Pascal name	Macro name
FInitQueue	_InitQueue
PBMountVol	_MountVol
PBGetVInfo	_GetVolInfo
PBGetVol	_GetVol
PBSetVol	_SetVol
PBFlushVol	_FlushVol
PBUnmountVol	_UnmountVol
PBOffLine	_OffLine
PBEject	_Eject
PBCreate	_Create
PBOpen	_Open
PBOpenRF	_OpenRF
PBRead	_Read
PBWrite	_Write
PBGetFPos	_GetFPos
PBSetFPos	_SetFPos
PBGetEOF	_GetEOF
PBSetEOF	_SetEOF
PBAllocate	_Allocate
PBFlushFile	_FlushFile
PBClose	_Close
PBGetFInfo	_GetFileInfo
PBSetFInfo	_SetFileInfo
PBSetFLock	_SetFilLock
PBRstFLock	_RstFilLock

4 File Manager

PBSetFVers   _SetFilType
PBRename   _Rename
PBDelete   _Delete

Variables

FSQHdr   File I/O queue header (10 bytes)
VCBQHdr   Volume-control-block queue header (10 bytes)
DefVCBPtr   Pointer to default volume control block
FCBSPtr   Pointer to file-control-block buffer
DrvQHdr   Drive queue header (10 bytes)
ToExtFS   Pointer to external file system

5 THE PRINTING MANAGER

5 Printing Manager

ABOUT THIS CHAPTER

The Printing Manager is a set of RAM-based routines and data types that allow you to use standard QuickDraw routines to print text or graphics on a printer. The Printing Manager calls the Printer Driver, a device driver in RAM. It also includes low-level calls to the Printer Driver so that you can implement alternate, low-level printing routines.

You should already be familiar with the following:

- the Resource Manager

- QuickDraw

- dialogs, as described in chapter 13 of Volume I

- the Device Manager, if you're interested in writing your own Printer Driver

ABOUT THE PRINTING MANAGER

The Printing Manager isn't in the Macintosh ROM; to access the Printing Manager routines, you must link with an object file or files provided as part of your development system.

The Macintosh user prints a document by choosing the Print command from the application's File menu; a dialog then requests information such as the print quality and number of copies. The Page Setup command in the File menu lets the user specify formatting information, such as the page size, that rarely needs to be changed and is saved with the document. The Printing Manager provides your application with two standard dialogs for obtaining Page Setup and Print information. The user can also print directly from the Finder by selecting one or more documents and choosing Print from the Finder's File menu; the Print dialog is then applied to all of the documents selected.

The Printing Manager is designed so that your application doesn't have to be concerned with what kind of printer is connected to the Macintosh; you call the same printing routines, regardless of the printer. This printer independence is possible because the actual printing code (which is different for different printers) is contained in a separate **printer resource file** on the user's disk. The printer resource file contains a device driver, called the **Printer Driver**, that communicates between the Printing Manager and the printer.

The user installs a new printer with the Choose Printer desk accessory, which gives the Printing Manager a new printer resource file. This process is transparent to your application, and your application should not make any assumptions about the printer type.

Figure 1 shows the flow of control for printing on the Macintosh.

You define the image to be printed by using a **printing grafPort**, a QuickDraw grafPort with additional fields that customize it for printing:

```
TYPE TPPrPort = ^TPrPort;
     TPrPort  = RECORD
                    gPort: GrafPort;  {grafPort to draw in}
                    {more fields for internal use}
                END;
```

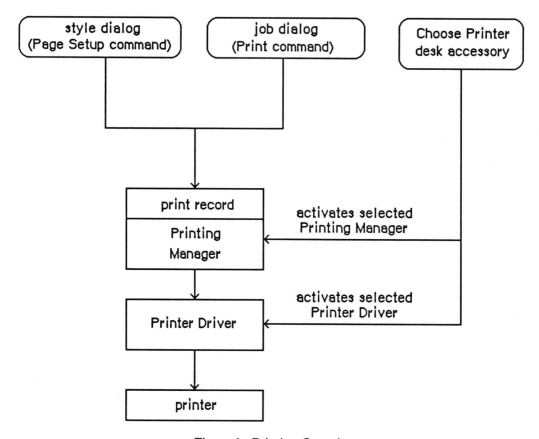

Figure 1. Printing Overview

The Printing Manager gives you a printing grafPort when you open a document for printing. You then print text and graphics by drawing into this port with QuickDraw, just as if you were drawing on the screen. The Printing Manager installs its own versions of QuickDraw's low-level drawing routines in the printing grafPort, causing your higher-level QuickDraw calls to drive the printer instead of drawing on the screen.

Warning: You should not try to do your own customization of QuickDraw routines in the printing grafPort unless you're sure of what you're doing.

PRINT RECORDS AND DIALOGS

To format and print a document, your application must know the following:

- the dimensions of the printable area of the page
- if the application must calculate the margins, the size of the physical sheet of paper and the printer's vertical and horizontal resolution
- which printing method is being used (draft or spool, explained below)

This information is contained in a data structure called a **print record**. The Printing Manager fills in the entire print record for you. Information that the user can specify is set through two standard dialogs.

The **style dialog** should be presented when the user selects the application's Page Setup command from the File menu. It lets the user specify any options that affect the page dimensions, that is, the information you need for formatting the document to match the printer. Figure 2 shows the standard style dialog for the Imagewriter printer.

Figure 2. The Style Dialog

The **job dialog** should be presented when the user chooses to start printing with the Print command. It requests information about how to print the document *this time,* such as the print quality (for printers that offer a choice of resolutions), the type of paper feed (such as fanfold or cut-sheet), the range of pages to print, and the number of copies. Figure 3 shows the standard job dialog for the Imagewriter.

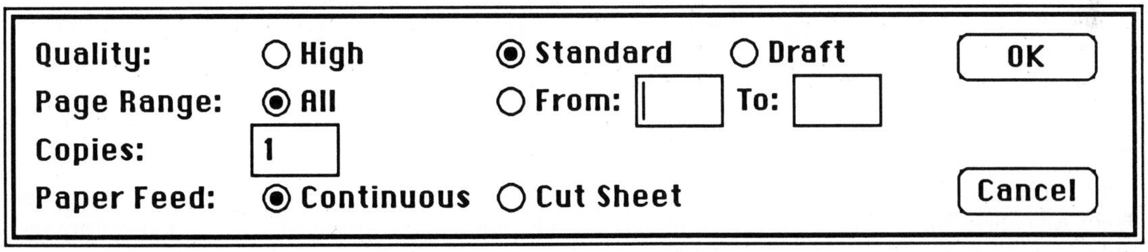

Figure 3. The Job Dialog

Note: The dialogs shown in Figures 2 and 3 are examples only; the actual content of these dialogs is customized for each printer.

Print records are referred to by handles. Their structure is as follows:

```
TYPE THPrint  =  ^TPPrint;
     TPPrint  =  ^TPrint;
     TPrint   =  RECORD
                     iPrVersion: INTEGER;   {Printing Manager version}
                     prInfo:     TPrInfo;   {printer information subrecord}
                     rPaper:     Rect;      {paper rectangle}
                     prStl:      TPrStl;    {additional device information}
                     prInfoPT:   TPrInfo;   {used internally}
                     prXInfo:    TPrXInfo;  {additional device information}
                     prJob:      TPrJob;    {job subrecord}
                     printX:     ARRAY[1..19] OF INTEGER  {not used}
                 END;
```

Warning: Your application should not change the data in the print record—be sure to use the standard dialogs for setting this information. The only fields you'll need to set directly are some containing optional information in the job subrecord (explained below). Attempting to set other values directly in the print record can produce unexpected results.

IPrVersion identifies the version of the Printing Manager that initialized this print record. If you try to use a print record that's invalid for the current version of the Printing Manager or for the currently installed printer, the Printing Manager will correct the record by filling it with default values.

The other fields of the print record are discussed in separate sections below.

Note: Whenever you save a document, you should write an appropriate print record in the document's resource file. This lets the document "remember" its own printing parameters for use the next time it's printed.

The Printer Information Subrecord

The printer information subrecord (field prInfo of the print record) gives you the information needed for page composition. It's defined as follows:

```
TYPE TPrInfo =  RECORD
                iDev:  INTEGER;    {used internally}
                iVRes: INTEGER;    {vertical resolution of printer}
                iHRes: INTEGER;    {horizontal resolution of printer}
                rPage: Rect        {page rectangle}
              END;
```

RPage is the **page rectangle**, representing the boundaries of the printable page: The printing grafPort's boundary rectangle, portRect, and clipRgn are set to this rectangle. Its top left corner always has coordinates (0,0); the coordinates of the bottom right corner give the maximum page height and width attainable on the given printer, in dots. Typically these are slightly less than the physical dimensions of the paper, because of the printer's mechanical limitations. RPage is set as a result of the style dialog.

The rPage rectangle is inside the **paper rectangle**, specified by the rPaper field of the print record. RPaper gives the physical paper size, defined in the same coordinate system as rPage (see Figure 4). Thus the top left coordinates of the paper rectangle are typically negative and its bottom right coordinates are greater than those of the page rectangle.

IVRes and iHRes give the printer's vertical and horizontal resolution in dots per inch. Thus, if you divide the width of rPage by iHRes, you get the width of the page rectangle in inches.

The Job Subrecord

The job subrecord (field prJob of the print record) contains information about a particular printing job. Its contents are set as a result of the job dialog.

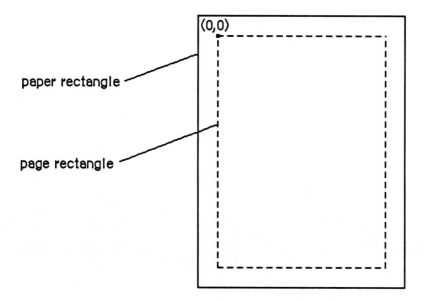

Figure 4. Page and Paper Rectangles

The job subrecord is defined as follows:

```
TYPE TPrJob =
        RECORD
            iFstPage:  INTEGER;      {first page to print}
            iLstPage:  INTEGER;      {last page to print}
            iCopies:   INTEGER;      {number of copies}
            bJDocLoop: SignedByte;   {printing method}
            fFromUsr:  BOOLEAN;      {used internally}
            pIdleProc: ProcPtr;      {background procedure}
            pFileName: StringPtr;    {spool file name}
            iFileVol:  INTEGER;      {spool file volume reference number}
            bFileVers: SignedByte;   {spool file version number}
            bJobX:     SignedByte    {used internally}
        END;
```

BJDocLoop designates the printing method that the Printing Manager will use. It will be one of the following predefined constants:

```
CONST bDraftLoop = 0;   {draft printing}
      bSpoolLoop = 1;   {spool printing}
```

Draft printing means that the document will be printed immediately. **Spool printing** means that printing may be deferred: The Printing Manager writes out a representation of the document's printed image to a disk file (or possibly to memory); this information is then converted into a bit image and printed. For details about the printing methods, see the "Methods of Printing" section below. The Printing Manager sets the bJDocLoop field; your application should not change it.

IFstPage and iLstPage designate the first and last pages to be printed. These page numbers are relative to the first page counted by the Printing Manager. The Printing Manager knows nothing about any page numbering placed by an application within a document.

ICopies is the number of copies to print. The Printing Manager automatically handles multiple copies for spool printing or for printing on the LaserWriter. Your application only needs this number for draft printing on the Imagewriter.

PIdleProc is a pointer to the background procedure (explained below) for this printing operation. In a newly initialized print record this field is set to NIL, designating the default background procedure, which just polls the keyboard and cancels further printing if the user types Command-period. You can install a background procedure of your own by storing a pointer to your procedure directly into the pIdleProc field.

For spool printing, your application may optionally provide a spool file name, volume reference number, and version number (described in chapter 4):

- PFileName is the name of the spool file. This field is initialized to NIL, and generally not changed by the application. NIL denotes the default file name (normally 'Print File') stored in the printer resource file.

- IFileVol is the volume reference number of the spool file. This field is initialized to 0, representing the default volume. You can use the File Manager function SetVol to change the default volume, or you can override the default setting by storing directly into this field.

- BFileVers is the version number of the spool file, initialized to 0.

Additional Device Information

The prStl and prXInfo fields of the print record provide device information that your application may need to refer to.

The prStl field of the print record is defined as follows:

```
TYPE TPrStl = RECORD
                wDev: INTEGER;     {high byte specifies device}
                {more fields for internal use}
              END;
```

The high-order byte of the wDev field indicates which printer is currently selected:

```
CONST bDevCItoh = 1;   {Imagewriter printer}
      bDevLaser = 3;   {LaserWriter printer}
```

A value of 0 indicates the Macintosh screen; other values are reserved for future use. The low-order byte of wDev is used internally.

The prXInfo field of the print record is defined as follows:

```
TYPE TPrXInfo = RECORD
                  iRowBytes: INTEGER;   {used internally}
                  iBandV:    INTEGER;   {used internally}
                  iBandH:    INTEGER;   {used internally}
                  iDevBytes: INTEGER;   {size of buffer}
                  {more fields for internal use}
                END;
```

IDevBytes is the number of bytes of memory required as a buffer for spool printing. (You need this information only if you choose to allocate your own buffer.)

METHODS OF PRINTING

There are two basic methods of printing documents: draft and spool. The Printing Manager determines which method to use; the two methods are implemented in different ways for different printers.

In draft printing, your QuickDraw calls are converted directly into command codes the printer understands, which are then immediately used to drive the printer:

- On the Imagewriter, draft printing is used for printing quick, low-quality drafts of text documents that are printed straight down the page from top to bottom and left to right.

- On the LaserWriter, draft printing is used to obtain high-quality output. (This typically requires 15K bytes of memory for your data and printing code.)

Spool printing is a two-stage process. First, the Printing Manager writes out ("spools") a representation of your document's printed image to a disk file or to memory. This information is then converted into a bit image and printed. On the Imagewriter, spool printing is used for standard or high-quality printing.

Spooling and printing are two separate stages because of memory considerations: Spooling a document takes only about 3K bytes of memory, but may require large portions of your application's code and data in memory; printing the spooled document typically requires from 20K to 40K for the printing code, buffers, and fonts, but most of your application's code and data are no longer needed. Normally you'll make your printing code a separate program segment, so you can swap the rest of your code and data out of memory during printing and swap it back in after you're finished (see chapter 2).

Note: This chapter frequently refers to spool files, although there may be cases when the document is spooled to memory. This difference will be transparent to the application.

Note: The internal format of spool files is private to the Printing Manager and may vary from one printer to another. This means that spool files destined for one printer can't be printed on another. In spool files for the Imagewriter, each page is stored as a QuickDraw picture. It's envisioned that most other printers will use this same approach, but there may be exceptions. Spool files can be identified by their file type ('PFIL') and creator ('PSYS'). File type and creator are discussed in chapter 1 of Volume III.

BACKGROUND PROCESSING

As mentioned above, the job subrecord includes a pointer, pIdleProc, to an optional **background procedure** to be run whenever the Printing Manager has directed output to the printer and is waiting for the printer to finish. The background procedure takes no parameters and returns no result; the Printing Manager simply runs it at every opportunity.

If you don't designate a background procedure, the Printing Manager uses a default procedure for canceling printing: The default procedure just polls the keyboard and sets a Printing Manager error code if the user types Command-period. If you use this option, you should display a dialog box during printing to inform the user that the Command-period option is available.

Note: If you designate a background procedure, you must set pIdleProc *after* presenting the dialogs, validating the print record, and initializing the printing grafPort: The routines that perform these operations reset pIdleProc to NIL.

Warning: If you write your own background procedure, you must be careful to avoid a number of subtle concurrency problems that can arise. For instance, if the background procedure uses QuickDraw, it must be sure to restore the printing grafPort as the current port before returning. It's particularly important not to attempt any printing from within the background procedure: The Printing Manager is *not* reentrant! If you use a background procedure that runs your application concurrently with printing, it should disable all menu items having to do with printing, such as Page Setup and Print.

USING THE PRINTING MANAGER

To use the Printing Manager, you must first initialize QuickDraw, the Font Manager, the Window Manager, the Menu Manager, TextEdit, and the Dialog Manager. The first Printing Manager routine to call is PrOpen; the last routine to call is PrClose.

Before you can print a document, you need a valid print record. You can either use an existing print record (for instance, one saved with a document), or initialize one by calling PrintDefault or PrValidate. If you use an existing print record, be sure to call PrValidate to make sure it's valid for the current version of the Printing Manager and for the currently installed printer. To create a new print record, you must first create a handle to it with the Memory Manager function NewHandle, as follows:

```
prRecHdl := THPrint(NewHandle(SIZEOF(TPrint)))
```

Print record information is obtained via the style and job dialogs:

- Call PrStlDialog when the user chooses the Page Setup commmand, to get the page dimensions. From the rPage field of the printer information subrecord, you can then determine where page breaks will be in the document. You can show rulers and margins correctly by using the information in the iVRes, iHRes, and rPaper fields.

- Call PrJobDialog when the user chooses the Print commmand, to get the specific information about that printing job, such as the page range and number of copies.

You can apply the results of one job dialog to several documents (when printing from the Finder, for example) by calling PrJobMerge.

After getting the job information, you should immediately print the document.

The Printing Loop

To print a document, you call the following procedures:

1. PrOpenDoc, which returns a printing grafPort that's set up for draft or spool printing (depending on the bJDocLoop field of the job subrecord)

2. PrOpenPage, which starts each new page (reinitializing the grafPort)

3. QuickDraw routines, for drawing the page in the printing grafPort created by PrOpenDoc

4. PrClosePage, which terminates the page

5. PrCloseDoc, at the end of the entire document, to close the printing grafPort

Each page is either printed immediately (draft printing) or written to the disk or to memory (spool printing). You should test to see whether spooling was done, and if so, print the spooled document: First, swap as much of your program out of memory as you can (see chapter 2), and then call PrPicFile.

It's a good idea to call PrError after each Printing Manager call, to check for any errors. To cancel a printing operation in progress, use PrSetError. If an error occurs and you cancel printing (or if the user aborts printing), be sure to exit normally from the printing loop so that all files are closed properly; that is, be sure that every PrOpenPage is matched by a PrClosePage and PrOpenDoc is matched by PrCloseDoc.

To sum up, your application's printing loop will typically use the following basic format for printing:

```
myPrPort := PrOpenDoc(prRecHdl,NIL,NIL); {open printing grafPort}
FOR pg := 1 TO myPgCount DO              {page loop: ALL pages of document}
   IF  PrError = noErr
      THEN
         BEGIN
         PrOpenPage(myPrPort,NIL);     {start new page}
         IF PrError = noErr
            THEN MyDrawingProc(pg);    {draw page with QuickDraw}
         PrClosePage(myPrPort);        {end current page}
         END;
PrCloseDoc(myPrPort);                  {close printing grafPort}
IF  prRecHdl^^.prJob.bJDocLoop = bSpoolLoop AND PrError = noErr
   THEN
      BEGIN
      MySwapOutProc;        {swap out code and data}
      PrPicFile(prRecHdl,NIL,NIL,NIL,myStRec); {print spooled document}
      END;
IF PrError <> noErr THEN MyPrErrAlertProc    {report any errors}
```

Note an important assumption in this example: The MyDrawingProc procedure must be able to determine the page boundaries without stepping through each page of the document.

Although spool printing may not be supported on all printers, you must be sure to include PrPicFile in your printing code, as shown above. The application should make no assumptions about the printing method.

Note: The maximum number of pages in a spool file is defined by the following constant:

```
CONST iPFMaxPgs = 128;
```

If you need to print more than 128 pages at one time, just repeat the printing loop (*without* calling PrValidate, PrStlDialog, or PrJobDialog).

Printing a Specified Range of Pages

The above example loops through every page of the document, regardless of which pages the user has selected; the Printing Manager draws each page but actually prints only the pages from iFstPage to iLstPage.

If you know the page boundaries in the document, it's much faster to loop through only the specified pages. You can do this by saving the values of iFstPage and iLstPage and then changing these fields in the print record: For example, to print pages 20 to 25, you would set iFstPage to 1 and iLstPage to 6 (or greater) and then begin printing at your page 20. You could implement this for all cases as follows:

```
myFirst := prRecHdl^^.prJob.iFstPage;    {save requested page numbers}
myLast := prRecHdl^^.prJob.iLstPage;
prRecHdl^^.prJob.iFstPage := 1;          {print "all" pages in loop}
prRecHdl^^.prJob.iLstPage := 999;
FOR pg := myFirst TO myLast DO           {page loop: requested pages only}
   . . .                                 {print as in first example}
```

Remember that iFstPage and iLstPage are relative to the first page counted by the Printing Manager. The Printing Manager counts one page each time PrOpenPage is called; the count begins at 1.

Using QuickDraw for Printing

When drawing to the printing grafPort, you should note the following:

- With each new page, you get a completely reinitialized grafPort, so you'll need to reset font information and other grafPort characteristics as desired.

- Don't make calls that don't do anything on the printer. For example, erase operations are quite time-consuming and normally aren't needed on the printer.

- Don't use clipping to select text to be printed. There are a number of subtle differences between how text appears on the screen and how it appears on the printer; you can't count on knowing the exact dimensions of the rectangle occupied by the text.

- Don't use fixed-width fonts to align columns. Since spacing gets adjusted on the printer, you should explicitly move the pen to where you want it.

For printing to the LaserWriter, you'll need to observe the following limitations:

- Regions aren't supported; try to simulate them with polygons.

- Clipping regions should be limited to rectangles.

- "Invert" routines aren't supported.

- Copy is the *only* transfer mode supported for all objects except text and bit images. For text, Bic is also supported. For bit images, the only transfer mode *not* supported is Xor.

- Don't change the grafPort's local coordinate system (with SetOrigin) within the printing loop (between PrOpenPage and PrClosePage).

For more information about optimizing your printing code for the LaserWriter, see the *Inside LaserWriter* manual.

Printing From the Finder

The Macintosh user can choose to print from the Finder as well as from an application. Your application should support both alternatives.

To print a document from the Finder, the user selects the document's icon and chooses the Print command from the File menu. Note that the user can select more than one document, or even a document and an application, which means that the application must verify that it can print the document before proceeding. When the Print command is chosen, the Finder starts up the application, and passes information to it indicating that the document is to be printed rather than opened (see chapter 2). Your application should then do the following, preferably without going through its entire startup sequence:

1. Call PrJobDialog. (If the user selected more than one document, you can use PrJobMerge to apply one job dialog to all of the documents.)

2. Print the document(s).

PRINTING MANAGER ROUTINES

This section describes the high-level Printing Manager routines; low-level routines are described below in the section "The Printer Driver".

Assembly-language note: There are no trap macros for these routines. To print from assembly language, call these Pascal routines from your program.

Initialization and Termination

```
PROCEDURE PrOpen;    [Not in ROM]
```

PrOpen prepares the Printing Manager for use. It opens the Printer Driver and the printer resource file. If either of these is missing, or if the printer resource file isn't properly formed, PrOpen will do nothing, and PrError will return a Resource Manager result code.

```
PROCEDURE PrClose;    [Not in ROM]
```

PrClose releases the memory used by the Printing Manager. It closes the printer resource file, allowing the file's resource map to be removed from memory. It doesn't close the Printer Driver.

Note: To close the Printer Driver, call the low-level routine PrDrvrClose, described in the section "The Printer Driver".

Print Records and Dialogs

`PROCEDURE PrintDefault (hPrint: THPrint);` [Not in ROM]

PrintDefault fills the fields of the specified print record with default values that are stored in the printer resource file. HPrint is a handle to the record, which may be a new print record that you've just allocated with NewHandle or an existing one (from a document, for example).

`FUNCTION PrValidate (hPrint: THPrint) : BOOLEAN;` [Not in ROM]

PrValidate checks the contents of the specified print record for compatibility with the current version of the Printing Manager and with the currently installed printer. If the record is valid, the function returns FALSE (no change); if invalid, the record is adjusted to the default values stored in the printer resource file, and the function returns TRUE.

PrValidate also makes sure all the information in the print record is internally self-consistent and updates the print record as necessary. These changes do *not* affect the function's Boolean result.

> **Warning:** You should never call PrValidate (or PrStlDialog or PrJobDialog, which call it) between pages of a document.

`FUNCTION PrStlDialog (hPrint: THPrint) : BOOLEAN;` [Not in ROM]

PrStlDialog conducts a style dialog with the user to determine the page dimensions and other information needed for page setup. The initial settings displayed in the dialog box are taken from the most recent print record. If the user confirms the dialog, the results of the dialog are saved in the specified print record, PrValidate is called, and the function returns TRUE. Otherwise, the print record is left unchanged and the function returns FALSE.

> **Note:** If the print record was taken from a document, you should update its contents in the document's resource file if PrStlDialog returns TRUE. This makes the results of the style dialog "stick" to the document.

`FUNCTION PrJobDialog (hPrint: THPrint) : BOOLEAN;` [Not in ROM]

PrJobDialog conducts a job dialog with the user to determine the print quality, range of pages to print, and so on. The initial settings displayed in the dialog box are taken from the printer resource file, where they were remembered from the previous job (with the exception of the page range, set to all, and the copies, set to 1).

If the user confirms the dialog, both the print record and the printer resource file are updated, PrValidate is called, and the function returns TRUE. Otherwise, the print record and printer resource file are left unchanged and the function returns FALSE.

> **Note:** Since the job dialog is associated with the Print command, you should proceed with the requested printing operation if PrJobDialog returns TRUE.

```
PROCEDURE PrJobMerge (hPrintSrc,hPrintDst: THPrint);   [Not in ROM]
```

PrJobMerge first calls PrValidate for each of the given print records. It then copies all of the information set as a result of a job dialog from hPrintSrc to hPrintDst. Finally, it makes sure that all the fields of hPrintDst are internally self-consistent.

PrJobMerge allows you to conduct a job dialog just once and then copy the job information to several print records, which means that you can print several documents with one dialog. This is useful when printing from the Finder.

Printing

```
FUNCTION PrOpenDoc (hPrint: THPrint; pPrPort: TPPrPort; pIOBuf:
        Ptr) : TPPrPort;   [Not in ROM]
```

PrOpenDoc initializes a printing grafPort for use in printing a document, makes it the current port, and returns a pointer to it.

HPrint is a handle to the print record for this printing operation; you should already have validated this print record.

Depending on the setting of the bJDocLoop field in the job subrecord, the printing grafPort will be set up for draft or spool printing. For spool printing, the spool file's name, volume reference number, and version number are taken from the job subrecord.

PPrPort and pIOBuf are normally NIL. PPrPort is a pointer to the printing grafPort; if it's NIL, PrOpenDoc allocates a new printing grafPort in the heap. Similarly, pIOBuf points to an area of memory to be used as an input/output buffer; if it's NIL, PrOpenDoc uses the volume buffer for the spool file's volume. If you allocate your own buffer, it must be 522 bytes long.

> **Note:** These parameters are provided because the printing grafPort and input/output buffer are both nonrelocatable objects; to avoid fragmenting the heap, you may want to allocate them yourself.

You must balance every call to PrOpenDoc with a call to PrCloseDoc.

```
PROCEDURE PrOpenPage (pPrPort: TPPrPort; pPageFrame: TPRect);
        [Not in ROM]
```

PrOpenPage begins a new page. The page is printed only if it falls within the page range given in the job subrecord.

For spool printing, the pPageFrame parameter is used for scaling. It points to a rectangle to be used as the QuickDraw picture frame for this page:

```
TYPE TPRect = ^Rect;
```

When you print the spooled document, this rectangle will be scaled (with the QuickDraw procedure DrawPicture) to coincide with the rPage rectangle in the printer information subrecord. Unless you want the printout to be scaled, you should set pPageFrame to NIL—this uses the rPage rectangle as the picture frame, so that the page will be printed with no scaling.

Warning: Don't call the QuickDraw function OpenPicture while a page is open (after a call to PrOpenPage and before the following PrClosePage). You can, however, call DrawPicture at any time.

Warning: The printing grafPort is completely reinitialized by PrOpenPage. Therefore, you must set grafPort features such as the font and font size for every page that you draw.

You must balance every call to PrOpenPage with a call to PrClosePage.

```
PROCEDURE PrClosePage (pPrPort: TPPrPort);    [Not in ROM]
```

PrClosePage finishes the printing of the current page. It lets the Printing Manager know that you're finished with this page, so that it can do whatever is required for the current printer and printing method.

```
PROCEDURE PrCloseDoc (pPrPort: TPPrPort);    [Not in ROM]
```

PrCloseDoc closes the printing grafPort. For draft printing, PrCloseDoc ends the printing job. For spool printing, PrCloseDoc ends the spooling process: The spooled document must now be printed. Before printing it, call PrError to find out whether spooling succeeded; if it did, you should swap out as much code as possible and then call PrPicFile.

```
PROCEDURE PrPicFile (hPrint: THPrint; pPrPort: TPPrPort; pIOBuf:
          Ptr; pDevBuf: Ptr; VAR prStatus: TPrStatus);    [Not in
          ROM]
```

PrPicFile prints a spooled document. If spool printing is being used, your application should normally call PrPicFile after PrCloseDoc.

HPrint is a handle to the print record for this printing job. The spool file's name, volume reference number, and version number are taken from the job subrecord of this print record. After printing is successfully completed, the Printing Manager deletes the spool file from the disk.

You'll normally pass NIL for pPrPort, pIOBuf, and pDevBuf. PPrPort is a pointer to the printing grafPort for this operation; if it's NIL, PrPicFile allocates a new printing grafPort in the heap. Similarly, pIOBuf points to an area of memory to be used as an input /output buffer for reading the spool file; if it's NIL, PrPicFile uses the volume buffer for the spool file's volume. PDevBuf points to a device-dependent buffer; if NIL, PrPicFile allocates a buffer in the heap.

Note: If you provide your own storage for pDevBuf, it has to be big enough to hold the number of bytes indicated by the iDevBytes field of the PrXInfo subrecord.

Warning: Be sure not to pass, in pPrPort, a pointer to the same printing grafPort you received from PrOpenDoc. If that port was allocated by PrOpenDoc itself (that is, if the pPrPort parameter to PrOpenDoc was NIL), then PrCloseDoc will have disposed of the port, making your pointer to it invalid. Of course, if you earlier provided your own storage to PrOpenDoc, there's no reason you can't use the same storage again for PrPicFile.

The prStatus parameter is a printer status record that PrPicFile will use to report on its progress:

```
TYPE TPrStatus = RECORD
                    iTotPages:    INTEGER;    {number of pages in spool file}
                    iCurPage:     INTEGER;    {page being printed}
                    iTotCopies:   INTEGER;    {number of copies requested}
                    iCurCopy:     INTEGER;    {copy being printed}
                    iTotBands:    INTEGER;    {used internally}
                    iCurBand:     INTEGER;    {used internally}
                    fPgDirty:     BOOLEAN;    {TRUE if started printing page}
                    fImaging:     BOOLEAN;    {used internally}
                    hPrint:       THPrint;    {print record}
                    pPrPort:      TPPrPort;   {printing grafPort}
                    hPic:         PicHandle   {used internally}
                 END;
```

The fPgDirty field is TRUE if anything has already been printed on the current page, FALSE if not.

Your background procedure (if any) can use this record to monitor the state of the printing operation.

Error Handling

```
FUNCTION PrError : INTEGER;    [Not in ROM]
```

PrError returns the result code left by the last Printing Manager routine. Some possible result codes are:

```
CONST noErr       =    0;   {no error}
      iPrSavPFil  =   -1;   {saving print file}
      controlErr  =  -17;   {unimplemented control instruction}
      iIOAbort    =  -27;   {I/O error}
      iMemFullErr = -108;   {not enough room in heap zone}
      iPrAbort    =  128;   {application or user requested abort}
```

ControlErr is returned by the Device Manager. Other Operating System or Toolbox result codes may also be returned; a list of all result codes is given in Appendix A (Volume III).

Assembly-language note: The current result code is contained in the global variable PrintErr.

```
PROCEDURE PrSetError (iErr: INTEGER);    [Not in ROM]
```

PrSetError stores the specified value into the global variable where the Printing Manager keeps its result code. This procedure is used for canceling a printing operation in progress. To do this, call:

```
IF PrError <> noErr THEN PrSetError(iPrAbort)
```

Assembly-language note: You can achieve the same effect as PrSetError by storing directly into the global variable PrintErr. You shouldn't, however, store into this variable if it already contains a nonzero value.

THE PRINTER DRIVER

The Printing Manager provides a high-level interface that interprets QuickDraw commands for printing; it also provides a low-level interface that lets you directly access the Printer Driver.

Note: You should not use the high-level and low-level calls together.

The Printer Driver is the device driver that communicates with a printer. You only need to read this section if you're interested in low-level printing or writing your own device driver. For more information, see chapter 6.

The printer resource file for each type of printer includes a device driver for that printer. When the user chooses a printer, the printer's device driver becomes the active Printer Driver.

You can communicate with the Printer Driver via the following low-level routines:

- PrDrvrOpen opens the Printer Driver; it remains open until you call PrDrvrClose.

- PrCtlCall enables you to perform low-level printing operations such as bit map printing and direct streaming of text to the printer.

- PrDrvrVers tells you the version number of the Printer Driver.

- PrDrvrDCE gets a handle to the driver's device control entry.

Note: Advanced programmers: You can also communicate with the Printer Driver through the standard Device Manager calls OpenDriver, CloseDriver, and Control. The driver name and driver reference number are available as predefined constants:

```
CONST sPrDrvr   = '.Print';   {Printer Driver resource name}
      iPrDrvrRef = -3;        {Printer Driver reference number}
```

Note also that when you make direct Device Manager calls, the driver I/O queue entries should be initialized to all zeroes.

Low-Level Driver Access Routines

The routines in this section are used for communicating directly with the Printer Driver.

Assembly-language note: See chapter 6 for information about how to make the Device Manager calls corresponding to these routines.

```
PROCEDURE PrDrvrOpen;    [Not in ROM]
```

PrDrvrOpen opens the Printer Driver, reading it into memory if necessary.

```
PROCEDURE PrDrvrClose;    [Not in ROM]
```

PrDrvrClose closes the Printer Driver, releasing the memory it occupies. (Notice that PrClose doesn't close the Printer Driver.)

```
PROCEDURE PrCtlCall (iWhichCtl: INTEGER; lParam1,lParam2,lParam3:
        LONGINT);    [Not in ROM]
```

PrCtlCall calls the Printer Driver's control routine. The iWhichCtl parameter identifies the operation to perform. The following values are predefined:

```
CONST  iPrBitsCtl = 4;    {bit map printing}
       iPrIOCtl   = 5;    {text streaming}
       iPrDevCtl  = 7;    {printer control}
```

These operations are described in detail in the following sections of this chapter. The meanings of the lParam1, lParam2, and lParam3 parameters depend on the operation.

> **Note:** Advanced programmers: If you're making a direct Device Manager Control call, iWhichCtl will be the csCode parameter, and lParam1, lParam2, and lParam3 will be csParam, csParam+4, and csParam+8.

```
FUNCTION PrDrvrDCE : Handle;    [Not in ROM]
```

PrDrvrDCE returns a handle to the Printer Driver's device control entry.

```
FUNCTION PrDrvrVers : INTEGER;    [Not in ROM]
```

PrDrvrVers returns the version number of the Printer Driver in the system resource file.

The version number of the Printing Manager is available as the predefined constant iPrRelease. You may want to compare the result of PrDrvrVers with iPrRelease to see if the Printer Driver in the resource file is the most recent version.

Printer Control

The iPrDevCtl parameter to PrCtlCall is used for several printer control operations. The high-order word of the lParam1 parameter specifies the operation to perform:

```
CONST  lPrReset    = $00010000;    {reset printer}
       lPrLineFeed = $00030000;    {carriage return only}
       lPrLFSixth  = $0003FFFF;    {standard 1/6-inch line feed}
       lPrPageEnd  = $00020000;    {end page}
```

The low-order word of lParam1 may specify additional information. The lParam2 and lParam3 parameters should always be 0.

Before starting to print, use

```
PrCtlCall(iPrDevCtl,lPrReset,0,0)
```

to reset the printer to its standard initial state. This call should be made only once per document. You can also specify the number of copies to make in the low-order byte of this parameter; for example, a value of $00010002 specifies two copies.

The lPrLineFeed and lPrLFSixth parameters allow you to achieve the effect of carriage returns and line feeds in a printer-independent way:

- LPrLineFeed specifies a carriage return only (with a line feed of 0).

- LPrLFSixth causes a carriage return and advances the paper by 1/6 inch (the standard "CR LF" sequence).

You can also specify the exact number of dots the paper advances in the low-order word of the lParam1 parameter. For example, a value of $00030008 for lParam1 causes a carriage return and advances the paper eight dots.

You should use these methods instead of sending carriage returns and line feeds directly to the printer.

The call

```
PrCtlCall(iPrDevCtl,lPrPageEnd,0,0)
```

does whatever is appropriate for the given printer at the end of each page, such as sending a form feed character and advancing past the paper fold. You should use this call instead of just sending a form feed yourself.

Bit Map Printing

To send all or part of a QuickDraw bit map directly to the printer, use

```
PrCtlCall(iPrBitsCtl,pBitMap,pPortRect,lControl)
```

The pBitMap parameter is a pointer to a QuickDraw bit map; pPortRect is a pointer to the rectangle to be printed, in the coordinates of the printing grafPort.

LControl should be one of the following predefined constants:

```
CONST lScreenBits = 0;    {default for printer}
      lPaintBits  = 1;    {square dots (72 by 72)}
```

The Imagewriter, in standard resolution, normally prints rectangular dots that are taller than they are wide (80 dots per inch horizontally by 72 vertically). Since the Macintosh 128K and 512K screen has square pixels (approximately 72 per inch both horizontally and vertically), lPaintBits gives a truer reproduction of the screen, although printing is somewhat slower.

On the LaserWriter, lControl should always be set to lPaintBits.

Putting all this together, you can print the entire screen at the default setting with

```
PrCtlCall(iPrBitsCtl,ORD(@screenBits),
                     ORD(@screenBits.bounds),lScreenBits)
```

To print the contents of a single window in square dots, use

```
PrCtlCall(iPrBitsCtl,ORD(@theWindow^.portBits),
                     ORD(@theWindow^.portRect),lPaintBits)
```

Text Streaming

Text streaming is useful for fast printing of text when speed is more important than fancy formatting or visual fidelity. It gives you full access to the printer's native text facilities (such as control or escape sequences for boldface, italic, underlining, or condensed or extended type), but makes no use of QuickDraw.

You can send a stream of characters (including control and escape sequences) directly to the printer with

```
PrCtlCall(iPrIOCtl,pBuf,lBufCount,0)
```

The pBuf parameter is a pointer to the beginning of the text. The low-order word of lBufCount is the number of bytes to transfer; the high-order word must be 0.

Warning: Relying on specific printer capabilities and control sequences will make your application printer-dependent. You can use iPrDevCtl to perform form feeds and line feeds in a printer-independent way.

Note: Advanced programmers who need more information about sending commands directly to the LaserWriter should see the *Inside LaserWriter* manual.

SUMMARY OF THE PRINTING MANAGER

Constants

```
CONST { Printing methods }

      bDraftLoop = 0;      {draft printing}
      bSpoolLoop = 1;      {spool printing}

      { Printer specification in prStl field of print record }

      bDevCItoh = 1;       {Imagewriter printer}
      bDevLaser = 3;       {LaserWriter printer}

      { Maximum number of pages in a spool file }

      iPFMaxPgs = 128;

      { Result codes }

      noErr       =  0;       {no error}
      iPrSavPFil  = -1;       {saving spool file}
      controlErr  = -17;      {unimplemented control instruction}
      iIOAbort    = -27;      {I/O abort error}
      iMemFullErr = -108;     {not enough room in heap zone}
      iPrAbort    = 128;      {application or user requested abort}

      { PrCtlCall parameters }

      iPrDevCtl   = 7;           {printer control}
      lPrReset    = $00010000;   {reset printer}
      lPrLineFeed = $00030000;   {carriage return only}
      lPrLFSixth  = $0003FFFF;   {standard 1/6-inch line feed}
      lPrPageEnd  = $00020000;   {end page}
      iPrBitsCtl  = 4;           {bit map printing}
      lScreenBits = 0;             {default for printer}
      lPaintBits  = 1;             {square dots (72 by 72)}
      iPrIOCtl    = 5;           {text streaming}

      { Printer Driver information }

      sPrDrvr    = '.Print';     {Printer Driver resource name}
      iPrDrvrRef = -3;           {Printer Driver reference number}
```

Data Types

```
TYPE TPPrPort = ^TPrPort;
     TPrPort  = RECORD
                    gPort: GrafPort;  {grafPort to draw in}
                    {more fields for internal use}
                END;

     THPrint  = ^TPPrint;
     TPPrint  = ^TPrint;
     TPrint   = RECORD
                    iPrVersion: INTEGER;  {Printing Manager version}
                    prInfo:     TPrInfo;  {printer information subrecord}
                    rPaper:     Rect;     {paper rectangle}
                    prStl:      TPrStl;   {additional device information}
                    prInfoPT:   TPrInfo;  {used internally}
                    prXInfo:    TPrXInfo; {additional device information}
                    prJob:      TPrJob;   {job subrecord}
                    printX:     ARRAY[1..19] OF INTEGER  {not used}
                END;

     TPrInfo = RECORD
                    iDev:  INTEGER;  {used internally}
                    iVRes: INTEGER;  {vertical resolution of printer}
                    iHRes: INTEGER;  {horizontal resolution of printer}
                    rPage: Rect      {page rectangle}
                END;

     TPrJob =
         RECORD
             iFstPage:  INTEGER;     {first page to print}
             iLstPage:  INTEGER;     {last page to print}
             iCopies:   INTEGER;     {number of copies}
             bJDocLoop: SignedByte;  {printing method}
             fFromUsr:  BOOLEAN;     {used internally}
             pIdleProc: ProcPtr;     {background procedure}
             pFileName: StringPtr;   {spool file name}
             iFileVol:  INTEGER;     {spool file volume reference number}
             bFileVers: SignedByte;  {spool file version number}
             bJobX:     SignedByte   {used internally}
         END;

     TPrStl = RECORD
                    wDev: INTEGER;   {high byte specifies device}
                    {more fields for internal use}
                END;
```

```
TPrXInfo = RECORD
              iRowBytes: INTEGER;      {used internally}
              iBandV:    INTEGER;      {used internally}
              iBandH:    INTEGER;      {used internally}
              iDevBytes: INTEGER;      {size of buffer}
              {more fields for internal use}
           END;


TPRect = ^Rect;


TPrStatus = RECORD
               iTotPages:  INTEGER;    {number of pages in spool file}
               iCurPage:   INTEGER;    {page being printed}
               iTotCopies: INTEGER;    {number of copies requested}
               iCurCopy:   INTEGER;    {copy being printed}
               iTotBands:  INTEGER;    {used internally}
               iCurBand:   INTEGER;    {used internally}
               fPgDirty:   BOOLEAN;    {TRUE if started printing page}
               fImaging:   BOOLEAN;    {used internally}
               hPrint:     THPrint;    {print record}
               pPrPort:    TPPrPort;   {printing grafPort}
               hPic:       PicHandle   {used internally}
            END;
```

Routines [Not in ROM]

Initialization and Termination

```
PROCEDURE PrOpen;
PROCEDURE PrClose;
```

Print Records and Dialogs

```
PROCEDURE PrintDefault (hPrint: THPrint);
FUNCTION  PrValidate   (hPrint: THPrint) : BOOLEAN;
FUNCTION  PrStlDialog  (hPrint: THPrint) : BOOLEAN;
FUNCTION  PrJobDialog  (hPrint: THPrint) : BOOLEAN;
PROCEDURE PrJobMerge   (hPrintSrc,hPrintDst: THPrint);
```

Printing

```
FUNCTION  PrOpenDoc    (hPrint: THPrint; pPrPort: TPPrPort; pIOBuf: Ptr) :
                        TPPrPort;
PROCEDURE PrOpenPage   (pPrPort: TPPrPort; pPageFrame: TPRect);
PROCEDURE PrClosePage  (pPrPort: TPPrPort);
PROCEDURE PrCloseDoc   (pPrPort: TPPrPort);
PROCEDURE PrPicFile    (hPrint: THPrint; pPrPort: TPPrPort; pIOBuf: Ptr;
                        pDevBuf: Ptr; VAR prStatus: TPrStatus);
```

Error Handling

```
FUNCTION  PrError :   INTEGER;
PROCEDURE PrSetError (iErr: INTEGER);
```

Low-Level Driver Access

```
PROCEDURE PrDrvrOpen;
PROCEDURE PrDrvrClose;
PROCEDURE PrCtlCall      (iWhichCtl: INTEGER; lParam1,lParam2,lParam3:
                          LONGINT);
FUNCTION  PrDrvrDCE :    Handle;
FUNCTION  PrDrvrVers :   INTEGER;
```

Assembly-Language Information

Constants

```
; Printing methods

bDraftLoop    .EQU   0     ;draft printing
bSpoolLoop    .EQU   1     ;spool printing

; Result codes

noErr         .EQU   0     ;no error
iPrSavPFil    .EQU   -1    ;saving spool file
controlErr    .EQU   -17   ;unimplemented control instruction
iIOAbort      .EQU   -27   ;I/O abort error
iMemFullErr   .EQU   -108  ;not enough room in heap zone
iPrAbort      .EQU   128   ;application or user requested abort

; Printer Driver Control call parameters

iPrDevCtl     .EQU   7     ;printer control
lPrReset      .EQU   1     ; reset printer
iPrLineFeed   .EQU   3     ; carriage return/paper advance
iPrLFSixth    .EQU   3     ;standard 1/6-inch line feed
lPrPageEnd    .EQU   2     ; end page
iPrBitsCtl    .EQU   4     ;bit map printing
lScreenBits   .EQU   0     ; default for printer
lPaintBits    .EQU   1     ; square dots (72 by 72)
iPrIOCtl      .EQU   5     ;text streaming

; Printer Driver information

iPrDrvrRef    .EQU   -3    ;Printer Driver reference number
```

Printing GrafPort Data Structure

gPort   GrafPort to draw in (portRec bytes)
iPrPortSize   Size in bytes of printing grafPort

Print Record Data Structure

iPrVersion   Printing Manager version (word)
prInfo   Printer information subrecord (14 bytes)
rPaper   Paper rectangle (8 bytes)
prStl   Additional device information (8 bytes)
prXInfo   Additional device information (16 bytes)
prJob   Job subrecord (iPrJobSize bytes)
iPrintSize   Size in bytes of print record

Structure of Printer Information Subrecord

iVRes   Vertical resolution of printer (word)
iHRes   Horizontal resolution of printer (word)
rPage   Page rectangle (8 bytes)

Structure of Job Subrecord

iFstPage   First page to print (word)
iLstPage   Last page to print (word)
iCopies   Number of copies (word)
bJDocLoop   Printing method (byte)
pIdleProc   Address of background procedure
pFileName   Pointer to spool file name (preceded by length byte)
iFileVol   Spool file volume reference number (word)
bFileVers   Spool file version number (byte)
iPrJobSize   Size in bytes of job subrecord

Structure of PrXInfo Subrecord

iDevBytes   Size of buffer (word)

Structure of Printer Status Record

iTotPages   Number of pages in spool file (word)
iCurPage   Page being printed (word)
iTotCopies   Number of copies requested (word)
iCurCopy   Copy being printed (word)
fPgDirty   Nonzero if started printing page (byte)
hPrint   Handle to print record
pPrPort   Pointer to printing grafPort
iPrStatSize   Size in bytes of printer status record

Variables

PrintErr   Result code from last Printing Manager routine (word)

6 THE DEVICE MANAGER

6 Device Manager

ABOUT THIS CHAPTER

This chapter describes the Device Manager, the part of the Operating System that controls the exchange of information between a Macintosh application and devices. It gives general information about using and writing device drivers, and also discusses interrupts: how the Macintosh uses them and how you can use them if you're writing your own device driver.

Note: Specific information about the standard Macintosh drivers is contained in separate chapters.

You should already be familiar with resources, as discussed in chapter 5 of Volume I.

ABOUT THE DEVICE MANAGER

The Device Manager is the part of the Operating System that handles communication between applications and devices. A **device** is a part of the Macintosh, or a piece of external equipment, that can transfer information into or out of the Macintosh. Macintosh devices include disk drives, two serial communications ports, and printers.

Note: The display screen is *not* a device; drawing on the screen is handled by QuickDraw.

There are two kinds of devices: character devices and block devices. A **character device** reads or writes a stream of characters, or bytes, one at a time: It can neither skip bytes nor go back to a previous byte. A character device is used to get information from or send information to the world outside of the Operating System and memory: It can be an input device, an output device, or an input/output device. The serial ports and printers are all character devices.

A **block device** reads and writes blocks of bytes at a time; it can read or write any accessible block on demand. Block devices are usually used to store and retrieve information; for example, disk drives are block devices.

Applications communicate with devices through the Device Manager—either directly or indirectly (through another part of the Operating System or Toolbox). For example, an application can communicate with a disk drive directly via the Device Manager, or indirectly via the File Manager (which calls the Device Manager). The Device Manager doesn't manipulate devices directly; it calls **device drivers** that do (see Figure 1). Device drivers are programs that take data coming from the Device Manager and convert them into actions of devices, or convert device actions into data for the Device Manager to process.

The Operating System includes three standard device drivers in ROM: the Disk Driver, the Sound Driver, and the ROM Serial Driver. There are also a number of standard RAM drivers, including the Printer Driver, the RAM Serial Driver, the AppleTalk drivers, and desk accessories. RAM drivers are resources, and are read from the system resource file as needed.

You can add other drivers independently or build on top of the existing drivers (for example, the Printer Driver is built on top of the Serial Driver); the section "Writing Your Own Device Drivers" describes how to do this. Desk accessories are a special type of device driver, and are manipulated via the routines of the Desk Manager.

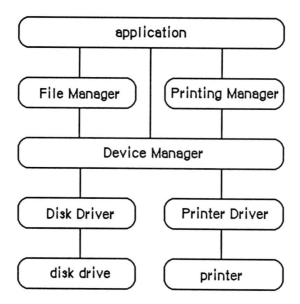

Figure 1. Communication with Devices

Warning: Information about desk accessories covered in chapter 14 of Volume I is not repeated here. Some information in this chapter may not apply to desk accessories.

A device driver can be either **open** or **closed**. The Sound Driver and Disk Driver are opened when the system starts up; the rest of the drivers are opened at the specific request of an application. After a driver has been opened, an application can read data from and write data to it. You can close device drivers that are no longer in use, and recover the memory used by them. Up to 32 device drivers may be open at any one time.

Before it's opened, you identify a device driver by its driver name; after it's opened, you identify it by its reference number. A **driver name** consists of a period (.) followed by any sequence of 1 to 254 printing characters. A RAM driver's name is the same as its resource name. You can use uppercase and lowercase letters when naming drivers, but the Device Manager ignores case when comparing names (it doesn't ignore diacritical marks).

Note: Although device driver names can be quite long, there's little reason for them to be more than a few characters in length.

The Device Manager assigns each open device driver a **driver reference number**, from –1 to –32, that's used instead of its driver name to refer to it.

Most communication between an application and an open device driver occurs by reading and writing data. Data read from a driver is placed in the application's **data buffer**, and data written to a driver is taken from the application's data buffer. A data buffer is memory allocated by the application for communication with drivers.

In addition to data that's read from or written to device drivers, drivers may require or provide other information. Information transmitted to a driver by an application is called **control information**; information provided by a driver is called **status information**. Control information may select modes of operation, start or stop processes, enable buffers, choose protocols, and so on. Status information may indicate the current mode of operation, the readiness of the device, the occurrence of errors, and so on. Each device driver may respond to a number of different types of control information and may provide a number of different types of status information.

Each of the standard Macintosh drivers includes predefined calls for transmitting control information and receiving status information. Explanations of these calls can be found in the chapters describing the drivers.

USING THE DEVICE MANAGER

You can call Device Manager routines via three different methods: high-level Pascal calls, low-level Pascal calls, and assembly language. The high-level Pascal calls are designed for Pascal programmers interested in using the Device Manager in a simple manner; they provide adequate device I/O and don't require much special knowledge to use. The low-level Pascal and assembly-language calls are designed for advanced Pascal programmers and assembly-language programmers interested in using the Device Manager to its fullest capacity; they require some special knowledge to be used most effectively.

> **Note:** The names used to refer to routines here are actually assembly-language macro names for the low-level routines, but the Pascal routine names are very similar.

The Device Manager is automatically initialized each time the system starts up.

Before an application can exchange information with a device driver, the driver must be opened. The Sound Driver and Disk Driver are opened when the system starts up; for other drivers, the application must call Open. The Open routine will return the driver reference number that you'll use every time you want to refer to that device driver.

An application can send data from its data buffer to an open driver with a Write call, and transfer data from an open driver to its data buffer with Read. An application passes control information to a device driver by calling Control, and receives status information from a driver by calling Status.

Whenever you want to stop a device driver from completing I/O initiated by a Read, Write, Control, or Status call, call KillIO. KillIO halts any current I/O and deletes any pending I/O.

When you're through using a driver, call Close. Close forces the device driver to complete any pending I/O, and then releases all the memory used by the driver.

DEVICE MANAGER ROUTINES

This section describes the Device Manager routines used to call drivers. It's divided into two parts: The first describes all the high-level Pascal routines of the Device Manager, and the second presents information about calling the low-level Pascal and assembly-language routines.

All the Device Manager routines in this section return an integer result code of type OSErr. Each routine description lists all of the applicable result codes, along with a short description of what the result code means. Lengthier explanations of all the result codes can be found in the summary at the end of this chapter.

High-Level Device Manager Routines

Note: As described in chapter 4, the FSRead and FSWrite routines are also used to read from and write to files.

```
FUNCTION OpenDriver (name: Str255; VAR refNum: INTEGER) : OSErr;
        [Not in ROM]
```

OpenDriver opens the device driver specified by name and returns its reference number in refNum.

Result codes   noErr   No error
                      badUnitErr   Bad reference number
                      dInstErr   Couldn't find driver in resource file
                      openErr   Driver can't perform the requested reading or writing
                      unitEmptyErr   Bad reference number

```
FUNCTION CloseDriver (refNum: INTEGER) : OSErr;   [Not in ROM]
```

CloseDriver closes the device driver having the reference number refNum. Any pending I/O is completed, and the memory used by the driver is released.

Warning: Before using this command to close a particular driver, refer to the chapter describing the driver for the consequences of closing it.

Result codes   noErr   No error
                      badUnitErr   Bad reference number
                      dRemoveErr   Attempt to remove an open driver
                      unitEmptyErr   Bad reference number

```
FUNCTION FSRead (refNum: INTEGER; VAR count: LONGINT; buffPtr:
        Ptr) : OSErr;   [Not in ROM]
```

FSRead attempts to read the number of bytes specified by the count parameter from the open device driver having the reference number refNum, and transfer them to the data buffer pointed to by buffPtr. After the read operation is completed, the number of bytes actually read is returned in the count parameter.

Result codes   noErr   No error
                      badUnitErr   Bad reference number
                      notOpenErr   Driver isn't open
                      unitEmptyErr   Bad reference number
                      readErr   Driver can't respond to Read calls

```
FUNCTION FSWrite (refNum: INTEGER; VAR count: LONGINT; buffPtr:
          Ptr) : OSErr;  [Not in ROM]
```

FSWrite takes the number of bytes specified by the count parameter from the buffer pointed to by buffPtr and attempts to write them to the open device driver having the reference number refNum. After the write operation is completed, the number of bytes actually written is returned in the count parameter.

Result codes
	noErr	No error
	badUnitErr	Bad reference number
	notOpenErr	Driver isn't open
	unitEmptyErr	Bad reference number
	writErr	Driver can't respond to Write calls

```
FUNCTION Control (refNum: INTEGER; csCode: INTEGER; csParamPtr:
          Ptr) : OSErr;  [Not in ROM]
```

Control sends control information to the device driver having the reference number refNum. The type of information sent is specified by csCode, and the information itself is pointed to by csParamPtr. The values passed in csCode and pointed to by csParamPtr depend on the driver being called.

Result codes
	noErr	No error
	badUnitErr	Bad reference number
	notOpenErr	Driver isn't open
	unitEmptyErr	Bad reference number
	controlErr	Driver can't respond to this Control call

```
FUNCTION Status (refNum: INTEGER; csCode: INTEGER; csParamPtr:
          Ptr) : OSErr;  [Not in ROM]
```

Status returns status information about the device driver having the reference number refNum. The type of information returned is specified by csCode, and the information itself is pointed to by csParamPtr. The values passed in csCode and pointed to by csParamPtr depend on the driver being called.

Result codes
	noErr	No error
	badUnitErr	Bad reference number
	notOpenErr	Driver isn't open
	unitEmptyErr	Bad reference number
	statusErr	Driver can't respond to this Status call

```
FUNCTION KillIO (refNum: INTEGER) : OSErr;   [Not in ROM]
```

KillIO terminates all current and pending I/O with the device driver having the reference number refNum.

6 Device Manager

Result codes	noErr	No error
	badUnitErr	Bad reference number
	unitEmptyErr	Bad reference number

Low-Level Device Manager Routines

This section contains special information for programmers using the low-level Pascal or assembly-language routines of the Device Manager, and describes them in detail.

Note: The Device Manager routines for writing device drivers are described in the section "Writing Your Own Device Drivers".

All low-level Device Manager routines can be executed either **synchronously** (meaning that the application can't continue until the routine is completed) or **asynchronously** (meaning that the application is free to perform other tasks while the routine is executing). Some cannot be executed asynchronously, because they use the Memory Manager to allocate and release memory.

When an application calls a Device Manager routine asynchronously, an **I/O request** is placed in the **driver I/O queue**, and control returns to the calling program—possibly even before the actual I/O is completed. Requests are taken from the queue one at a time, and processed; meanwhile, the calling program is free to work on other things.

The calling program may specify a **completion routine** to be executed at the end of an asynchronous operation.

Routine parameters passed by an application to the Device Manager and returned by the Device Manager to an application are contained in a **parameter block**, which is a data structure in the heap or stack. All low-level Pascal calls to the Device Manager are of the form

```
FUNCTION PBCallName (paramBlock: ParmBlkPtr; async: BOOLEAN) : OSErr;
```

PBCallName is the name of the routine. ParamBlock points to the parameter block containing the parameters for the routine. If async is TRUE, the call is executed asynchronously; otherwise the call is executed synchronously. Each call returns an integer result code of type OSErr.

Assembly-language note: When you call a Device Manager routine, A0 must point to a parameter block containing the parameters for the routine. If you want the routine to be executed asynchronously, set bit 10 of the routine trap word. You can do this by supplying the word ASYNC as the second argument to the routine macro. For example:

```
_Read    ,ASYNC
```

You can set or test bit 10 of a trap word by using the global constant asyncTrpBit.

If you want a routine to be executed immediately (bypassing the driver I/O queue), set bit 9 of the routine trap word. This can be accomplished by supplying the word IMMED as the second argument to the routine macro. (The driver must be able to handle immediate calls for this to work.) For example:

```
_Write   ,IMMED
```

You can set or test bit 9 of a trap word by using the global constant noQueueBit. You can specify either ASYNC or IMMED, but not both. (The syntax shown above applies to the Lisa Workshop Assembler; programmers using another development system should consult its documentation for the proper syntax.)

All routines return a result code in D0.

Routine Parameters

There are two different kinds of parameter blocks you'll pass to Device Manager routines: one for I/O routines and another for Control and Status calls.

The lengthy, variable-length data structure of a parameter block is given below. The Device Manager and File Manager use this same data structure, but only the parts relevant to the Device Manager are discussed here. Each kind of parameter block contains eight fields of standard information and three to nine fields of additional information:

```
TYPE  ParamBlkType  = (ioParam,fileParam,volumeParam,cntrlParam);

      ParamBlockRec =
          RECORD
              qLink:       QElemPtr;   {next queue entry}
              qType:       INTEGER;    {queue type}
              ioTrap:      INTEGER;    {routine trap}
              ioCmdAddr:   Ptr;        {routine address}
              ioCompletion: ProcPtr;   {completion routine}
              ioResult:    OSErr;      {result code}
              ioNamePtr:   StringPtr;  {driver name}
              ioVRefNum:   INTEGER;    {volume reference or drive number}
              CASE ParamBlkType OF
                  ioParam:
                      . . . {I/O routine parameters}
                  fileParam:
                      . . . {used by the File Manager}
                  volumeParam:
                      . . . {used by the File Manager}
                  cntrlParam:
                      . . . {Control and Status call parameters}
          END;

      ParmBlkPtr = ^ParamBlockRec;
```

The first four fields in each parameter block are handled entirely by the Device Manager, and most programmers needn't be concerned with them; programmers who are interested in them should see the section "The Structure of a Device Driver".

IOCompletion contains a pointer to a completion routine to be executed at the end of an asynchronous call; it should be NIL for asynchronous calls with no completion routine, and is automatically set to NIL for all synchronous calls.

Warning: Completion routines are executed at the interrupt level and must preserve all registers other than A0, A1, and D0-D2. Your completion routine must not make any calls to the Memory Manager, directly or indirectly, and can't depend on handles to unlocked blocks being valid. If it uses application globals, it must also ensure that register A5 contains the address of the boundary between the application globals and the application parameters; for details, see SetUpA5 and RestoreA5 in chapter 13.

Assembly-language note: When your completion routine is called, register A0 points to the parameter block of the asynchronous call and register D0 contains the result code.

Routines that are executed asynchronously return control to the calling program with the result code noErr as soon as the call is placed in the driver I/O queue. This isn't an indication of successful call completion, but simply indicates that the call was successfully queued. To determine when the call is actually completed, you can poll the ioResult field; this field is set to 1 when the call is made, and receives the actual result code upon completion of the call. Completion routines are executed after the result code is placed in ioResult.

IONamePtr is a pointer to the name of a driver and is used only for calls to the Open function. IOVRefNum is used by the Disk Driver to identify drives.

I/O routines use the following additional fields:

```
ioParam:
   (ioRefNum:    INTEGER;       {driver reference number}
    ioVersNum:   SignedByte;    {not used}
    ioPermssn:   SignedByte;    {read/write permission}
    ioMisc:      Ptr;           {not used}
    ioBuffer:    Ptr;           {pointer to data buffer}
    ioReqCount:  LONGINT;       {requested number of bytes}
    ioActCount:  LONGINT;       {actual number of bytes}
    ioPosMode:   INTEGER;       {positioning mode}
    ioPosOffset: LONGINT);      {positioning offset}
```

IOPermssn requests permission to read from or write to a driver when the driver is opened, and must contain one of the following values:

```
CONST fsCurPerm   = 0;    {whatever is currently allowed}
      fsRdPerm    = 1;    {request to read only}
      fsWrPerm    = 2;    {request to write only}
      fsRdWrPerm  = 3;    {request to read and write}
```

This request is compared with the capabilities of the driver (some drivers are read-only, some are write-only). If the driver is incapable of performing as requested, a result code indicating the error is returned.

IOBuffer points to a data buffer into which data is written by Read calls and from which data is read by Write calls. IOReqCount specifies the requested number of bytes to be read or written. IOActCount contains the number of bytes actually read or written.

IOPosMode and ioPosOffset contain positioning information used for Read and Write calls by drivers of block devices. IOPosMode contains the positioning mode; bits 0 and 1 indicate where an operation should begin relative to the physical beginning of the block-formatted medium (such as a disk). You can use the following predefined constants to test or set the value of these bits:

```
CONST fsAtMark    = 0;    {at current position}
      fsFromStar  = 1;    {offset relative to beginning of medium}
      fsFromMark  = 3;    {offset relative to current position}
```

IOPosOffset specifies the byte offset (either positive or negative), relative to the position specified by the positioning mode, where the operation will be performed (except when the positioning mode is fsAtMark, in which case ioPosOffset is ignored). IOPosOffset must be a 512-byte multiple.

To verify that data written to a block device matches the data in memory, make a Read call right after the Write call. The parameters for a read-verify operation are the same as for a standard Read call, except that the following constant must be added to the positioning mode:

```
CONST rdVerify = 64;   {read-verify mode}
```

The result code ioErr is returned if any of the data doesn't match.

Control and Status calls use three additional fields:

```
cntrlParam:
   (ioCRefNum: INTEGER;       {driver reference number}
    csCode:    INTEGER;       {type of Control or Status call}
    csParam:   ARRAY[0..10] OF INTEGER); {control or status information}
```

IOCRefNum contains the reference number of the device driver. The csCode field contains a number identifying the type of call; this number may be interpreted differently by each driver. The csParam field contains the control or status information for the call; it's declared as up to 22 bytes of information because its exact contents will vary from one Control or Status call to the next. To store information in this field, you must perform the proper type coercion.

Routine Descriptions

This section describes the procedures and functions. Each routine description includes the low-level Pascal form of the call and the routine's assembly-language macro. A list of the fields in the parameter block affected by the call is also given.

Assembly-language note: The field names given in these descriptions are those of the ParamBlockRec data type; see the summary at the end of this chapter for the names of the corresponding assembly-language offsets. (The names for some offsets differ from their Pascal equivalents, and in certain cases more than one name for the same offset is provided.)

The number next to each parameter name indicates the byte offset of the parameter from the start of the parameter block pointed to by register A0; only assembly-language programmers need be concerned with it. An arrow next to each parameter name indicates whether it's an input, output, or input/output parameter:

Arrow	**Meaning**
→	Parameter is passed to the routine
←	Parameter is returned by the routine
↔	Parameter is passed to and returned by the routine

Note: As described in chapter 4, the Open and Close functions are also used to open and close files.

```
FUNCTION PBOpen (paramBlock: ParmBlkPtr; async: BOOLEAN) : OSErr;
```

Trap macro   _Open

Parameter block

→	12	ioCompletion	pointer
←	16	ioResult	word
→	18	ioNamePtr	pointer
←	24	ioRefNum	word
→	27	ioPermssn	byte

PBOpen opens the device driver specified by ioNamePtr, reading it into memory if necessary, and returns its reference number in ioRefNum. IOPermssn specifies the requested read/write permission.

Result codes	noErr	No error
	badUnitErr	Bad reference number
	dInstErr	Couldn't find driver in resource file
	openErr	Driver can't perform the requested reading or writing
	unitEmptyErr	Bad reference number

```
FUNCTION PBClose (paramBlock: ParmBlkPtr; async: BOOLEAN) : OSErr;
```

Trap macro   _Close

Parameter block

→	12	ioCompletion	pointer
←	16	ioResult	word
→	24	ioRefNum	word

PBClose closes the device driver having the reference number ioRefNum. Any pending I/O is completed, and the memory used by the driver is released.

Result codes	noErr	No error
	badUnitErr	Bad reference number
	dRemovErr	Attempt to remove an open driver
	unitEmptyErr	Bad reference number

```
FUNCTION PBRead (paramBlock: ParmBlkPtr; async: BOOLEAN) : OSErr;
```

Trap macro   _Read

Parameter block

→	12	ioCompletion	pointer
←	16	ioResult	word
→	22	ioVRefNum	word
→	24	ioRefNum	word
→	32	ioBuffer	pointer
→	36	ioReqCount	long word
←	40	ioActCount	long word
→	44	ioPosMode	word
↔	46	ioPosOffset	long word

PBRead attempts to read ioReqCount bytes from the device driver having the reference number ioRefNum, and transfer them to the data buffer pointed to by ioBuffer. The drive number, if any, of the device to be read from is specified by ioVRefNum. After the read is completed, the position is returned in ioPosOffset and the number of bytes actually read is returned in ioActCount.

Result codes	noErr	No error
	badUnitErr	Bad reference number
	notOpenErr	Driver isn't open
	unitEmptyErr	Bad reference number
	readErr	Driver can't respond to Read calls

```
FUNCTION PBWrite (paramBlock: ParmBlkPtr; async: BOOLEAN) :
         OSErr;
```

Trap macro   _Write

Parameter block

→	12	ioCompletion	pointer
←	16	ioResult	word
→	22	ioVRefNum	word
→	24	ioRefNum	word
→	32	ioBuffer	pointer
→	36	ioReqCount	long word
←	40	ioActCount	long word
→	44	ioPosMode	word
↔	46	ioPosOffset	long word

PBWrite takes ioReqCount bytes from the buffer pointed to by ioBuffer and attempts to write them to the device driver having the reference number ioRefNum. The drive number, if any, of the device to be written to is specified by ioVRefNum. After the write is completed, the position is returned in ioPosOffset and the number of bytes actually written is returned in ioActCount.

Result codes	noErr	No error
	badUnitErr	Bad reference number
	notOpenErr	Driver isn't open
	unitEmptyErr	Bad reference number
	writErr	Driver can't respond to Write calls

6 Device Manager

```
FUNCTION PBControl (paramBlock: ParmBlkPtr; async: BOOLEAN) :
          OSErr;
```

Trap macro   _Control

Parameter block

→	12	ioCompletion	pointer
←	16	ioResult	word
→	22	ioVRefNum	word
→	24	ioRefNum	word
→	26	csCode	word
→	28	csParam	record

PBControl sends control information to the device driver having the reference number ioRefNum; the drive number, if any, is specified by ioVRefNum. The type of information sent is specified by csCode, and the information itself begins at csParam. The values passed in csCode and csParam depend on the driver being called.

Result codes	noErr	No error
	badUnitErr	Bad reference number
	notOpenErr	Driver isn't open
	unitEmptyErr	Bad reference number
	controlErr	Driver can't respond to this Control call

```
FUNCTION PBStatus (paramBlock: ParmBlkPtr; async: BOOLEAN) :
          OSErr;
```

Trap macro   _Status

Parameter block

→	12	ioCompletion	pointer
←	16	ioResult	word
→	22	ioVRefNum	word
→	24	ioRefNum	word
→	26	csCode	word
←	28	csParam	record

PBStatus returns status information about the device driver having the reference number ioRefNum; the drive number, if any, is specified by ioVRefNum. The type of information returned is specified by csCode, and the information itself begins at csParam. The values passed in csCode and csParam depend on the driver being called.

Result codes	noErr	No error
	badUnitErr	Bad reference number
	notOpenErr	Driver isn't open
	unitEmptyErr	Bad reference number
	statusErr	Driver can't respond to this Status call

```
FUNCTION PBKillIO (paramBlock: ParmBlkPtr; async: BOOLEAN) :
          OSErr;
```

Trap macro   _KillIO

Parameter block

→	12	ioCompletion	pointer
←	16	ioResult	word
→	24	ioRefNum	word

PBKillIO stops any current I/O request being processed, and removes all pending I/O requests from the I/O queue of the device driver having the reference number ioRefNum. The completion routine of each pending I/O request is called, with the ioResult field of each request equal to the result code abortErr.

Result codes	noErr	No error
	badUnitErr	Bad reference number
	unitEmptyErr	Bad reference number

THE STRUCTURE OF A DEVICE DRIVER

This section describes the structure of device drivers for programmers interested in writing their own driver or manipulating existing drivers. Some of the information presented here is accessible only through assembly language.

RAM drivers are stored in resource files. The resource type for drivers is 'DRVR'. The resource name is the driver name. The resource ID for a driver is its unit number (explained below) and must be between 0 and 31 inclusive.

Warning: Don't use the unit number of an existing driver unless you want the existing driver to be replaced.

As shown in Figure 2, a driver begins with a few words of flags and other data, followed by offsets to the routines that do the work of the driver, an optional title, and finally the routines themselves.

Every driver contains a routine to handle Open and Close calls, and may contain routines to handle Read, Write, Control, Status, and KillIO calls. The driver routines that handle Device Manager calls are as follows:

Device Manager call	Driver routine
Open	Open
Read	Prime
Write	Prime
Control	Control
KillIO	Control
Status	Status
Close	Close

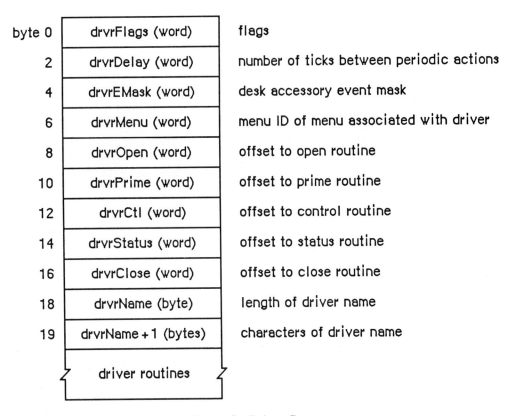

byte 0	drvrFlags (word)	flags
2	drvrDelay (word)	number of ticks between periodic actions
4	drvrEMask (word)	desk accessory event mask
6	drvrMenu (word)	menu ID of menu associated with driver
8	drvrOpen (word)	offset to open routine
10	drvrPrime (word)	offset to prime routine
12	drvrCtl (word)	offset to control routine
14	drvrStatus (word)	offset to status routine
16	drvrClose (word)	offset to close routine
18	drvrName (byte)	length of driver name
19	drvrName + 1 (bytes)	characters of driver name
	driver routines	

Figure 2. Driver Structure

For example, when a KillIO call is made to a driver, the driver's control routine must implement the call.

Each bit of the *high-order* byte of the drvrFlags word contains a flag:

```
dReadEnable    .EQU    0   ;set if driver can respond to Read calls
dWritEnable    .EQU    1   ;set if driver can respond to Write calls
dCtlEnable     .EQU    2   ;set if driver can respond to Control calls
dStatEnable    .EQU    3   ;set if driver can respond to Status calls
dNeedGoodBye   .EQU    4   ;set if driver needs to be called before the
                           ; application heap is reinitialized
dNeedTime      .EQU    5   ;set if driver needs time for performing a
                           ; periodic action
dNeedLock      .EQU    6   ;set if driver will be locked in memory as
                           ; soon as it's opened (always set for ROM
                           ; drivers)
```

Bits 8-11 (bits 0-3 of the high-order byte) indicate which Device Manager calls the driver's routines can respond to.

Unlocked RAM drivers in the application heap will be lost every time the heap is reinitialized (when an application starts up, for example). If dNeedGoodBye is set, the control routine of the device driver will be called before the heap is reinitialized, and the driver can perform any "clean-up" actions it needs to. The driver's control routine identifies this "good-bye" call by checking the csCode parameter—it will be the global constant

```
goodBye   .EQU   -1   ;heap will be reinitialized, clean up if necessary
```

Device drivers may need to perform predefined actions periodically. For example, a network driver may want to poll its input buffer every ten seconds to see if it has received any messages. If the dNeedTime flag is set, the driver *does* need to perform a periodic action, and the drvrDelay word contains a tick count indicating how often the periodic action should occur. A tick count of 0 means it should happen as often as possible, 1 means it should happen at most every sixtieth of a second, 2 means at most every thirtieth of a second, and so on. Whether the action actually occurs this frequently depends on how often the application calls the Desk Manager procedure SystemTask. SystemTask calls the driver's control routine (if the time indicated by drvrDelay has elapsed), and the control routine must perform whatever predefined action is desired. The driver's control routine identifies the SystemTask call by checking the csCode parameter—it will be the global constant

```
accRun   .EQU   65   ;take the periodic action, if any, for this driver
```

Note: Some drivers may not want to rely on the application to call SystemTask. They can instead install a task to be executed during the vertical retrace interrupt. There are, however, certain restrictions on tasks performed during interrupts, such as not being able to make calls to the Memory Manager. For more information on these restrictions, see chapter 11. Periodic actions performed in response to SystemTask calls are not performed via an interrupt and so don't have these restrictions.

DrvrEMask and drvrMenu are used only for desk accessories and are discussed in chapter 14 of Volume I.

Following drvrMenu are the offsets to the driver routines, a title for the driver (preceded by its length in bytes), and the routines that do the work of the driver.

Note: Each of the driver routines must be aligned on a word boundary.

Device Control Entry

The first time a driver is opened, information about it is read into a structure in memory called a **device control entry**. A device control entry contains the header of the driver's I/O queue, the location of the driver's routines, and other information. A device control entry is a 40-byte relocatable block located in the system heap. It's locked while the driver is open, and unlocked while the driver is closed.

Most of the data in the device control entry is stored and accessed only by the Device Manager, but in some cases the driver itself must store into it. The structure of a device control entry is shown below; note that the first four words of the driver are copied into the dCtlFlags, dCtlDelay, dCtlEMask, and dCtlMenu fields.

```
TYPE DCtlEntry =
  RECORD
    dCtlDriver:   Ptr;         {pointer to ROM driver or handle to RAM driver}
    dCtlFlags:    INTEGER;     {flags}
    dCtlQHdr:     QHdr;        {driver I/O queue header}
    dCtlPosition: LONGINT;     {byte position used by Read and Write calls}
    dCtlStorage:  Handle;      {handle to RAM driver's private storage}
    dCtlRefNum:   INTEGER;     {driver reference number}
    dCtlCurTicks: LONGINT;     {used internally}
    dCtlWindow:   WindowPtr;   {pointer to driver's window}
    dCtlDelay:    INTEGER;     {number of ticks between periodic actions}
    dCtlEMask:    INTEGER;     {desk accessory event mask}
    dCtlMenu:     INTEGER      {menu ID of menu associated with driver}
  END;

    DCtlPtr    = ^DCtlEntry;
    DCtlHandle = ^DCtlPtr;
```

The low-order byte of the dCtlFlags word contains the following flags:

Bit number	Meaning
5	Set if driver is open
6	Set if driver is RAM-based
7	Set if driver is currently executing

Assembly-language note: These flags can be accessed with the global constants
dOpened, dRAMBased, and drvrActive.

The high-order byte of the dCtlFlags word contains flags copied from the drvrFlags word of the
driver, as described above.

DCtlQHdr contains the header of the driver's I/O queue (described below). DCtlPosition is used
only by drivers of block devices, and indicates the current source or destination position of a
Read or Write call. The position is given as a number of bytes beyond the physical beginning of
the medium used by the device. For example, if one logical block of data has just been read from
a 3 1/2-inch disk via the Disk Driver, dCtlPosition will be 512.

ROM drivers generally use locations in low memory for their local storage. RAM drivers may
reserve memory within their code space, or allocate a relocatable block and keep a handle to it in
dCtlStorage (if the block resides in the application heap, its handle will be set to NIL when the
heap is reinitialized).

You can get a handle to a driver's device control entry by calling the Device Manager function
GetDCtlEntry.

```
FUNCTION GetDCtlEntry (refNum: INTEGER) : DCtlHandle;   [Not in ROM]
```

GetDCtlEntry returns a handle to the device control entry of the device driver having the reference
number refNum.

Assembly-language note: You can get a handle to a driver's device control entry from the unit table, as described below.

The Driver I/O Queue

Each device driver has a driver I/O queue; this is a standard Operating System queue (described in chapter 13) that contains the parameter blocks for all asynchronous routines awaiting execution. Each time a routine is called, the driver places an entry in the queue; each time a routine is completed, its entry is removed from the queue. The queue's header is located in the dCtlQHdr field of the driver's device control entry. The low-order byte of the queue flags field in the queue header contains the version number of the driver, and can be used for distinguishing between different versions of the same driver.

Each entry in the driver I/O queue consists of a parameter block for the routine that was called. Most of the fields of this parameter block contain information needed by the specific Device Manager routines; these fields are explained above in the section "Low-Level Device Manager Routines". The first four fields of this parameter block, shown below, are used by the Device Manager in processing the I/O requests in the queue.

```
TYPE ParamBlockRec = RECORD
                        qLink:     QElemPtr;   {next queue entry}
                        qType:     INTEGER;    {queue type}
                        ioTrap:    INTEGER;    {routine trap}
                        ioCmdAddr: Ptr;        {routine address}
                        . . .                  {rest of block}
                     END;
```

QLink points to the next entry in the queue, and qType indicates the queue type, which must always be ORD(ioQType). IOTrap and ioCmdAddr contain the trap and address of the Device Manager routine that was called.

The Unit Table

The location of each device control entry is maintained in a list called the **unit table**. The unit table is a 128-byte nonrelocatable block containing 32 four-byte entries. Each entry has a number, from 0 to 31, called the **unit number**, and contains a handle to the device control entry for a driver. The unit number can be used as an index into the unit table to locate the handle to a specific driver's device control entry; it's equal to

$$-1 * (refNum + 1)$$

where refNum is the driver reference number. For example, the Sound Driver's reference number is –4 and its unit number is 3.

Figure 3 shows the layout of the unit table with the standard drivers and desk accessories installed.

byte 0	reserved	unit number 0
4	hard disk driver (XL only)	1
8	Printer Driver	2
12	Sound Driver	3
16	Disk Driver	4
20	Serial Driver port A input	5
24	Serial Driver port A output	6
28	Serial Driver port B input	7
32	Serial Driver port B output	8
36	AppleTalk .MPP Driver	9
40	AppleTalk .ATP Driver	10
44	reserved	11
48	Calculator	12
52	Alarm Clock	13
56	Key Caps	14·
60	Puzzle	15
64	Note Pad	16
68	Scrapbook	17
72	Control Panel	18
	not used	
124	not used	31

Figure 3. The Unit Table

Warning: Any new drivers contained in resource files should have resource IDs that don't conflict with the unit numbers of existing drivers—unless you want an existing driver to be replaced. Be sure to check the unit table before installing a new driver; the base address of the unit table is stored in the global variable UTableBase.

WRITING YOUR OWN DEVICE DRIVERS

Drivers are usually written in assembly language. The structure of your driver must match that shown in the previous section. The routines that do the work of the driver should be written to operate the device in whatever way you require. Your driver must contain routines to handle Open and Close calls, and may choose to handle Read, Write, Control, Status, and KillIO calls as well.

> **Warning:** A device driver doesn't "own" the hardware it operates, and has no way of determining whether another driver is attempting to use that hardware at the same time. There's a possiblity of conflict in situations where two drivers that operate the same device are installed concurrently.

When the Device Manager executes a driver routine to handle an application call, it passes a pointer to the call's parameter block in register A0 and a pointer to the driver's device control entry in register A1. From this information, the driver can determine exactly what operations are required to fulfill the call's requests, and do them.

Open and close routines must execute synchronously and return via an RTS instruction. They needn't preserve any registers that they use. Close routines should put a result code in register D0. Since the Device Manager sets D0 to 0 upon return from an Open call, open routines should instead place the result code in the ioResult field of the parameter block.

The **open routine** must allocate any private storage required by the driver, store a handle to it in the device control entry (in the dCtlStorage field), initialize any local variables, and then be ready to receive a Read, Write, Status, Control, or KillIO call. It might also install interrupt handlers, change interrupt vectors, and store a pointer to the device control entry somewhere in its local storage for its interrupt handlers to use. The **close routine** must reverse the effects of the open routine, by releasing all used memory, removing interrupt handlers, and replacing changed interrupt vectors. If anything about the operational state of the driver should be saved until the next time the driver is opened, it should be kept in the relocatable block of memory pointed to by dCtlStorage.

Prime, control, and status routines must be able to respond to queued calls and asynchronous calls, and should be interrupt-driven. Asynchronous portions of the routines can use registers A0-A3 and D0-D3, but must preserve any other registers used; synchronous portions can use all registers. Prime, control, and status routines should return a result code in D0. They must return via an RTS if called immediately (with noQueueBit set in the ioTrap field) or if the device couldn't complete the I/O request right away, or via a JMP to the IODone routine (explained below) if not called immediately and if the device completed the request.

> **Warning:** If the prime, control, and status routines can be called as the result of an interrupt, they must preserve all registers other than A0, A1, and D0-D2. They can't make any calls to the Memory Manager and cannot depend on unlocked handles being valid. If they use application globals, they must also ensure that register A5 contains the address of the boundary between the application globals and the application parameters; for details, see SetUpA5 and RestoreA5 in chapter 13.

The **prime routine** implements Read and Write calls made to the driver. It can distinguish between Read and Write calls by comparing the low-order byte of the ioTrap field with the following predefined constants:

```
aRdCmd      .EQU    2       ;Read call
aWrCmd      .EQU    3       ;Write call
```

You may want to use the Fetch and Stash routines (described below) to read and write characters. If the driver is for a block device, it should update the dCtlPosition field of the device control entry after each read or write.

The **control routine** accepts the control information passed to it, and manipulates the device as requested. The **status routine** returns requested status information. Since both the control and status routines may be subjected to Control and Status calls sending and requesting a variety of information, they must be prepared to respond correctly to all types. The control routine must handle KillIO calls. The driver identifies KillIO calls by checking the csCode parameter—it will be the global constant

```
killCode    .EQU    1       ;handle the KillIO call
```

Warning: KillIO calls must return via an RTS, and shouldn't jump (via JMP) to the IODone routine.

Routines for Writing Drivers

The Device Manager includes three routines—Fetch, Stash, and IODone—that provide low-level support for driver routines. These routines can be used only with a pending, asynchronous request; include them in the code of your device driver if they're useful to you. A pointer to the device control entry is passed to each of these routines in register A1. The device control entry contains the driver I/O queue header, which is used to locate the pending request. If there are no pending requests, these routines generate the system error dsIOCoreErr (see chapter 12 for more information).

Fetch, Stash, and IODone are invoked via "jump vectors" (stored in the global variables JFetch, JStash, and JIODone) rather than macros, in the interest of speed. You use a jump vector by moving its address onto the stack. For example:

```
        MOVE.L          JIODone,-(SP)
        RTS
```

Fetch and Stash don't return a result code; if an error occurs, the System Error Handler is invoked. IODone may return a result code.

Fetch function

Jump vector	JFetch
On entry	A1: pointer to device control entry
On exit	D0: character fetched; bit 15=1 if it's the last character in data buffer

Fetch gets the next character from the data buffer pointed to by ioBuffer and places it in D0. IOActCount is incremented by 1. If ioActCount equals ioReqCount, bit 15 of D0 is set. After receiving the last byte requested, the driver should call IODone.

Stash function

Jump vector	JStash
On entry	A1: pointer to device control entry D0: character to stash
On exit	D0: bit 15=1 if it's the last character requested

Stash places the character in D0 into the data buffer pointed to by ioBuffer, and increments ioActCount by 1. If ioActCount equals ioReqCount, bit 15 of D0 is set. After stashing the last byte requested, the driver should call IODone.

IODone function

Jump vector	JIODone
On entry	A1: pointer to device control entry D0: result code (word)

IODone removes the current I/O request from the driver I/O queue, marks the driver inactive, unlocks the driver and its device control entry (if it's allowed to by the dNeedLock bit of the dCtlFlags word), and executes the completion routine (if there is one). Then it begins executing the next I/O request in the driver I/O queue.

> **Warning:** Due to the way the File Manager does directory lookups, block device drivers should take care to support asynchronous I/O operations. If the driver's prime routine has completed an asynchronous Read or Write call just prior to calling IODone *and* its completion routine starts an additional Read or Write, large amounts of the stack may be used (potentially causing the stack to expand into the heap). To avoid this problem, the prime routine should exit via an RTS instruction and then jump to IODone via an interrupt.

INTERRUPTS

This section discusses how **interrupts** are used on the Macintosh 128K and 512K; only programmers who want to write interrupt-driven device drivers need read this section.

> **Warning:** Only the Macintosh 128K and 512K are covered in this section. Much of the information presented here is hardware-dependent; programmers are encouraged to write code that's hardware-independent to ensure compatibility with future versions of the Macintosh.

An interrupt is a form of **exception**: an error or abnormal condition detected by the processor in the course of program execution. Specifically, an interrupt is an exception that's signaled to the processor by a device, as distinct from a trap, which arises directly from the execution of an instruction. Interrupts are used by devices to notify the processor of a change in condition of the device, such as the completion of an I/O request. An interrupt causes the processor to suspend normal execution, save the address of the next instruction and the processor's internal status on the stack, and execute an **interrupt handler**.

The MC68000 recognizes seven different levels of interrupt, each with its own interrupt handler. The addresses of the various handlers, called **interrupt vectors**, are kept in a **vector table** in low memory. Each level of interrupt has its own vector located in the vector table. When an interrupt occurs, the processor fetches the proper vector from the table, uses it to locate the interrupt handler for that level of interrupt, and jumps to the handler. On completion, the handler restores the internal status of the processor from the stack and resumes normal execution from the point of suspension.

There are three devices that can create interrupts: the Synertek SY6522 Versatile Interface Adapter (VIA), the Zilog Z8530 Serial Communications Controller (SCC), and the debugging switch. They send a three-bit number called the **interrupt priority level** to the processor. This number indicates which device is interrupting, and which interrupt handler should be executed:

Level	Interrupting device
0	None
1	VIA
2	SCC
3	VIA and SCC
4-7	Debugging switch

A level-3 interrupt occurs when both the VIA and the SCC interrupt at the same instant; the interrupt handler for a level-3 interrupt is simply an RTE instruction. Debugging interrupts shouldn't occur during the normal execution of an application.

The interrupt priority level is compared with the **processor priority** in bits 8-10 of the status register. If the interrupt priority level is greater than the processor priority, the MC68000 acknowledges the interrupt and initiates interrupt processing. The processor priority determines which interrupting devices are ignored, and which are serviced:

Level	Services
0	All interrupts
1	SCC and debugging interrupts only
2-6	Debugging interrupts only
7	No interrupts

When an interrupt is acknowledged, the processor priority is set to the interrupt priority level, to prevent additional interrupts of equal or lower priority, until the interrupt handler has finished servicing the interrupt.

The interrupt priority level is used as an index into the primary interrupt vector table. This table contains seven long words beginning at address $64. Each long word contains the starting address of an interrupt handler (see Figure 4).

Execution jumps to the interrupt handler at the address specified in the table. The interrupt handler must identify and service the interrupt. Then it must restore the processor priority, status register, and program counter to the values they contained before the interrupt occurred.

$64	autoInt1	vector to level-1 interrupt handler
$68	autoInt2	vector to level-2 interrupt handler
$6C	autoInt3	vector to level-3 interrupt handler
$70	autoInt4	vector to level-4 interrupt handler
$74	autoInt5	vector to level-5 interrupt handler
$78	autoInt6	vector to level-6 interrupt handler
$7C	autoInt7	vector to level-7 interrupt handler

Figure 4. Primary Interrupt Vector Table

Level-1 (VIA) Interrupts

Level-1 interrupts are generated by the VIA. You'll need to read the Synertek manual describing the VIA to use most of the information provided in this section. The level-1 interrupt handler determines the source of the interrupt (via the VIA's interrupt flag register and interrupt enable register) and then uses a table of secondary vectors in low memory to determine which interrupt handler to call (see Figure 5).

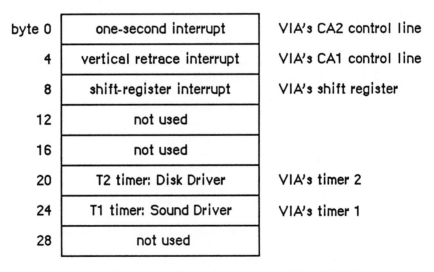

byte 0	one-second interrupt	VIA's CA2 control line
4	vertical retrace interrupt	VIA's CA1 control line
8	shift-register interrupt	VIA's shift register
12	not used	
16	not used	
20	T2 timer: Disk Driver	VIA's timer 2
24	T1 timer: Sound Driver	VIA's timer 1
28	not used	

Figure 5. Level-1 Secondary Interrupt Vector Table

The level-1 secondary interrupt vector table is stored in the global variable Lvl1DT. Each vector in the table points to the interrupt handler for a different source of interrupt. The interrupts are handled in order of their entry in the table, and only one interrupt handler is called per level-1 interrupt (even if two or more sources are interrupting). This allows the level-1 interrupt handler to be reentrant; interrupt handlers should lower the processor priority as soon as possible in order to enable other pending interrupts to be processed.

The one-second interrupt updates the global variable Time (explained in chapter 13); it's also used for inverting ("blinking") the apple symbol in the menu bar when the alarm goes off. Vertical retrace interrupts are generated once every vertical retrace interval; control is passed to the Vertical Retrace Manager, which performs recurrent system tasks (such as updating the global variable Ticks) and executes tasks installed by the application. (For more information, see chapter 11.)

If the cumulative elapsed time for all tasks during a vertical retrace interrupt exceeds about 16 milliseconds (one video frame), the vertical retrace interrupt may itself be interrupted by another vertical retrace interrupt. In this case, tasks to be performed during the second vertical retrace interrupt are ignored, with one exception: The global variable Ticks will still be updated.

The shift-register interrupt is used by the keyboard and mouse interrupt handlers. Whenever the Disk Driver or Sound Driver isn't being used, you can use the T1 and T2 timers for your own needs; there's no way to tell, however, when they'll be needed again by the Disk Driver or Sound Driver.

The base address of the VIA (stored in the global variable VIA) is passed to each interrupt handler in register A1.

Level-2 (SCC) Interrupts

Level-2 interrupts are generated by the SCC. You'll need to read the Zilog manual describing the SCC to effectively use the information provided in this section. The level-2 interrupt handler determines the source of the interrupt, and then uses a table of secondary vectors in low memory to determine which interrupt handler to call (see Figure 6).

byte 0	channel B transmit buffer empty	
4	channel B external/status change	mouse vertical
8	channel B receive character available	
12	channel B special receive condition	
16	channel A transmit buffer empty	
20	channel A external/status change	mouse horizontal
24	channel A receive character available	
28	channel A special receive condition	

Figure 6. Level-2 Secondary Interrupt Vector Table

The level-2 secondary interrupt vector table is stored in the global variable Lvl2DT. Each vector in the table points to the interrupt handler for a different source of interrupt. The interrupts are handled according to the following fixed priority:

> channel A receive character available and special receive
> channel A transmit buffer empty
> channel A external/status change
> channel B receive character available and special receive
> channel B transmit buffer empty
> channel B external/status change

Only one interrupt handler is called per level-2 interrupt (even if two or more sources are interrupting). This allows the level-2 interrupt handler to be reentrant; interrupt handlers should lower the processor priority as soon as possible in order to enable other pending interrupts to be processed.

External/status interrupts pass through a tertiary vector table in low memory to determine which interrupt handler to call (see Figure 7).

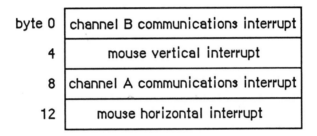

> | byte 0 | channel B communications interrupt |
> |---|---|
> | 4 | mouse vertical interrupt |
> | 8 | channel A communications interrupt |
> | 12 | mouse horizontal interrupt |

Figure 7. Level-2 External/Status Interrupt Vector Table

The external/status interrupt vector table is stored in the global variable ExtStsDT. Each vector in the table points to the interrupt handler for a different source of interrupt. Communications interrupts (break/abort, for example) are always handled before mouse interrupts.

When a level-2 interrupt handler is called, D0 contains the address of the SCC read register 0 (external/status interrupts only), and D1 contains the bits of read register 0 that have changed since the last external/status interrupt. A0 points to the SCC channel A or channel B control read address and A1 points to SCC channel A or channel B control write address, depending on which channel is interrupting. The SCC's data read address and data write address are located four bytes beyond A0 and A1, respectively; they're also contained in the global variables SCCWr and

SCCRd. You can use the following predefined constants as offsets from these base addresses to locate the SCC control and data lines:

```
aData       .EQU      6       ;channel A data in or out
aCtl        .EQU      2       ;channel A control
bData       .EQU      4       ;channel B data in or out
bCtl        .EQU      0       ;channel B control
```

Writing Your Own Interrupt Handlers

You can write your own interrupt handlers to replace any of the standard interrupt handlers just described. Be sure to place a vector that points to your interrupt handler in one of the vector tables.

Both the level-1 and level-2 interrupt handlers preserve registers A0-A3 and D0-D3. Every interrupt handler (except for external/status interrupt handlers) is responsible for clearing the source of the interrupt, and for saving and restoring any additional registers used. Interrupt handlers should return directly via an RTS instruction, unless the interrupt is completing an asynchronous call, in which case they should jump (via JMP) to the IODone routine.

SUMMARY OF THE DEVICE MANAGER

Constants

```
CONST { Values for requesting read/write access }

        fsCurPerm    = 0;    {whatever is currently allowed}
        fsRdPerm     = 1;    {request to read only}
        fsWrPerm     = 2;    {request to write only}
        fsRdWrPerm   = 3;    {request to read and write}


        { Positioning modes }

        fsAtMark     = 0;    {at current position}
        fsFromStart  = 1;    {offset relative to beginning of medium}
        fsFromMark   = 3;    {offset relative to current position}
        rdVerify     = 64;   {add to above for read-verify}
```

Data Types

```
TYPE  ParamBlkType  = (ioParam,fileParam,volumeParam,cntrlParam);

      ParmBlkPtr     = ^ParamBlockRec;
      ParamBlockRec  = RECORD
          qLink:         QElemPtr;      {next queue entry}
          qType:         INTEGER;       {queue type}
          ioTrap:        INTEGER;       {routine trap}
          ioCmdAddr:     Ptr;           {routine address}
          ioCompletion:  ProcPtr;       {completion routine}
          ioResult:      OSErr;         {result code}
          ioNamePtr:     StringPtr;     {driver name}
          ioVRefNum:     INTEGER;       {volume reference or drive number}
      CASE ParamBlkType OF
        ioParam:
        (ioRefNum:       INTEGER;       {driver reference number}
         ioVersNum:      SignedByte;    {not used}
         ioPermssn:      SignedByte;    {read/write permission}
         ioMisc:         Ptr;           {not used}
         ioBuffer:       Ptr;           {pointer to data buffer}
         ioReqCount:     LONGINT;       {requested number of bytes}
         ioActCount:     LONGINT;       {actual number of bytes}
         ioPosMode:      INTEGER;       {positioning mode}
         ioPosOffset:    LONGINT);      {positioning offset}
        fileParam:
        . . . {used by File Manager}
        volumeParam:
        . . . {used by File Manager}
```

6 Device Manager

```
      cntrlParam:
        (ioCRefNum: INTEGER;    {driver reference number}
         csCode:    INTEGER;    {type of Control or Status call}
         csParam:   ARRAY[0..10] OF INTEGER) {control or status information}
      END;

      DCtlHandle = ^DCtlPtr;
      DCtlPtr    = ^DCtlEntry;
      DCtlEntry  =
        RECORD
          dCtlDriver:   Ptr;        {pointer to ROM driver or handle to }
                                    { RAM driver}
          dCtlFlags:    INTEGER;    {flags}
          dCtlQHdr:     QHdr;       {driver I/O queue header}
          dCtlPosition: LONGINT;    {byte position used by Read and }
                                    { Write calls}
          dCtlStorage:  Handle;     {handle to RAM driver's private }
                                    { storage}
          dCtlRefNum:   INTEGER;    {driver reference number}
          dCtlCurTicks: LONGINT;    {used internally}
          dCtlWindow:   WindowPtr;  {pointer to driver's window}
          dCtlDelay:    INTEGER;    {number of ticks between periodic }
                                    { actions}
          dCtlEMask:    INTEGER;    {desk accessory event mask}
          dCtlMenu:     INTEGER     {menu ID of menu associated with }
                                    { driver}
        END;
```

High-Level Routines [Not in ROM]

```
FUNCTION OpenDriver    (name: Str255; VAR refNum: INTEGER) : OSErr;
FUNCTION CloseDriver   (refNum: INTEGER) : OSErr;
FUNCTION FSRead        (refNum: INTEGER; VAR count: LONGINT; buffPtr: Ptr)
                         : OSErr;
FUNCTION FSWrite       (refNum: INTEGER; VAR count: LONGINT; buffPtr: Ptr)
                         : OSErr;
FUNCTION Control       (refNum: INTEGER; csCode: INTEGER; csParamPtr: Ptr)
                         : OSErr;
FUNCTION Status        (refNum: INTEGER; csCode: INTEGER; csParamPtr: Ptr)
                         : OSErr;
FUNCTION KillIO        (refNum: INTEGER) : OSErr;
```

Low-Level Routines

```
FUNCTION PBOpen (paramBlock: ParmBlkPtr; async: BOOLEAN) : OSErr;
    →   12      ioCompletion      pointer
    ←   16      ioResult          word
    →   18      ioNamePtr         pointer
    ←   24      ioRefNum          word
    →   27      ioPermssn         byte
```

```
FUNCTION PBClose (paramBlock: ParmBlkPtr; async: BOOLEAN) : OSErr;
    →   12      ioCompletion        pointer
    ←   16      ioResult            word
    →   24      ioRefNum            word


FUNCTION PBRead (paramBlock: ParmBlkPtr; async: BOOLEAN) : OSErr;
    →   12      ioCompletion        pointer
    ←   16      ioResult            word
    →   22      ioVRefNum           word
    →   24      ioRefNum            word
    →   32      ioBuffer            pointer
    →   36      ioReqCount          long word
    ←   40      ioActCount          long word
    →   44      ioPosMode           word
    ↔   46      ioPosOffset         long word


FUNCTION PBWrite (paramBlock: ParmBlkPtr; async: BOOLEAN) : OSErr;
    →   12      ioCompletion        pointer
    ←   16      ioResult            word
    →   22      ioVRefNum           word
    →   24      ioRefNum            word
    →   32      ioBuffer            pointer
    →   36      ioReqCount          long word
    ←   40      ioActCount          long word
    →   44      ioPosMode           word
    ↔   46      ioPosOffset         long word


FUNCTION PBControl (paramBlock: ParmBlkPtr; async: BOOLEAN) : OSErr;
    →   12      ioCompletion        pointer
    ←   16      ioResult            word
    →   22      ioVRefNum           word
    →   24      ioRefNum            word
    →   26      csCode              word
    →   28      csParam             record


FUNCTION PBStatus (paramBlock: ParmBlkPtr; async: BOOLEAN) : OSErr;
    →   12      ioCompletion        pointer
    ←   16      ioResult            word
    →   22      ioVRefNum           word
    →   24      ioRefNum            word
    →   26      csCode              word
    ←   28      csParam             record


FUNCTION PBKillIO (paramBlock: ParmBlkPtr; async: BOOLEAN) : OSErr;
    →   12      ioCompletion        pointer
    ←   16      ioResult            word
    →   24      ioRefNum            word
```

Accessing a Driver's Device Control Entry

```
FUNCTION GetDCtlEntry (refNum: INTEGER) : DCtlHandle;   [Not in ROM]
```

Result Codes

Name	Value	Meaning
abortErr	−27	I/O request aborted by KillIO
badUnitErr	−21	Driver reference number doesn't match unit table
controlErr	−17	Driver can't respond to this Control call
dInstErr	−26	Couldn't find driver in resource file
dRemovErr	−25	Attempt to remove an open driver
noErr	0	No error
notOpenErr	−28	Driver isn't open
openErr	−23	Requested read/write permission doesn't match driver's open permission
readErr	−19	Driver can't respond to Read calls
statusErr	−18	Driver can't respond to this Status call
unitEmptyErr	−22	Driver reference number specifies NIL handle in unit table
writErr	−20	Driver can't respond to Write calls

Assembly-Language Information

Constants

```
; Flags in trap words

asnycTrpBit     .EQU     10      ;set for an asynchronous call
noQueueBit      .EQU      9      ;set for immediate execution

; Values for requesting read/write access

fsCurPerm       .EQU      0      ;whatever is currently allowed
fsRdPerm        .EQU      1      ;request to read only
fsWrPerm        .EQU      2      ;request to write only
fsRdWrPerm      .EQU      3      ;request to read and write

; Positioning modes

fsAtMark        .EQU      0      ;at current position
fsFromStart     .EQU      1      ;offset relative to beginning of medium
fsFromMark      .EQU      3      ;offset relative to current position
rdVerify        .EQU     64      ;add to above for read-verify
```

```
; Driver flags

dReadEnable      .EQU    0    ;set if driver can respond to Read calls
dWritEnable      .EQU    1    ;set if driver can respond to Write calls
dCtlEnable       .EQU    2    ;set if driver can respond to Control calls
dStatEnable      .EQU    3    ;set if driver can respond to Status calls
dNeedGoodBye     .EQU    4    ;set if driver needs to be called before the
                             ; application heap is reinitialized
dNeedTime        .EQU    5    ;set if driver needs time for performing a
                             ; periodic action
dNeedLock        .EQU    6    ;set if driver will be locked in memory as
                             ; soon as it's opened (always set for ROM
                             ; drivers)

; Device control entry flags

dOpened          .EQU    5    ;set if driver is open
dRAMBased        .EQU    6    ;set if driver is RAM-based
drvrActive       .EQU    7    ;set if driver is currently executing

; csCode values for driver control routine

accRun           .EQU    65   ;take the periodic action, if any, for this
                             ; driver
goodBye          .EQU   -1    ;heap will be reinitialized, clean up if
                             ; necessary
killCode         .EQU    1    ;handle the KillIO call

; Low-order byte of Device Manager traps

aRdCmd           .EQU    2    ;Read call (trap $A002)
aWrCmd           .EQU    3    ;Write call (trap $A003)

; Offsets from SCC base addresses

aData            .EQU    6    ;channel A data in or out
aCtl             .EQU    2    ;channel A control
bData            .EQU    4    ;channel B data in or out
bCtl             .EQU    0    ;channel B control
```

Standard Parameter Block Data Structure

qLink	Pointer to next queue entry
qType	Queue type (word)
ioTrap	Routine trap (word)
ioCmdAddr	Routine address
ioCompletion	Address of completion routine
ioResult	Result code (word)
ioVNPtr	Pointer to driver name (preceded by length byte)
ioVRefNum	Volume reference number (word)
ioDrvNum	Drive number (word)

Control and Status Parameter Block Data Structure

ioRefNum	Driver reference number (word)
csCode	Type of Control or Status call (word)
csParam	Parameters for Control or Status call (22 bytes)

I/O Parameter Block Data Structure

ioRefNum	Driver reference number (word)
ioPermssn	Open permission (byte)
ioBuffer	Pointer to data buffer
ioReqCount	Requested number of bytes (long)
ioActCount	Actual number of bytes (long)
ioPosMode	Positioning mode (word)
ioPosOffset	Positioning offset (long)

Device Driver Data Structure

drvrFlags	Flags (word)
drvrDelay	Number of ticks between periodic actions (word)
drvrEMask	Desk accessory event mask (word)
drvrMenu	Menu ID of menu associated with driver (word)
drvrOpen	Offset to open routine (word)
drvrPrime	Offset to prime routine (word)
drvrCtl	Offset to control routine (word)
drvrStatus	Offset to status routine (word)
drvrClose	Offset to close routine (word)
drvrName	Driver name (preceded by length byte)

Device Control Entry Data Structure

dCtlDriver	Pointer to ROM driver or handle to RAM driver
dCtlFlags	Flags (word)
dCtlQueue	Queue flags: low-order byte is driver's version number (word)
dCtlQHead	Pointer to first entry in driver's I/O queue
dCtlQTail	Pointer to last entry in driver's I/O queue
dCtlPosition	Byte position used by Read and Write calls (long)
dCtlStorage	Handle to RAM driver's private storage
dCtlRefNum	Driver's reference number (word)
dCtlWindow	Pointer to driver's window
dCtlDelay	Number of ticks between periodic actions (word)
dCtlEMask	Desk accessory event mask (word)
dCtlMenu	Menu ID of menu associated with driver (word)

Structure of Primary Interrupt Vector Table

autoInt1	Vector to level-1 interrupt handler
autoInt2	Vector to level-2 interrupt handler

autoInt3   Vector to level-3 interrupt handler
autoInt4   Vector to level-4 interrupt handler
autoInt5   Vector to level-5 interrupt handler
autoInt6   Vector to level-6 interrupt handler
autoInt7   Vector to level-7 interrupt handler

Macro Names

Pascal name	Macro name
PBRead	_Read
PBWrite	_Write
PBControl	_Control
PBStatus	_Status
PBKillIO	_KillIO

Routines for Writing Drivers

Routine	Jump vector	On entry	On exit
Fetch	JFetch	A1: ptr to device control entry	D0: character fetched; bit 15=1 if last character in buffer
Stash	JStash	A1: ptr to device control entry D0: character to stash	D0: bit 15=1 if last character requested
IODone	JIODone	A1: ptr to device control entry D0: result code (word)	

Variables

UTableBase	Base address of unit table
JFetch	Jump vector for Fetch function
JStash	Jump vector for Stash function
JIODone	Jump vector for IODone function
Lvl1DT	Level-1 secondary interrupt vector table (32 bytes)
Lvl2DT	Level-2 secondary interrupt vector table (32 bytes)
VIA	VIA base address
ExtStsDT	External/status interrupt vector table (16 bytes)
SCCWr	SCC write base address
SCCRd	SCC read base address

6 Device Manager

7   THE DISK DRIVER

7 Disk Driver

ABOUT THIS CHAPTER

The Disk Driver is a Macintosh device driver used for storing and retrieving information on Macintosh 3 1/2-inch disk drives. This chapter describes the Disk Driver in detail. It's intended for programmers who want to access Macintosh drives directly, bypassing the File Manager.

You should already be familiar with:

- events, as discussed in chapter 8 of Volume I and in chapter 3 of this volume
- files and disk drives, as described in chapter 4
- interrupts and the use of devices and device drivers, as described in chapter 6

ABOUT THE DISK DRIVER

The Disk Driver is a standard Macintosh device driver in ROM. It allows Macintosh applications to read from disks, write to disks, and eject disks.

Note: The Disk Driver cannot format disks; this task is accomplished by the Disk Initialization Package.

Information on disks is stored in 512-byte **sectors**. There are 800 sectors on one 400K-byte Macintosh disk. Each sector consists of an **address mark** that contains information used by the Disk Driver to determine the position of the sector on the disk, and a **data mark** that primarily contains data stored in that sector.

Consecutive sectors on a disk are grouped into **tracks**. There are 80 tracks on one 400K-byte Macintosh disk. Track 0 is the outermost and track 79 is the innermost. Each track corresponds to a ring of constant radius around the disk.

Macintosh disks are formatted in a manner that allows a more efficient use of disk space than most microcomputer formatting schemes: The tracks are divided into five groups of 16 tracks each, and each group of tracks is accessed at a different rotational speed from the other groups. (Those at the edge of the disk are accessed at slower speeds than those toward the center.)

Each group of tracks contains a different number of sectors:

Tracks	Sectors per track	Sectors
0-15	12	0-191
16-31	11	192-367
32-47	10	368-527
48-63	9	528-671
64-79	8	672-799

An application can read or write data in *whole* disk sectors only. The application must specify the data to be read or written in 512-byte multiples, and the Disk Driver automatically calculates which sector to access. The application specifies where on the disk the data should be read or

7 Disk Driver

written by providing a positioning mode and a positioning offset. Data can be read from or written to the disk:

- at the current sector on the disk (the sector following the last sector read or written)

- from a position relative to the current sector on the disk

- from a position relative to the beginning of first sector on the disk

The following constants are used to specify the positioning mode:

```
CONST fsAtMark     = 0;   {at current sector}
      fsFromStart  = 1;   {relative to first sector}
      fsFromMark   = 3;   {relative to current sector}
```

If the positioning mode is relative to a sector (fsFromStart or fsFromMark), the relative offset from that sector must be given as a 512-byte multiple.

In addition to the 512 bytes of standard information, each sector contains 12 bytes of **file tags**. The file tags are designed to allow easy reconstruction of files from a volume whose directory or other file-access information has been destroyed. Whenever the Disk Driver reads a sector from a disk, it places the sector's file tags at a special location in low memory called the **file tags buffer** (the remaining 512 bytes in the sector are passed on to the File Manager). Each time one sector's file tags are written there, the previous file tags are overwritten. Conversely, whenever the Disk Driver writes a sector on a disk, it takes the 12 bytes in the file tags buffer and writes them on the disk.

Assembly-language note: The information in the file tags buffer can be accessed through the following global variables:

Name	Contents
BufTgFNum	File number (long)
BufTgFFlag	Flags (word: bit 1=1 if resource fork)
BufTgFBkNum	Logical block number (word)
BufTgDate	Date and time of last modification (long)

The logical block number indicates which relative portion of a file the block contains—the first logical block of a file is numbered 0, the second is numbered 1, and so on.

The Disk Driver disables interrupts during disk accesses. While interrupts are disabled, it stores any serial data received via the modem port and later passes the data to the Serial Driver. This allows the modem port to be used simultaneously with disk accesses without fear of hardware overrun errors. (For more information, see chapter 9.)

USING THE DISK DRIVER

The Disk Driver is opened automatically when the system starts up. It allocates space in the system heap for variables, installs entries in the drive queue for each drive that's attached to the

Macintosh, and installs a task into the vertical retrace queue. The Disk Driver's name is '.Sony', and its reference number is –5.

To write data onto a disk, make a Device Manager Write call. You must pass the following parameters:

- the driver reference number –5

- the drive number 1 (internal drive) or 2 (external drive)

- a positioning mode indicating where on the disk the information should be written

- a positioning offset that's a multiple of 512 bytes

- a buffer that contains the data you want to write

- the number of bytes (in multiples of 512) that you want to write

The Disk Driver's prime routine returns one of the following result codes to the Write function:

noErr	No error
nsDrvErr	No such drive
paramErr	Bad positioning information
wPrErr	Volume is locked by a hardware setting
firstDskErr through lastDskErr	Low-level disk error

To read data from a disk, make a Device Manager Read call. You must pass the following parameters:

- the driver reference number –5

- the drive number 1 (internal drive) or 2 (external drive)

- a positioning mode indicating where on the disk the information should be read from

- a positioning offset that's a multiple of 512 bytes

- a buffer to receive the data that's read

- the number of bytes (in multiples of 512) that you want to read

The Disk Driver's prime routine returns one of the following result codes to the Read function:

noErr	No error
nsDrvErr	No such drive
paramErr	Bad positioning information
firstDskErr through lastDskErr	Low-level disk error

To verify that data written to a disk exactly matches the data in memory, make a Device Manager Read call right after the Write call. The parameters for a read-verify operation are the same as for a standard Read call, except that the following constant must be added to the positioning mode:

```
CONST rdVerify = 64;   {read-verify mode}
```

The result code dataVerErr will be returned if any of the data doesn't match.

The Disk Driver can read and write sectors in any order, and therefore operates faster on one large data request than it would on a series of equivalent but smaller data requests.

There are three different calls you can make to the Disk Driver's control routine:

- KillIO causes all current I/O requests to be aborted. KillIO is a Device Manager call.

- SetTagBuffer specifies the information to be used in the file tags buffer.

- DiskEject ejects a disk from a drive.

An application using the File Manager should always unmount the volume in a drive before ejecting the disk.

You can make one call, DriveStatus, to the Disk Driver's status routine, to learn about the state of the driver.

An application can bypass the implicit mounting of volumes done by the File Manager by calling the Operating System Event Manager function GetOSEvent and looking for disk-inserted events. Once the volume has been inserted in the drive, it can be read from normally.

DISK DRIVER ROUTINES

The Disk Driver routines return an integer result code of type OSErr; each routine description lists all of the applicable result codes.

```
FUNCTION DiskEject (drvNum: INTEGER) : OSErr;   [Not in ROM]
```

Assembly-language note: DiskEject is equivalent to a Control call with csCode equal to the global constant ejectCode.

DiskEject ejects the disk from the internal drive if drvNum is 1, or from the external drive if drvNum is 2.

Result codes   noErr   No error
                nsDrvErr   No such drive

```
FUNCTION SetTagBuffer (buffPtr: Ptr) : OSErr;   [Not in ROM]
```

Assembly-language note: SetTagBuffer is equivalent to a Control call with csCode equal to the global constant tgBuffCode.

An application can change the information used in the file tags buffer by calling SetTagBuffer. The buffPtr parameter points to a buffer that contains the information to be used. If buffPtr is NIL, the information in the file tags buffer isn't changed.

If buffPtr isn't NIL, every time the Disk Driver reads a sector from the disk, it stores the file tags in the file tags buffer and in the buffer pointed to by buffPtr. Every time the Disk Driver writes a sector onto the disk, it reads 12 bytes from the buffer pointed to by buffPtr, places them in the file tags buffer, and then writes them onto the disk.

The contents of the buffer pointed to by buffPtr are overwritten at the end of every read request (which can be composed of a number of sectors) instead of at the end of every sector. Each read request places 12 bytes in the buffer for *each* sector, always beginning at the start of the buffer. This way an application can examine the file tags for a number of sequentially read sectors. If a read request is composed of a number of sectors, the Disk Driver places 12 bytes in the buffer for each sector. For example, for a read request of five sectors, the Disk Driver will place 60 bytes in the buffer.

Result codes   noErr   No error

```
FUNCTION DriveStatus (drvNum: INTEGER; VAR status: DrvSts) :
         OSErr;   [Not in ROM]
```

Assembly-language note: DriveStatus is equivalent to a Status call with csCode equal to the global constant drvStsCode; status is returned in csParam through csParam+21.

DriveStatus returns information about the internal drive if drvNum is 1, or about the external drive if drvNum is 2. The information is returned in a record of type DrvSts:

```
TYPE DrvSts  = RECORD
               track:       INTEGER;      {current track}
               writeProt:   SignedByte;   {bit 7=1 if volume is locked}
               diskInPlace: SignedByte;   {disk in place}
               installed:   SignedByte;   {drive installed}
               sides:       SignedByte;   {bit 7=0 if single-side drive}
               qLink:       QElemPtr;     {next queue entry}
               qType:       INTEGER;      {reserved for future use}
               dQDrive:     INTEGER;      {drive number}
               dQRefNum:    INTEGER;      {driver reference number}
               dQFSID:      INTEGER;      {file-system identifier}
               twoSideFmt:  SignedByte;   {-1 if two-sided disk}
               needsFlush:  SignedByte;   {reserved for future use}
               diskErrs:    INTEGER       {error count}
             END;
```

The diskInPlace field is 0 if there's no disk in the drive, 1 or 2 if there is a disk in the drive, or –4 to –1 if the disk was ejected in the last 1.5 seconds. The installed field is 1 if the drive is connected to the Macintosh, 0 if the drive might be connected to the Macintosh, and –1 if the drive isn't installed. The value of twoSideFmt is valid only when diskInPlace=2. The value of diskErrs is incremented every time an error occurs internally within the Disk Driver.

Result codes   noErr   No error
                nsDrvErr   No such drive

ASSEMBLY-LANGUAGE EXAMPLE

The following assembly-language example ejects the disk in drive 1:

```
MyEject   MOVEQ     #<ioVQElSize/2>-1,D0      ;prepare an I/O
@1        CLR.W     -(SP)                     ; parameter block
          DBRA      D0,@1                     ; on the stack
          MOVE.L    SP,A0                     ;A0 points to it
          MOVE.W    #-5,ioRefNum(A0)          ;driver refNum
          MOVE.W    #1,ioDrvNum(A0)           ;internal drive
          MOVE.W    #ejectCode,csCode(A0)     ;eject control code
          _Eject                              ;synchronous call
          ADD       #ioVQElSize,SP            ;clean up stack
```

To asynchronously read sector 4 from the disk in drive 1, you would do the following:

```
MyRead    MOVEQ     #<ioQElSize/2>-1,D0       ;prepare an I/O
@1        CLR.W     -(SP)                     ; parameter block
          DBRA      D0,@1                     ; on the stack
          MOVE.L    SP,A0                     ;A0 points to it
          MOVE.W    #-5,ioRefNum(A0)          ;driver refNum
          MOVE.W    #1,ioDrvNum(A0)           ;internal drive
          MOVE.W    #1,ioPosMode(A0)          ;absolute positioning
          MOVE.L    #<512*4>,ioPosOffset(A0)  ;sector 4

          MOVE.L    #512,ioReqCount(A0)       ;read one sector
          LEA       myBuffer,A1
          MOVE.L    A1,ioBuffer(A0)           ;buffer address
          _Read     ,ASYNC                    ;read data

; Do any other processing here.  Then, when the sector is needed:

@2        MOVE.W    ioResult(A0),D0           ;wait for completion
          BGT.S     @2
          ADD       #ioQElSize,SP             ;clean up stack

myBuffer  .BLOCK    512,0
```

II-216 Assembly-Language Example

SUMMARY OF THE DISK DRIVER

Constants

```
CONST { Positioning modes }

      fsAtMark     = 0;    {at current sector}
      fsFromStart  = 1;    {relative to first sector}
      fsFromMark   = 3;    {relative to current sector}
      rdVerify     = 64;   {add to above for read-verify}
```

Data Types

```
TYPE DrvSts = RECORD
              track:        INTEGER;     {current track}
              writeProt:    SignedByte;  {bit 7=1 if volume is locked}
              diskInPlace:  SignedByte;  {disk in place}
              installed:    SignedByte;  {drive installed}
              sides:        SignedByte;  {bit 7=0 if single-sided drive}
              qLink:        QElemPtr;    {next queue entry}
              qType:        INTEGER;     {reserved for future use}
              dQDrive:      INTEGER;     {drive number}
              dQRefNum:     INTEGER;     {driver reference number}
              dQFSID:       INTEGER;     {file-system identifier}
              twoSideFmt:   SignedByte;  {-1 if two-sided disk}
              needsFlush:   SignedByte;  {reserved for future use}
              diskErrs:     INTEGER      {error count}
            END;
```

Routines [Not in ROM]

```
FUNCTION DiskEject    (drvNum: INTEGER) : OSErr;
FUNCTION SetTagBuffer (buffPtr: Ptr) : OSErr;
FUNCTION DriveStatus  (drvNum: INTEGER; VAR status: DrvSts) : OSErr;
```

Result Codes

Name	Value	Meaning
noErr	0	No error
nsDrvErr	–56	No such drive
paramErr	–50	Bad positioning information
wPrErr	–44	Volume is locked by a hardware setting

Name	Value	Meaning
firstDskErr	–84	First of the range of low-level disk errors
sectNFErr	–81	Can't find sector
seekErr	–80	Drive error
spdAdjErr	–79	Can't correctly adjust disk speed
twoSideErr	–78	Tried to read side 2 of a disk in a single-sided drive
initIWMErr	–77	Can't initialize disk controller chip
tk0BadErr	–76	Can't find track 0
cantStepErr	–75	Drive error
wrUnderrun	–74	Write underrun occurred
badDBtSlp	–73	Bad data mark
badDCksum	–72	Bad data mark
noDtaMkErr	–71	Can't find data mark
badBtSlpErr	–70	Bad address mark
badCksmErr	–69	Bad address mark
dataVerErr	–68	Read-verify failed
noAdrMkErr	–67	Can't find an address mark
noNybErr	–66	Disk is probably blank
offLinErr	–65	No disk in drive
noDriveErr	–64	Drive isn't connected
lastDskErr	–64	Last of the range of low-level disk errors

Assembly-Language Information

Constants

```
; Positioning modes

fsAtMark      .EQU    0     ;at current sector
fsFromStart   .EQU    1     ;relative to first sector
fsFromMark    .EQU    3     ;relative to current sector
rdVerify      .EQU    64    ;add to above for read-verify

; csCode values for Control/Status calls

ejectCode     .EQU    7     ;Control call, DiskEject
tgBuffCode    .EQU    8     ;Control call, SetTagBuffer
drvStsCode    .EQU    8     ;Status call, DriveStatus
```

Structure of Status Information

dsTrack	Current track (word)
dsWriteProt	Bit 7=1 if volume is locked (byte)
dsDiskInPlace	Disk in place (byte)
dsInstalled	Drive installed (byte)
dsSides	Bit 7=0 if single-sided drive (byte)
dsQLink	Pointer to next queue entry
dsDQDrive	Drive number (word)

dsDQRefNum   Driver reference number (word)
dsDQFSID   File-system identifier (word)
dsTwoSideFmt   −1 if two-sided disk (byte)
dsDiskErrs   Error count (word)

Equivalent Device Manager Calls

Pascal routine	**Call**
DiskEject	Control with csCode=ejectCode
SetTagBuffer	Control with csCode=tgBuffCode
DriveStatus	Status with csCode=drvStsCode, status returned in csParam through csParam+21

Variables

BufTgFNum   File tags buffer: file number (long)
BufTgFFlag   File tags buffer: flags (word: bit 1=1 if resource fork)
BufTgFBkNum   File tags buffer: logical block number (word)
BufTgDate   File tags buffer: date and time of last modification (long)

8 THE SOUND DRIVER

ABOUT THIS CHAPTER

The Sound Driver is a Macintosh device driver for handling sound and music generation in a Macintosh application. This chapter describes the Sound Driver in detail.

You should already be familiar with:

■ events, as discussed in chapter 8 of Volume I

■ the Memory Manager

■ the use of devices and device drivers, as described in chapter 6

ABOUT THE SOUND DRIVER

The Sound Driver is a standard Macintosh device driver in ROM that's used to synthesize sound. You can generate sound characterized by any kind of waveform by using the three different sound synthesizers in the Sound Driver:

■ The **four-tone synthesizer** is used to make simple harmonic tones, with up to four "voices" producing sound simultaneously; it requires about 50% of the microprocessor's attention during any given time interval.

■ The **square-wave synthesizer** is used to produce less harmonic sounds such as beeps, and requires about 2% of the processor's time.

■ The **free-form synthesizer** is used to make complex music and speech; it requires about 20% of the processor's time.

The Macintosh XL is equipped only with a square-wave synthesizer; all information in this chapter about four-tone and free-form sound applies only to the Macintosh 128K and 512K.

Figure 1 depicts the **waveform** of a typical sound wave, and the terms used to describe it. The **magnitude** is the vertical distance between any given point on the wave and the horizontal line about which the wave oscillates; you can think of the magnitude as the volume level. The **amplitude** is the maximum magnitude of a periodic wave. The **wavelength** is the horizontal extent of one complete cycle of the wave. Magnitude and wavelength can be measured in any unit of distance. The **period** is the time elapsed during one complete cycle of a wave. The **frequency** is the reciprocal of the period, or the number of cycles per second—also called hertz (Hz). The **phase** is some fraction of a wave cycle (measured from a fixed point on the wave).

There are many different types of waveforms, three of which are depicted in Figure 2. Sine waves are generated by objects that oscillate periodically at a single frequency (such as a tuning fork). Square waves are generated by objects that toggle instantly between two states at a single frequency (such as an electronic "beep"). Free-form waves are the most common of all, and are generated by objects that vibrate at rapidly changing frequencies with rapidly changing magnitudes (such as your vocal cords).

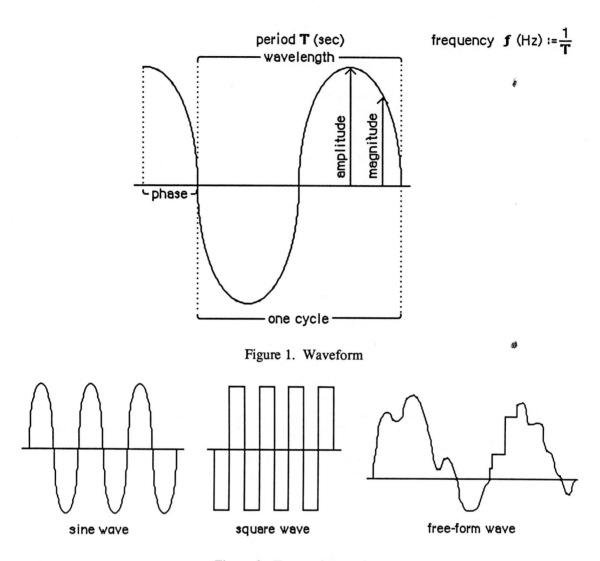

Figure 1. Waveform

Figure 2. Types of Waveforms

Figure 3 shows analog and digital representations of a waveform. The Sound Driver represents waveforms digitally, so all waveforms must be converted from their analog representation to a digital representation. The rows of numbers at the bottom of the figure are digital representations of the waveform. The numbers in the upper row are the magnitudes relative to the horizontal zero-magnitude line. The numbers in the lower row all represent the same relative magnitudes, but have been normalized to positive numbers; you'll use numbers like these when calling the Sound Driver.

A digital representation of a waveform is simply a sequence of wave magnitudes measured at fixed intervals. This sequence of magnitudes is stored in the Sound Driver as a sequence of bytes, each one of which specifies an instantaneous voltage to be sent to the speaker. The bytes are stored in a data structure called a **waveform description**. Since a sequence of bytes can only represent a group of numbers whose maximum and minimum values differ by less than 256, the magnitudes of your waveforms must be constrained to these same limits.

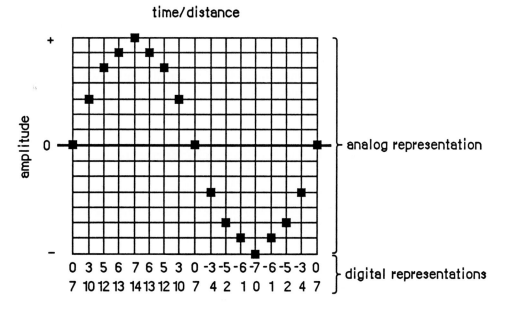

Figure 3. Analog and Digital Representations of a Waveform

SOUND DRIVER SYNTHESIZERS

A description of the sound to be generated by a synthesizer is contained in a data structure called a **synthesizer buffer**. A synthesizer buffer contains the duration, pitch, phase, and waveform of the sound the synthesizer will generate. The exact structure of a synthesizer buffer differs for each type of synthesizer being used. The first word in every synthesizer buffer is an integer that identifies the synthesizer, and must be one of the following predefined constants:

```
CONST swMode = -1;  {square-wave synthesizer}
      ftMode =  1;  {four-tone synthesizer}
      ffMode =  0;  {free-form synthesizer}
```

Square-Wave Synthesizer

The square-wave synthesizer is used to make sounds such as beeps. A square-wave synthesizer buffer has the following structure:

```
TYPE  SWSynthRec = RECORD
                     mode:     INTEGER;   {always swMode}
                     triplets: Tones      {sounds}
                   END;

      SWSynthPtr = ^SWSynthRec;

      Tones = ARRAY[0..5000] OF Tone;
      Tone  = RECORD
                count:     INTEGER;   {frequency}
                amplitude: INTEGER;   {amplitude, 0-255}
                duration:  INTEGER    {duration in ticks}
              END;
```

Each tone triplet contains the count, amplitude, and duration of a different sound. You can store as many triplets in a synthesizer buffer as there's room for.

The count integer can range in value from 0 to 65535. The actual frequency the count corresponds to is given by the relationship:

frequency (Hz) = 783360 / count

A partial list of count values and corresponding frequencies for notes is given in the summary at the end of this chapter.

The type Tones is declared with 5001 elements to allow you to pass up to 5000 sounds (the last element must contain 0). To be space-efficient, your application shouldn't declare a variable of type Tones; instead, you can do something like this:

```
VAR myPtr: Ptr;
    myHandle: Handle;
    mySWPtr: SWSynthPtr;
    . . .

myHandle := NewHandle(buffSize);      {allocate space for the buffer}
HLock(myHandle);                      {lock the buffer}
myPtr := myHandle^;                   {dereference the handle}
mySWPtr := SWSynthPtr(myPtr);         {coerce type to SWSynthPtr}
mySWPtr^.mode := swMode;              {identify the synthesizer}
mySWPtr^.triplets[0].count := 2;      {fill the buffer with values }
    . . .                             { describing the sound}
StartSound(myPtr,buffSize,POINTER(-1));   {produce the sound}
HUnlock(myHandle)                     {unlock the buffer}
```

where buffSize contains the number of bytes in the synthesizer buffer. This example dereferences handles instead of using pointers directly, to minimize the number of nonrelocatable objects in the heap.

Assembly-language note: The global variable CurPitch contains the current value of the count field.

The amplitude can range from 0 to 255. The duration specifies the number of ticks that the sound will be generated.

The list of tones ends with a triplet in which all fields are set to 0. When the square-wave synthesizer is used, the sound specified by each triplet is generated once, and then the synthesizer stops.

Four-Tone Synthesizer

The four-tone synthesizer is used to produce harmonic sounds such as music. It can simultaneously generate four different sounds, each with its own frequency, phase, and waveform.

A four-tone synthesizer buffer has the following structure:

```
TYPE FTSynthRec = RECORD
                    mode:   INTEGER;      {always ftMode}
                    sndRec: FTSndRecPtr   {tones to play}
                  END;


     FTSynthPtr = ^FTSynthRec;
```

The sndRec field points to a **four-tone record,** which describes the four tones:

```
TYPE FTSoundRec = RECORD
                    duration:    INTEGER;   {duration in ticks}
                    sound1Rate:  Fixed;     {tone 1 cycle rate}
                    sound1Phase: LONGINT;   {tone 1 byte offset}
                    sound2Rate:  Fixed;     {tone 2 cycle rate}
                    sound2Phase: LONGINT;   {tone 2 byte offset}
                    sound3Rate:  Fixed;     {tone 3 cycle rate}
                    sound3Phase: LONGINT;   {tone 3 byte offset}
                    sound4Rate:  Fixed;     {tone 4 cycle rate}
                    sound4Phase: LONGINT;   {tone 4 byte offset}
                    sound1Wave:  WavePtr;   {tone 1 waveform}
                    sound2Wave:  WavePtr;   {tone 2 waveform}
                    sound3Wave:  WavePtr;   {tone 3 waveform}
                    sound4Wave:  WavePtr    {tone 4 waveform}
                  END;


     FTSndRecPtr = ^FTSoundRec:

     Wave       = PACKED ARRAY[0..255] OF Byte;
     WavePtr    = ^Wave;
```

Assembly-language note: The address of the four-tone record currently in use is stored in the global variable SoundPtr.

The duration integer indicates the number of ticks that the sound will be generated. Each phase long integer indicates the byte within the waveform description at which the synthesizer should begin producing sound (the first byte is byte number 0). Each rate value determines the speed at which the synthesizer cycles through the waveform, from 0 to 255.

The four-tone synthesizer creates sound by starting at the byte in the waveform description specified by the phase, and skipping ahead the number of bytes specified by the rate field every 44.93 microseconds; when the time specified by the duration has elapsed, the synthesizer stops. The rate field determines how the waveform will be "sampled", as shown in Figure 4. For nonperiodic waveforms, this is best illustrated by example: If the rate field is 1, each byte value in the waveform will be used, each producing sound for 44.93 microseconds. If the rate field is 0.1, each byte will be used 10 times, each therefore producing sound for a total of 449.3 microseconds. If the rate field is 5, only every fifth byte in the waveform will be sampled, each producing sound for 44.93 microseconds.

If the waveform contains one wavelength, the frequency that the rate corresponds to is given by:

frequency (Hz) = 1000000 / (44.93 / (rate/256))

You can use the Toolbox Utility routines FixMul and FixRatio to calculate this, as follows:

```
frequency := FixMul(rate,FixRatio(22257,256))
```

The maximum rate of 256 corresponds to approximately 22.3 kilohertz if the waveform contains one wavelength, and a rate of 0 produces no sound. A partial list of rate values and corresponding frequencies for notes is given in the summary at the end of this chapter.

Free-Form Synthesizer

The free-form synthesizer is used to synthesize complex music and speech. The sound to be produced is represented as a waveform whose complexity and length are limited only by available memory.

A free-form synthesizer buffer has the following structure:

```
TYPE  FFSynthRec = RECORD
                    mode:       INTEGER;    {always ffMode}
                    count:      Fixed;      {"sampling" factor}
                    waveBytes:  FreeWave    {waveform description}
                  END;

      FFSynthPtr = ^FFSynthRec;

      FreeWave   = PACKED ARRAY[0..30000] OF Byte;
```

The type FreeWave is declared with 30001 elements to allow you to pass a very long waveform. To be space-efficient, your application shouldn't declare a variable of type FreeWave; instead, you can do something like this:

```
VAR myPtr: Ptr;
    myHandle: Handle;
    myFFPtr: FFSynthPtr;
    . . .

myHandle := NewHandle(buffSize);      {allocate space for the buffer}
HLock(myHandle);                      {lock the buffer}
myPtr := myHandle^;                   {dereference the handle}
myFFPtr := FFSynthPtr(myPtr);         {coerce type to FFSynthPtr}
myFFPtr^.mode := ffMode;              {identify the synthesizer}
myFFPtr^.count := FixRatio(1,1);      {fill the buffer with values }
myFFPtr^.waveBytes[0] := 0;           { describing the sound}
    . . .
StartSound(myPtr,buffSize,POINTER(-1));  {produce the sound}
HUnlock(myHandle)                     {unlock the buffer}
```

where buffSize contains the number of bytes in the synthesizer buffer. This example dereferences handles instead of using pointers directly, to minimize the number of nonrelocatable objects in the heap.

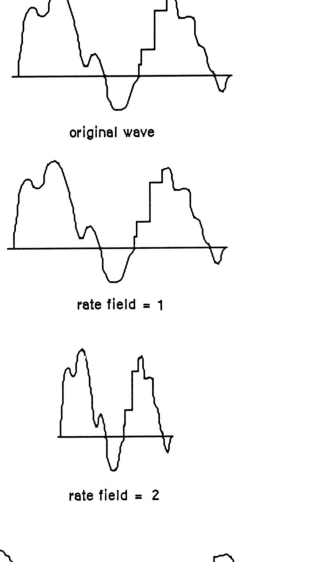

original wave

rate field = 1

rate field = 2

rate field = .5

Figure 4. Effect of the Rate Field

8 Sound Driver

The free-form synthesizer creates sound by starting at the first byte in the waveform and skipping ahead the number of bytes specified by count every 44.93 microseconds. The count field determines how the waveform will be "sampled"; it's analogous to the rate field of the four-tone synthesizer (see Figure 4 above). When the end of the waveform is reached, the synthesizer will stop.

For periodic waveforms, you can determine the frequency of the wave cycle by using the following relationship:

frequency (Hz) = 1000000 / (44.93 * (wavelength/count))

You can calculate this with Toolbox Utility routines as follows:

```
frequency := FixMul(count,FixRatio(22257,wavelength))
```

The wavelength is given in bytes. For example, the frequency of a wave with a 100-byte wavelength played at a count value of 2 would be approximately 445 Hz.

USING THE SOUND DRIVER

The Sound Driver is opened automatically when the system starts up. Its driver name is '.Sound', and its driver reference number is –4. To close or open the Sound Driver, you can use the Device Manager Close and Open functions. Because the driver is in ROM, there's really no reason to close it.

To use one of the three types of synthesizers to generate sound, you can do the following: Use the Memory Manager function NewHandle to allocate heap space for a synthesizer buffer; then lock the buffer, fill it with values describing the sound, and make a StartSound call to the Sound Driver. StartSound can be called either synchronously or asynchronously (with an optional completion routine). When called synchronously, control returns to your application after the sound is completed. When called asynchronously, control returns to your application immediately, and your application is free to perform other tasks while the sound is produced.

To produce continuous, unbroken sounds, it's sometimes advantageous to preallocate space for all the synthesizer buffers you require before you make the first StartSound call. Then, while one asynchronous StartSound call is being completed, you can calculate the waveform values for the next call.

To avoid the click that may occur between StartSound calls when using the four-tone synthesizer, set the duration field to a large value and just change the value of one of the rate fields to start a new sound. To avoid the clicks that may occur during four-tone and free-form sound generation, fill the waveform description with multiples of 740 bytes.

> **Warning:** The Sound Driver uses interrupts to produce sound. If other device drivers are in use, they may turn off interrupts, making sound production unreliable. For instance, if the Disk Driver is accessing a disk during sound generation, a "crackling" sound may be produced.

To determine when the sound initiated by a StartSound call has been completed, you can poll the SoundDone function. You can cancel any current StartSound call and any pending asynchronous StartSound calls by calling StopSound. By calling GetSoundVol and SetSoundVol, you can get and set the current speaker volume level.

SOUND DRIVER ROUTINES

```
PROCEDURE StartSound (synthRec: Ptr; numBytes: LONGINT;
            completionRtn: ProcPtr);   [Not in ROM]
```

Assembly-language note: StartSound is equivalent to a Device Manager Write call with ioRefNum=–4, ioBuffer=synthRec, and ioReqCount=numBytes.

StartSound begins producing the sound described by the synthesizer buffer pointed to by synthRec. NumBytes indicates the size of the synthesizer buffer (in bytes), and completionRtn points to a completion routine to be executed when the sound finishes:

- If completionRtn is POINTER(–1), the sound will be produced synchronously.

- If completionRtn is NIL, the sound will be produced asynchronously, but no completion routine will be executed.

- Otherwise, the sound will be produced asynchronously and the routine pointed to by completionRtn will be executed when the sound finishes.

Warning: You may want the completion routine to start the next sound when one sound finishes, but beware: Completion routines are executed at the interrupt level and must preserve all registers other than A0, A1, and D0-D2. They must not make any calls to the Memory Manager, directly or indirectly, and can't depend on handles to unlocked blocks being valid; be sure to preallocate all the space you'll need. Or, instead of starting the next sound itself, the completion routine can post an application-defined event and your application's main event loop can start the next sound when it gets the event.

Because the type of pointer for each type of synthesizer buffer is different and the type of the synthRec parameter is Ptr, you'll need to do something like the following example (which applies to the free-form synthesizer):

```
VAR myPtr: Ptr;
    myHandle: Handle;
    myFFPtr: FFSynthPtr;
    . . .

myHandle := NewHandle(buffSize);      {allocate space for the buffer}
HLock(myHandle);                      {lock the buffer}
myPtr := myHandle^;                   {dereference the handle}
myFFPtr := FFSynthPtr(myPtr);         {coerce type to FFSynthPtr}
myFFPtr^.mode := ffMode;              {identify the synthesizer}
    . . .                             {fill the buffer with values }
                                      { describing the sound}
StartSound(myPtr,buffSize,POINTER(-1));    {produce the sound}
HUnlock(myHandle)                     {unlock the buffer}
```

where buffSize is the number of bytes in the synthesizer buffer.

The sounds are generated as follows:

■ Free-form synthesizer: The magnitudes described by each byte in the waveform description are generated sequentially until the number of bytes specified by the numBytes parameter have been written.

■ Square-wave synthesizer: The sounds described by each sound triplet are generated sequentially until either the end of the buffer has been reached (indicated by a count, amplitude, and duration of 0 in the square-wave buffer), or the number of bytes specified by the numBytes parameter have been written.

■ Four-tone synthesizer: All four sounds are generated for the length of time specified by the duration integer in the four-tone record.

PROCEDURE StopSound;   [Not in ROM]

StopSound immediately stops the current StartSound call (if any), executes the current StartSound call's completion routine (if any), and cancels any pending asynchronous StartSound calls.

Assembly-language note: To stop sound from assembly language, you can make a Device Manager KillIO call (and, when using the square-wave synthesizer, set the global variable CurPitch to 0). Although StopSound executes the completion routine of only the current StartSound call, KillIO executes the completion routine of every pending asynchronous call.

FUNCTION SoundDone : BOOLEAN;   [Not in ROM]

SoundDone returns TRUE if the Sound Driver isn't currently producing sound and there are no asynchronous StartSound calls pending; otherwise it returns FALSE.

Assembly-language note: Assembly-language programmers can poll the ioResult field of the most recent Device Manager Write call's parameter block to determine when the Write call finishes.

PROCEDURE GetSoundVol (VAR level: INTEGER);   [Not in ROM]

GetSoundVol returns the current speaker volume, from 0 (silent) to 7 (loudest).

Assembly-language note: Assembly-language programmers can get the speaker volume level from the low-order three bits of the global variable SdVolume.

```
PROCEDURE SetSoundVol (level: INTEGER);   [Not in ROM]
```

SetSoundVol immediately sets the speaker volume to the specified level, from 0 (silent) to 7 (loudest); it doesn't, however, change the volume setting that's under user control via the Control Panel desk accessory. If your application calls SetSoundVol, it should save the current volume (using GetSoundVol) when it starts up and restore it (with SetSoundVol) upon exit; this resets the actual speaker volume to match the Control Panel setting.

Assembly-language note: To set the speaker volume level from assembly language, call this Pascal procedure from your program. As a side effect, it will set the low-order three bits of the global variable SdVolume to the specified level.

Note: The Control Panel volume setting is stored in parameter RAM; if you're writing a similar desk accessory and want to change this setting, see the discussion of parameter RAM in chapter 13.

SOUND DRIVER HARDWARE

The information in this section applies to the Macintosh 128K and 512K, but not the Macintosh XL.

This section briefly describes how the Sound Driver uses the Macintosh hardware to produce sound, and how assembly-language programmers can intervene in this process to control the square-wave synthesizer. You can skip this section if it doesn't interest you, and you'll still be able to use the Sound Driver as described.

Note: For more information about the hardware used by the Sound Driver, see chapter 2 of Volume III.

The Sound Driver and disk speed-control circuitry share a special 740-byte buffer in memory, of which the Sound Driver uses the 370 even-numbered bytes to generate sound. Every horizontal blanking interval (every 44.93 microseconds—when the beam of the display tube moves from the right edge of the screen to the left), the MC68000 automatically fetches two bytes from this buffer and sends the high-order byte to the speaker.

Note: The period of any four-tone or free-form sound generated by the Sound Driver is a multiple of this 44.93-microsecond interval; the highest frequency is 11128 Hz, which corresponds to twice this interval.

Every vertical blanking interval (every 16.6 milliseconds—when the beam of the display tube moves from the bottom of the screen to the top), the Sound Driver fills its half of the 740-byte buffer with the next set of values. For square-wave sound, the buffer is filled with a constant value; for more complex sound, it's filled with many values.

From assembly language, you can cause the square-wave synthesizer to start generating sound, and then change the amplitude of the sound being generated any time you wish:

1. Make an asynchronous Device Manager Write call to the Sound Driver specifying the count, amplitude, and duration of the sound you want. The amplitude you specify will be placed in the 740-byte buffer, and the Sound Driver will begin producing sound.

2. Whenever you want to change the sound being generated, make an *immediate* Control call to the Sound Driver with the following parameters: ioRefNum must be –4, csCode must be 3, and csParam must provide the new amplitude level. The amplitude you specify will be placed in the 740-byte buffer, and the sound will change. You can continue to change the sound until the time specified by the duration has elapsed.

When the immediate Control call is completed, the Device Manager will execute the completion routine (if any) of the currently executing Write call. For this reason, the Write call shouldn't have a completion routine.

Note: You can determine the amplitude placed in the 740-byte buffer from the global variable SoundLevel.

SUMMARY OF THE SOUND DRIVER

Constants

```
CONST { Mode values for synthesizers }

    swMode = -1;    {square-wave synthesizer}
    ftMode =  1;    {four-tone synthesizer}
    ffMode =  0;    {free-form synthesizer}
```

Data Types

```
TYPE { Free-form synthesizer }

    FFSynthPtr =  ^FFSynthRec;
    FFSynthRec =  RECORD
                    mode:      INTEGER;    {always ffMode}
                    count:     Fixed;      {"sampling" factor}
                    waveBytes: FreeWave    {waveform description}
                  END;


    FreeWave    = PACKED ARRAY[0..30000] OF Byte;

    { Square-wave synthesizer }

    SWSynthPtr = ^SWSynthRec;
    SWSynthRec = RECORD
                    mode:      INTEGER;    {always swMode}
                    triplets:  Tones       {sounds}
                  END;

    Tones = ARRAY[0..5000] OF Tone;
    Tone  = RECORD
                    count:     INTEGER;  {frequency}
                    amplitude: INTEGER;  {amplitude, 0-255}
                    duration:  INTEGER   {duration in ticks}
                  END;

    { Four-tone synthesizer }

    FTSynthPtr  = ^FTSynthRec;
    FTSynthRec  = RECORD
                    mode:   INTEGER;      {always ftMode}
                    sndRec: FTSndRecPtr   {tones to play}
                  END;
```

```
FTSndRecPtr =  ^FTSoundRec;
FTSoundRec  =  RECORD
                   duration:     INTEGER;     {duration in ticks}
                   sound1Rate:   Fixed;       {tone 1 cycle rate}
                   sound1Phase:  LONGINT;     {tone 1 byte offset}
                   sound2Rate:   Fixed;       {tone 2 cycle rate}
                   sound2Phase:  LONGINT;     {tone 2 byte offset}
                   sound3Rate:   Fixed;       {tone 3 cycle rate}
                   sound3Phase:  LONGINT;     {tone 3 byte offset}
                   sound4Rate:   Fixed;       {tone 4 cycle rate}
                   sound4Phase:  LONGINT;     {tone 4 byte offset}
                   sound1Wave:   WavePtr;     {tone 1 waveform}
                   sound2Wave:   WavePtr;     {tone 2 waveform}
                   sound3Wave:   WavePtr;     {tone 3 waveform}
                   sound4Wave:   WavePtr      {tone 4 waveform}
               END;

WavePtr = ^Wave;
Wave    = PACKED ARRAY[0..255] OF Byte;
```

Routines [Not in ROM]

```
PROCEDURE StartSound    (synthRec: Ptr; numBytes: LONGINT; completionRtn:
                         ProcPtr);
PROCEDURE StopSound;
FUNCTION  SoundDone :   BOOLEAN;
PROCEDURE GetSoundVol (VAR level: INTEGER);
PROCEDURE SetSoundVol (level: INTEGER);
```

Assembly-Language Information

Routines

Pascal name	Equivalent for assembly language
StartSound	Call Write with ioRefNum=–4, ioBuffer=synthRec, ioReqCount=numBytes
StopSound	Call KillIO and (for square-wave) set CurPitch to 0
SoundDone	Poll ioResult field of most recent Write call's parameter block
GetSoundVol	Get low-order three bits of variable SdVolume
SetSoundVol	Call this Pascal procedure from your program

Variables

SdVolume	Speaker volume (byte: low-order three bits only)
SoundPtr	Pointer to four-tone record
SoundLevel	Amplitude in 740-byte buffer (byte)
CurPitch	Value of count in square-wave synthesizer buffer (word)

Sound Driver Values for Notes

The following table contains values for the rate field of a four-tone synthesizer and the count field of a square-wave synthesizer. A just-tempered scale—in the key of C, as an example—is given in the first four columns; you can use a just-tempered scale for perfect tuning in a particular key. The last four columns give an equal-tempered scale, for applications that may use any key; this scale is appropriate for most Macintosh sound applications. Following this table is a list of the ratios used in calculating these values, and instructions on how to calculate them for a just-tempered scale in any key.

| | Just-Tempered Scale | | | | Equal-Tempered Scale | | | |
| | Rate for Four-Tone | | Count for Square-Wave | | Rate for Four-Tone | | Count for Square-Wave | |
Note	Long	Fixed	Word	Integer	Long	Fixed	Word	Integer
3 octaves below middle C								
C	612B	0.37956	5CBA	23738	604C	0.37616	5D92	23954
C#	667C	0.40033	57EB	22507	6606	0.39853	5851	22609
Db	67A6	0.40488	56EF	22255				
D	6D51	0.42702	526D	21101	6C17	0.42223	535C	21340
Ebb	6E8F	0.43187	5180	20864				
D#	71DF	0.44481	4F21	20257	7284	0.44733	4EAF	20143
Eb	749A	0.45547	4D46	19782				
E	7976	0.47446	4A2F	18991	7953	0.47392	4A44	19012
F	818F	0.50609	458C	17804	808A	0.50211	4619	17945
F#	88A5	0.53377	41F0	16880	882F	0.53197	422A	16938
Gb	8A32	0.53983	4133	16691				
G	91C1	0.56935	3DD1	15825	9048	0.56360	3E73	15987
G#	97D4	0.59308	3B58	15192	98DC	0.59711	3AF2	15090
Ab	9B79	0.60732	39F4	14836				
A	A1F3	0.63261	37A3	14243	A1F3	0.63261	37A3	14243
Bbb	A3CA	0.63980	3703	14083				
A#	AA0C	0.66425	34FD	13565	AB94	0.67023	3484	13444
Bb	ACBF	0.67479	3429	13353				
B	B631	0.71169	3174	12660	B5C8	0.71008	3191	12689
2 octaves below middle C								
C	C257	0.75914	2E5D	11869	C097	0.75230	2EC9	11977
C#	CCF8	0.80066	2BF6	11254	CC0B	0.79704	2C29	11305
Db	CF4C	0.80975	2B77	11127				
D	DAA2	0.85403	2936	10550	D82D	0.84444	29AE	10670
Ebb	DD1D	0.86372	28C0	10432				
D#	E3BE	0.88962	2790	10128	E508	0.89465	2757	10071
Eb	E935	0.91096	26A3	9891				
E	F2ED	0.94893	2517	9495	F2A6	0.94785	2522	9506
F	1031E	1.01218	22C6	8902	10114	1.00421	230C	8972
F#	1114A	1.06754	20F8	8440	1105D	1.06392	2115	8469
Gb	11465	1.07967	2099	8345				
G	12382	1.13870	1EE9	7913	12090	1.12720	1F3A	7994

Note	Long	Fixed	Word	Integer	Long	Fixed	Word	Integer
2 octaves below middle C								
G#	12FA8	1.18616	1DAC	7596	131B8	1.19421	1D79	7545
Ab	136F1	1.21461	1CFA	7418				
A	143E6	1.26523	1BD1	7121	143E6	1.26523	1BD1	7121
Bbb	14794	1.27960	1B81	7041				
A#	15418	1.32849	1A7E	6782	15729	1.34047	1A42	6722
Bb	1597E	1.34958	1A14	6676				
B	16C63	1.42339	18BA	6330	16B90	1.42017	18C8	6344
1 octave below middle C								
C	184AE	1.51828	172F	5935	1812F	1.50462	1764	5988
C#	199EF	1.60130	15FB	5627	19816	1.59409	1614	5652
Db	19E97	1.61949	15BC	5564				
D	1B543	1.70805	149B	5275	1B05A	1.68887	14D7	5335
Ebb	1BA3B	1.72746	1460	5216				
D#	1C77B	1.77922	13C8	5064	1CA10	1.78931	13AC	5036
Eb	1D26A	1.82193	1351	4945				
E	1E5D9	1.89784	128C	4748	1E54D	1.89571	1291	4753
F	2063D	2.02437	1163	4451	20228	2.00842	1186	4486
F#	22294	2.13507	107C	4220	220BB	2.12785	108A	4234
Gb	228C9	2.15932	104D	4173				
G	24704	2.27740	F74	3956	2411F	2.25438	F9D	3997
G#	25F4F	2.37230	ED6	3798	26370	2.38843	EBC	3772
Ab	26DE3	2.42924	E7D	3709				
A	287CC	2.53046	DE9	3561	287CC	2.53046	DE9	3561
Bbb	28F28	2.55920	DC1	3521				
A#	2A830	2.65698	D3F	3391	2AE51	2.68092	D21	3361
Bb	2B2FC	2.69916	D0A	3338				
B	2D8C6	2.84677	C5D	3165	2D721	2.84035	C64	3172
Middle C								
C	3095B	3.03654	B97	2967	3025D	3.00923	BB2	2994
C#	333DE	3.20261	AFD	2813	3302C	3.18817	B0A	2826
Db	33D2E	3.23898	ADE	2782				
D	36A87	3.41612	A4E	2638	360B5	3.37776	A6C	2668
Ebb	37476	3.45493	A30	2608				
D#	38EF7	3.55846	9E4	2532	39420	3.57861	9D6	2518
Eb	3A4D4	3.64386	9A9	2473				
E	3CBB2	3.79568	946	2374	3CA99	3.79140	949	2377
F	40C7A	4.04874	8B1	2225	40450	4.01685	8C3	2243
F#	44528	4.27014	83E	2110	44176	4.25571	845	2117
Gb	45193	4.31865	826	2086				
G	48E09	4.55482	7BA	1978	4823E	4.50876	7CE	1998
G#	4BE9F	4.74461	76B	1899	4C6E1	4.77687	75E	1886
Ab	4DBC5	4.85847	73F	1855				
A	50F98	5.06091	6F4	1780	50F98	5.06091	6F4	1780

Note	Long	Fixed	Word	Integer	Long	Fixed	Word	Integer
Middle C								
Bbb	51E4F	5.11839	6E0	1760				
A#	55060	5.31396	6A0	1696	55CA2	5.36185	690	1680
Bb	565F8	5.39832	685	1669				
B	5B18B	5.69353	62F	1583	5AE41	5.68068	632	1586
1 octave above middle C								
C	612B7	6.07310	5CC	1484	604BB	6.01848	5D9	1497
C#	667BD	6.40523	57F	1407	66059	6.37636	585	1413
Db	67A5C	6.47797	56F	1391				
D	6D50D	6.83223	527	1319	6C169	6.75551	536	1334
Ebb	6E8EB	6.90984	518	1304				
D#	71DEE	7.11691	4F2	1266	7283F	7.15721	4EB	1259
Eb	749A8	7.28772	4D4	1236				
E	79764	7.59137	4A3	1187	79533	7.58281	4A4	1188
F	818F3	8.09746	459	1113	808A1	8.03371	462	1122
F#	88A51	8.54030	41F	1055	882EC	8.51141	423	1059
Gb	8A326	8.63730	413	1043				
G	91C12	9.10965	3DD	989	9047D	9.01753	3E7	999
G#	97D3D	9.48921	3B6	950	98DC2	9.55374	3AF	943
Ab	9B78B	9.71696	39F	927				
A	A1F30	10.12183	37A	890	A1F30	10.12183	37A	890
Bbb	A3C9F	10.23680	370	880				
A#	AA0BF	10.62791	350	848	AB945	10.72371	348	840
Bb	ACBEF	10.79662	343	835				
B	B6316	11.38705	317	791	B5C83	11.36137	319	793
2 octaves above middle C								
C	C256D	12.14619	2E6	742	C0976	12.03696	2ED	749
C#	CCF79	12.81044	2BF	703	CC0B1	12.75270	2C3	707
Db	CF4B9	12.95595	2B7	695				
D	DAA1B	13.66447	293	659	D82D2	13.51102	29B	667
Ebb	DD1D6	13.81967	28C	652				
D#	E3BDC	14.23383	279	633	E507E	14.31442	275	629
Eb	E9350	14.57544	26A	618				
E	F2EC8	15.18274	251	593	F2A65	15.16560	252	594
F	1031E7	16.19493	22C	556	101141	16.06740	231	561
F#	1114A1	17.08058	210	528	1105D8	17.02283	211	529
Gb	11464C	17.27460	20A	522				
G	123824	18.21930	1EF	495	1208F9	18.03505	1F4	500
G#	12FA7B	18.97844	1DB	475	131B83	19.10747	1D8	472
Ab	136F15	19.43391	1D0	464				
A	143E61	20.24367	1BD	445	143E61	20.24367	1BD	445
Bbb	14793D	20.47359	1B8	440				
A#	15417F	21.25584	1A8	424	15728A	21.44742	1A4	420
Bb	1597DE	21.59323	1A1	417				
B	16C62D	22.77412	18C	396	16B906	22.72275	18D	397

8 Sound Driver

Note	Long	Fixed	Word	Integer	Long	Fixed	Word	Integer
3 octaves above middle C								
C	184ADA	24.29239	173	371	1812EB	24.07390	176	374
C#	199EF2	25.62088	160	352	198163	25.50542	161	353
Db	19E971	25.91188	15C	348				
D	1B5436	27.32895	14A	330	1B05A5	27.02205	14D	333
Ebb	1BA3AC	27.63934	146	326				
D#	1C77B8	28.46765	13D	317	1CA0FD	28.62886	13B	315
Eb	1D26A0	29.15088	135	309				
E	1E5D91	30.36549	129	297	1E54CB	30.33122	129	297
F	2063CE	32.38986	116	278	202283	32.13481	118	280
F#	222943	34.16118	108	264	220BAF	34.04564	109	265
Gb	228C97	34.54918	105	261				
G	247047	36.43858	F7	247	2411F2	36.07010	FA	250
G#	25F4F5	37.95686	ED	237	263706	38.21494	EC	236
Ab	26DE2A	38.86783	E8	232				
A	287CC1	40.48732	DF	223	287CC1	40.48732	DF	223
Bbb	28F27A	40.94717	DC	220				
A#	2A82FE	42.51169	D4	212	2AE513	42.89482	D2	210
Bb	2B2FBD	43.18648	D1	209				
B	2D8C59	45.54823	C6	198	2D720B	45.44548	C6	198

The following table gives the ratios used in calculating the above values. It shows the relationship between the notes making up the just-tempered scale in the key of C; should you need to implement a just-tempered scale in some other key, you can do so as follows: First get the value of the root note in the proper octave in the equal-tempered scale (from the above table). Then use the following table to determine the values of the intervals for the other notes in the key by multiplying the ratio by the root note.

Chromatic interval	Note	Just-tempered frequency ratio	Equal-tempered frequency ratio	Interval type
0	C	1.00000	1.00000	Unison
1	C#	1.05469	1.05946	Minor second as chromatic semitone
	Db	1.06667		Minor second as diatonic semitone
2	D	1.11111	1.12246	Major second as minor tone
	D	1.12500		Major second as major tone
	Ebb	1.13778		Diminished third
3	D#	1.17188	1.18921	Augmented second
	Eb	1.20000		Minor third
4	E	1.25000	1.25992	Major third
5	F	1.33333	1.33484	Fourth
6	F#	1.40625	1.41421	Tritone as augmented fourth
	Gb	1.42222		Tritone as diminished fifth
7	G	1.50000	1.49831	Fifth

Chromatic interval	Note	Just-tempered frequency ratio	Equal-tempered frequency ratio	Interval type
8	G#	1.56250	1.58740	Augmented fifth
	Ab	1.60000		Minor sixth
9	A	1.66667	1.68179	Major sixth
	Bbb	1.68560		Diminished seventh
10	A#	1.75000	1.78180	Augmented sixth
	Bb	1.77778		Minor seventh
11	B	1.87500	1.88775	Major seventh
12	C	2.00000	2.00000	Octave

9 THE SERIAL DRIVERS

ABOUT THIS CHAPTER

The Macintosh RAM Serial Driver and ROM Serial Driver are Macintosh device drivers for handling asynchronous serial communication between a Macintosh application and serial devices. This chapter describes the Serial Drivers in detail.

You should already be familiar with:

- resources, as discussed in chapter 5 of Volume I

- events, as discussed in chapter 8 of Volume I

- the Memory Manager

- interrupts and the use of devices and device drivers, as described in chapter 6

- asynchronous serial data communication

SERIAL COMMUNICATION

The Serial Drivers support full-duplex asynchronous serial communication. **Serial data** is transmitted over a single-path communication line, one bit at a time (as opposed to parallel data, which is transmitted over a multiple-path communication line, multiple bits at a time). **Full-duplex** means that the Macintosh and another serial device connected to it can transmit data simultaneously (as opposed to half-duplex operation, in which data can be transmitted by only one device at a time). **Asynchronous communication** means that the Macintosh and other serial devices communicating with it don't share a common timer, and no timing data is transmitted. The time interval between characters transmitted asynchronously can be of any length. The format of asynchronous serial data communication used by the Serial Drivers is shown in Figure 1.

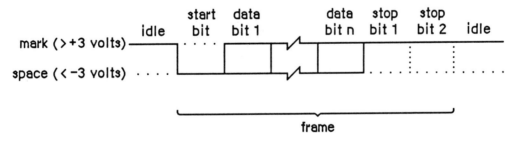

Figure 1. Asynchronous Data Transmission

When a transmitting serial device is idle (not sending data), it maintains the transmission line in a continuous state ("mark" in Figure 1). The transmitting device may begin sending a character at any time by sending a **start bit**. The start bit tells the receiving device to prepare to receive a character. The transmitting device then transmits 5, 6, 7, or 8 **data bits**, optionally followed by a **parity bit**. The value of the parity bit is chosen such that the number of 1's among the data and parity bits is even or odd, depending on whether the parity is even or odd, respectively. Finally, the transmitting device sends 1, 1.5, or 2 **stop bits**, indicating the end of the character. The measure of the total number of bits sent over the transmission line per second is called the **baud rate**.

If a parity bit is set incorrectly, the receiving device will note a **parity error**. The time elapsed from the start bit to the last stop bit is called a **frame**. If the receiving device doesn't get a stop bit after the data and parity bits, it will note a **framing error**. After the stop bits, the transmitting device may send another character or maintain the line in the mark state. If the line is held in the "space" state (Figure 1) for one frame or longer, a **break** occurs. Breaks are used to interrupt data transmission.

ABOUT THE SERIAL DRIVERS

There are two Macintosh device drivers for serial communication: the RAM Serial Driver and the ROM Serial Driver. The two drivers are nearly identical, although the RAM driver has a few features the ROM driver doesn't. Both allow Macintosh applications to communicate with serial devices via the two serial ports on the back of the Macintosh.

> **Note:** There are actually two versions of the RAM Serial Driver; one is for the Macintosh 128K and 512K, the other is for the Macintosh XL. If you want your application to run on all versions of the Macintosh, you should install both drivers in your application resource file, as resources of type 'SERD'. The resource ID should be 1 for the Macintosh 128K and 512K driver, and 2 for the Macintosh XL driver.

Each Serial Driver actually consists of four drivers: one input driver and one output driver for the modem port, and one input driver and one output driver for the printer port (Figure 2). Each **input driver** receives data via a serial port and transfers it to the application. Each **output driver** takes data from the application and sends it out through a serial port. The input and output drivers for a port are closely related, and share some of the same routines. Each driver does, however, have a separate device control entry, which allows the Serial Drivers to support full-duplex communication. An individual port can both transmit and receive data at the same time. The serial ports are controlled by the Macintosh's Zilog Z8530 Serial Communications Controller (SCC). Channel A of the SCC controls the modem port, and channel B controls the printer port.

Data received via a serial port passes through a three-character buffer in the SCC and then into a buffer in the input driver for the port. Characters are removed from the input driver's buffer each time an application issues a Read call to the driver. Each input driver's buffer can initially hold up to 64 characters, but your application can specify a larger buffer if necessary. The following errors may occur:

- If the SCC buffer ever overflows (because the input driver doesn't read it often enough), a **hardware overrun error** occurs.

- If an input driver's buffer ever overflows (because the application doesn't issue Read calls to the driver often enough), a **software overrun error** occurs.

The printer port should be used for output-only connections to devices such as printers, or at low baud rates (300 baud or less). The modem port has no such restrictions. It may be used simultaneously with disk accesses without fear of hardware overrun errors, because whenever the Disk Driver must turn off interrupts for longer than 100 microseconds, it stores any data received via the modem port and later passes the data to the modem port's input driver.

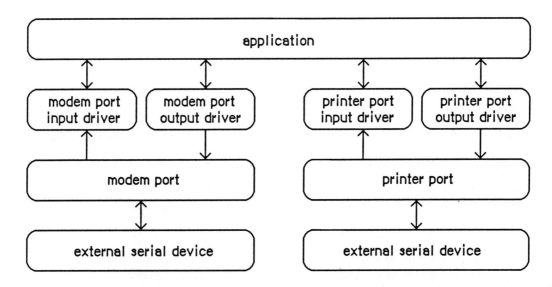

Figure 2. Input and Output Drivers of a Serial Driver

All four drivers default to 9600 baud, eight data bits per character, no parity bit, and two stop bits. You can change any of these options. The Serial Drivers support Clear To Send (CTS) hardware handshake and XOn/XOff software flow control.

> **Note:** The ROM Serial Driver defaults to hardware handshake only; it doesn't support XOn/XOff input flow control—only output flow control. Use the RAM Serial Driver if you want XOn/XOff input flow control. The RAM Serial Driver defaults to no hardware handshake and no software flow control.

Whenever an input driver receives a break, it terminates any pending Read requests, but not Write requests. You can choose to have the input drivers terminate Read requests whenever a parity, overrun, or framing error occurs.

> **Note:** The ROM Serial Driver always terminates input requests when an error occurs. Use the RAM Serial Driver if you don't want input requests to be terminated by errors.

You can request the Serial Drivers to post device driver events whenever a change in the hardware handshake status or a break occurs, if you want your application to take some specific action upon these occurrences.

USING THE SERIAL DRIVERS

This section introduces you to the Serial Driver routines described in detail in the next section, and discusses other calls you can make to communicate with the Serial Drivers.

Drivers are referred to by name and reference number:

Driver	Driver name	Reference number
Modem port input	.AIn	–6
Modem port output	.AOut	–7
Printer port input	.BIn	–8
Printer port output	.BOut	–9

Before you can receive data through a port, both the input and output drivers for the port must be opened. Before you can send data through a port, the output driver for the port must be opened. To open the ROM input and output drivers, call the Device Manager Open function; to open the RAM input and output drivers, call the Serial Driver function RAMSDOpen. The RAM drivers occupy less than 2K bytes of memory in the application heap.

When you open an output driver, the Serial Driver initializes local variables for the output driver and the associated input driver, allocates and locks buffer storage for both drivers, installs interrupt handlers for both drivers, and initializes the correct SCC channel (ROM Serial Driver only). When you open an input driver, the Serial Driver only notes the location of its device control entry.

You shouldn't ever close the ROM Serial Driver with a Device Manager Close call. If you wish to replace it with a RAM Serial Driver, the RAMSDOpen call will automatically close the ROM driver for you. You must close the RAM Serial Driver with a call to RAMSDClose before your application terminates; this will also release the memory occupied by the driver itself. When you close an output driver, the Serial Driver resets the appropriate SCC channel, releases all local variable and buffer storage space, and restores any changed interrupt vectors.

To transmit serial data out through a port, make a Device Manager Write call to the output driver for the port. You must pass the following parameters:

- the driver reference number –7 or –9, depending on whether you're using the modem port or the printer port

- a buffer that contains the data you want to transmit

- the number of bytes you want to transmit

To receive serial data from a port, make a Device Manager Read call to the input driver for the port. You must pass the following parameters:

- the driver reference number –6 or –8, depending on whether you're using the modem port or the printer port

- a buffer to receive the data

- the number of bytes you want to receive

There are six different calls you can make to the Serial Driver's control routine:

- KillIO causes all current I/O requests to be aborted and any bytes remaining in both input buffers to be discarded. KillIO is a Device Manager call.

- SerReset resets and reinitializes a driver with new data bits, stop bits, parity bit, and baud rate information.

- SerSetBuf allows you to specify a new input buffer, replacing the driver's 64-character default buffer.

- SerHShake allows you to specify handshake options.

```
baud3600    =  30;      {3600 baud}
baud4800    =  22;      {4800 baud}
baud7200    =  14;      {7200 baud}
baud9600    =  10;      {9600 baud}
baud19200   =  4;       {19200 baud}
baud57600   =  0;       {57600 baud}
stop10      =  16384;   {1 stop bit}
stop15      = -32768;   {1.5 stop bits}
stop20      = -16384;   {2 stop bits}
noParity    =  0;       {no parity}
oddParity   =  4096;    {odd parity}
evenParity  =  12288;   {even parity}
data5       =  0;       {5 data bits}
data6       =  2048;    {6 data bits}
data7       =  1024;    {7 data bits}
data8       =  3072;    {8 data bits}
```

For example, the default setting of 9600 baud, eight data bits, two stop bits, and no parity bit is equivalent to passing the following value in serConfig: baud9600 + data8 + stop20 + noParity.

Result codes   noErr   No error

```
FUNCTION SerSetBuf (refNum: INTEGER; serBPtr: Ptr; serBLen:
        INTEGER) : OSErr;   [Not in ROM]
```

Assembly-language note: SerSetBuf is equivalent to a Control call with csCode=9, csParam=serBPtr, and csParam+4=serBLen.

SerSetBuf specifies a new input buffer for the input driver having the reference number refNum. SerBPtr points to the buffer, and serBLen specifies the number of bytes in the buffer. To restore the driver's default buffer, call SerSetBuf with serBLen set to 0.

Warning: You must lock a new input buffer while it's in use.

Result codes   noErr   No error

```
FUNCTION SerHShake (refNum: INTEGER; flags: SerShk) : OSErr;   [Not
        in ROM]
```

Assembly-language note: SerHShake is equivalent to a Control call with csCode=10 and csParam through csParam+6 flags.

SerHShake sets handshake options and other control information, as specified by the flags parameter, for the input or output driver having the reference number refNum. The flags parameter has the following data structure:

```
TYPE SerShk =  PACKED RECORD
                    fXOn: Byte;   {XOn/XOff output flow control flag}
                    fCTS: Byte;   {CTS hardware handshake flag}
                    xOn:  CHAR;   {XOn character}
                    xOff: CHAR;   {XOff character}
                    errs: Byte;   {errors that cause abort}
                    evts: Byte;   {status changes that cause events}
                    fInX: Byte;   {XOn/XOff input flow control flag}
                    null: Byte    {not used}
               END;
```

If fXOn is nonzero, XOn/XOff output flow control is enabled; if fInX is nonzero, XOn/XOff input flow control is enabled. XOn and xOff specify the XOn character and XOff character used for XOn/XOff flow control. If fCTS is nonzero, CTS hardware handshake is enabled. The errs field indicates which errors will cause input requests to be aborted; for each type of error, there's a predefined constant in which the corresponding bit is set:

```
CONST parityErr     = 16;   {set if parity error}
      hwOverrunErr  = 32;   {set if hardware overrun error}
      framingErr    = 64;   {set if framing error}
```

Note: The ROM Serial Driver doesn't support XOn/XOff input flow control or aborts caused by error conditions.

The evts field indicates whether changes in the CTS or break status will cause the Serial Driver to post device driver events. You can use the following predefined constants to set or test the value of evts:

```
CONST ctsEvent   = 32;   {set if CTS change will cause event to be }
                         { posted}
      breakEvent = 128;  {set if break status change will cause event }
                         { to be posted}
```

Warning: Use of this option is discouraged because of the long time that interrupts are disabled while such an event is posted.

Result codes   noErr   No error

```
FUNCTION SerSetBrk (refNum: INTEGER) : OSErr;   [Not in ROM]
```

Assembly-language note: SerSetBrk is equivalent to a Control call with csCode=12.

SerSetBrk sets break mode in the input or output driver having the reference number refNum.

Result codes   noErr   No error

```
FUNCTION SerClrBrk (refNum: INTEGER) : OSErr;    [Not in ROM]
```

Assembly-language note: SerClrBrk is equivalent to a Control call with csCode=11.

SerClrBrk clears break mode in the input or output driver having the reference number refNum.

Result codes   noErr   No error

Getting Serial Driver Information

```
FUNCTION SerGetBuf (refNum: INTEGER; VAR count: LONGINT) : OSErr;
        [Not in ROM]
```

Assembly-language note: SerGetBuf is equivalent to a Status call with csCode=2; count is returned in csParam as a long word.

SerGetBuf returns, in the count parameter, the number of bytes in the buffer of the input driver having the reference number refNum.

Result codes   noErr   No error

```
FUNCTION SerStatus (refNum: INTEGER; VAR serSta: SerStaRec) :
         OSErr;   [Not in ROM]
```

Assembly-language note: SerStatus is equivalent to a Status call with csCode=8; serSta is returned in csParam through csParam+5.

SerStatus returns in serSta three words of status information for the input or output driver having the reference number refNum. SerSta has the following data structure:

```
TYPE SerStaRec = PACKED RECORD
                   cumErrs:  Byte;   {cumulative errors}
                   xOffSent: Byte;   {XOff sent as input flow control}
                   rdPend:   Byte;   {read pending flag}
                   wrPend:   Byte;   {write pending flag}
                   ctsHold:  Byte;   {CTS flow control hold flag}
                   xOffHold: Byte    {XOff flow control hold flag}
                 END;
```

9 Serial Drivers

CumErrs indicates which errors have occurred since the last time SerStatus was called:

```
CONST swOverrunErr = 1;    {set if software overrun error}
      parityErr    = 16;   {set if parity error}
      hwOverrunErr = 32;   {set if hardware overrun error}
      framingErr   = 64;   {set if framing error}
```

If the driver has sent an XOff character, xOffSent will be equal to the following predefined constant:

```
CONST xOffWasSent = $80; {XOff character was sent}
```

If the driver has a Read or Write call pending, rdPend or wrPend, respectively, will be nonzero. If output has been suspended because the hardware handshake was disabled, ctsHold will be nonzero. If output has been suspended because an XOff character was received, xOffHold will be nonzero.

Result codes   noErr   No error

ADVANCED CONTROL CALLS

This section describes the calls that advanced programmers can make to the RAM Serial Driver's control routine via a Device Manager Control call.

csCode = 13   csParam = baudRate

This call provides an additional way (besides SerReset) to set the baud rate. CsParam specifies the actual baud rate as an integer (for instance, 9600). The closest baud rate that the Serial Driver will generate is returned in csParam.

csCode = 19   csParam = char

After this call is made, all incoming characters with parity errors will be replaced by the character specified by the ASCII code in csParam. If csParam is 0, no character replacement will be done.

csCode = 21

This call unconditionally sets XOff for output flow control. It's equivalent to receiving an XOff character. Data transmission is halted until an XOn is received or a Control call with csCode=24 is made.

csCode = 22

This call unconditionally clears XOff for output flow control. It's equivalent to receiving an XOn character.

csCode = 23

This call sends an XOn character for input flow control if the last input flow control character sent was XOff.

csCode = 24

This call unconditionally sends an XOn character for input flow control, regardless of the current state of input flow control.

csCode = 25

This call sends an XOff character for input flow control if the last input flow control character sent was XOn.

csCode = 26

This call unconditionally sends an XOff character for input flow control, regardless of the current state of input flow control.

csCode = 27

This call lets you reset the SCC channel belonging to the driver specified by ioRefNum before calling RAMSDClose or SerReset.

SUMMARY OF THE SERIAL DRIVERS

Constants

```
CONST  { Driver reset information }

        baud300     =   380;      {300 baud}
        baud600     =   189;      {600 baud}
        baud1200    =   94;       {1200 baud}
        baud1800    =   62;       {1800 baud}
        baud2400    =   46;       {2400 baud}
        baud3600    =   30;       {3600 baud}
        baud4800    =   22;       {4800 baud}
        baud7200    =   14;       {7200 baud}
        baud9600    =   10;       {9600 baud}
        baud19200   =   4;        {19200 baud}
        baud57600   =   0;        {57600 baud}
        stop10      =   16384;    {1 stop bit}
        stop15      =   -32768;   {1.5 stop bits}
        stop20      =   -16384;   {2 stop bits}
        noParity    =   0;        {no parity}
        oddParity   =   4096;     {odd parity}
        evenParity  =   12288;    {even parity}
        data5       =   0;        {5 data bits}
        data6       =   2048;     {6 data bits}
        data7       =   1024;     {7 data bits}
        data8       =   3072;     {8 data bits}

        { Masks for errors }

        swOverrunErr = 1;    {set if software overrun error}
        parityErr    = 16;   {set if parity error}
        hwOverrunErr = 32;   {set if hardware overrun error}
        framingErr   = 64;   {set if framing error}

        { Masks for changes that cause events to be posted }

        ctsEvent    = 32;    {set if CTS change will cause event to be }
                             { posted}
        breakEvent  = 128;   {set if break status change will cause event }
                             { to be posted}

        { Indication that an XOff character was sent }

        xOffWasSent = $80;

        { Result codes }

        noErr   =   0;    {no error}
        openErr = -23;    {attempt to open RAM Serial Driver failed}
```

Data Types

```
TYPE  SPortSel = (sPortA,  {modem port}
                  sPortB   {printer port});

      SerShk = PACKED RECORD
                  fXOn: Byte;  {XOn/XOff output flow control flag}
                  fCTS: Byte;  {CTS hardware handshake flag}
                  xOn:  CHAR;  {XOn character}
                  xOff: CHAR;  {XOff character}
                  errs: Byte;  {errors that cause abort}
                  evts: Byte;  {status changes that cause events}
                  fInX: Byte;  {XOn/XOff input flow control flag}
                  null: Byte   {not used}
               END;

      SerStaRec = PACKED RECORD
                     cumErrs:  Byte;  {cumulative errors}
                     xOffSent: Byte;  {XOff sent as input flow control}
                     rdPend:   Byte;  {read pending flag}
                     wrPend:   Byte;  {write pending flag}
                     ctsHold:  Byte;  {CTS flow control hold flag}
                     xOffHold: Byte   {XOff flow control hold flag}
                  END;
```

Routines [Not in ROM]

Opening and Closing the RAM Serial Driver

```
FUNCTION  RAMSDOpen  (whichPort: SPortSel) : OSErr;
PROCEDURE RAMSDClose (whichPort: SPortSel);
```

Changing Serial Driver Information

```
FUNCTION SerReset  (refNum: INTEGER; serConfig: INTEGER) : OSErr;
FUNCTION SerSetBuf (refNum: INTEGER; serBPtr: Ptr; serBLen: INTEGER) :
                    OSErr;
FUNCTION SerHShake (refNum: INTEGER; flags: SerShk) : OSErr;
FUNCTION SerSetBrk (refNum: INTEGER) : OSErr;
FUNCTION SerClrBrk (refNum: INTEGER) : OSErr;
```

Getting Serial Driver Information

```
FUNCTION SerGetBuf (refNum: INTEGER; VAR count: LONGINT) : OSErr;
FUNCTION SerStatus (refNum: INTEGER; VAR serSta: SerStaRec) : OSErr;
```

9 Serial Drivers

Advanced Control Calls (RAM Serial Driver)

csCode	csParam	Effect
13	baudRate	Set baud rate (actual rate, as an integer)
19	char	Replace parity errors
21		Unconditionally set XOff for output flow control
22		Unconditionally clear XOff for input flow control
23		Send XOn for input flow control if XOff was sent last
24		Unconditionally send XOn for input flow control
25		Send XOff for input flow control if XOn was sent last
26		Unconditionally send XOff for input flow control
27		Reset SCC channel

Driver Names and Reference Numbers

Driver	Driver name	Reference number
Modem port input	.AIn	−6
Modem port output	.AOut	−7
Printer port input	.BIn	−8
Printer port output	.BOut	−9

Assembly-Language Information

Constants

```
; Result codes

noErr     .EQU   0     ;no error
openErr   .EQU   -23   ;attempt to open RAM Serial Driver failed
```

Structure of Control Information for SerHShake

shFXOn	XOn/XOff output flow control flag (byte)
shFCTS	CTS hardware handshake flag (byte)
shXOn	XOn character (byte)
shXOff	XOff character (byte)
shErrs	Errors that cause abort (byte)
shEvts	Status changes that cause events (byte)
shFInX	XOn/XOff input flow control flag (byte)

Structure of Status Information for SerStatus

ssCumErrs	Cumulative errors (byte)
ssXOffSent	XOff sent as input flow control (byte)
ssRdPend	Read pending flag (byte)
ssWrPend	Write pending flag (byte)
ssCTSHold	CTS flow control hold flag (byte)
ssXOffHold	XOff flow control hold flag (byte)

Equivalent Device Manager Calls

Pascal routine	Call
SerReset	Control with csCode=8, csParam=serConfig
SerSetBuf	Control with csCode=8, csParam=serBPtr, csParam+4=serBLen
SerHShake	Control with csCode=10, csParam through csParam+6=flags
SerSetBrk	Control with csCode=12
SerClrBrk	Control with csCode=11
SerGetBuf	Status with csCode=2; count returned in csParam
SerStatus	Status with csCode=8; serSta returned in csParam through csParam+5

10 THE APPLETALK MANAGER

ABOUT THIS CHAPTER

The AppleTalk Manager is an interface to a pair of RAM device drivers that allow Macintosh programs to send and receive information via an AppleTalk network. This chapter describes the AppleTalk Manager in detail.

You should already be familiar with:

■ events, as discussed in chapter 8 of Volume I

■ interrupts and the use of devices and device drivers, as described in chapter 6, if you want to write your own assembly-language additions to the AppleTalk Manager

■ the *Inside AppleTalk* manual, if you want to understand AppleTalk protocols in detail

APPLETALK PROTOCOLS

The AppleTalk Manager provides a variety of services that allow Macintosh programs to interact with programs in devices connected to an AppleTalk network. This interaction, achieved through the exchange of variable-length blocks of data (known as packets) over AppleTalk, follows well-defined sets of rules known as **protocols**.

Although most programmers using AppleTalk needn't understand the details of these protocols, they should understand the information in this section—what the services provided by the different protocols are, and how the protocols are interrelated. Detailed information about AppleTalk protocols is available in *Inside AppleTalk*.

The AppleTalk system architecture consists of a number of protocols arranged in layers. Each protocol in a specific layer provides services to higher-level layers (known as the protocol's clients) by building on the services provided by lower-level layers. A Macintosh program can use services provided by any of the layers in order to construct more sophisticated or more specialized services.

The AppleTalk Manager contains the following protocols:

■ AppleTalk Link Access Protocol

■ Datagram Delivery Protocol

■ Routing Table Maintenance Protocol

■ Name-Binding Protocol

■ AppleTalk Transaction Protocol

Figure 1 illustrates the layered structure of the protocols in the AppleTalk Manager; the heavy connecting lines indicate paths of interaction. Note that the Routing Table Maintenance Protocol isn't directly accessible to Macintosh programs.

The **AppleTalk Link Access Protocol** (ALAP) provides the lowest-level services of the AppleTalk system. Its main function is to control access to the AppleTalk network among various competing devices. Each device connected to an AppleTalk network, known as a **node**, is assigned an eight-bit **node ID** number that identifies the node. ALAP ensures that each node

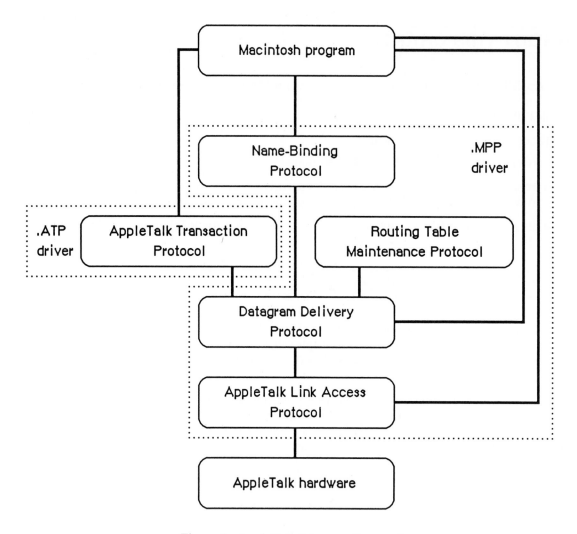

Figure 1. AppleTalk Manager Protocols

on an AppleTalk network has a unique node ID, assigned dynamically when the node is started up.

ALAP provides its clients with node-to-node delivery of data frames on a *single* AppleTalk network. An **ALAP frame** is a variable-length packet of data preceded and followed by control information referred to as the ALAP **frame header** and **frame trailer,** respectively. The ALAP frame header includes the node IDs of the frame's destination and source nodes. The AppleTalk hardware uses the destination node ID to deliver the frame. The frame's source node ID allows a program in the receiving node to determine the identity of the source. A sending node can ask ALAP to send a frame to all nodes on the AppleTalk network; this **broadcast service** is obtained by specifying a destination node ID of 255.

ALAP can have multiple clients in a single node. When a frame arrives at a node, ALAP determines which client it should be delivered to by reading the frame's **ALAP protocol type.** The ALAP protocol type is an eight-bit quantity, contained in the frame's header, that identifies the ALAP client to whom the frame will be sent. ALAP calls the client's **protocol handler,** which is a software process in the node that reads in and then services the frames. The protocol handlers for a node are listed in a **protocol handler table**.

An ALAP frame trailer contains a 16-bit **frame check sequence** generated by the AppleTalk hardware. The receiving node uses the frame check sequence to detect transmission errors, and discards frames with errors. In effect, a frame with an error is "lost" in the AppleTalk network, because ALAP doesn't attempt to recover from errors by requesting the sending node to retransmit such frames. Thus ALAP is said to make a "best effort" to deliver frames, without any guarantee of delivery.

An ALAP frame can contain up to 600 bytes of client data. The first two bytes must be an integer equal to the length of the client data (including the length bytes themselves).

Datagram Delivery Protocol (DDP) provides the next-higher level protocol in the AppleTalk architecture, managing socket-to-socket delivery of datagrams over AppleTalk internets. DDP is an ALAP client, and uses the node-to-node delivery service provided by ALAP to send and receive datagrams. **Datagrams** are packets of data transmitted by DDP. A DDP datagram can contain up to 586 bytes of client data. **Sockets** are logical entities within the nodes of a network; each socket within a given node has a unique eight-bit **socket number**.

On a single AppleTalk network, a socket is uniquely identified by its **AppleTalk address**—its socket number together with its node ID. To identify a socket in the scope of an AppleTalk internet, the socket's AppleTalk address and **network number** are needed. **Internets** are formed by interconnecting AppleTalk networks via intelligent nodes called **bridges**. A network number is a 16-bit number that uniquely identifies a network in an internet. A socket's AppleTalk address together with its network number provide an internet-wide unique socket identifier called an **internet address**.

Sockets are owned by **socket clients**, which typically are software processes in the node. Socket clients include code called the **socket listener**, which receives and services datagrams addressed to that socket. Socket clients must open a socket before datagrams can be sent or received through it. Each node contains a **socket table** that lists the listener for each open socket.

A datagram is sent from its source socket through a series of AppleTalk networks, being passed on from bridge to bridge, until it reaches its destination network. The ALAP in the destination network then delivers the datagram to the node containing the destination socket. Within that node the datagram is received by ALAP calling the DDP protocol handler, and by the DDP protocol handler in turn calling the destination socket listener, which for most applications will be a higher-level protocol such as the AppleTalk Transaction Protocol. You can't send a datagram between two sockets in the same node.

Bridges on AppleTalk internets use the **Routing Table Maintenance Protocol** (RTMP) to maintain **routing tables** for routing datagrams through the internet. In addition, nonbridge nodes use RTMP to determine the number of the network to which they're connected and the node ID of one bridge on their network. The RTMP code in nonbridge nodes contains only a subset of RTMP (the **RTMP stub**), and is a DDP client owning socket number 1 (the **RTMP socket**).

Socket clients are also known as **network-visible entities**, because they're the primary accessible entities on an internet. Network-visible entities can choose to identify themselves by an **entity name**, an identifier of the form

    object:type@zone

Each of the three fields of this name is an alphanumeric string of up to 32 characters. The object and type fields are arbitrary identifiers assigned by a socket client, to provide itself with a name and type descriptor (for example, abs:Mailbox). The zone field identifies the zone in which the socket client is located; a **zone** is an arbitrary subset of AppleTalk networks in an internet. A socket client can identify itself by as many different names as it chooses. These **aliases** are all treated as independent identifiers for the same socket client.

The **Name-Binding Protocol** (NBP) maintains a **names table** in each node that contains the name and internet address of each entity in *that* node. These name-address pairs are called **NBP tuples**. The collection of names tables in an internet is known as the **names directory**.

NBP allows its clients to add or delete their name-address tuples from the node's names table. It also allows its clients to obtain the internet addresses of entities from their names. This latter operation, known as **name lookup** (in the names directory), requires that NBP install itself as a DDP client and broadcast special name-lookup packets to the nodes in a specified zone. These datagrams are sent by NBP to the **names information socket**—socket number 2 in every node using NBP.

NBP clients can use special meta-characters in place of one or more of the three fields of the name of an entity it wishes to look up. The character "=" in the object or type field signifies "all possible values". The zone field can be replaced by "*", which signifies "this zone"—the zone in which the NBP client's node is located. For example, an NBP client performing a lookup with the name

    =:Mailbox@*

will obtain in return the entity names and internet addresses of all mailboxes in the client's zone (excluding the client's own names and addresses). The client can specify whether one or all of the matching names should be returned.

NBP clients specify how thorough a name lookup should be by providing NBP with the number of times (**retry count**) that NBP should broadcast the lookup packets and the time interval (**retry interval**) between these retries.

As noted above, ALAP and DDP provide "best effort" delivery services with no recovery mechanism when packets are lost or discarded because of errors. Although for many situations such a service suffices, the **AppleTalk Transaction Protocol** (ATP) provides a reliable loss-free transport service. ATP uses **transactions**, consisting of a **transaction request** and a **transaction response**, to deliver data reliably. Each transaction is assigned a 16-bit **transaction ID** number to distinguish it from other transactions. A transaction request is retransmitted by ATP until a complete response has been received, thus allowing for recovery from packet-loss situations. The retry interval and retry count are specified by the ATP client sending the request.

Although transaction requests must be contained in a single datagram, transaction responses can consist of as many as eight datagrams. Each datagram in a response is assigned a **sequence number** from 0 to 7, to indicate its ordering within the response.

ATP is a DDP client, and uses the services provided by DDP to transmit requests and responses. ATP supports both **at-least-once** and **exactly-once** transactions. Four of the bytes in an ATP header, called the **user bytes**, are provided for use by ATP's clients—they're ignored by ATP.

ATP's transaction model and means of recovering from datagram loss are covered in detail below.

APPLETALK TRANSACTION PROTOCOL

This section covers ATP in greater depth, providing more detail about three of its fundamental concepts: transactions, buffer allocation, and recovery of lost datagrams.

Transactions

A transaction is a interaction between two ATP clients, known as the requester and the responder. The requester calls the .ATP driver in its node to send a transaction request (TReq) to the responder, and then awaits a response. The TReq is received by the .ATP driver in the responder's node and is delivered to the responder. The responder then calls its .ATP driver to send back a transaction response (TResp), which is received by the requester's .ATP driver and delivered to the requester. Figure 2 illustrates this process.

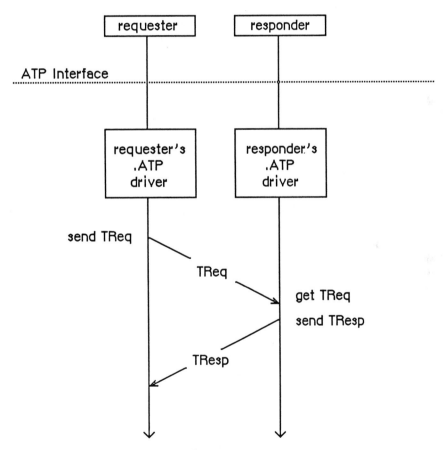

Figure 2. Transaction Process

Simple examples of transactions are:

- read a counter, reset it and send back the value read

- read six sectors of a disk and send back the data read

- write the data sent in the TReq to a printer

A basic assumption of the transaction model is that the amount of ATP data sent in the TReq specifying the operation to be performed is small enough to fit in a single datagram. A TResp, on the other hand, may span several datagrams, as in the second example. Thus, a TReq is a single datagram, while a TResp consists of up to eight datagrams, each of which is assigned a sequence number from 0 to 7 to indicate its position in the response.

The requester must, before calling for a TReq to be sent, set aside enough buffer space to receive the datagram(s) of the TResp. The number of buffers allocated (in other words, the maximum number of datagrams that the responder can send) is indicated in the TReq by an eight-bit bit map. The bits of this bit map are numbered 0 to 7 (the least significant bit being number 0); each bit corresponds to the response datagram with the respective sequence number.

Datagram Loss Recovery

The way that ATP recovers from datagram loss situations is best explained by an example; see Figure 3. Assume that the requester wants to read six sectors of 512 bytes each from the responder's disk. The requester puts aside six 512-byte buffers (which may or may not be contiguous) for the response datagrams, and calls ATP to send a TReq. In this TReq the bit map is set to binary 00111111 or decimal 63. The TReq carries a 16-bit transaction ID, generated by the requester's .ATP driver before sending it. (This example assumes that the requester and responder have already agreed that each buffer can hold 512 bytes.) The TReq is delivered to the responder, which reads the six disk sectors and sends them back, through ATP, in TResp datagrams bearing sequence numbers 0 through 5. Each TResp datagram also carries exactly the same transaction ID as the TReq to which they're responding.

There are several ways that datagrams may be lost in this case. The original TReq could be lost for one of many reasons. The responding node might be too busy to receive the TReq or might be out of buffers for receiving it, there could be an undetected collision on the network, a bit error in the transmission line, and so on. To recover from such errors, the requester's .ATP driver maintains an ATP retry timer for each transaction sent. If this timer expires and the complete TResp has not been received, the TReq is retransmitted and the retry timer is restarted.

A second error situation occurs when one or more of the TResp datagrams isn't received correctly by the requester's .ATP driver (datagram 1 in Figure 3). Again, the retry timer will expire and the complete TResp will not have been received; this will result in a retransmission of the TReq. However, to avoid unnecessary retransmission of the TResp datagrams already properly received, the bit map of this retransmitted TReq is modified to reflect only those datagrams not yet received. Upon receiving this TReq, the responder retransmits only the missing response datagrams.

Another possible failure is that the responder's .ATP driver goes down or the responder becomes unreachable through the underlying network system. In this case, retransmission of the TReq could continue indefinitely. To avoid this situation, the requester provides a maximum retry count; if this count is exceeded, the requester's .ATP driver returns an appropriate error message to the requester.

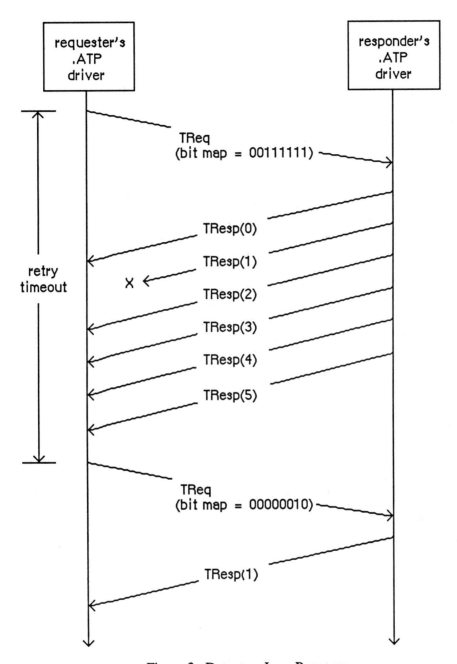

Figure 3. Datagram Loss Recovery

Note: There may be situations where, due to an anticipated delay, you'll want a request to be retransmitted more than 255 times; specifying a retry count of 255 indicates "infinite retries" to ATP and will cause a message to be retransmitted until the request has either been serviced, or been cancelled through a specific call.

Finally, in our example, what if the responder is able to provide only four disk sectors (having reached the end of the disk) instead of the six requested? To handle this situation, there's an end-of-message (EOM) flag in each TResp datagram. In this case, the TResp datagram numbered 3 would come with this flag set. The reception of this datagram informs the requester's .ATP driver that TResps numbered 4 and 5 will not be sent and should not be expected.

When the transaction completes successfully (all expected TResp datagrams are received or TResp datagrams numbered 0 to n are received with datagram n's EOM flag set), the requester is informed and can then use the data received in the TResp.

ATP provides two classes of service: at-least-once (ALO) and exactly-once (XO). The TReq datagram contains an XO flag that's set if XO service is required and cleared if ALO service is adequate. The main difference between the two is in the sequence of events that occurs when the TReq is received by the responder's .ATP driver.

In the case of ALO service, each time a TReq is received (with the XO flag cleared), it's delivered to the responder by its .ATP driver; this is true even for retransmitted TReqs of the same transaction. Each time the TReq is delivered, the responder performs the requested operation and sends the necessary TResp datagrams. Thus, the requested operation is performed at least once, and perhaps several times, until the transaction is completed at the requester's end.

The at-least-once service is satisfactory in a variety of situations—for instance, if the requester wishes to read a clock or a counter being maintained at the responder's end. However, in other circumstances, repeated execution of the requested operation is unacceptable. This is the case, for instance, if the requester is sending data to be printed at the responding end; exactly-once service is designed for such situations.

The responder's .ATP driver maintains a transactions list of recently received XO TReqs. Whenever a TReq is received with its XO flag set, the driver goes through this list to see if this is a retransmitted TReq. If it's the first TReq of a transaction, it's entered into the list and delivered to the responder. The responder executes the requested operation and calls its driver to send a TResp. Before sending it out, the .ATP driver *saves* the TResp in the list.

When a retransmitted TReq for the same XO transaction is received, the responder's .ATP driver will find a corresponding entry in the list. The retransmitted TReq is *not* delivered to the responder; instead, the driver automatically retransmits the response datagrams that were saved in the list. In this way, the responder never sees the retransmitted TReqs and the requested operation is performed only once.

ATP must include a mechanism for eventually removing XO entries from the responding end's transaction list; two provisions are made for this. When the requester's .ATP driver has received all the TResp datagrams of a particular transaction, it sends a datagram known as a transaction release (TRel); this tells the responder's .ATP driver to remove the transaction from the list. However, the TRel could be lost in the network (or the responding end may die, and so on), leaving the entry in the list forever. To account for this situation, the responder's .ATP driver maintains a **release timer** for each transaction. If this timer expires and no activity has occurred for the transaction, its entry is removed from the transactions list.

the Macintosh and confirms that the node ID isn't already being used by another node on the network.

> **Warning:** For this reason it's imperative that the Macintosh be connected to the AppleTalk network through serial port B (the printer port) *before* being switched on.

The AppleTalk Manager also provides Pascal routines for opening and closing the .MPP and .ATP drivers. The open calls allow a program to load AppleTalk code at times other than system startup. The close calls allow a program to remove the AppleTalk code from the Macintosh; the use of close calls is highly discouraged, since other co-resident programs are then "disconnected" from AppleTalk. Both sets of calls are described in detail under "Calling the AppleTalk Manager from Pascal".

> **Warning:** If, at system startup, serial port B isn't available for use by AppleTalk, the .MPP driver won't open. However, a driver doesn't return an error message when it fails to open. Pascal programmers must ensure the proper opening of AppleTalk by calling one of the two routines for opening the AppleTalk drivers (either MPPOpen or ATPLoad). If AppleTalk was successfully loaded at system startup, these calls will have no effect; otherwise they'll check the availability of port B, attempt to load the AppleTalk code, and return an appropriate result code.

> **Assembly-language note:** Assembly-language programmers can use the Pascal routines for opening AppleTalk. They can also check the availability of port B themselves and then decide whether to open MPP or ATP. Detailed information on how to do this is provided in the section "Calling the AppleTalk Manager from Assembly Language".

CALLING THE APPLETALK MANAGER FROM PASCAL

This section discusses how to use the AppleTalk Manager from Pascal. Equivalent assembly-language information is given in the next section.

You can execute many AppleTalk Manager routines either **synchronously** (meaning that the application can't continue until the routine is completed) or **asynchronously** (meaning that the application is free to perform other tasks while the routine is being executed).

When an application calls an AppleTalk Manager routine asynchronously, an I/O request is placed in the appropriate driver's I/O queue, and control returns to the calling program—possibly even before the actual I/O is completed. Requests are taken from the queue one at a time, and processed; meanwhile, the calling program is free to work on other things.

The routines that can be executed asynchronously contain a Boolean parameter called async. If async is TRUE, the call is executed asynchronously; otherwise the call is executed synchronously. Every time an asynchronous routine call is completed, the AppleTalk Manager posts a network event. The message field of the event record will contain a handle to the parameter block that was used to make that call.

Most AppleTalk Manager routines return an integer result code of type OSErr. Each routine description lists all of the applicable result codes generated by the AppleTalk Manager, along with a short description of what the result code means. Lengthier explanations of all the result codes can be found in the summary at the end of the chapter. Result codes from other parts of the

Operating System may also be returned. (See Appendix A in Volume III for a list of all result codes.)

Many Pascal calls to the AppleTalk Manager require information passed in a parameter block of type ABusRecord. The exact content of an ABusRecord depends on the protocol being called:

```
TYPE ABProtoType = (lapProto,ddpProto,nbpProto,atpProto);

     ABusRecord  = RECORD
                       abOpcode:        ABCallType; {type of call}
                       abResult:        INTEGER;    {result code}
                       abUserReference: LONGINT;    {for your use}
                       CASE ABProtoType OF
                         lapProto:
                           . . .  {ALAP parameters}
                         ddpProto:
                           . . .  {DDP parameters}
                         nbpProto:
                           . . .  {NBP parameters}
                         atpProto:
                           . . .  {ATP parameters}
                       END;
                   END;

     ABRecPtr    = ^ABusRecord;
     ABRecHandle = ^ABRecPtr;
```

The value of the abOpcode field is inserted by the AppleTalk Manager when the call is made, and is always a member of the following set:

```
TYPE ABCallType = (tLAPRead,tLAPWrite,tDDPRead,tDDPWrite,tNBPLookup,
                   tNBPConfirm,tNBPRegister,tATPSndRequest,
                   tATPGetRequest,tATPSdRsp,tATPAddRsp,tATPRequest,
                   tATPRespond);
```

The abUserReference field is available for use by the calling program in any way it wants. This field isn't used by the AppleTalk Manager routines or drivers.

The size of an ABusRecord data structure in bytes is given by one of the following constants:

```
CONST lapSize = 20;
      ddpSize = 26;
      nbpSize = 26;
      atpSize = 56;
```

Variables of type ABusRecord must be allocated in the heap with Memory Manager NewHandle calls. For example:

```
myABRecord := ABRecHandle(NewHandle(ddpSize))
```

Warning: These Memory Manager calls can't be made inside interrupts.

Routines that are executed asynchronously return control to the calling program with the result code noErr as soon as the call is placed in the driver's I/O queue. This isn't an indication of successful call completion; it simply indicates that the call was successfully queued to the appropriate driver. To determine when the call is actually completed, you can either check for a network event or poll the abResult field of the call's ABusRecord. The abResult field, set to 1 when the call is made, receives the actual result code upon completion of the call.

> **Warning:** A data structure of type ABusRecord is often used by the AppleTalk Manager during an asynchronous call, and so is locked by the AppleTalk Manager. Don't attempt to unlock or use such a variable.

Each routine description includes a list of the ABusRecord fields affected by the routine. The arrow next to each field name indicates whether it's an input, output, or input/output parameter:

Arrow	Meaning
→	Parameter is passed to the routine
←	Parameter is returned by the routine
↔	Parameter is passed to and returned by the routine

Opening and Closing AppleTalk

```
FUNCTION MPPOpen : OSErr;    [Not in ROM]
```

MPPOpen first checks whether the .MPP driver has already been loaded; if it has, MPPOpen does nothing and returns noErr. If MPP hasn't been loaded, MPPOpen attempts to load it into the system heap. If it succeeds, it then initializes the driver's variables and goes through the process of dynamically assigning a node ID to that Macintosh. On a Macintosh 512K or XL, it also loads the .ATP driver and NBP code into the system heap.

If serial port B isn't configured for AppleTalk, or is already in use, the .MPP driver isn't loaded and an appropriate result code is returned.

Result codes	noErr	No error
	portInUse	Port B is already in use
	portNotCf	Port B not configured for AppleTalk

```
FUNCTION MPPClose : OSErr;    [Not in ROM]
```

MPPClose removes the .MPP driver, and any data structures associated with it, from memory. If the .ATP driver or NBP code were also installed, they're removed as well. MPPClose also returns the use of port B to the Serial Driver.

> **Warning:** Since other co-resident programs may be using AppleTalk, it's strongly recommended that you never use this call. MPPClose will completely disable AppleTalk; the only way to restore AppleTalk is to call MPPOpen again.

AppleTalk Link Access Protocol

Data Structures

ALAP calls use the following ABusRecord fields:

```
lapProto:
  (lapAddress:   LAPAdrBlock; {destination or source node ID}
   lapReqCount:  INTEGER;    {length of frame data or buffer size in bytes}
   lapActCount:  INTEGER;    {number of frame data bytes actually received}
   lapDataPtr:   Ptr);       {pointer to frame data or pointer to buffer}
```

When an ALAP frame is sent, the lapAddress field indicates the ID of the destination node. When an ALAP frame is received, lapAddress returns the ID of the source node. The lapAddress field also indicates the ALAP protocol type of the frame:

```
TYPE LAPAdrBlock =  PACKED RECORD
                      dstNodeID:   Byte;    {destination node ID}
                      srcNodeID:   Byte;    {source node ID}
                      lapProtType: ABByte   {ALAP protocol type}
                    END;
```

When an ALAP frame is sent, lapReqCount indicates the size of the frame data in bytes and lapDataPtr points to a buffer containing the frame data to be sent. When an ALAP frame is received, lapDataPtr points to a buffer in which the incoming data can be stored and lapReqCount indicates the size of the buffer in bytes. The number of bytes actually sent or received is returned in the lapActCount field.

Each ALAP frame contains an eight-bit ALAP protocol type in the header. ALAP protocol types 128 through 255 are reserved for internal use by ALAP, hence the declaration:

```
TYPE ABByte = 1..127;   {ALAP protocol type}
```

Warning: Don't use ALAP protocol type values 1 and 2; they're reserved for use by DDP. Value 3 through 15 are reserved for internal use by Apple and also shouldn't be used.

Using ALAP

Most programs will never need to call ALAP, because higher-level protocols will automatically call it as necessary. If you do want to send a frame directly via ALAP, call the LAPWrite function. If you want to read ALAP frames, you have two choices:

■ Call LAPOpenProtocol with NIL for protoPtr (see below); this installs the default protocol handler provided by the AppleTalk Manager. Then call LAPRead to receive frames.

■ Write your own protocol handler, and call LAPOpenProtocol to add it to the node's protocol handler table. The ALAP code will examine every incoming frame and send all those with the correct ALAP protocol type to your protocol handler. See the section "Protocol Handlers and Socket Listeners" for information on how to write a protocol handler.

When your program no longer wants to receive frames with a particular ALAP protocol type value, it can call LAPCloseProtocol to remove the corresponding protocol handler from the protocol handler table.

ALAP Routines

```
FUNCTION LAPOpenProtocol (theLAPType: ABByte; protoPtr: Ptr) :
         OSErr;   [Not in ROM]
```

LAPOpenProtocol adds the ALAP protocol type specified by theLAPType to the node's protocol table. If you provide a pointer to a protocol handler in protoPtr, ALAP will send each frame with an ALAP protocol type of theLAPType to that protocol handler.

If protoPtr is NIL, the default protocol handler will be used for receiving frames with an ALAP protocol type of theLAPType. In this case, to receive a frame you must call LAPRead to provide the default protocol handler with a buffer for placing the data. If, however, you've written your own protocol handler and protoPtr points to it, your protocol handler will have the responsibility for receiving the frame and it's not necessary to call LAPRead.

Result codes	noErr	No error
	lapProtErr	Error attaching protocol type

```
FUNCTION LAPCloseProtocol (theLAPType: ABByte) : OSErr;   [Not in
         ROM]
```

LAPCloseProtocol removes from the node's protocol table the specified ALAP protocol type, as well as its protocol handler.

Warning: Don't close ALAP protocol type values 1 or 2. If you close these protocol types, DDP will be disabled; once disabled, the only way to restore DDP is to restart the system, or to close and then reopen AppleTalk.

Result codes	noErr	No error
	lapProtErr	Error detaching protocol type

```
FUNCTION LAPWrite (abRecord: ABRecHandle; async: BOOLEAN) :
         OSErr;   [Not in ROM]
```

ABusRecord

←	abOpcode	{always tLAPWrite}
←	abResult	{result code}
→	abUserReference	{for your use}
→	lapAddress.dstNodeID	{destination node ID}
→	lapAddress.lapProtType	{ALAP protocol type}
→	lapReqCount	{length of frame data}
→	lapDataPtr	{pointer to frame data}

LAPWrite sends a frame to another node. LAPReqCount and lapDataPtr specify the length and location of the data to send. The lapAddress.lapProtType field indicates the ALAP protocol type of the frame and the lapAddress.dstNodeID indicates the node ID of the node to which the frame should be sent.

Note: The first two bytes of an ALAP frame's data must contain the length in bytes of that data, including the length bytes themselves.

Result codes	noErr	No error
	excessCollsns	Unable to contact destination node; packet not sent
	ddpLenErr	ALAP data length too big
	lapProtErr	Invalid ALAP protocol type

```
FUNCTION LAPRead (abRecord: ABRecHandle; async: BOOLEAN) : OSErr;
         [Not in ROM]
```

ABusRecord

←	abOpcode	{always tLAPRead}
←	abResult	{result code}
→	abUserReference	{for your use}
←	lapAddress.dstNodeID	{destination node ID}
←	lapAddress.srcNodeID	{source node ID}
→	lapAddress.lapProtType	{ALAP protocol type}
→	lapReqCount	{buffer size in bytes}
←	lapActCount	{number of frame data bytes actually received}
→	lapDataPtr	{pointer to buffer}

LAPRead receives a frame from another node. LAPReqCount and lapDataPtr specify the size and location of the buffer that will receive the frame data. If the buffer isn't large enough to hold all of the incoming frame data, the extra bytes will be discarded and buf2SmallErr will be returned. The number of bytes actually received is returned in lapActCount. Only frames with ALAP protocol type equal to lapAddress.lapProtType will be received. The node IDs of the frame's source and destination nodes are returned in lapAddress.srcNodeID and lapAddress.dstNodeID. You can determine whether the packet was broadcast to you by examining the value of lapAddress.dstNodeID—if the packet was broadcast it's equal to 255, otherwise it's equal to your node ID.

Note: You should issue LAPRead calls only for ALAP protocol types that were opened (via LAPOpenProtocol) to use the default protocol handler.

Warning: If you close a protocol type for which there are still LAPRead calls pending, the calls will be canceled but the memory occupied by their ABusRecords will not be released. For this reason, before closing a protocol type, call LAPRdCancel to cancel any pending LAPRead calls associated with that protocol type.

Result codes	noErr	No error
	buf2SmallErr	Frame too large for buffer
	readQErr	Invalid protocol type or protocol type not found in table

```
FUNCTION LAPRdCancel (abRecord: ABRecHandle) : OSErr;    [Not in ROM]
```

Given the handle to the ABusRecord of a previously made LAPRead call, LAPRdCancel
dequeues the LAPRead call, provided that a packet satisfying the LAPRead has not already
arrived. LAPRdCancel returns noErr if the LAPRead call is successfully removed from the
queue. If LAPRdCancel returns recNotFnd, check the abResult field to verify that the LAPRead
has been completed and determine its outcome.

Result codes	noErr	No error
	readQErr	Invalid protocol type or protocol type not found in table
	recNotFnd	ABRecord not found in queue

Example

This example sends an ALAP packet synchronously and waits asynchronously for a response.
Assume that both nodes are using a known protocol type (in this case, 73) to receive packets, and
that the destination node has a node ID of 4.

```
VAR myABRecord: ABRecHandle;
    myBuffer: PACKED ARRAY[0..599] OF CHAR; {buffer for both send and }
                                            { receive}

    myLAPType: Byte;
    errCode,index,dataLen: INTEGER;
    someText: Str255;
    async: BOOLEAN;

BEGIN
errCode := MPPOpen;
IF errCode <> noErr
   THEN
     WRITELN('Error in opening AppleTalk')
     {Maybe serial port B isn't available for use by AppleTalk}
   ELSE
     BEGIN
     {Call Memory Manager to allocate ABusRecord}
     myABRecord := ABRecHandle(NewHandle(lapSize));
     myLAPType := 73;
     {Enter myLAPType into protocol handler table and install default }
     { handler to service frames of that ALAP type.  No packets of }
     { that ALAP type will be received until we call LAPRead.}
     errCode := LAPOpenProtocol(myLAPType,NIL);
     IF errCode <> noErr
       THEN
         WRITELN('Error while opening the protocol type')
         {Have we opened too many protocol types?  Remember that DDP }
         { uses two of them.}
       ELSE
         BEGIN
         {Prepare data to be sent}
         someText := 'This data will be in the ALAP data area';
```

```
{The .MPP implementation requires that the first two bytes }
{ of the ALAP data field contain the length of the data, }
{ including the length bytes themselves.}
dataLen := LENGTH(someText)+2;
buffer[0] := CHR(dataLen DIV 256); {high byte of data length}
buffer[1] := CHR(dataLen MOD 256); {low byte of data length}
FOR index := 1 TO dataLen-2 DO {stuff buffer with packet data}
  buffer[index+1] := someText[index];
async := FALSE;
WITH myABRecord^^ DO    {fill parameters in the ABusRecord}
  BEGIN
  lapAddress.lapProtType := myLAPType;
  lapAddress.dstNodeID := 4;
  lapReqCount := dataLen;
  lapDataPtr := @buffer;
  END;
{Send the frame}
errCode := LAPWrite(myABRecord,async);
{In the case of a sync call, errCode and the abResult field of }
{ the myABRecord will contain the same result code.  We can also }
{ reuse myABRecord, since we know whether the call has completed.}
IF errCode <> noErr
  THEN
    WRITELN('Error while writing out the packet')
    {Maybe the receiving node wasn't on-line}
  ELSE
    BEGIN
    {We have sent out the packet and are now waiting for a }
    { response.  We issue an async LAPRead call so that we don't }
    { "hang" waiting for a response that may not come.}
    async := TRUE;
    WITH myABRecord^^ DO
      BEGIN
      lapAddress.lapProtType := myLAPType; {ALAP type we want }
                                           { to receive}
      lapReqCount := 600;  {our buffer is maximum size}
      lapDataPtr := @buffer;
      END;
    errCode := LAPRead(myABRecord,async);    {wait for a packet}
    IF errCode <> noErr
      THEN
        WRITELN('Error while trying to queue up a LAPRead')
        {Was the protocol handler installed correctly?}
      ELSE
        BEGIN
        {We can either sit here in a loop and poll the abResult }
        { field or just exit our code and use the event }
        { mechanism to flag us when the packet arrives.}
        CheckForMyEvent;   {your procedure for checking for a }
                           { network event}
        errCode := LAPCloseProtocol(myLAPType);
```

```
                        IF errCode <> noErr
                          THEN
                            WRITELN('Error while closing the protocol type');
                      END;
                  END;
              END;
          END;
  END.
```

Datagram Delivery Protocol

Data Structures

DDP calls use the following ABusRecord fields:

```
ddpProto:
   (ddpType:      Byte;        {DDP protocol type}
    ddpSocket:    Byte;        {source or listening socket number}
    ddpAddress:   AddrBlock;   {destination or source socket address}
    ddpReqCount:  INTEGER;     {length of datagram data or buffer size }
                               { in bytes}
    ddpActCount:  INTEGER;     {number of bytes actually received}
    ddpDataPtr:   Ptr;         {pointer to buffer}
    ddpNodeID:    Byte);       {original destination node ID}
```

When a DDP datagram is sent, ddpReqCount indicates the size of the datagram data in bytes and ddpDataPtr points to a buffer containing the datagram data. DDPSocket specifies the socket from which the datagram should be sent. DDPAddress is the internet address of the socket to which the datagram should be sent:

```
TYPE AddrBlock =  PACKED RECORD
                    aNet:    INTEGER;    {network number}
                    aNode:   Byte;       {node ID}
                    aSocket: Byte        {socket number}
                  END;
```

Note: The network number you specify in ddpAddress.aNet tells MPP whether to create a long header (for an internet) or a short header (for a local network only). A short DDP header will be sent if ddpAddress.aNet is 0 or equal to the network number of the local network.

When a DDP datagram is received, ddpDataPtr points to a buffer in which the incoming data can be stored and ddpReqCount indicates the size of the buffer in bytes. The number of bytes actually sent or received is returned in the ddpActCount field. DDPAddress is the internet address of the socket from which the datagram was sent.

DDPType is the DDP protocol type of the datagram, and ddpSocket specifies the socket that will receive the datagram.

Warning: DDP protocol types 1 through 15 and DDP socket numbers 1 through 63 are reserved by Apple for internal use. Socket numbers 64 through 127 are available for experimental use. Use of these experimental sockets isn't recommended for commercial products, since there's no mechanism for eliminating conflicting usage by different developers.

Using DDP

Before it can use a socket, the program must call DDPOpenSocket, which adds a socket and its socket listener to the socket table. When a program is finished using a socket, call DDPCloseSocket, which removes the socket's entry from the socket table. To send a datagram via DDP, call DDPWrite. To receive datagrams, you have two choices:

■ Call DDPOpenSocket with NIL for sktListener (see below); this installs the default socket listener provided by the AppleTalk Manager. Then call DDPRead to receive datagrams.

■ Write your own socket listener and call DDPOpenSocket to install it. DDP will call your socket listener for every incoming datagram for that socket; in this case, you shouldn't call DDPRead. For information on how to write a socket listener, see the section "Protocol Handlers and Socket Listeners".

To cancel a previously issued DDPRead call (provided it's still in the queue), call DDPRdCancel.

DDP Routines

```
FUNCTION DDPOpenSocket (VAR theSocket: Byte; sktListener: Ptr) :
        OSErr;   [Not in ROM]
```

DDPOpenSocket adds a socket and its socket listener to the socket table. If theSocket is nonzero, it must be in the range 64 to 127, and it specifies the socket's number; if theSocket is 0, DDPOpenSocket dynamically assigns a socket number in the range 128 to 254, and returns it in theSocket. SktListener contains a pointer to the socket listener; if it's NIL, the default listener will be used.

If you're using the default socket listener, you must then call DDPRead to receive a datagram (in order to specify buffer space for the default socket listener). If, however, you've written your own socket listener and sktListener points to it, your listener will provide buffers for receiving datagrams and you shouldn't use DDPRead calls.

DDPOpenSocket will return ddpSktErr if you pass the number of an already opened socket, if you pass a socket number greater than 127, or if the socket table is full.

> **Note:** The range of static socket numbers 1 through 63 is reserved by Apple for internal use. Socket numbers 64 through 127 are available for unrestricted experimental use.

Result codes   noErr   No error
                           ddpSktErr   Socket error

```
FUNCTION DDPCloseSocket (theSocket: Byte) : OSErr;   [Not in ROM]
```

DDPCloseSocket removes the entry of the specified socket from the socket table and cancels all pending DDPRead calls that have been made for that socket. If you pass a socket number of 0, or if you attempt to close a socket that isn't open, DDPCloseSocket will return ddpSktErr.

Result codes   noErr   No error
                             ddpSktErr   Socket error

```
FUNCTION DDPWrite (abRecord: ABRecHandle; doChecksum: BOOLEAN;
        async: BOOLEAN) : OSErr;   [Not in ROM]
```

ABusRecord

←	abOpcode	{always tDDPWrite}
←	abResult	{result code}
→	abUserReference	{for your use}
→	ddpType	{DDP protocol type}
→	ddpSocket	{source socket number}
→	ddpAddress	{destination socket address}
→	ddpReqCount	{length of datagram data}
→	ddpDataPtr	{pointer to buffer}

DDPWrite sends a datagram to another socket. DDPReqCount and ddpDataPtr specify the length and location of the data to send. The ddpType field indicates the DDP protocol type of the frame, and ddpAddress is the complete internet address of the socket to which the datagram should be sent. DDPSocket specifies the socket from which the datagram should be sent. Datagrams sent over the internet to a node on an AppleTalk network different from the sending node's network have an optional software checksum to detect errors that might occur inside the intermediate bridges. If doChecksum is TRUE, DDPWrite will compute this checksum; if it's FALSE, this software checksum feature is ignored.

Note: The destination socket can't be in the same node as the program making the DDPWrite call.

Result codes   noErr   No error
                            ddpLenErr   Datagram length too big
                            ddpSktErr   Source socket not open
                            noBridgeErr   No bridge found

```
FUNCTION DDPRead (abRecord: ABRecHandle; retCksumErrs: BOOLEAN;
        async: BOOLEAN) : OSErr;   [Not in ROM]
```

ABusRecord

←	abOpcode	{always tDDPRead}
←	abResult	{result code}
→	abUserReference	{for your use}
←	ddpType	{DDP protocol type}
→	ddpSocket	{listening socket number}
←	ddpAddress	{source socket address}
→	ddpReqCount	{buffer size in bytes}
←	ddpActCount	{number of bytes actually received}
→	ddpDataPtr	{pointer to buffer}
←	ddpNodeID	{original destination node ID}

DDPRead receives a datagram from another socket. The size and location of the buffer that will receive the data are specified by ddpReqCount and ddpDataPtr. If the buffer isn't large enough to hold all of the incoming frame data, the extra bytes will be discarded and buf2SmallErr will be returned. The number of bytes actually received is returned in ddpActCount. DDPSocket specifies the socket to receive the datagram (the "listening" socket). The node to which the packet was sent is returned in ddpNodeID; if the packet was broadcast ddpNodeID will contain 255. The address of the socket that sent the packet is returned in ddpAddress. If retCksumErrs is FALSE, DDPRead will discard any packets received with an invalid checksum and inform the caller of the error. If retCksumErrs is TRUE, DDPRead will deliver all packets, whether or not the checksum is valid; it will also notify the caller when there's a checksum error.

Note: The sender of the datagram must be in a different node from the receiver. You should issue DDPRead calls only for receiving datagrams for sockets opened with the default socket listener; see the description of DDPOpenSocket.

Note: If the buffer provided isn't large enough to hold all of the incoming frame data (buf2SmallErr), the checksum can't be calculated; in this case, DDPRead will deliver packets even if retCksumErrs is FALSE.

Result codes	noErr	No error
	buf2SmallErr	Datagram too large for buffer
	cksumErr	Checksum error
	ddpLenErr	Datagram length too big
	ddpSktErr	Socket error
	readQErr	Invalid socket or socket not found in table

```
FUNCTION DDPRdCancel (abRecord: ABRecHandle) : OSErr;    [Not in ROM]
```

Given the handle to the ABusRecord of a previously made DDPRead call, DDPRdCancel dequeues the DDPRead call, provided that a packet satisfying the DDPRead hasn't already arrived. DDPRdCancel returns noErr if the DDPRead call is successfully removed from the queue. If DDPRdCancel returns recNotFnd, check the abResult field of abRecord to verify that the DDPRead has been completed and determine its outcome.

Result codes	noErr	No error
	readQErr	Invalid socket or socket not found in table
	recNotFnd	ABRecord not found in queue

Example

This example sends a DDP packet synchronously and waits asynchronously for a response. Assume that both nodes are using a known socket number (in this case, 30) to receive packets. Normally, you would want to use NBP to look up your destination's socket address.

```
    VAR myABRecord: ABRecHandle;
        myBuffer: PACKED ARRAY[0..599] OF CHAR;      {buffer for both send and }
                                                     { receive}

        mySocket: Byte;
        errCode,index,dataLen: INTEGER;
        someText: Str255;
        async,retCksumErrs,doChecksum: BOOLEAN;

BEGIN
errCode := MPPOpen;
IF errCode <> noErr
  THEN
      WRITELN('Error in opening AppleTalk')
      {Maybe serial port B isn't available for use by AppleTalk}
  ELSE
      BEGIN
      {Call Memory Manager to allocate ABusRecord}
      myABRecord := ABRecHandle(NewHandle(ddpSize));
      mySocket := 30;
      {Add mySocket to socket table and install default socket listener }
      { to service datagrams addressed to that socket.  No packets }
      { addressed to mySocket will be received until we call DDPRead.}
      errCode := DDPOpenSocket(mySocket,NIL);
IF errCode <> noErr
  THEN
      WRITELN('Error while opening the socket')
      {Have we opened too many socket listeners?  Remember that DDP }
      { uses two of them.}
  ELSE
      BEGIN
      {Prepare data to be sent}
      someText := 'This is a sample datagram';
      dataLen := LENGTH(someText);
      FOR index := 0 TO dataLen-1 DO  {stuff buffer with packet data}
         myBuffer[index] := someText[index+1];
      async := FALSE;
      WITH myABRecord^^ DO  {fill the parameters in the ABusRecord}
         BEGIN
         ddpType := 5;
         ddpAddress.aNet := 0;   {send on "our" network}
         ddpAddress.aNode := 34;
         ddpAddress.aSocket := mySocket;
         ddpReqCount := dataLen;
         ddpDataPtr := @myBuffer;
         END;
      doChecksum := FALSE;
      {If packet contains a DDP long header, compute checksum and insert }
      { it into the header.}
      errCode := DDPWrite(myABRecord,doChecksum,async); {send packet}
      {In the case of a sync call, errCode and the abResult field of }
      { myABRecord will contain the same result code.  We can also reuse }
      { myABRecord, since we know whether the call has completed.}
```

```
    IF errCode <> noErr
        THEN
            WRITELN('Error while writing out the packet')
            {Maybe the receiving node wasn't on-line}
        ELSE
        BEGIN
        {We have sent out the packet and are now waiting for a }
        { response.  We issue an async DDPRead call so that we }
        { don't "hang" waiting for a response that may not come. }
        { To cancel the async read call, we must close the socket }
        { associated with the call or call DDPRdCancel.}
        async := TRUE;
        retCksumErrs := TRUE;   {return packets even if they have a }
                                { checksum error}
        WITH myABRecord^^ DO
            BEGIN
            ddpSocket := mySocket;
            ddpReqCount := 600; {our reception buffer is max size}
            ddpDataPtr := @myBuffer;
            END;
        {Wait for a packet asynchronously}
        errCode := DDPRead(myABRecord,retCksumErrs,async);
        IF errCode <> noErr
            THEN
                WRITELN('Error while trying to queue up a DDPRead')
                {Was the socket listener installed correctly?}
            ELSE
                BEGIN
                {We can either sit here in a loop and poll the }
                { abResult field or just exit our code and use the }
                { event mechanism to flag us when the packet arrives.}
                CheckForMyEvent;  {your procedure for checking for a }
                                  { network event}
                {If there were no errors, a packet is inside the array }
                { mybuffer, the length is in ddpActCount, and the }
                { address of the sending socket is in ddpAddress. }
                { Process the packet received here and report any errors.}
                errCode := DDPCloseSocket(mySocket); {we're done with it}
                IF errCode <> noErr
                    THEN
                        WRITELN('Error while closing the socket');
                END;
            END;
        END;
    END;
END.
```

AppleTalk Transaction Protocol

Data Structures

ATP calls use the following ABusRecord fields:

```
atpProto:
 (atpSocket:      Byte;         {listening or responding socket number}
  atpAddress:     AddrBlock;    {destination or source socket address}
  atpReqCount:    INTEGER;      {request size or buffer size}
  atpDataPtr:     Ptr;          {pointer to buffer}
  atpRspBDSPtr:   BDSPtr;       {pointer to response BDS}
  atpBitMap:      BitMapType;   {transaction bit map}
  atpTransID:     INTEGER;      {transaction ID}
  atpActCount:    INTEGER;      {number of bytes actually received}
  atpUserData:    LONGINT;      {user bytes}
  atpXO:          BOOLEAN;      {exactly-once flag}
  atpEOM:         BOOLEAN;      {end-of-message flag}
  atpTimeOut:     Byte;         {retry timeout interval in seconds}
  atpRetries:     Byte;         {maximum number of retries}
  atpNumBufs:     Byte;         {number of elements in response BDS or }
                                { number of response packets sent}
  atpNumRsp:      Byte;         {number of response packets received or }
                                { sequence number}
  atpBDSSize:     Byte;         {number of elements in response BDS}
  atpRspUData:    LONGINT;      {user bytes sent or received in transaction }
                                { response}
  atpRspBuf:      Ptr;          {pointer to response message buffer}
  atpRspSize:     INTEGER);     {size of response message buffer}
```

The socket receiving the request or sending the response is identified by atpSocket. ATPAddress is the address of either the destination or the source socket of a transaction, depending on whether the call is sending or receiving data, respectively. ATPDataPtr and atpReqCount specify the location and size (in bytes) of a buffer that either contains a request or will receive a request. The number of bytes actually received in a request is returned in atpActCount. ATPTransID specifies the transaction ID. The transaction bit map is contained in atpBitMap, in the form:

```
TYPE BitMapType = PACKED ARRAY[0..7] OF BOOLEAN;
```

Each bit in the bit map corresponds to one of the eight possible packets in a response. For example, when a request is made for which five response packets are expected, the bit map sent is binary 00011111 or decimal 31. If the second packet in the response is lost, the requesting socket will retransmit the request with a bit map of binary 00000010 or decimal 2.

ATPUserData contains the user bytes of an ATP header. ATPXO is TRUE if the transaction is to be made with exactly-once service. ATPEOM is TRUE if the response packet is the last packet of a transaction. If the number of responses is less than the number that were requested, then ATPEOM must also be TRUE. ATPNumRsp contains either the number of responses received or the sequence number of a response.

The timeout interval in seconds and the maximum number of times that a request should be made are indicated by atpTimeOut and atpRetries, respectively.

Note: Setting atpRetries to 255 will cause the request to be retransmitted indefinitely, until a full response is received or the call is canceled.

ATP provides a data structure, known as a response buffer data structure (**response BDS**), for allocating buffer space to receive the datagram(s) of the response. A response BDS is an array of one to eight elements. Each BDS element defines the size and location of a buffer for receiving one response datagram; they're numbered 0 to 7 to correspond to the sequence numbers of the response datagrams.

ATP needs a separate buffer for each response datagram expected, since packets may not arrive in the proper sequence. It does not, however, require you to set up and use the BDS data structure to describe the response buffers; if you don't, ATP will do it for you. Two sets of calls are provided for both requests and responses; one set requires you to allocate a response BDS and the other doesn't.

Assembly-language note: The two calls that don't require you to define a BDS data structure (ATPRequest and ATPResponse) are available in Pascal only.

The number of BDS elements allocated (in other words, the maximum number of datagrams that the responder can send) is indicated in the TReq by an eight-bit bit map. The bits of this bit map are numbered 0 to 7 (the least significant bit being number 0); each bit corresponds to the response datagram with the respective sequence number.

ATPRspBDSPtr and atpBDSSize indicate the location and number of elements in the response BDS, which has the following structure:

```
TYPE  BDSElement =
            RECORD
                buffSize:  INTEGER;    {buffer size in bytes}
                buffPtr:   Ptr;        {pointer to buffer}
                dataSize:  INTEGER;    {number of bytes actually received}
                userBytes: LONGINT     {user bytes}
            END;

      BDSType = ARRAY[0..7] OF BDSElement; {response BDS}
      BDSPtr  = ^BDSType;
```

ATPNumBufs indicates the number of elements in the response BDS that contain information. In most cases, you can allocate space for your variables of BDSType statically with a VAR declaration. However, you can allocate only the minimum space required by your ATP calls by doing the following:

```
VAR myBDSPtr: BDSPtr;

    . . .

numOfBDS := 3; {number of elements needed}
myBDSPtr := BDSPtr(NewPtr(SIZEOF(BDSElement) * numOfBDS));
```

Note: The userBytes field of the BDSElement and the atpUserData field of the ABusRecord represent the same information in the datagram. Depending on the ATP call made, one or both of these fields will be used.

Using ATP

Before you can use ATP on a Macintosh 128K, the .ATP driver must be read from the system resource file via an ATPLoad call. The .ATP driver loads itself into the application heap and installs a task into the vertical retrace queue.

Warning: When another application starts up, the application heap is reinitialized; on a Macintosh 128K, this means that the ATP code is lost (and must be reloaded by the next application).

When you're through using ATP on a Macintosh 128K, call ATPUnload—the system will be returned to the state it was in before the .ATP driver was opened.

On a Macintosh 512K or XL, the .ATP driver will have been loaded into the system heap either at system startup or upon execution of MPPOpen or ATPLoad. ATPUnload has no effect on a Macintosh 512K or XL.

To send a transaction request, call ATPSndRequest or ATPRequest. The .ATP driver will automatically select and open a socket through which the request datagram will be sent, and through which the response datagrams will be received. The transaction requester can't specify the number of this socket. However, the requester must specify the full network address (network number, node ID, and socket number) of the socket to which the request is to be sent. This socket is known as the responding socket, and its address must be known in advance by the requester.

Note: The requesting and responding sockets can't be in the same node.

At the responder's end, before a transaction request can be received, a responding socket must be opened, and the appropriate calls be made, to receive a request. To do this, the responder first makes an ATPOpenSocket call which allows the responder to specify the address (or part of it) of the requesters from whom it's willing to accept transaction requests. Then it issues an ATPGetRequest call to provide ATP with a buffer for receiving a request; when a request is received, ATPGetRequest is completed. The responder can queue up several ATPGetRequest calls, each of which will be completed as requests are received.

Upon receiving a request, the responder performs the requested operation, and then prepares the information to be returned to the requester. It then calls ATPSndRsp (or ATPResponse) to send the response. Actually, the responder can issue the ATPSndRsp call with only part (or none) of the response specified. Additional portions of the response can be sent later by calling ATPAddRsp.

The ATPSndRsp and ATPAddRsp calls provide flexibility in the design (and range of types) of transaction responders. For instance, the responder may, for some reason, be forced to send the responses out of sequence. Also, there might be memory constraints that force sending the complete transaction response in parts. Even though eight response datagrams might need to be sent, the responder might have only enough memory to build one datagram at a time. In this case, it would build the first response datagram and call ATPSndRsp to send it. It would then build the second response datagram in the same buffer and call ATPAddRsp to send it; and so on, for the third through eighth response datagrams.

A responder can close a responding socket by calling ATPCloseSocket. This call cancels all pending ATP calls for that socket, such as ATPGetRequest, ATPSndRsp, and ATPResponse.

For exactly-once transactions, the ATPSndRsp and ATPAddRsp calls don't terminate until the entire transaction has completed (that is, the responding end receives a release packet, or the release timer has expired).

To cancel a pending, asynchronous ATPSndRequest or ATPRequest call, call ATPReqCancel. To cancel a pending, asynchronous ATPSndRsp or ATPResponse call, call ATPRspCancel. Pending asynchronous ATPGetRequest calls can be canceled only by issuing the ATPCloseSocket call, but that will cancel all outstanding calls for that socket.

Warning: You cannot reuse a variable of type ABusRecord passed to an ATP routine until the entire transaction has either been completed or canceled.

ATP Routines

```
FUNCTION ATPLoad : OSErr;   [Not in ROM]
```

ATPLoad first verifies that the .MPP driver is loaded and running. If it isn't, ATPLoad verifies that port B is configured for AppleTalk and isn't in use, and then loads MPP into the system heap.

ATPLoad then loads the .ATP driver, unless it's already in memory. On a Macintosh 128K, ATPLoad reads the .ATP driver from the system resource file into the application heap; on a Macintosh 512K or XL, ATP is read into the system heap.

Note: On a Macintosh 512K or XL, ATPLoad and MPPOpen perform essentially the same function.

Result codes	noErr	No error
	portInUse	Port B is already in use
	portNotCf	Port B not configured for AppleTalk

```
FUNCTION ATPUnload : OSErr;   [Not in ROM]
```

ATPUnload makes the .ATP driver purgeable; the space isn't actually released by the Memory Manager until necessary.

Note: This call applies only to a Macintosh 128K; on a Macintosh 512K or Macintosh XL, ATPUnload has no effect.

Result codes	noErr	No error

```
FUNCTION ATPOpenSocket (addrRcvd: AddrBlock; VAR atpSocket: Byte)
              : OSErr;   [Not in ROM]
```

ATPOpenSocket opens a socket for the purpose of receiving requests. ATPSocket contains the socket number of the socket to open; if it's 0, a number is dynamically assigned and returned in atpSocket. AddrRcvd contains a filter of the sockets from which requests will be accepted. A 0 in the network number, node ID, or socket number field of the addrRcvd record acts as a "wild card"; for instance, a 0 in the socket number field means that requests will be accepted from all sockets in the node(s) specified by the network and node fields.

Result codes   noErr   No error
                        tooManySkts   Socket table full
                        noDataArea   Too many outstanding ATP calls

Note: If you're only going to send requests and receive responses to these requests, you don't need to open an ATP socket. When you make the ATPSndRequest or ATPRequest call, ATP automatically opens a dynamically assigned socket for that purpose.

```
FUNCTION ATPCloseSocket (atpSocket: Byte) : OSErr;   [Not in ROM]
```

ATPCloseSocket closes the responding socket whose number is specified by atpSocket. It releases the data structures associated with all pending, asynchronous calls involving that socket; these pending calls are completed immediately and return the result code sktClosed.

Result codes   noErr   No error
                        noDataArea   Too many outstanding ATP calls

```
FUNCTION ATPSndRequest (abRecord: ABRecHandle; async: BOOLEAN) :
          OSErr;   [Not in ROM]
```

ABusRecord

←	abOpcode	{always tATPSndRequest}
←	abResult	{result code}
→	abUserReference	{for your use}
→	atpAddress	{destination socket address}
→	atpReqCount	{request size in bytes}
→	atpDataPtr	{pointer to buffer}
→	atpRspBDSPtr	{pointer to response BDS}
→	atpUserData	{user bytes}
→	atpXO	{exactly-once flag}
←	atpEOM	{end-of-message flag}
→	atpTimeOut	{retry timeout interval in seconds}
→	atpRetries	{maximum number of retries}
→	atpNumBufs	{number of elements in response BDS}
←	atpNumRsp	{number of response packets actually received}

ATPSndRequest sends a request to another socket. ATPAddress is the internet address of the socket to which the request should be sent. ATPDataPtr and atpReqCount specify the location and size of a buffer that contains the request information to be sent. ATPUserData contains the user bytes for the ATP header.

ATPSndRequest requires you to allocate a response BDS. ATPRspBDSPtr is a pointer to the response BDS; atpNumBufs indicates the number of elements in the BDS (this is also the maximum number of response datagrams that will be accepted). The number of response datagrams actually received is returned in atpNumRsp; if a nonzero value is returned, you can examine the response BDS to determine which packets of the transaction were actually received. If the number returned is less than requested, one of the following is true:

■ Some of the packets have been lost and the retry count has been exceeded.

■ ATPEOM is TRUE; this means that the response consisted of fewer packets than were expected, but that all packets sent were received (the last packet came with the atpEOM flag set).

ATPTimeOut indicates the length of time that ATPSndRequest should wait for a response before retransmitting the request. ATPRetries indicates the maximum number of retries ATPSndRequest should attempt. ATPXO should be TRUE if you want the request to be part of an exactly-once transaction.

ATPSndRequest completes when either the transaction is completed or the retry count is exceeded.

Result codes	noErr	No error
	reqFailed	Retry count exceeded
	tooManyReqs	Too many concurrent requests
	noDataArea	Too many outstanding ATP calls

```
FUNCTION ATPRequest (abRecord: ABRecHandle; async: BOOLEAN) :
            OSErr;   [Not in ROM]
```

ABusRecord

←	abOpcode	{always tATPRequest}
←	abResult	{result code}
→	abUserReference	{for your use}
→	atpAddress	{destination socket address}
→	atpReqCount	{request size in bytes}
→	atpDataPtr	{pointer to buffer}
←	atpActCount	{number of bytes actually received}
→	atpUserData	{user bytes}
→	atpXO	{exactly-once flag}
←	atpEOM	{end-of-message flag}
→	atpTimeOut	{retry timeout interval in seconds}
→	atpRetries	{maximum number of retries}
←	atpRspUData	{user bytes received in transaction response}
→	atpRspBuf	{pointer to response message buffer}
→	atpRspSize	{size of response message buffer}

ATPRequest is functionally analogous to ATPSndRequest. It sends a request to another socket, but doesn't require the caller to set up and use the BDS data structure to describe the response buffers. ATPAddress indicates the socket to which the request should be sent. ATPDataPtr and atpReqCount specify the location and size of a buffer that contains the request information to be sent. ATPUserData contains the user bytes to be sent in the request's ATP header. ATPTimeOut indicates the length of time that ATPRequest should wait for a response before retransmitting the request. ATPRetries indicates the maximum number of retries ATPRequest should attempt.

To use this call, you must have an area of contiguous buffer space that's large enough to receive all expected datagrams. The various datagrams will be assembled in this buffer and returned to you as a complete message upon completion of the transaction. The location and size of this buffer are passed in atpRspBuf and atpRspSize. Upon completion of the call, the size of the received response message is returned in atpActCount. The user bytes received in the ATP header of the first response packet are returned in atpRspUData. ATPXO should be TRUE if you want the request to be part of an exactly-once transaction.

Although you don't provide a BDS, ATPRequest in fact creates one and calls the .ATP driver (as in an ATPSndRequest call). For this reason, the abRecord fields atpRspBDSPtr and atpNumBufs are used by ATPRequest; you should not expect these fields to remain unaltered during or after the function's execution.

For ATPRequest to receive and correctly deliver the response as a single message, the responding end must, upon receiving the request (with an ATPGetRequest call), generate the complete response as a message in a single buffer and then call ATPResponse.

> **Note:** The responding end could also use ATPSndRsp and ATPAddRsp provided that each response packet (except the last one) contains exactly 578 ATP data bytes; the last packet in the response can contain less than 578 ATP data bytes. Also, if this method is used, only the ATP user bytes of the first response packet will be delivered to the requester; any information in the user bytes of the remaining response packets will not be delivered.

ATPRequest completes when either the transaction is completed or the retry count is exceeded.

Result codes	noErr	No error
	reqFailed	Retry count exceeded
	tooManyReqs	Too many concurrent requests
	sktClosed	Socket closed by a cancel call
	noDataArea	Too many outstanding ATP calls

```
FUNCTION ATPReqCancel (abRecord: ABRecHandle; async: BOOLEAN) :
        OSErr;   [Not in ROM]
```

Given the handle to the ABusRecord of a previously made ATPSndRequest or ATPRequest call, ATPReqCancel dequeues the ATPSndRequest or ATPRequest call, provided that the call hasn't already completed. ATPReqCancel returns noErr if the ATPSndRequest or ATPRequest call is successfully removed from the queue. If it returns cbNotFound, check the abResult field of abRecord to verify that the ATPSndRequest or ATPRequest call has completed and determine its outcome.

Result codes	noErr	No error
	cbNotFound	ATP control block not found

```
FUNCTION ATPGetRequest (abRecord: ABRecHandle; async: BOOLEAN) :
        OSErr;   [Not in ROM]
```

ABusRecord

←	abOpcode	{always tATPGetRequest}
←	abResult	{result code}
→	abUserReference	{for your use}
→	atpSocket	{listening socket number}
←	atpAddress	{source socket address}
→	atpReqCount	{buffer size in bytes}
→	atpDataPtr	{pointer to buffer}
←	atpBitMap	{transaction bit map}
←	atpTransID	{transaction ID}

←	atpActCount	{number of bytes actually received}
←	atpUserData	{user bytes}
←	atpXO	{exactly-once flag}

ATPGetRequest sets up the mechanism to receive a request sent by either an ATPSndRequest or an ATPRequest call. ATPSocket contains the socket number of the socket that should listen for a request; this socket must already have been opened by calling ATPOpenSocket. The address of the socket from which the request was sent is returned in atpAddress. ATPDataPtr specifies a buffer to store the incoming request; atpReqCount indicates the size of the buffer in bytes. The number of bytes actually received in the request is returned in atpActCount. ATPUserData contains the user bytes from the ATP header. The transaction bit map is returned in atpBitMap. The transaction ID is returned in atpTransID. ATPXO will be TRUE if the request is part of an exactly-once transaction.

ATPGetRequest completes when a request is received. To cancel an asynchronous ATPGetRequest call, you must call ATPCloseSocket, but this cancels all pending calls involving that socket.

Result codes	noErr	No error
	badATPSkt	Bad responding socket
	sktClosed	Socket closed by a cancel call

```
FUNCTION ATPSndRsp (abRecord: ABRecHandle; async: BOOLEAN) :
        OSErr;   [Not in ROM]
```

ABusRecord

←	abOpcode	{always tATPSdRsp}
←	abResult	{result code}
→	abUserReference	{for your use}
→	atpSocket	{responding socket number}
→	atpAddress	{destination socket address}
→	atpRspBDSPtr	{pointer to response BDS}
→	atpTransID	{transaction ID}
→	atpEOM	{end-of-message flag}
→	atpNumBufs	{number of response packets being sent}
→	atpBDSSize	{number of elements in response BDS}

ATPSndRsp sends a response to another socket. ATPSocket contains the socket number from which the response should be sent and atpAddress contains the internet address of the socket to which the response should be sent. ATPTransID must contain the transaction ID. ATPEOM is TRUE if the response BDS contains the final packet in a transaction composed of a group of packets and the number of packets in the response is less than expected. ATPRspBDSPtr points to the buffer data structure containing the responses to be sent. ATPBDSSize indicates the number of elements in the response BDS, and must be in the range 1 to 8. ATPNumBufs indicates the number of response packets being sent with this call, and must be in the range 0 to 8.

> **Note:** In some situations, you may want to send only part (or possibly none) of your response message back immediately. For instance, you might be requested to send back seven disk blocks, but have only enough internal memory to store one block. In this case,

set atpBDSSize to 7 (total number of response packets), atpNumBufs to 0 (number of response packets currently being sent), and call ATPSndRsp. Then as you read in one block at a time, call ATPAddRsp until all seven response datagrams have been sent.

During exactly-once transactions, ATPSndRsp won't complete until the release packet is received or the release timer expires.

Result codes	noErr	No error
	badATPSkt	Bad responding socket
	noRelErr	No release received
	sktClosed	Socket closed by a cancel call
	noDataArea	Too many outstanding ATP calls
	badBuffNum	Bad sequence number

```
FUNCTION ATPAddRsp (abRecord: ABRecHandle) : OSErr;   [Not in ROM]
```

ABusRecord

←	abOpcode	{always tATPAddRsp}
←	abResult	{result code}
→	abUserReference	{for your use}
→	atpSocket	{responding socket number}
→	atpAddress	{destination socket address}
→	atpReqCount	{buffer size in bytes}
→	atpDataPtr	{pointer to buffer}
→	atpTransID	{transaction ID}
→	atpUserData	{user bytes}
→	atpEOM	{end-of-message flag}
→	atpNumRsp	{sequence number}

ATPAddRsp sends one additional response packet to a socket that has already been sent the initial part of a response via ATPSndRsp. ATPSocket contains the socket number from which the response should be sent and atpAddress contains the internet address of the socket to which the response should be sent. ATPTransID must contain the transaction ID. ATPDataPtr and atpReqCount specify the location and size of a buffer that contains the information to send; atpNumRsp is the sequence number of the response. ATPEOM is TRUE if this response datagram is the final packet in a transaction composed of a group of packets. ATPUserData contains the user bytes to be sent in this response datagram's ATP header.

Note: No BDS is needed with ATPAddRsp because all pertinent information is passed within the record.

Result codes	noErr	No error
	badATPSkt	Bad responding socket
	badBuffNum	Bad sequence number
	noSendResp	ATPAddRsp issued before ATPSndRsp
	noDataArea	Too many outstanding ATP calls

```
FUNCTION ATPResponse (abRecord: ABRecHandle; async: BOOLEAN) :
          OSErr;   [Not in ROM]
```

ABusRecord

←	abOpcode	{always tATPResponse}
←	abResult	{result code}
→	abUserReference	{for your use}
→	atpSocket	{responding socket number}
→	atpAddress	{destination socket address}
→	atpTransID	{transaction ID)
→	atpRspUData	{user bytes sent in transaction response}
→	atpRspBuf	{pointer to response message buffer}
→	atpRspSize	{size of response message buffer}

ATPResponse is functionally analogous to ATPSndRsp. It sends a response to another socket, but doesn't require the caller to provide a BDS. ATPAddress must contain the complete network address of the socket to which the response should be sent (taken from the data provided by an ATPGetRequest call). ATPTransID must contain the transaction ID. ATPSocket indicates the socket from which the response should be sent (the socket on which the corresponding ATPGetRequest was issued). ATPRspBuf points to the buffer containing the response message; the size of this buffer must be passed in atpRspSize. The four user bytes to be sent in the ATP header of the first response packet are passed in atpRspUData. The last packet of the transaction response is sent with the EOM flag set.

Although you don't provide a BDS, ATPResponse in fact creates one and calls the .ATP driver (as in an ATPSndRsp call). For this reason, the abRecord fields atpRspBDSPtr and atpNumBufs are used by ATPResponse; you should not expect these fields to remain unaltered during or after the function's execution.

During exactly-once transactions ATPResponse won't complete until the release packet is received or the release timer expires.

> **Warning:** The maximum permissible size of the response message is 4624 bytes.

Result codes	noErr	No error
	badATPSkt	Bad responding socket
	noRelErr	No release received
	atpLenErr	Response too big
	sktClosed	Socket closed by a cancel call
	noDataArea	Too many outstanding ATP calls

```
FUNCTION ATPRspCancel (abRecord: ABRecHandle; async: BOOLEAN) :
          OSErr;   [Not in ROM]
```

Given the handle to the ABusRecord of a previously made ATPSndRsp or ATPResponse call, ATPRspCancel dequeues the ATPSndRsp or ATPResponse call, provided that the call hasn't already completed. ATPRspCancel returns noErr if the ATPSndRsp or ATPResponse call is successfully removed from the queue. If it returns cbNotFound, check the abResult field of abRecord to verify that the ATPSndRsp or ATPResponse call has completed and determine its outcome.

Result codes   noErr   No error
                          cbNotFound   ATP control block not found

Example

This example shows the requesting side of an ATP transaction that asks for a 512-byte disk block from the responding end. The block number of the file is a byte and is contained in myBuffer[0].

```
VAR  myABRecord: ABRecHandle;
     myBDSPtr: BDSPtr;
     myBuffer: PACKED ARRAY[0..511] OF CHAR;
     errCode: INTEGER;
     async: BOOLEAN;

BEGIN
errCode := ATPLoad;
IF errCode <> noErr
  THEN
    WRITELN('Error in opening AppleTalk')
    {Maybe serial port B isn't available for use by AppleTalk}
  ELSE
    BEGIN
    {Prepare the BDS; allocate space for a one-element BDS}
    myBDSPtr := BDSPtr(NewPtr(SIZEOF(BDSElement)));
    WITH myBDSPtr^[0] DO
      BEGIN
      buffSize := 512;       {size of our buffer used in reception}
      buffPtr := @myBuffer;  {pointer to the buffer}
      END;
    {Prepare the ABusRecord}
    myBuffer[0] := CHR(1);    {requesting disk block number 1}
    myABRecord := ABRecHandle(NewHandle(atpSize));
    WITH myABRecord^^ DO
      BEGIN
      atpAddress.aNet := 0;
      atpAddress.aNode := 30;     {we probably got this from an NBP call}
      atpAddress.aSocket := 15;   {socket to send request to}
      atpReqCount := 1;         {size of request data field (disk block #)}
      atpDataPtr := @myBuffer;    {ptr to request to be sent}
      atpRspBDSPtr := @myBDSPtr;
      atpUserData := 0;       {for your use}
      atpXO := FALSE;         {at-least-once service}
      atpTimeOut := 5;        {5-second timeout}
      atpRetries := 3;        {3 retries; request will be sent 4 times max}
      atpNumBufs := 1;        {we're only expecting 1 block to be returned}
      END;
    async := FALSE;
    {Send the request and wait for the response}
    errCode := ATPSndRequest(myABRecord,async);
```

```
      IF errCode <> noErr
        THEN
          WRITELN('An error occurred in the ATPSndRequest call')
        ELSE
          BEGIN
          {The disk block requested is now in myBuffer.  We can verify }
          { that atpNumRsp contains 1, meaning one response received.}
          . . .
          END;
      END;
  END.
```

Name-Binding Protocol

Data Structures

NBP calls use the following fields:

```
nbpProto:
(nbpEntityPtr:       EntityPtr;      {pointer to entity name}
 nbpBufPtr:          Ptr;            {pointer to buffer}
 nbpBufSize:         INTEGER;        {buffer size in bytes}
 nbpDataField:       INTEGER;        {number of addresses or socket }
                                     { number}
 nbpAddress:         AddrBlock;      {socket address}
 nbpRetransmitInfo: RetransType); {retransmission information}
```

When data is sent via NBP, nbpBufSize indicates the size of the data in bytes and nbpBufPtr points to a buffer containing the data. When data is received via NBP, nbpBufPtr points to a buffer in which the incoming data can be stored and nbpBufSize indicates the size of the buffer in bytes. NBPAddress is used in some calls to give the internet address of a named entity. The AddrBlock data type is described above under "Datagram Delivery Protocol".

NBPEntityPtr points to a variable of type EntityName, which has the following data structure:

```
TYPE EntityName = RECORD
                    objStr: Str32;  {object}
                    typeStr: Str32; {type}
                    zoneStr: Str32  {zone}
                  END;

     EntityPtr = ^EntityName;

     Str32 = STRING[32];
```

NBPRetransmitInfo contains information about the number of times a packet should be transmitted and the interval between retransmissions:

```
TYPE RetransType =
       PACKED RECORD
         retransInterval: Byte; {retransmit interval in 8-tick units}
         retransCount:    Byte  {total number of attempts}
       END;
```

RetransCount contains the *total* number of times a packet should be transmitted, including the first transmission. If retransCount is 0, the packet will be transmitted a total of 255 times.

Using NBP

On a Macintosh 128K, the AppleTalk Manager's NBP code is read into the application heap when any one of the NBP (Pascal) routines is called; you can call the NBPLoad function yourself if you want to load the NBP code explicitly. When you're finished with the NBP code and want to reclaim the space it occupies, call NBPUnload. On a Macintosh 512K or XL, the NBP code is read in when the .MPP driver is loaded.

> **Note:** When another application starts up, the application heap is reinitialized; on a Macintosh 128K, this means that the NBP code is lost (and must be reloaded by the next application).

When an entity wants to communicate via an AppleTalk network, it should call NBPRegister to place its name and internet address in the names table. When an entity no longer wants to communicate on the network, or is being shut down, it should call NBPRemove to remove its entry from the names table.

To determine the address of an entity you know only by name, call NBPLookup, which returns a list of all entities with the name you specify. Call NBPExtract to extract entity names from the list.

If you already know the address of an entity, and want only to confirm that it still exists, call NBPConfirm. NBPConfirm is more efficient than NBPLookup in terms of network traffic.

NBP Routines

```
FUNCTION NBPRegister (abRecord: ABRecHandle; async: BOOLEAN) :
         OSErr;   [Not in ROM]
```

ABusRecord

←	abOpcode	{always tNBPRegister}
←	abResult	{result code}
→	abUserReference	{for your use}
→	nbpEntityPtr	{pointer to entity name}
→	nbpBufPtr	{pointer to buffer}
→	nbpBufSize	{buffer size in bytes}
→	nbpAddress.aSocket	{socket address}
→	nbpRetransmitInfo	{retransmission information}

NBPRegister adds the name and address of an entity to the node's names table. NBPEntityPtr points to a variable of type EntityName containing the entity's name. If the name is already registered, NBPRegister returns the result code nbpDuplicate. NBPAddress indicates the socket for which the name should be registered. NBPBufPtr and nbpBufSize specify the location and size of a buffer for NBP to use internally.

While the variable of type EntityName is declared as three 32-byte strings, only the actual characters of the name are placed in the buffer pointed to by nbpBufPtr. For this reason, nbpBufSize needs only to be equal to the actual length of the name, plus an additional 12 bytes for use by NBP.

Warning: This buffer must not be altered or released until the name is removed from the names table via an NBPRemove call. If you allocate the buffer through a NewHandle call, you must lock it as long as the name is registered.

Warning: The zone field of the entity name must be set to the meta-character "*".

Result codes	noErr	No error
	nbpDuplicate	Duplicate name already exists

```
FUNCTION NBPLookup (abRecord: ABRecHandle; async: BOOLEAN) :
        OSErr;   [Not in ROM]
```

ABusRecord

←	abOpcode	{always tNBPLookup}
←	abResult	{result code}
→	abUserReference	{for your use}
→	nbpEntityPtr	{pointer to entity name}
→	nbpBufPtr	{pointer to buffer}
→	nbpBufSize	{buffer size in bytes}
↔	nbpDataField	{number of addresses received}
→	nbpRetransmitInfo	{retransmission information}

NBPLookup returns the addresses of all entities with a specified name. NBPEntityPtr points to a variable of type EntityName containing the name of the entity whose address should be returned. (Meta-characters are allowed in the entity name.) NBPBufPtr and nbpBufSize contain the location and size of an area of memory in which the entity names and their corresponding addresses should be returned. NBPDataField indicates the maximum number of matching names to find addresses for; the actual number of addresses found is returned in nbpDataField. NBPRetransmitInfo contains the retry interval and the retry count.

When specifying nbpBufSize, for each NBP tuple expected, allow space for the actual characters of the name, the address, and four bytes for use by NBP.

Result codes	noErr	No error
	nbpBuffOvr	Buffer overflow

```
FUNCTION NBPExtract (theBuffer: Ptr; numInBuf: INTEGER; whichOne:
        INTEGER; VAR abEntity: EntityName; VAR address:
        AddrBlock) : OSErr;   [Not in ROM]
```

NBPExtract returns one address from the list of addresses returned by NBPLookup. TheBuffer and numInBuf indicate the location and number of tuples in the buffer. WhichOne specifies which one of the tuples in the buffer should be returned in the abEntity and address parameters.

Result codes	noErr	No error
	extractErr	Can't find tuple in buffer

```
FUNCTION NBPConfirm (abRecord: ABRecHandle; async: BOOLEAN) :
        OSErr;    [Not in ROM]
```

ABusRecord

←	abOpcode	{always tNBPConfirm}
←	abResult	{result code}
→	abUserReference	{for your use}
→	nbpEntityPtr	{pointer to entity name}
←	nbpDataField	{socket number}
→	nbpAddress	{socket address}
→	nbpRetransmitInfo	{retransmission information}

NBPConfirm confirms that an entity known by name and address still exists (is still entered in the names directory). NBPEntityPtr points to a variable of type EntityName that contains the name to confirm, and nbpAddress specifies the address to be confirmed. (No meta-characters are allowed in the entity name.) NBPRetransmitInfo contains the retry interval and the retry count. The socket number of the entity is returned in nbpDataField. NBPConfirm is more efficient than NBPLookup in terms of network traffic.

Result codes	noErr	No error
	nbpConfDiff	Name confirmed for different socket
	nbpNoConfirm	Name not confirmed

```
FUNCTION NBPRemove (abEntity: EntityPtr) : OSErr;    [Not in ROM]
```

NBPRemove removes an entity name from the names table of the given entity's node.

Result codes	noErr	No error
	nbpNotFound	Name not found

```
FUNCTION NBPLoad : OSErr;    [Not in ROM]
```

On a Macintosh 128K, NBPLoad reads the NBP code from the system resource file into the application heap. On a Macintosh 512K or XL, NBPLoad has no effect since the NBP code should have already been loaded when the .MPP driver was opened. Normally you'll never need to call NBPLoad, because the AppleTalk Manager calls it when necessary.

Result codes	noErr	No error

```
FUNCTION NBPUnload : OSErr;    [Not in ROM]
```

On a Macintosh 128K, NBPUnload makes the NBP code purgeable; the space isn't actually released by the Memory Manager until necessary. On a Macintosh 512K or Macintosh XL, NBPUnload has no effect.

Result codes	noErr	No error

10 AppleTalk Manager

Example

This example of NBP registers our node as a print spooler, searches for any print spoolers
registered on the network, and then extracts the information for the first one found.

```
CONST mySocket = 20;

VAR  myABRecord: ABRecHandle;
     myEntity: EntityName;
     entityAddr: AddrBlock;
     nbpNamePtr: Ptr;
     myBuffer: PACKED ARRAY[0..999] OF CHAR;
     errCode: INTEGER;
     async: BOOLEAN;

BEGIN
errCode := MPPOpen;
IF errCode <> noErr
  THEN
     WRITELN('Error in opening AppleTalk')
     {Maybe serial port B isn't available for use by AppleTalk}
  ELSE
     BEGIN
     {Call Memory Manager to allocate ABusRecord}
     myABRecord := ABRecHandle(NewHandle(nbpSize));
     {Set up our entity name to register}
     WITH myEntity DO
       BEGIN
       objStr := 'Gene Station';    {we are called 'Gene Station' }
       typeStr := 'PrintSpooler';   { and are of type 'PrintSpooler'}
       zoneStr := '*';
       {Allocate data space for the entity name (used by NBP)}
       nbpNamePtr := NewPtr(LENGTH(objStr)+LENGTH(typeStr)+
                                              LENGTH(zoneStr)+12);
       END;
     {Set up the ABusRecord for the NBPRegister call}
     WITH myABRecord^^ DO
       BEGIN
       nbpEntityPtr := @myEntity;
       nbpBufPtr := nbpNamePtr;     {buffer used by NBP internally}
       nbpBufSize := nbpNameBufSize;
       nbpAddress.aSocket := mySocket; {socket to register us on}
       nbpRetransmitInfo.retransInterval := 8; {retransmit every 64 }
       nbpRetransmitInfo.retransCount := 3;    { ticks and try 3 times}
       END;
     async := FALSE;
     errCode := NBPRegister(myABRecord,async);
     IF errCode <> noErr
       THEN
         WRITELN('Error occurred in the NBPRegister call')
         {Maybe the name is already registered somewhere else on the }
         { network.}
```

```
      ELSE
        BEGIN
        {Now that we've registered our name, find others of type }
        { 'PrintSpooler'.}
        WITH myEntity DO
          BEGIN
          objStr := '=';                  {any one of type }
          typeStr := 'PrintSpooler';  { "PrintSpooler" }
          zoneStr := '*';                 { in our zone}
          END;
        WITH myABRecord^^ DO
          BEGIN
          nbpEntityPtr := @myEntity;
          nbpBufPtr := @myBuffer;  {buffer to place responses in}
          nbpBufSize := SIZEOF(myBuffer);
          {The field nbpDataField, before the NBPLookup call, }
          { represents an approximate number of responses.  After the }
          { call, nbpDataField contains the actual number of responses }
          { received.}
          nbpDataField := 100;  {we want about 100 responses back}
          END;
        errCode := NBPLookup(myABRecord,async);    {make sync call}
        IF errCode <> noErr
          THEN
            WRITELN('An error occurred in the NBPLookup')
            {Did the buffer overflow?}
          ELSE
            BEGIN
            {Get the first reply}
            errCode := NBPExtract(@mybuffer,myABRecord^^.nbpDataField,1,
                                      myEntity,entityAddr);
            {The socket address and name of the entity are returned here. }
            { If we want all of them, we'll have to loop for each one in }
            { the buffer.}
            IF errCode <> noErr
              THEN
                WRITELN('Error in NBPExtract');
                {Maybe the one we wanted wasn't in the buffer}
            END;
        END;
      END;
  END.
```

Miscellaneous Routines

```
FUNCTION GetNodeAddress (VAR myNode,myNet: INTEGER) : OSErr;
            [Not in ROM]
```

GetNodeAddress returns the current node ID and network number of the caller. If the .MPP driver isn't installed, it returns noMPPErr. If myNet contains 0, this means that a bridge hasn't yet been found.

Result codes	noErr	No error
	noMPPErr	MPP driver not installed

```
FUNCTION IsMPPOpen : BOOLEAN;    [Not in ROM]
```

IsMPPOpen returns TRUE if the .MPP driver is loaded and running.

```
FUNCTION IsATPOpen : BOOLEAN;    [Not in ROM]
```

IsATPOpen returns TRUE if the .ATP driver is loaded and running.

CALLING THE APPLETALK MANAGER FROM ASSEMBLY LANGUAGE

This section discusses how to use the AppleTalk Manager from assembly language. Equivalent Pascal information is given in the preceding section.

All routines make Device Manager Control calls. The description of each routine includes a list of the fields needed. Some of these fields are part of the parameter block described in chapter 6; additional fields are provided for the AppleTalk Manager.

The number next to each field name indicates the byte offset of the field from the start of the parameter block pointed to by A0. An arrow next to each parameter name indicates whether it's an input, output, or input/output parameter:

Arrow	Meaning
→	Parameter is passed to the routine
←	Parameter is returned by the routine
↔	Parameter is passed to and returned by the routine

All Device Manager Control calls return an integer result code of type OSErr in the ioResult field. Each routine description lists all of the applicable result codes generated by the AppleTalk Manager, along with a short description of what the result code means. Lengthier explanations of all the result codes can be found in the summary at the end of this chapter. Result codes from other parts of the Operating System may also be returned. (See Appendix A in Volume III for a list of all result codes.)

Opening AppleTalk

Two tests are made at system startup to determine whether the .MPP driver should be opened at that time. If port B is already in use, or isn't configured for AppleTalk, .MPP isn't opened until explicitly requested by an application; otherwise it's opened at system startup.

It's the application's responsibility to test the availability of port B before opening AppleTalk. Assembly-language programmers can use the Pascal calls MPPOpen and ATPLoad to open the .MPP and .ATP drivers.

The global variable SPConfig is used for configuring the serial ports; it's copied from a byte in parameter RAM (which is discussed in chapter 13). The low-order four bits of this variable contain the current configuration of port B. The following use types are provided as global constants for testing or setting the configuration of port B:

```
useFree         .EQU      0      ;unconfigured
useATalk        .EQU      1      ;configured for AppleTalk
useAsync        .EQU      2      ;configured for the Serial Driver
```

The application shouldn't attempt to open AppleTalk unless SPConfig is equal to either useFree or useATalk.

A second test involves the global variable PortBUse; the low-order four bits of this byte are used to monitor the current use of port B. If PortBUse is negative, the program is free to open AppleTalk. If PortBUse is positive, the program should test to see whether port B is already being used by AppleTalk; if it is, the low-order four bits of PortBUse will be equal to the use type useATalk.

The .MPP driver sets PortBUse to the correct value (useATalk) when it's opened and resets it to $FF when it's closed. Bits 4-6 of this byte are used for driver-specific information; ATP uses bit 4 to indicate whether it's currently opened:

```
atpLoadedBit    .EQU      4      ;set if ATP is opened
```

Example

The following code illustrates the use of the SPConfig and PortBUse variables.

```
                MOVE      #-<atpUnitNum+1>,atpRefNum(A0)    ;save known ATP refNum
                                                           ; in case ATP not opened
OpenAbus  SUB       #ioQElSize,SP        ;allocate queue entry
          MOVE.L    SP,A0                ;A0 -> queue entry
          CLR.B     ioPermssn(A0)        ;make sure permission's clear
          MOVE.B    PortBUse,D1          ;is port B in use?
          BPL.S     @10                  ;if so, make sure by AppleTalk
          MOVEQ     #portNotCf,D0        ;assume port not configured for
                                         ; AppleTalk
          MOVE.B    SPConfig,D1          ;get configuration data
          AND.B     #$0F,D1              ;mask it to low 4 bits
          SUBQ.B    #useATalk,D1         ;unconfigured or configured for
                                         ; AppleTalk
          BGT.S     @30                  ;if not, return error
          LEA       mppName,A1           ;A1 = address of driver name
          MOVE.L    A1,ioFileName(A0)    ;set in queue entry
          _Open                          ;open MPP
          BNE.S     @30                  ;return error, if it can't load it
          BRA.S     @20                  ;otherwise, go check ATP
@10       MOVEQ     #portInUse,D0        ;assume port in use error
          AND.B     #$0F,D1              ;clear all but use bits
          SUBQ.B    #useATalk,D1         ;is AppleTalk using it?
          BNE.S     @30                  ;if not, then error
@20       MOVEQ     #0,D0                ;assume no error
          BTST      #atpLoadedBit,PortBUse  ;ATP already open?
          BNE.S     @30                  ;just return if so
          LEA       atpName,A1           ;A1 = address of driver name
```

```
            MOVE.L    A1,ioFileName(A0)  ;set in queue entry
            _Open                        ;open ATP
@30         ADD       #ioQElSize,SP      ;deallocate queue entry
            RTS                          ;and return
mppName     .BYTE     4                  ;length of .MPP driver name
            .ASCII    '.MPP'             ;name of .MPP driver
atpName     .BYTE     4                  ;length of .ATP driver name
            .ASCII    '.ATP'             ;name of .ATP driver
```

AppleTalk Link Access Protocol

Data Structures

An ALAP frame is composed of a three-byte header, up to 600 bytes of data, and a two-byte frame check sequence (Figure 5). You can use the following global constants to access the contents of an ALAP header:

```
    lapDstAdr    .EQU    0        ;destination node ID
    lapSrcAdr    .EQU    1        ;source node ID
    lapType      .EQU    2        ;ALAP protocol type
    lapHdSz      .EQU    3        ;ALAP header size
```

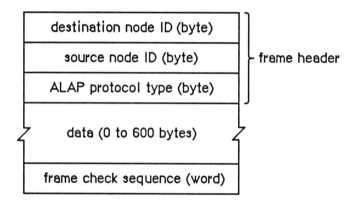

Figure 5. ALAP Frame

Two of the protocol handlers in every node are used by DDP. These protocol handlers service frames with ALAP protocol types equal to the following global constants:

```
    shortDDP    .EQU    1        ;short DDP header
    longDDP     .EQU    2        ;long DDP header
```

When you call ALAP to send a frame, you pass it information about the frame in a **write data structure**, which has the format shown in Figure 6.

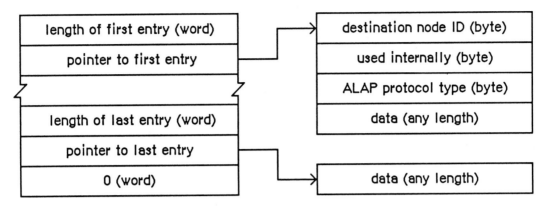

Figure 6. Write Data Structure for ALAP

Using ALAP

Most programs will never need to call ALAP, because higher-level protocols will automatically call ALAP as necessary. If you do want to send a frame directly via an ALAP, call the WriteLAP function. There's no ReadLAP function in assembly language; if you want to read ALAP frames, you must call AttachPH to add your protocol handler to the node's protocol handler table. The ALAP module will examine every incoming frame and call your protocol handler for each frame received with the correct ALAP protocol. When your program no longer wants to receive frames with a particular ALAP protocol type value, it can call DetachPH to remove the corresponding protocol handler from the protocol handler table.

See the "Protocol Handlers and Socket Listeners" section for information on how to write a protocol handler.

ALAP Routines

WriteLAP function

Parameter block

→	26	csCode	word	;always writeLAP
→	30	wdsPointer	pointer	;write data structure

WriteLAP sends a frame to another node. The frame data and destination of the frame are described by the write data structure pointed to by wdsPointer. The first two data bytes of an ALAP frame sent to another computer using the AppleTalk Manager must indicate the length of the frame in bytes. The ALAP protocol type byte must be in the range 1 to 127.

Result codes	noErr	No error
	excessCollsns	No CTS received after 32 RTS's
	ddpLengthErr	Packet length exceeds maximum
	lapProtErr	Invalid ALAP protocol type

AttachPH function

Parameter block

→	26	csCode	word	;always attachPH
→	28	protType	byte	;ALAP protocol type
→	30	handler	pointer	;protocol handler

AttachPH adds the protocol handler pointed to by handler to the node's protocol table. ProtType specifies what kind of frame the protocol handler can service. After AttachPH is called, the protocol handler is called for each incoming frame whose ALAP protocol type equals protType.

Result codes	noErr	No error
	lapProtErr	Error attaching protocol type

DetachPH function

Parameter block

→	26	csCode	word	;always detachPH
→	28	protType	byte	;ALAP protocol type

DetachPH removes from the node's protocol table the specified ALAP protocol type and corresponding protocol handler.

Result codes	noErr	No error
	lapProtErr	Error detaching protocol type

Datagram Delivery Protocol

Data Structures

A DDP datagram consists of a header followed by up to 586 bytes of actual data (Figure 7). The headers can be of two different lengths; they're identified by the following ALAP protocol types:

```
shortDDP   .EQU    1      ;short DDP header
longDDP    .EQU    2      ;long DDP header
```

Long DDP headers (13 bytes) are used for sending datagrams between two or more different AppleTalk networks. You can use the following global constants to access the contents of a long DDP header:

```
ddpHopCnt    .EQU    0      ;count of bridges passed (4 bits)
ddpLength    .EQU    0      ;datagram length (10 bits)
ddpChecksum  .EQU    2      ;checksum
ddpDstNet    .EQU    4      ;destination network number
ddpSrcNet    .EQU    6      ;source network number
ddpDstNode   .EQU    8      ;destination node ID
ddpSrcNode   .EQU    9      ;source node ID
```

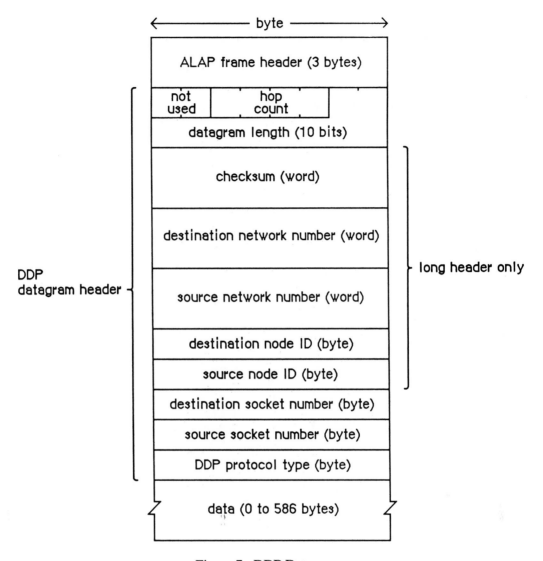

Figure 7. DDP Datagram

```
ddpDstSkt      .EQU      10      ;destination socket number
ddpSrcSkt      .EQU      11      ;source socket number
ddpType        .EQU      12      ;DDP protocol type
```

The size of a DDP long header is given by the following constant:

```
ddpHSzLong     .EQU      ddpType+1
```

The short headers (five bytes) are used for datagrams sent to sockets within the same network as the source socket. You can use the following global constants to access the contents of a short DDP header:

```
ddpLength      .EQU     0              ;datagram length
sDDPDstSkt     .EQU     ddpChecksum    ;destination socket number
sDDPSrcSkt     .EQU     sDDPDstSkt+1   ;source socket number
sDDPType       .EQU     sDDPSrcSkt+1   ;DDP protocol type
```

The size of a DDP short header is given by the following constant:

```
ddpHSzShort    .EQU     sDDPType+1
```

The datagram length is a ten-bit field. You can use the following global constant as a mask for these bits:

```
ddpLenMask     .EQU     $03FF
```

The following constant indicates the maximum length of a DDP datagram:

```
ddpMaxData     .EQU     586
```

When you call DDP to send a datagram, you pass it information about the datagram in a write data structure with the format shown in Figure 8.

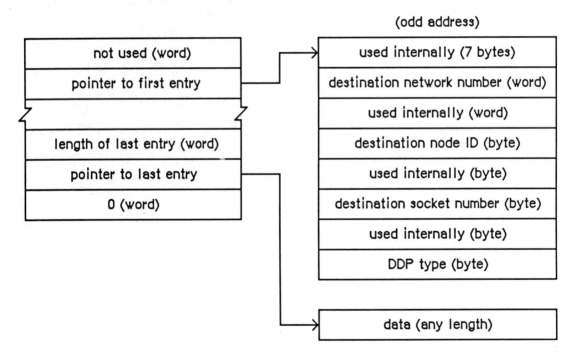

Figure 8. Write Data Structure for DDP

The first seven bytes are used internally for the ALAP header and the DDP datagram length and checksum. The other bytes used internally store the network number, node ID, and socket number of the socket client sending the datagram.

Warning: The first entry in a DDP write data structure must begin at an odd address.

If you specify a node ID of 255, the datagram will be broadcast to all nodes within the destination network. A network number of 0 means the local network to which the node is connected.

Warning: DDP always destroys the high-order byte of the destination network number when it sends a datagram with a short header. Therefore, if you want to reuse the first entry of a DDP write data structure entry, you must restore the destination network number.

Using DDP

Before it can use a socket, the program must call OpenSkt, which adds a socket and its socket listener to the socket table. When a client is finished using a socket, call CloseSkt, which removes the socket's entry from the socket table. To send a datagram via DDP, call WriteDDP. If you want to read DDP datagrams, you must write your own socket listener. DDP will send every incoming datagram for that socket to your socket listener.

See the "Protocol Handlers and Socket Listeners" section for information on how to write a socket listener.

DDP Routines

OpenSkt function

Parameter block

→	26	csCode	word	;always openSkt
↔	28	socket	byte	;socket number
→	30	listener	pointer	;socket listener

OpenSkt adds a socket and its socket listener to the socket table. If the socket parameter is nonzero, it must be in the range 64 to 127, and it specifies the socket's number; if socket is 0, OpenSkt opens a socket with a socket number in the range 128 to 254, and returns it in the socket parameter. Listener contains a pointer to the socket listener.

OpenSkt will return ddpSktErr if you pass the number of an already opened socket, if you pass a socket number greater than 127, or if the socket table is full (the socket table can hold a maximum of 12 sockets).

Result codes	noErr	No error
	ddpSktErr	Socket error

CloseSkt function

Parameter block

→	26	csCode	word	;always closeSkt
→	28	socket	byte	;socket number

CloseSkt removes the entry of the specified socket from the socket table. If you pass a socket number of 0, or if you attempt to close a socket that isn't open, CloseSkt will return ddpSktErr.

Result codes	noErr	No error
	ddpSktErr	Socket error

WriteDDP function

Parameter block

→	26	csCode	word	;always writeDDP
→	28	socket	byte	;socket number
→	29	checksumFlag	byte	;checksum flag
→	30	wdsPointer	pointer	;write data structure

WriteDDP sends a datagram to another socket. WDSPointer points to a write data structure containing the datagram and the address of the destination socket. If checksumFlag is TRUE, WriteDDP will compute the checksum for all datagrams requiring long headers.

Result codes	noErr	No error
	ddpLenErr	Datagram length too big
	ddpSktErr	Socket error
	noBridgeErr	No bridge found

AppleTalk Transaction Protocol

Data Structures

An ATP packet consists of an ALAP header, DDP header, and ATP header, followed by actual data (Figure 9). You can use the following global constants to access the contents of an ATP header:

```
atpControl      .EQU    0       ;control information
atpBitMap       .EQU    1       ;bit map
atpRespNo       .EQU    1       ;sequence number
atpTransID      .EQU    2       ;transaction ID
atpUserData     .EQU    4       ;user bytes
```

The size of an ATP header is given by the following constant:

```
atpHdSz         .EQU    8
```

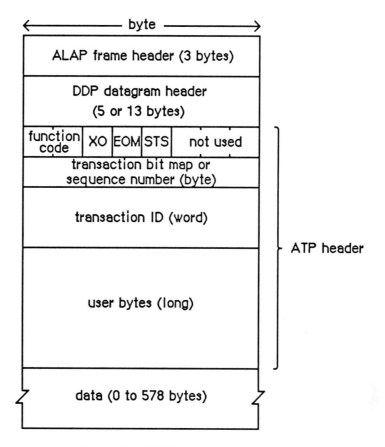

Figure 9. ATP Packet

ATP packets are identified by the following DDP protocol type:

```
atp              .EQU     3
```

The control information contains a function code and various control bits. The function code identifies either a TReq, TResp, or TRel packet with one of the following global constants:

```
atpReqCode       .EQU     $40      ;TReq packet
atpRspCode       .EQU     $80      ;TResp packet
atpRelCode       .EQU     $C0      ;TRel packet
```

The send-transmission-status, end-of-message, and exactly-once bits in the control information are accessed via the following global constants:

```
atpSTSBit        .EQU     3        ;send-transmission-status bit
atpEOMBit        .EQU     4        ;end-of-message bit
atpXOBit         .EQU     5        ;exactly-once bit
```

Many ATP calls require a field called atpFlags (Figure 10), which contains the above three bits plus the following two bits:

```
sendChk        .EQU    0       ;send-checksum bit
tidValid       .EQU    1       ;transaction ID validity bit
```

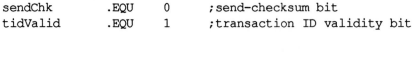

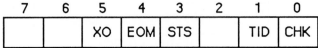

Figure 10. ATPFlags Field

The maximum number of response packets in an ATP transaction is given by the following global constant:

```
atpMaxNum      .EQU    8
```

When you call ATP to send responses, you pass the responses in a response BDS, which is a list of up to eight elements, each of which contains the following:

```
bdsBuffSz      .EQU    0       ;size of data to send
bdsBuffAddr    .EQU    2       ;pointer to data
bdsUserData    .EQU    8       ;user bytes
```

When you call ATP to receive responses, you pass it a response BDS with up to eight elements, each in the following format:

```
bdsBuffSz      .EQU    0       ;buffer size in bytes
bdsBuffAddr    .EQU    2       ;pointer to buffer
bdsDataSz      .EQU    6       ;number of bytes actually received
bdsUserData    .EQU    8       ;user bytes
```

The size of a BDS element is given by the following constant:

```
bdsEntrySz     .EQU    12
```

ATP clients are identified by internet addresses in the form shown in Figure 11.

```
┌─────────────────────────────┐
│   network number (word)     │
├─────────────────────────────┤
│      node ID (byte)         │
├─────────────────────────────┤
│   socket number (byte)      │
└─────────────────────────────┘
```

Figure 11. Internet Address

Using ATP

Before you can use ATP on a Macintosh 128K, the .ATP driver must be read from the system resource file via a Device Manager Open call. The name of the .ATP driver is '.ATP' and its reference number is −11. When the .ATP driver is opened, it reads its ATP code into the application heap and installs a task into the vertical retrace queue.

> **Warning:** When another application starts up, the application heap is reinitialized; on a Macintosh 128K, this means that the ATP code is lost (and must be reloaded by the next application).

When you're through using ATP on a Macintosh 128K, call the Device Manager Close routine—the system will be returned to the state it was in before the .ATP driver was opened.

On a Macintosh 512K or XL, the .ATP driver will have been loaded into the system heap either at system startup or upon execution of a Device Manager Open call loading MPP. You shouldn't close the .ATP driver on a Macintosh 512K or XL; AppleTalk expects it to remain open on these systems.

To send a request to another socket and get a response, call SendRequest. The call terminates when either an entire response is received or a specified retry timeout interval elapses. To open a socket for the purpose of responding to requests, call OpenATPSkt. Then call GetRequest to receive a request; when a request is received, the call is completed. After receiving and servicing a request, call SendResponse to return response information. If you cannot or do not want to send the entire response all at once, make a SendResponse call to send some of the response, and then call AddResponse later to send the remainder of the response. To close a socket opened for the purpose of sending responses, call CloseATPSkt.

During exactly-once transactions, SendResponse doesn't terminate until the transaction is completed via a TRel packet, or the retry count is exceeded.

> **Warning:** Don't modify the parameter block passed to an ATP call until the call is completed.

ATP Routines

OpenATPSkt function

Parameter block

→	26	csCode	word	;always openATPSkt
↔	28	atpSocket	byte	;socket number
→	30	addrBlock	long word	;socket request specification

OpenATPSkt opens a socket for the purpose of receiving requests. ATPSocket contains the socket number of the socket to open. If it's 0, a number is dynamically assigned and returned in atpSocket. AddrBlock contains a specification of the socket addresses from which requests will be accepted. A 0 in the network number, node ID, or socket number field of addrBlock means that requests will be accepted from every network, node, or socket, respectively.

Result codes	noErr	No error
	tooManySkts	Too many responding sockets
	noDataArea	Too many outstanding ATP calls

CloseATPSkt function

Parameter block

→	26	csCode	word	;always closeATPSkt
→	28	atpSocket	byte	;socket number

CloseATPSkt closes the socket whose number is specified by atpSocket, for the purpose of receiving requests.

Result codes	noErr	No error
	noDataArea	Too many outstanding ATP calls

SendRequest function

Parameter block

→	18	userData	long word	;user bytes
←	22	reqTID	word	;transaction ID used in request
→	26	csCode	word	;always sendRequest
←	28	currBitMap	byte	;bit map
↔	29	atpFlags	byte	;control information
→	30	addrBlock	long word	;destination socket address
→	34	reqLength	word	;request size in bytes
→	36	reqPointer	pointer	;pointer to request data
→	40	bdsPointer	pointer	;pointer to response BDS
→	44	numOfBuffs	byte	;number of responses expected
→	45	timeOutVal	byte	;timeout interval
←	46	numOfResps	byte	;number of responses received
↔	47	retryCount	byte	;number of retries

SendRequest sends a request to another socket and waits for a response. UserData contains the four user bytes. AddrBlock indicates the socket to which the request should be sent. ReqLength and reqPointer contain the size and location of the request to send. BDSPointer points to a response BDS where the responses are to be returned; numOfBuffs indicates the number of responses requested. The number of responses received is returned in numOfResps. If a nonzero value is returned in numOfResps, you can examine currBitMap to determine which packets of the transaction were actually received and to detect pieces for higher-level recovery, if desired.

TimeOutVal indicates the number of seconds that SendRequest should wait for a response before resending the request. RetryCount indicates the maximum number of retries SendRequest should attempt. The end-of-message flag of atpFlags will be set if the EOM bit is set in the last packet received in a valid response sequence. The exactly-once flag should be set if you want the request to be part of an exactly-once transaction.

To cancel a SendRequest call, you need the transaction ID; it's returned in reqTID. You can examine reqTID before the completion of the call, but its contents are valid only after the tidValid bit of atpFlags has been set.

SendRequest completes when either an entire response is received or the retry count is exceeded.

Note: The value provided in retryCount will be modified during SendRequest if any retries are made. This field is used to monitor the number of retries; for each retry, it's decremented by 1.

Result codes	noErr	No error
	reqFailed	Retry count exceeded
	tooManyReqs	Too many concurrent requests
	noDataArea	Too many outstanding ATP calls
	reqAborted	Request canceled by user

GetRequest function

Parameter block

←	18	userData	long word	;user bytes
→	26	csCode	word	;always getRequest
→	28	atpSocket	byte	;socket number
←	29	atpFlags	byte	;control information
←	30	addrBlock	long word	;source of request
↔	34	reqLength	word	;request buffer size
→	36	reqPointer	pointer	;pointer to request buffer
←	44	bitMap	byte	;bit map
←	46	transID	word	;transaction ID

GetRequest sets up the mechanism to receive a request sent by a SendRequest call. UserData returns the four user bytes from the request. ATPSocket contains the socket number of the socket that should listen for a request. The internet address of the socket from which the request was sent is returned in addrBlock. ReqLength and reqPointer indicate the size (in bytes) and location of a buffer to store the incoming request. The actual size of the request is returned in reqLength. The transaction bit map and transaction ID will be returned in bitMap and transID. The exactly-once flag in atpFlags will be set if the request is part of an exactly-once transaction.

GetRequest completes when a request is received.

Result codes	noErr	No error
	badATPSkt	Bad responding socket

SendResponse function

Parameter block

←	18	userData	long word	;user bytes from TRel
→	26	csCode	word	;always sendResponse
→	28	atpSocket	byte	;socket number
→	29	atpFlags	byte	;control information
→	30	addrBlock	long word	;response destination
→	40	bdsPointer	pointer	;pointer to response BDS
→	44	numOfBuffs	byte	;number of response packets being sent
→	45	bdsSize	byte	;BDS size in elements
→	46	transID	word	;transaction ID

SendResponse sends a response to a socket. If the response was part of an exactly-once transaction, userData will contain the user bytes from the TRel packet. ATPSocket contains the socket number from which the response should be sent. The end-of-message flag in atpFlags should be set if the response contains the final packet in a transaction composed of a group of packets and the number of responses is less than requested. AddrBlock indicates the address of the socket to which the response should be sent. BDSPointer points to a response BDS containing room for the maximum number of responses to be sent; bdsSize contains this maximum number. NumOfBuffs contains the number of response packets to be sent in this call; you may wish to make AddResponse calls to complete the response. TransID indicates the transaction ID of the associated request.

During exactly-once transactions, SendResponse doesn't complete until either a TRel packet is received from the socket that made the request, or the retry count is exceeded.

Result codes	noErr	No error
	badATPSkt	Bad responding socket
	noRelErr	No release received
	noDataArea	Too many outstanding ATP calls
	badBuffNum	Sequence number out of range

AddResponse function

Parameter block

→	18	userData	long word	;user bytes
→	26	csCode	word	;always addResponse
→	28	atpSocket	byte	;socket number
→	29	atpFlags	byte	;control information
→	30	addrBlock	long word	;response destination
→	34	reqLength	word	;response size
→	36	reqPointer	pointer	;pointer to response
→	44	rspNum	byte	;sequence number
→	46	transID	word	;transaction ID

AddResponse sends an additional response packet to a socket that has already been sent the initial part of a response via SendResponse. UserData contains the four user bytes. ATPSocket contains the socket number from which the response should be sent. The end-of-message flag in atpFlags should be set if this response packet is the final packet in a transaction composed of a group of packets and the number of responses is less than requested. AddrBlock indicates the socket to which the response should be sent. ReqLength and reqPointer contain the size (in bytes) and location of the response to send; rspNum indicates the sequence number of the response (in the range 0 to 7). TransID must contain the transaction ID.

Warning: If the transaction is part of an exactly-once transaction, the buffer used in the AddResponse call must not be altered or released until the corresponding SendResponse call has completed.

Result codes   noErr   No error
                        badATPSkt   Bad responding socket
                        noSendResp   AddResponse issued before SendResponse
                        badBuffNum   Sequence number out of range
                        noDataArea   Too many outstanding ATP calls

RelTCB function

Parameter block

→	26	csCode	word	;always relTCB
→	30	addrBlock	long word	;destination of request
→	46	transID	word	;transaction ID of request

RelTCB dequeues the specified SendRequest call and returns the result code reqAborted for the aborted call. The transaction ID can be obtained from the reqTID field of the SendRequest queue entry; see the description of SendRequest for details.

Result codes   noErr   No error
                        cbNotFound   ATP control block not found
                        noDataArea   Too many outstanding ATP calls

RelRspCB function

Parameter block

→	26	csCode	word	;always relRspCB
→	28	atpSocket	byte	;socket number that request was received on
→	30	addrBlock	long word	;source of request
→	46	transID	word	;transaction ID of request

In an exactly-once transaction, RelRspCB cancels the specified SendResponse, without waiting for the release timer to expire or a TRel packet to be received. No error is returned for the SendResponse call. Whan called to cancel a transaction that isn't using exactly-once service, RelRspCB returns cbNotFound. The transaction ID can be obtained from the reqTID field of the SendResponse queue entry; see the description of SendResponse for details.

Result codes   noErr   No error
                        cbNotFound   ATP control block not found

Name-Binding Protocol

Data Structures

The first two bytes in the NBP header (Figure 12) indicate the type of the packet, the number of tuples in the packet, and an NBP packet identifier. You can use the following global constants to access these bytes:

```
nbpControl      .EQU    0    ;packet type
nbpTCount       .EQU    0    ;tuple count
nbpID           .EQU    1    ;packet identifier
nbpTuple        .EQU    2    ;start of first tuple
```

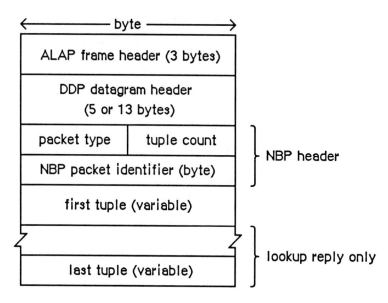

Figure 12. NBP Packet

NBP packets are identified by the following DDP protocol type:

```
nbp             .EQU    2
```

NBP uses the following global constants in the nbpControl field to identify NBP packets:

```
brRq            .EQU    1    ;broadcast request
lkUp            .EQU    2    ;lookup request
lkUpReply       .EQU    3    ;lookup reply
```

NBP entities are identified by internet address in the form shown in Figure 13 below. Entities are also identified by tuples, which include both an internet address and an entity name. You can use the following global constants to access information in tuples:

```
tupleNet        .EQU    0    ;network number
tupleNode       .EQU    2    ;node ID
tupleSkt        .EQU    3    ;socket number
tupleEnum       .EQU    4    ;used internally
tupleName       .EQU    5    ;entity name
```

The meta-characters in an entity name can be identified with the following global constants:

```
equals          .EQU    '='    ;"wild-card" meta-character
star            .EQU    '*'    ;"this zone" meta-character
```

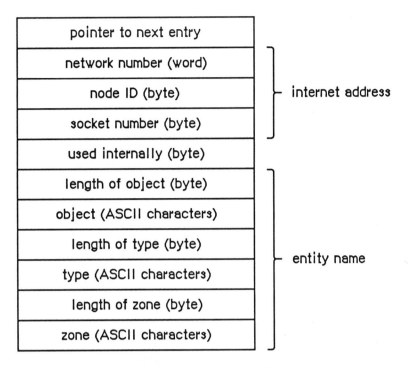

Figure 13. Names Table Entry

The maximum number of tuples in an NBP packet is given by the following global constant:

```
tupleMax      .EQU      15
```

Entity names are mapped to sockets via the names table. Each entry in the names table has the structure shown in Figure 13.

You can use the following global constants to access some of the elements of a names table entry:

```
ntLink        .EQU      0      ;pointer to next entry
ntTuple       .EQU      4      ;tuple
ntSocket      .EQU      7      ;socket number
ntEntity      .EQU      9      ;entity name
```

The socket number of the names information socket is given by the following global constant:

```
nis           .EQU      2
```

Using NBP

On a Macintosh 128K, before calling any other NBP routines, call the LoadNBP function, which reads the NBP code from the system resource file into the application heap. (The NBP code is part of the .MPP driver, which has a driver reference number of –10.) When you're finished with NBP and want to reclaim the space its code occupies, call UnloadNBP. On a Macintosh 512K or XL, the NBP code is read in when the .MPP driver is loaded.

Warning: When an application starts up, the application heap is reinitialized; on a Macintosh 128K, this means that the NBP code is lost (and must be reloaded by the next application).

When an entity wants to communicate via an AppleTalk network, it should call RegisterName to place its name and internet address in the names table. When an entity no longer wants to communicate on the network, or is being shut down, it should call RemoveName to remove its entry from the names table.

To determine the address of an entity you know only by name, call LookupName, which returns a list of all entities with the name you specify. If you already know the address of an entity, and want only to confirm that it still exists, call ConfirmName. ConfirmName is more efficient than LookupName in terms of network traffic.

NBP Routines

RegisterName function

Parameter block

→	26	csCode	word	;always registerName
→	28	interval	byte	;retry interval
↔	29	count	byte	;retry count
→	30	ntQElPtr	pointer	;names table element pointer
→	34	verifyFlag	byte	;set if verify needed

RegisterName adds the name and address of an entity to the node's names table. NTQElPtr points to a names table entry containing the entity's name and internet address (in the form shown in Figure 13 above). Meta-characters aren't allowed in the object and type fields of the entity name; the zone field, however, *must* contain the meta-character "*". If verifyFlag is TRUE, RegisterName checks on the network to see if the name is already in use, and returns a result code of nbpDuplicate if so. Interval and count contain the retry interval in eight-tick units and the retry count. When a retry is made, the count field is modified.

Warning: The names table entry passed to RegisterName remains the property of NBP until removed from the names table. Don't attempt to remove or modify it. If you've allocated memory using a NewHandle call, you must lock it as long as the name is registered.

Warning: VerifyFlag should normally be set before calling RegisterName.

Result codes	noErr	No error
	nbpDuplicate	Duplicate name already exists
	nbpNISErr	Error opening names information socket

LookupName function

Parameter block

→	26	csCode	word	;always lookupName
→	28	interval	byte	;retry interval
↔	29	count	byte	;retry count
→	30	entityPtr	pointer	;pointer to entity name
→	34	retBuffPtr	pointer	;pointer to buffer
→	38	retBuffSize	word	;buffer size in bytes
→	40	maxToGet	word	;matches to get
←	42	numGotten	word	;matches found

LookupName returns the addresses of all entities with a specified name. EntityPtr points to the entity's name (in the form shown in Figure 13 above). Meta-characters are allowed in the entity name. RetBuffPtr and retBuffSize contain the location and size of an area of memory in which the tuples describing the entity names and their corresponding addresses should be returned. MaxToGet indicates the maximum number of matching names to find addresses for; the actual number of addresses found is returned in numGotten. Interval and count contain the retry interval and the retry count. LookupName completes when either the number of matches is equal to or greater than maxToGet, or the retry count has been exceeded. The count field is decremented for each retransmission.

> **Note:** NumGotten is first set to 0 and then incremented with each match found. You can test the value in this field, and can start examining the received addresses in the buffer while the lookup continues.

Result codes	noErr	No error
	nbpBuffOvr	Buffer overflow

ConfirmName function

Parameter block

→	26	csCode	word	;always confirmName
→	28	interval	byte	;retry interval
↔	29	count	byte	;retry count
→	30	entityPtr	pointer	;pointer to entity name
→	34	confirmAddr	pointer	;entity address
←	38	newSocket	byte	;socket number

ConfirmName confirms that an entity known by name and address still exists (is still entered in the names directory). EntityPtr points to the entity's name (in the form shown in Figure 13 above). ConfirmAddr specifies the address to confirmed. No meta-characters are allowed in the entity name. Interval and count contain the retry interval and the retry count. The socket number of the entity is returned in newSocket. ConfirmName is more efficient than LookupName in terms of network traffic.

Result codes	noErr	No error
	nbpConfDiff	Name confirmed for different socket
	nbpNoConfirm	Name not confirmed

RemoveName function

Parameter block

→	26	csCode	word	;always removeName
→	30	entityPtr	pointer	;pointer to entity name

RemoveName removes an entity name from the names table of the given entity's node.

Result codes	noErr	No error
	nbpNotFound	Name not found

LoadNBP function

Parameter block

→	26	csCode	word	;always loadNBP

On a Macintosh 128K, LoadNBP reads the NBP code from the system resource file into the application heap; on a Macintosh 512K or XL it has no effect.

Result codes	noErr	No error

UnloadNBP function

Parameter block

→	26	csCode	word	;always unloadNBP

On a Macintosh 128K, UnloadNBP makes the NBP code purgeable; the space isn't actually released by the Memory Manager until necessary. On a Macintosh 512K or XL, UnloadNBP has no effect.

Result codes	noErr	No error

PROTOCOL HANDLERS AND SOCKET LISTENERS

This section describes how to write your own protocol handlers and socket listeners. If you're only interested in using the default protocol handlers and socket listeners provided by the Pascal interface, you can skip this section. Protocol handlers and socket listeners must be written in assembly language because they'll be called by the .MPP driver with parameters in various registers not directly accessible from Pascal.

The .MPP and .ATP drivers have been designed to maximize overall throughput while minimizing code size. Two principal sources of loss of throughput are unnecessary buffer copying and inefficient mechanisms for dispatching (routing) packets between the various layers of the network protocol architecture. The AppleTalk Manager completely eliminates buffer copying by using simple, efficient dispatching mechanisms at two important points of the data reception path: protocol handlers and socket listeners. To write your own, you should understand the flow of control in this path.

Data Reception in the AppleTalk Manager

When the SCC detects an ALAP frame addressed to the particular node (or a broadcast frame), it interrupts the Macintosh's MC68000. An interrupt handler built into the .MPP driver gets control and begins servicing the interrupt. Meanwhile, the frame's ALAP header bytes are coming into the SCC's data reception buffer; this is a three-byte FIFO buffer. The interrupt handler must remove these bytes from the SCC's buffer to make room for the bytes right behind; for this purpose, MPP has an internal buffer, known as the Read Header Area (RHA), into which it places these three bytes.

The third byte of the frame contains the ALAP protocol type field. If the most significant bit of this field is set (that is, ALAP protocol types 128 to 255), the frame is an ALAP control frame. Since ALAP control frames are only three bytes long (plus two CRC bytes), for such frames the interrupt handler simply confirms that the CRC bytes indicate an error-free frame and then performs the specified action.

If, however, the frame being received is a data frame (that is, ALAP protocol types 1 to 127), intended for a higher layer of the protocol architecture implemented on that Macintosh, this means that additional data bytes are coming right behind. The interrupt handler must immediately pass control to the protocol handler corresponding to the protocol type specified in the third byte of the ALAP frame for continued reception of the frame. To allow for such a dispatching mechanism, the ALAP code in MPP maintains a protocol table. This consists of a list of currently used ALAP protocol types with the memory addresses of their corresponding protocol handlers. To allow MPP to transfer control to a protocol handler you've written, you must make an appropriate entry in the protocol table with a valid ALAP protocol type and the memory address of your code module.

To enter your protocol handler into the protocol table, issue the LAPOpenProtocol call from Pascal or an AttachPH call from assembly language. Thereafter, whenever an ALAP header with your ALAP protocol type is received, MPP will call your protocol handler. When you no longer wish to receive packets of that ALAP protocol type, call LAPCloseProtocol from Pascal or DetachPH from assembly language.

> **Warning:** Remember that ALAP protocol types 1 and 2 are reserved by DDP for the default protocol handler and that types 128 to 255 are used by ALAP for its control frames.

A protocol handler is a piece of assembly-language code that controls the reception of AppleTalk packets of a given ALAP protocol type. More specifically, a protocol handler must carry out the reception of the rest of the frame following the ALAP header. The nature of a particular protocol handler depends on the characteristics of the protocol for which it was written. In the simplest case, the protocol handler simply reads the entire packet into an internal buffer. A more sophisticated protocol handler might read in the header of its protocol, and on the basis of information contained in it, decide where to put the rest of the packet's data. In certain cases, the protocol handler might, after examining the header corresponding to its own protocol, in turn transfer control to a similar piece of code at the next-higher level of the protocol architecture (for example, in the case of DDP, its protocol handler must call the socket listener of the datagram's destination socket).

In this way, protocol handlers are used to allow "on the fly" decisions regarding the intended recipient of the packets's data, and thus avoid buffer copying. By using protocol handlers and their counterparts in higher layers (for instance, socket listeners), data sent over the AppleTalk network is read directly from the network into the destination's buffer.

Writing Protocol Handlers

When the .MPP driver calls your protocol handler, it has already read the first five bytes of the packet into the RHA. These are the three-byte ALAP header and the next two bytes of the packet. The two bytes following the header must contain the length in bytes of the data in the packet, including these two bytes themselves, but excluding the ALAP header.

Note: Since ALAP packets can have at most 600 data bytes, only the lower ten bits of this length value are significant.

After determining how many bytes to read and where to put them, the protocol handler must call one or both of two functions that perform all the low-level manipulation of the SCC required to read bytes from the network. ReadPacket can be called repeatedly to read in the packet piecemeal or ReadRest can be called to read the rest of the packet. Any number of ReadPacket calls can be used, as long as a ReadRest call is made to read the final piece of the packet. This is necessary because ReadRest restores state information and verifies that the hardware-generated CRC is correct. An error will be returned if the protocol handler attempts to use ReadPacket to read more bytes than remain in the packet.

When MPP passes control to your protocol handler, it passes various parameters and pointers in the processor's registers:

Register(s)	Contents
A0-A1	SCC addresses used by MPP
A2	Pointer to MPP's local variables (discussed below)
A3	Pointer to next free byte in RHA
A4	Pointer to ReadPacket and ReadRest jump table
D1 (word)	Number of bytes left to read in packet

These registers, with the exception of A3, must be preserved until ReadRest is called. A3 is used as an input parameter to ReadPacket and ReadRest, so its contents may be changed. D0, D2, and D3 are free for your use. In addition, register A5 has been saved by MPP and may be used by the protocol handler until ReadRest is called. When control returns to the protocol handler from ReadRest, MPP no longer needs the data in these registers. At that point, standard interrupt routine conventions apply and the protocol handler can freely use A0-A3 and D0-D3 (they're restored by the interrupt handler).

D1 contains the number of bytes left to be read in the packet as derived from the packet's length field. A transmission error could corrupt the length field or some bytes in the packet might be lost, but this won't be discovered until the end of the packet is reached and the CRC checked.

When the protocol handler is first called, the first five bytes of the packet (ALAP destination node ID, source node ID, ALAP protocol type, and length) can be read from the RHA. Since A3 is pointing to the next free position in the RHA, these bytes can be read using negative offsets from A3. For instance, the ALAP source node ID is at −4(A3), the packet's data length (given in D1) is also pointed to by –2(A3), and so on. Alternatively, they can be accessed as positive offsets from the top of the RHA. The effective address of the top of the RHA is toRHA(A2), so the following code could be used to obtain the ALAP type field:

```
LEA      toRHA(A2),A5      ;A5 points to top of RHA
MOVE.B   lapType(A5),D2    ;load D2 with type field
```

These methods are valid only as long as SCC interrupts remain locked out (which they are when the protocol handler is first called). If the protocol handler lowers the interrupt level, another packet could arrive over the network and invalidate the contents of the RHA.

You can call ReadPacket by jumping through the jump table in the following way:

```
JSR   (A4)
```

On entry D3: number of bytes to be read (word)
          A3: pointer to a buffer to hold the bytes

On exit   D0: modified
          D1: number of bytes left to read in packet (word)
          D2: preserved
          D3: = 0   if requested number of bytes were read
               <> 0 if error
          A0-A2: preserved
          A3: pointer to one byte past the last byte read

ReadPacket reads the number of bytes specified in D3 into the buffer pointed to by A3. The number of bytes remaining to be read in the packet is returned in D1. A3 points to the byte following the last byte read.

You can call ReadRest by jumping through the jump table in the following way:

```
JSR   2(A4)
```

On entry A3: pointer to a buffer to hold the bytes
          D3: size of the buffer (word)

On exit   D0-D1: modified
          D2: preserved
          D3: = 0 if packet was exactly the size of the buffer
               < 0 if packet was (–D3) bytes too large to fit in buffer and was
                    truncated
               > 0 if D3 bytes weren't read (packet is smaller than buffer)
          A0-A2: preserved
          A3: pointer to one byte past the last byte read

ReadRest reads the remaining bytes of the packet into the buffer whose size is given in D3 and whose location is pointed to by A3. The result of the operation is returned in D3.

ReadRest can be called with D3 set to a buffer size greater than the packet size; ReadPacket cannot (it will return an error).

Warning: Remember to always call ReadRest to read the last part of a packet; otherwise the system will eventually crash.

If at any point before it has read the last byte of a packet, the protocol handler wants to discard the remaining data, it should terminate by calling ReadRest as follows:

```
MOVEQ    #0,D3        ;byte count of 0
JSR      2(A4)        ;call ReadRest
RTS
```

Or, equivalently:

```
MOVEQ    #0,D3        ;byte count of 0
JMP      2(A4)        ;JMP to ReadRest, not JSR
```

In all other cases, the protocol handler should end with an RTS, even if errors were detected. If MPP returns an error from a ReadPacket call, the protocol handler must quit via an RTS without calling ReadRest at all (in this case it has already been called by MPP).

The Z (Zero) condition code is set upon return from these routines to indicate the presence of errors (CRC, overrun, and so on). Zero bit set means no error was detected; a nonzero condition code implies an error of some kind.

Up to 24 bytes of temporary storage are available in MPP's RHA. When the protocol handler is called, 19 of these bytes are free for its use. It may read several bytes (at least four are suggested) into this area to empty the SCC's buffer and buy some time for further processing.

MPP's globals include some variables that you may find useful. They're allocated as a block of memory pointed to by the contents of the global variable ABusVars, but a protocol handler can access them by offsets from A2:

Name	Contents
sysLAPAddr	This node's node ID (byte)
toRHA	Top of the Read Header Area (24 bytes)
sysABridge	Node ID of a bridge (byte)
sysNetNum	This node's network number (word)
vSCCEnable	Status Register (SR) value to re-enable SCC interrupts (word)

Warning: Under no circumstances should your protocol handler modify these variables. It can read them to find the node's ID, its network number, and the node ID of a bridge on the AppleTalk internet.

If, after reading the entire packet from the network and using the data in the RHA, the protocol handler needs to do extensive post-processing, it can load the value in vSCCEnable into the SR to enable interrupts. To allow your programs to run transparently on any Macintosh, use the value in vSCCEnable rather than directly manipulating the interrupt level by changing specific bits in the SR.

Additional information, such as the driver's version number or reference number and a pointer (or handle) to the driver itself, may be obtained from MPP's device control entry. This can be found by dereferencing the handle in the unit table's entry corresponding to unit number 9; for more information, see the section "The Structure of a Device Driver" in chapter 6.

Timing Considerations

Once it's been called by MPP, your protocol handler has complete responsibility for receiving the rest of the packet. The operation of your protocol handler is time-critical. Since it's called just after MPP has emptied the SCC's three-byte buffer, the protocol handler has approximately 95 microseconds (best case) before it must call ReadPacket or ReadRest. Failure to do so will result in an overrun of the SCC's buffer and loss of packet information. If, within that time, the protocol handler can't determine where to put the entire incoming packet, it should call ReadPacket to read at least four bytes into some private buffer (possibly the RHA). Doing this will again empty the SCC's buffer and buy another 95 microseconds. You can do this as often as necessary, as long as the processing time between successive calls to ReadPacket doesn't exceed 95 microseconds.

Writing Socket Listeners

A socket listener is a piece of assembly-language code that receives datagrams delivered by the DDP built-in protocol handler and delivers them to the client owning that socket.

When a datagram (a packet with ALAP protocol type 1 or 2) is received by the ALAP, DDP's built-in protocol handler is called. This handler reads the DDP header into the RHA, examines the destination socket number, and determines whether this socket is open by searching DDP's socket table. This table lists the socket number and corresponding socket listener address for each open socket. If an entry is found matching the destination socket, the protocol handler immediately transfers control to the appropriate socket listener. (To allow DDP to recognize and branch to a socket listener you've written, call DDPOpenSocket from Pascal or OpenSkt from assembly language.)

At this point, the registers are set up as follows:

Register(s)	Contents
A0-A1	SCC addresses used by MPP
A2	Pointer to MPP's local variables (discussed above)
A3	Pointer to next free byte in RHA
A4	Pointer to ReadPacket and ReadRest jump table
D0	This packet's destination socket number (byte)
D1	Number of bytes left to read in packet (word)

The entire ALAP and DDP headers are in the RHA; these are the only bytes of the packet that have been read in from the SCC's buffer. The socket listener can get the destination socket number from D0 to select a buffer into which the packet can be read. The listener then calls ReadPacket and ReadRest as described under "Writing Protocol Handlers" above. The timing considerations discussed in that section apply as well, as do the issues related to accessing the MPP local variables.

The socket listener may examine the ALAP and DDP headers to extract the various fields relevant to its particular client's needs. To do so, it must first examine the ALAP protocol type field (three bytes from the beginning of the RHA) to decide whether a short (ALAP protocol type=1) or long (ALAP protocol type=2) header has been received.

A long DDP header containing a nonzero checksum field implies that the datagram was checksummed at the source. In this case, the listener can recalculate the checksum using the received datagram, and compare it with the checksum value. The following subroutine can be used for this purpose:

```
DoChksum    ;
            ; D1 (word) = number of bytes to checksum
            ; D3 (word) = current checksum
            ; A1 points to the bytes to checksum
            ;
            CLR.W     D0          ;clear high byte
            SUBQ.W    #1,D1       ;decrement count for DBRA
Loop        MOVE.B    (A1)+,D0    ;read a byte into D0
            ADD.W     D0,D3       ;accumulate checksum
            ROL.W     #1,D3       ;rotate left one bit
            DBRA      D1,Loop     ;loop if more bytes
            RTS
```

Note: D0 is modified by DoChksum.

The checksum must be computed for all bytes starting with the DDP header byte following the checksum field up to the last data byte (not including the CRC bytes). The socket listener must start by first computing the checksum for the DDP header fields in the RHA. This is done as follows:

```
            CLR.W     D3          ;set checksum to 0
            MOVEQ     #ddpHSzLong-ddpDstNet,D1
                                  ;length of header part to checksum
            LEA       toRHA+lapHdSz+ddpDstNet(A2),A1
                                  ;point to destination network number
            JSR       DoChksum
            ; D3 = accumulated checksum of DDP header part
```

The socket listener must now continue to set up D1 and A1 for each subsequent portion of the datagram, and call DoChksum for each. It must not alter the value in D3.

The situation of the calculated checksum being equal to 0 requires special attention. For such packets, the source sends a value of –1 to distinguish them from unchecksummed packets. At the end of its checksum computation, the socket listener must examine the value in D3 to see if it's 0. If so, it's converted to –1 and compared with the received checksum to determine whether there was a checksum error:

```
            TST.W     D3          ;is calculated value 0?
            BNE.S     @1          ;no -- go and use it
            SUBQ.W    #1,D3       ;it is 0; make it -1
@1          CMP.W     toRHA+lapHdSz+ddpChecksum(A2),D3
            BNE       ChksumError
```

SUMMARY OF THE APPLETALK MANAGER

Constants

```
CONST lapSize = 20;     {ABusRecord size for ALAP}
      ddpSize = 26;     {ABusRecord size for DDP}
      nbpSize = 26;     {ABusRecord size for NBP}
      atpSize = 56;     {ABusRecord size for ATP}
```

Data Types

```
TYPE ABProtoType = (lapProto,ddpProto,nbpProto,atpProto);

     ABRecHandle = ^ABRecPtr;
     ABRecPtr    = ^ABusRecord;
     ABusRecord  =
       RECORD
           abOpcode:       ABCallType;   {type of call}
           abResult:       INTEGER;      {result code}
           abUserReference: LONGINT;     {for your use}
           CASE ABProtoType OF
             lapProto:
               (lapAddress: LAPAdrBlock; {destination or source node ID}
                lapReqCount: INTEGER;    {length of frame data or buffer }
                                         { size in bytes}
                lapActCount  INTEGER;    {number of frame data bytes }
                                         { actually received}
                lapDataPtr: Ptr);        {pointer to frame data or pointer }
                                         { to buffer}
             ddpProto:
               (ddpType:     Byte;       {DDP protocol type}
                ddpSocket:   Byte;       {source or listening socket number}
                ddpAddress:  AddrBlock;  {destination or source socket address}
                ddpReqCount: INTEGER;    {length of datagram data or buffer }
                                         { size in bytes}
                ddpActCount: INTEGER;    {number of bytes actually received}
                ddpDataPtr:  Ptr;        {pointer to buffer}
                ddpNodeID:   Byte);      {original destination node ID}
             nbpProto:
               (nbpEntityPtr:     EntityPtr;  {pointer to entity name}
                nbpBufPtr:        Ptr;        {pointer to buffer}
                nbpBufSize:       INTEGER;    {buffer size in bytes}
                nbpDataField:     INTEGER;    {number of addresses or }
                                              { socket number}
                nbpAddress:       AddrBlock;  {socket address}
                nbpRetransmitInfo: RetransType); {retransmission information}
```

```
        atpProto:
           (atpSocket:      Byte;          {listening or responding socket }
                                           { number}
              atpAddress:     AddrBlock;     {destination or source socket }
                                             { address}
              atpReqCount:    INTEGER;       {request size or buffer size}
              atpDataPtr      Ptr;           {pointer to buffer}
              atpRspBDSPtr:   BDSPtr;        {pointer to response BDS}
              atpBitMap:      BitMapType;    {transaction bit map}
              atpTransID:     INTEGER;       {transaction ID}
              atpActCount:    INTEGER;       {number of bytes actually received}
              atpUserData:    LONGINT;       {user bytes}
              atpXO:          BOOLEAN;       {exactly-once flag}
              atpEOM:         BOOLEAN;       {end-of-message flag}
              atpTimeOut:     Byte;          {retry timeout interval in seconds}
              atpRetries:     Byte;          {maximum number of retries}
              atpNumBufs:     Byte;          {number of elements in response }
                                             { BDS or number of response }
                                             { packets sent}
              atpNumRsp:      Byte;          {number of response packets }
                                             { received or sequence number}
              atpBDSSize:     Byte;          {number of elements in response BDS}
              atpRspUData:    LONGINT;       {user bytes sent or received in }
                                             { transaction response}
              atpRspBuf:      Ptr;           {pointer to response message buffer}
              atpRspSize:     INTEGER);      {size of response message buffer}
      END;


   ABCallType = (tLAPRead,tLAPWrite,tDDPRead,tDDPWrite,tNBPLookup,
                 tNBPConfirm,tNBPRegister,tATPSndRequest,
                 tATPGetRequest,tATPSdRsp,tATPAddRsp,tATPRequest,
                 tATPResponse);


   LAPAdrBlock = PACKED RECORD
                   dstNodeID:   Byte;    {destination node ID}
                   srcNodeID:   Byte;    {source node ID}
                   lapProtType: ABByte   {ALAP protocol type}
                 END;


   ABByte = 1..127; {ALAP protocol type}


   AddrBlock = PACKED RECORD
                 aNet:    INTEGER; {network number}
                 aNode:   Byte;    {node ID}
                 aSocket: Byte     {socket number}
               END;


   BDSPtr    = ^BDSType;
   BDSType   = ARRAY[0..7] OF BDSElement; {response BDS}
```

```
BDSElement = RECORD
                 buffSize:  INTEGER;  {buffer size in bytes}
                 buffPtr:   Ptr;      {pointer to buffer}
                 dataSize:  INTEGER;  {number of bytes actually received}
                 userBytes: LONGINT   {user bytes}
             END;

BitMapType = PACKED ARRAY[0..7] OF BOOLEAN;

EntityPtr  = ^EntityName;
EntityName = RECORD
                 objStr:   Str32;  {object}
                 typeStr:  Str32;  {type}
                 zoneStr:  Str32   {zone}
             END;

Str32 = STRING[32];

RetransType =
    PACKED RECORD
      retransInterval: Byte;  {retransmit interval in 8-tick units}
      retransCount:    Byte   {total number of attempts}
    END;
```

Routines [Not in ROM]

Opening and Closing AppleTalk

```
FUNCTION MPPOpen :  OSErr;
FUNCTION MPPClose : OSErr;
```

AppleTalk Link Access Protocol

```
FUNCTION LAPOpenProtocol  (theLAPType: ABByte; protoPtr: Ptr) : OSErr;
FUNCTION LAPCloseProtocol (theLAPType: ABByte) : OSErr;

FUNCTION LAPWrite (abRecord: ABRecHandle; async: BOOLEAN) : OSErr;
```

←	abOpcode	{always tLAPWrite}
←	abResult	{result code}
→	abUserReference	{for your use}
→	lapAddress.dstNodeID	{destination node ID}
→	lapAddress.lapProtType	{ALAP protocol type}
→	lapReqCount	{length of frame data}
→	lapDataPtr	{pointer to frame data}

```
FUNCTION LAPRead (abRecord: ABRecHandle; async: BOOLEAN) : OSErr;
```
←	abOpcode	{always tLAPRead}
←	abResult	{result code}
→	abUserReference	{for your use}
←	lapAddress.dstNodeID	{destination node ID}
←	lapAddress.srcNodeID	{source node ID}
→	lapAddress.lapProtType	{ALAP protocol type}
→	lapReqCount	{buffer size in bytes}
←	lapActCount	{number of frame data bytes actually received}
→	lapDataPtr	{pointer to buffer}

```
FUNCTION LAPRdCancel (abRecord: ABRecHandle) : OSErr;
```

Datagram Delivery Protocol

```
FUNCTION DDPOpenSocket  (VAR theSocket: Byte; sktListener: Ptr) : OSErr;
FUNCTION DDPCloseSocket (theSocket: Byte) : OSErr;

FUNCTION DDPWrite (abRecord: ABRecHandle; doChecksum: BOOLEAN; async:
                BOOLEAN) : OSErr;
```
←	abOpcode	{always tDDPWrite}
←	abResult	{result code}
→	abUserReference	{for your use}
→	ddpType	{DDP protocol type}
→	ddpSocket	{source socket number}
→	ddpAddress	{destination socket address}
→	ddpReqCount	{length of datagram data}
→	ddpDataPtr	{pointer to buffer}

```
FUNCTION DDPRead (abRecord: ABRecHandle; retCksumErrs: BOOLEAN; async:
                BOOLEAN) : OSErr;
```
←	abOpcode	{always tDDPRead}
←	abResult	{result code}
→	abUserReference	{for your use}
←	ddpType	{DDP protocol type}
→	ddpSocket	{listening socket number}
←	ddpAddress	{source socket address}
→	ddpReqCount	{buffer size in bytes}
←	ddpActCount	{number of bytes actually received}
→	ddpDataPtr	{pointer to buffer}
←	ddpNodeID	{original destination node ID}

```
FUNCTION DDPRdCancel (abRecord: ABRecHandle) : OSErr;
```

AppleTalk Transaction Protocol

```
FUNCTION ATPLoad :        OSErr;
FUNCTION ATPUnload :      OSErr;
FUNCTION ATPOpenSocket (addrRcvd: AddrBlock; VAR atpSocket: Byte) : OSErr;
FUNCTION ATPCloseSocket (atpSocket: Byte) : OSErr;
```

```
FUNCTION ATPSndRequest (abRecord: ABRecHandle; async: BOOLEAN) : OSErr;
```
←	abOpcode	{always tATPSndRequest}
←	abResult	{result code}
→	abUserReference	{for your use}
→	atpAddress	{destination socket address}
→	atpReqCount	{request size in bytes}
→	atpDataPtr	{pointer to buffer}
→	atpRspBDSPtr	{pointer to response BDS}
→	atpUserData	{user bytes}
→	atpXO	{exactly-once flag}
←	atpEOM	{end-of-message flag}
→	atpTimeOut	{retry timeout interval in seconds}
→	atpRetries	{maximum number of retries}
→	atpNumBufs	{number of elements in response BDS}
←	atpNumRsp	{number of response packets actually received}

```
FUNCTION ATPRequest (abRecord: ABRecHandle; async: BOOLEAN) : OSErr;
```
←	abOpcode	{always tATPRequest}
←	abResult	{result code}
→	abUserReference	{for your use}
→	atpAddress	{destination socket address}
→	atpReqCount	{request size in bytes}
→	atpDataPtr	{pointer to buffer}
←	atpActCount	{number of bytes actually received}
→	atpUserData	{user bytes}
→	atpXO	{exactly-once flag}
←	atpEOM	{end-of-message flag}
→	atpTimeOut	{retry timeout interval in seconds}
→	atpRetries	{maximum number of retries}
←	atpRspUData	{user bytes received in transaction response}
→	atpRspBuf	{pointer to response message buffer}
→	atpRspSize	{size of response message buffer}

```
FUNCTION ATPReqCancel (abRecord: ABRecHandle; async: BOOLEAN) : OSErr;

FUNCTION ATPGetRequest (abRecord: ABRecHandle; async: BOOLEAN) : OSErr;
```
←	abOpcode	{always tATPGetRequest}
←	abResult	{result code}
→	abUserReference	{for your use}
→	atpSocket	{listening socket number}
←	atpAddress	{source socket address}
→	atpReqCount	{buffer size in bytes}
→	atpDataPtr	{pointer to buffer}
←	atpBitMap	{transaction bit map}
←	atpTransID	{transaction ID}
←	atpActCount	{number of bytes actually received}
←	atpUserData	{user bytes}
←	atpXO	{exactly-once flag}

```
FUNCTION ATPSndRsp (abRecord: ABRecHandle; async: BOOLEAN) : OSErr;
```
←	abOpcode	{always tATPSdRsp}
←	abResult	{result code}
→	abUserReference	{for your use}
→	atpSocket	{responding socket number}
→	atpAddress	{destination socket address}
→	atpRspBDSPtr	{pointer to response BDS}
→	atpTransID	{transaction ID}
→	atpEOM	{end-of-message flag}
→	atpNumBufs	{number of response packets being sent}
→	atpBDSSize	{number of elements in response BDS}

```
FUNCTION ATPAddRsp (abRecord: ABRecHandle) : OSErr;
```
←	abOpcode	{always tATPAddRsp}
←	abResult	{result code}
→	abUserReference	{for your use}
→	atpSocket	{responding socket number}
→	atpAddress	{destination socket address}
→	atpReqCount	{buffer size in bytes}
→	atpDataPtr	{pointer to buffer}
→	atpTransID	{transaction ID}
→	atpUserData	{user bytes}
→	atpEOM	{end-of-message flag}
→	atpNumRsp	{sequence number}

```
FUNCTION ATPResponse (abRecord: ABRecHandle; async: BOOLEAN) : OSErr;
```
←	abOpcode	{always tATPResponse}
←	abResult	{result code}
→	abUserReference	{for your use}
→	atpSocket	{responding socket number}
→	atpAddress	{destination socket address}
→	atpTransID	{transaction ID)
→	atpRspUData	{user bytes sent in transaction response}
→	atpRspBuf	{pointer to response message buffer}
→	atpRspSize	{size of response message buffer}

```
FUNCTION ATPRspCancel (abRecord: ABRecHandle; async: BOOLEAN) : OSErr;
```

Name-Binding Protocol

```
FUNCTION NBPRegister (abRecord: ABRecHandle; async: BOOLEAN) : OSErr;
```
←	abOpcode	{always tNBPRegister}
←	abResult	{result code}
→	abUserReference	{for your use}
→	nbpEntityPtr	{pointer to entity name}
→	nbpBufPtr	{pointer to buffer}
→	nbpBufSize	{buffer size in bytes}
→	nbpAddress.aSocket	{socket address}
→	nbpRetransmitInfo	{retransmission information}

```
FUNCTION NBPLookup (abRecord: ABRecHandle; async: BOOLEAN) : OSErr;
```
←	abOpcode	{always tNBPLookup}
←	abResult	{result code}
→	abUserReference	{for your use}
→	nbpEntityPtr	{pointer to entity name}
→	nbpBufPtr	{pointer to buffer}
→	nbpBufSize	{buffer size in bytes}
↔	nbpDataField	{number of addresses received}
→	nbpRetransmitInfo	{retransmission information}

```
FUNCTION NBPExtract (theBuffer: Ptr; numInBuf: INTEGER; whichOne:
                     INTEGER; VAR abEntity: EntityName; VAR address:
                     AddrBlock) : OSErr;
```

```
FUNCTION NBPConfirm (abRecord: ABRecHandle; async: BOOLEAN) : OSErr;
```
←	abOpcode	{always tNBPConfirm}
←	abResult	{result code}
→	abUserReference	{for your use}
→	nbpEntityPtr	{pointer to entity name}
←	nbpDataField	{socket number}
→	nbpAddress	{socket address}
→	nbpRetransmitInfo	{retransmission information}

```
FUNCTION NBPRemove  (abEntity: EntityPtr) : OSErr;
FUNCTION NBPLoad :    OSErr;
FUNCTION NBPUnload : OSErr;
```

Miscellaneous Routines

```
FUNCTION GetNodeAddress (VAR myNode,myNet: INTEGER) : OSErr;
FUNCTION IsMPPOpen :      BOOLEAN;
FUNCTION IsATPOpen :      BOOLEAN;
```

Result Codes

Name	Value	Meaning
atpBadRsp	−3107	Bad response from ATPRequest
atpLenErr	−3106	ATP response message too large
badATPSkt	−1099	ATP bad responding socket
badBuffNum	−1100	ATP bad sequence number
buf2SmallErr	−3101	ALAP frame too large for buffer DDP datagram too large for buffer
cbNotFound	−1102	ATP control block not found
cksumErr	−3103	DDP bad checksum
ddpLenErr	−92	DDP datagram or ALAP data length too big

Name	Value	Meaning
ddpSktErr	−91	DDP socket error: socket already active; not a well-known socket; socket table full; all dynamic socket numbers in use
excessCollsns	−95	ALAP no CTS received after 32 RTS's, or line sensed in use 32 times (not necessarily caused by collisions)
extractErr	−3104	NBP can't find tuple in buffer
lapProtErr	−94	ALAP error attaching/detaching ALAP protocol type: attach error when ALAP protocol type is negative, not in range, already in table, or when table is full; detach error when ALAP protocol type isn't in table
nbpBuffOvr	−1024	NBP buffer overflow
nbpConfDiff	−1026	NBP name confirmed for different socket
nbpDuplicate	−1027	NBP duplicate name already exists
nbpNISErr	−1029	NBP names information socket error
nbpNoConfirm	−1025	NBP name not confirmed
nbpNotFound	−1028	NBP name not found
noBridgeErr	−93	No bridge found
noDataArea	−1104	Too many outstanding ATP calls
noErr	0	No error
noMPPError	−3102	MPP driver not installed
noRelErr	−1101	ATP no release received
noSendResp	−1103	ATPAddRsp issued before ATPSndRsp
portInUse	−97	Driver Open error, port already in use
portNotCf	−98	Driver Open error, port not configured for this connection
readQErr	−3105	Socket or protocol type invalid or not found in table
recNotFnd	−3108	ABRecord not found
reqAborted	−1105	Request aborted
reqFailed	−1096	ATPSndRequest failed: retry count exceeded
sktClosedErr	−3109	Asynchronous call aborted because socket was closed before call was completed
tooManyReqs	−1097	ATP too many concurrent requests
tooManySkts	−1098	ATP too many responding sockets

Assembly-Language Information

Constants

```
; Serial port use types

useFree         .EQU    0       ;unconfigured
useATalk        .EQU    1       ;configured for AppleTalk
useASync        .EQU    2       ;configured for the Serial Driver

; Bit in PortBUse for .ATP driver status

atpLoadedBit    .EQU    4       ;set if .ATP driver is opened

; Unit numbers for AppleTalk drivers

mppUnitNum      .EQU    9       ;.MPP driver
atpUnitNum      .EQU    10      ;.ATP driver

; csCode values for Control calls (MPP)

writeLAP        .EQU    243
detachPH        .EQU    244
attachPH        .EQU    245
writeDDP        .EQU    246
closeSkt        .EQU    247
openSkt         .EQU    248
loadNBP         .EQU    249
confirmName     .EQU    250
lookupName      .EQU    251
removeName      .EQU    252
registerName    .EQU    253
killNBP         .EQU    254
unloadNBP       .EQU    255

; csCode values for Control calls (ATP)

relRspCB        .EQU    249
closeATPSkt     .EQU    250
addResponse     .EQU    251
sendResponse    .EQU    252
getRequest      .EQU    253
openATPSkt      .EQU    254
sendRequest     .EQU    255
relTCB          .EQU    256

; ALAP header

lapDstAdr       .EQU    0       ;destination node ID
lapSrcAdr       .EQU    1       ;source node ID
lapType         .EQU    2       ;ALAP protocol type
```

```
; ALAP header size

lapHdSz          .EQU    3

; ALAP protocol type values

shortDDP         .EQU    1       ;short DDP header
longDDP          .EQU    2       ;long DDP header

; Long DDP header

ddpHopCnt        .EQU    0       ;count of bridges passed (4 bits)
ddpLength        .EQU    0       ;datagram length (10 bits)
ddpChecksum      .EQU    2       ;checksum
ddpDstNet        .EQU    4       ;destination network number
ddpSrcNet        .EQU    6       ;source network number
ddpDstNode       .EQU    8       ;destination node ID
ddpSrcNode       .EQU    9       ;source node ID
ddpDstSkt        .EQU    10      ;destination socket number
ddpSrcSkt        .EQU    11      ;source socket number
ddpType          .EQU    12      ;DDP protocol type

; DDP long header size

ddpHSzLong       .EQU    ddpType+1

; Short DDP header

ddpLength        .EQU    0               ;datagram length
sDDPDstSkt       .EQU    ddpChecksum     ;destination socket number
sDDPSrcSkt       .EQU    sDDPDstSkt+1    ;source socket number
sDDPType         .EQU    sDDPSrcSkt+1    ;DDP protocol type

; DDP short header size

ddpHSzShort      .EQU    sDDPType+1

; Mask for datagram length

ddpLenMask       .EQU    $03FF

; Maximum size of DDP data

ddpMaxData       .EQU    586

; ATP header

atpControl       .EQU    0       ;control information
atpBitMap        .EQU    1       ;bit map
atpRespNo        .EQU    1       ;sequence number
atpTransID       .EQU    2       ;transaction ID
atpUserData      .EQU    4       ;user bytes
```

```
; ATP header size

atpHdSz        .EQU    8

; DDP protocol type for ATP packets

atp            .EQU    3

; ATP function code

atpReqCode     .EQU    $40     ;TReq packet
atpRspCode     .EQU    $80     ;TResp packet
atpRelCode     .EQU    $C0     ;TRel packet

; ATPFlags control information bits

sendChk        .EQU    0       ;send-checksum bit
tidValid       .EQU    1       ;transaction ID validity bit
atpSTSBit      .EQU    3       ;send-transmission-status bit
atpEOMBit      .EQU    4       ;end-of-message bit
atpXOBit       .EQU    5       ;exactly-once bit

; Maximum number of ATP request packets

atpMaxNum      .EQU    8

; ATP buffer data structure

bdsBuffSz      .EQU    0       ;size of data to send or buffer size
bdsBuffAddr    .EQU    2       ;pointer to data or buffer
bdsDataSz      .EQU    6       ;number of bytes actually received
bdsUserData    .EQU    8       ;user bytes

; BDS element size

bdsEntrySz     .EQU    12

; NBP packet

nbpControl     .EQU    0       ;packet type
nbpTCount      .EQU    0       ;tuple count
nbpID          .EQU    1       ;packet identifier
nbpTuple       .EQU    2       ;start of first tuple

; DDP protocol type for NBP packets

nbp            .EQU    2
```

```
; NBP packet types

brRq            .EQU    1       ;broadcast request
lkUp            .EQU    2       ;lookup request
lkUpReply       .EQU    3       ;lookup reply

; NBP tuple

tupleNet        .EQU    0       ;network number
tupleNode       .EQU    2       ;node ID
tupleSkt        .EQU    3       ;socket number
tupleEnum       .EQU    4       ;used internally
tupleName       .EQU    5       ;entity name

; Maximum number of tuples in NBP packet

tupleMax        .EQU    15

; NBP meta-characters

equals          .EQU    '='     ;"wild-card" meta-character
star            .EQU    '*'     ;"this zone" meta-character

; NBP names table entry

ntLink          .EQU    0       ;pointer to next entry
ntTuple         .EQU    4       ;tuple
ntSocket        .EQU    7       ;socket number
ntEntity        .EQU    9       ;entity name

; NBP names information socket number

nis             .EQU    2
```

Routines

Link Access Protocol

WriteLAP function

→	26	csCode	word	;always writeLAP
→	30	wdsPointer	pointer	;write data structure

AttachPH function

→	26	csCode	word	;always attachPH
→	28	protType	byte	;ALAP protocol type
→	30	handler	pointer	;protocol handler

DetachPH function

→	26	csCode	word	;always detachPH
→	28	protType	byte	;ALAP protocol type

Datagram Delivery Protocol

OpenSkt function

→	26	csCode	word	;always openSkt
↔	28	socket	byte	;socket number
→	30	listener	pointer	;socket listener

CloseSkt function

→	26	csCode	word	;always closeSkt
→	28	socket	byte	;socket number

WriteDDP function

→	26	csCode	word	;always writeDDP
→	28	socket	byte	;socket number
→	29	checksumFlag	byte	;checksum flag
→	30	wdsPointer	pointer	;write data structure

AppleTalk Transaction Protocol

OpenATPSkt function

→	26	csCode	word	;always openATPSkt
↔	28	atpSocket	byte	;socket number
→	30	addrBlock	long word	;socket request specification

CloseATPSkt function

→	26	csCode	word	;always closeATPSkt
→	28	atpSocket	byte	;socket number

SendRequest function

→	18	userData	long word	;user bytes
←	22	reqTID	word	;transaction ID used in request
→	26	csCode	word	;always sendRequest
←	28	currBitMap	byte	;bit map
↔	29	atpFlags	byte	;control information
→	30	addrBlock	long word	;destination socket address
→	34	reqLength	word	;request size in bytes
→	36	reqPointer	pointer	;pointer to request data
→	40	bdsPointer	pointer	;pointer to response BDS
→	44	numOfBuffs	byte	;number of responses expected
→	45	timeOutVal	byte	;timeout interval
←	46	numOfResps	byte	;number of responses received
↔	47	retryCount	byte	;number of retries

GetRequest function

←	18	userData	long word	;user bytes
→	26	csCode	word	;always getRequest
→	28	atpSocket	byte	;socket number
←	29	atpFlags	byte	;control information
←	30	addrBlock	long word	;source of request
↔	34	reqLength	word	;request buffer size
→	36	reqPointer	pointer	;pointer to request buffer
←	44	bitMap	byte	;bit map
←	46	transID	word	;transaction ID

SendResponse function

←	18	userData	long word	;user bytes from TRel
→	26	csCode	word	;always sendResponse
→	28	atpSocket	byte	;socket number
→	29	atpFlags	byte	;control information
→	30	addrBlock	long word	;response destination
→	40	bdsPointer	pointer	;pointer to response BDS
→	44	numOfBuffs	byte	;number of response packets being sent
→	45	bdsSize	byte	;BDS size in elements
→	46	transID	word	;transaction ID

AddResponse function

→	18	userData	long word	;user bytes
→	26	csCode	word	;always addResponse
→	28	atpSocket	byte	;socket number
→	29	atpFlags	byte	;control information
→	30	addrBlock	long word	;response destination
→	34	reqLength	word	;response size
→	36	reqPointer	pointer	;pointer to response
→	44	rspNum	byte	;sequence number
→	46	transID	word	;transaction ID

RelTCB function

→	26	csCode	word	;always relTCB
→	30	addrBlock	long word	;destination of request
→	46	transID	word	;transaction ID of request

RelRspCB function

→	26	csCode	word	;always relRspCB
→	28	atpSocket	byte	;socket number that request was received on
→	30	addrBlock	long word	;source of request
→	46	transID	word	;transaction ID of request

Name-Binding Protocol

RegisterName function

→	26	csCode	word	;always registerName
→	28	interval	byte	;retry interval
↔	29	count	byte	;retry count
→	30	ntQElPtr	pointer	;names table element pointer
→	34	verifyFlag	byte	;set if verify needed

LookupName function

→	26	csCode	word	;always lookupName
→	28	interval	byte	;retry interval
↔	29	count	byte	;retry count
→	30	entityPtr	pointer	;pointer to entity name
→	34	retBuffPtr	pointer	;pointer to buffer
→	38	retBuffSize	word	;buffer size in bytes
→	40	maxToGet	word	;matches to get
←	42	numGotten	word	;matches found

ConfirmName function

→	26	csCode	word	;always confirmName
→	28	interval	byte	;retry interval
↔	29	count	byte	;retry count
→	30	entityPtr	pointer	;pointer to entity name
→	34	confirmAddr	pointer	;entity address
←	38	newSocket	byte	;socket number

RemoveName function

→	26	csCode	word	;always removeName
→	30	entityPtr	pointer	;pointer to entity name

LoadNBP function

→	26	csCode	word	;always loadNBP

UnloadNBP function

→	26	csCode	word	;always unloadNBP

Variables

SPConfig	Use types for serial ports (byte) (bits 0-3: current configuration of serial port B bits 4-6: current configuration of serial port A)
PortBUse	Current availability of serial port B (byte) (bit 7: 1 = not in use, 0 = in use bits 0-3: current use of port bits bits 4-6: driver-specific)
ABusVars	Pointer to AppleTalk variables

11   THE VERTICAL RETRACE MANAGER

ABOUT THIS CHAPTER

This chapter describes the Vertical Retrace Manager, the part of the Operating System that schedules and performs recurrent tasks during vertical retrace interrupts. It describes how your application can install and remove its own recurrent tasks.

You should already be familiar with:

■ events, as discussed in chapter 8 of Volume I

■ interrupts, as described in chapter 6

ABOUT THE VERTICAL RETRACE MANAGER

The Macintosh video circuitry generates a **vertical retrace interrupt**, also known as the **vertical blanking** (or VBL) **interrupt**, 60 times a second while the beam of the display tube returns from the bottom of the screen to the top to display the next frame. This interrupt is used as a convenient time for performing the following sequence of recurrent system tasks:

1. Increment the number of ticks since system startup (every interrupt). You can get this number by calling the Toolbox Event Manager function TickCount.

2. Check whether the stack has expanded into the heap; if so, it calls the System Error Handler (every interrupt).

3. Handle cursor movement (every interrupt).

4. Post a mouse event if the state of the mouse button changed from its previous state and then remained unchanged for four interrupts (every other interrupt).

5. Reset the keyboard if it's been reattached after having been detached (every 32 interrupts).

6. Post a disk-inserted event if the user has inserted a disk or taken any other action that requires a volume to be mounted (every 30 interrupts).

These tasks must execute at regular intervals based on the "heartbeat" of the Macintosh, and shouldn't be changed.

Tasks performed during the vertical retrace interrupt are known as **VBL tasks**. An application can add any number of its own VBL tasks for the Vertical Retrace Manager to execute. VBL tasks can be set to execute at any frequency (up to once per vertical retrace interrupt). For example, an electronic mail application might add a VBL task that checks every tenth of a second (every six interrupts) to see if it has received any messages. These tasks can perform any desired action as long as they don't make any calls to the Memory Manager, directly or indirectly, and don't depend on handles to unlocked blocks being valid. They must preserve all registers other than A0-A3 and D0-D3. If they use application globals, they must also ensure that register A5 contains the address of the boundary between the application globals and the application parameters; for details, see SetUpA5 and RestoreA5 in chapter 13.

Warning: When interrupts are disabled (such as during a disk access), or when VBL tasks take longer than about a sixtieth of a second to perform, one or more vertical retrace interrupts may be missed, thereby affecting the performance of certain VBL tasks. For instance, while a disk is being accessed, the updating of the cursor movement may be irregular.

Note: To perform periodic actions that do allocate and release memory, you can use the Desk Manager procedure SystemTask. Or, since the first thing the Vertical Retrace Manager does during a vertical retrace interrupt is increment the tick count, you can call TickCount repeatedly and perform periodic actions whenever a specific number of ticks have elapsed.

Information describing each VBL task is contained in the **vertical retrace queue**. The vertical retrace queue is a standard Macintosh Operating System queue, as described in chapter 13. Each entry in the vertical retrace queue has the following structure:

```
TYPE VBLTask =  RECORD
                    qLink:    QElemPtr;   {next queue entry}
                    qType:    INTEGER;    {queue type}
                    vblAddr:  ProcPtr;    {pointer to task}
                    vblCount: INTEGER;    {task frequency}
                    vblPhase: INTEGER     {task phase}
                END;
```

QLink points to the next entry in the queue, and qType indicates the queue type, which must be ORD(vType).

VBLAddr contains a pointer to the task. VBLCount specifies the number of ticks between successive calls to the task. This value is decremented each sixtieth of a second until it reaches 0, at which point the task is called. The task must then reset vblCount, or its entry will be removed from the queue after it has been executed. VBLPhase contains an integer (smaller than vblCount) used to modify vblCount when the task is first added to the queue. This ensures that two or more tasks added to the queue at the same time with the same vblCount value will be out of phase with each other, and won't be called during the same interrupt. Unless there are many tasks to be added to the queue at the same time, vblPhase can usually be set to 0.

The Vertical Retrace Manager uses bit 6 of the queue flags field in the queue header to indicate when a task is being executed:

Bit	Meaning
6	Set if a task is being executed

Assembly-language note: Assembly-programmers can use the global constant inVBL to test this bit.

USING THE VERTICAL RETRACE MANAGER

The Vertical Retrace Manager is automatically initialized each time the system starts up. To add a VBL task to the vertical retrace queue, call VInstall. When your application no longer wants a task to be executed, it can remove the task from the vertical retrace queue by calling VRemove. A VBL task shouldn't call VRemove to remove its entry from the queue—either the application should call VRemove, or the task should simply not reset the vblCount field of the queue entry.

Assembly-language note: VBL tasks may use registers A0-A3 and D0-D3, and must save and restore any additional registers used. They must exit with an RTS instruction.

If you'd like to manipulate the contents of the vertical retrace queue directly, you can get a pointer to the header of the vertical retrace queue by calling GetVBLQHdr.

VERTICAL RETRACE MANAGER ROUTINES

```
FUNCTION VInstall (vblTaskPtr: QElemPtr) : OSErr;
```

Trap macro	_VInstall
On entry	A0: vblTaskPtr (pointer)
On exit	D0: result code (word)

VInstall adds the VBL task specified by vblTaskPtr to the vertical retrace queue. Your application must fill in all fields of the task except qLink. VInstall returns one of the result codes listed below.

Result codes	noErr	No error
	vTypErr	QType field isn't ORD(vType)

```
FUNCTION VRemove (vblTaskPtr: QElemPtr) : OSErr;
```

Trap macro	_VRemove
On entry	A0: vblTaskPtr (pointer)
On exit	D0: result code (word)

VRemove removes the VBL task specified by vblTaskPtr from the vertical retrace queue. It returns one of the result codes listed below.

Result codes   noErr   No error
                          vTypErr   QType field isn't ORD(vType)
                          qErr   Task entry isn't in the queue

```
FUNCTION GetVBLQHdr : QHdrPtr;    [Not in ROM]
```

GetVBLQHdr returns a pointer to the header of the vertical retrace queue.

Assembly-language note: The global variable VBLQueue contains the header of the vertical retrace queue.

SUMMARY OF THE VERTICAL RETRACE MANAGER

Constants

```
CONST { Result codes }

     noErr   =  0;   {no error}
     qErr    = -1;   {task entry isn't in the queue}
     vTypErr = -2;   {qType field isn't ORD(vType)}
```

Data Types

```
TYPE VBLTask = RECORD
                qLink:     QElemPtr;   {next queue entry}
                qType:     INTEGER;    {queue type}
                vblAddr:   ProcPtr;    {pointer to task}
                vblCount:  INTEGER;    {task frequency}
                vblPhase:  INTEGER     {task phase}
              END;
```

Routines

```
FUNCTION VInstall    (vblTaskPtr: QElemPtr) : OSErr;
FUNCTION VRemove     (vblTaskPtr: QElemPtr) : OSErr;
FUNCTION GetVBLQHdr :  QHdrPtr;  [Not in ROM]
```

Assembly-Language Information

Constants

```
inVBL    .EQU   6    ;set if Vertical Retrace Manager is executing a task

; Result codes

noErr    .EQU   0   ;no error
qErr     .EQU  -1   ;task entry isn't in the queue
vTypErr  .EQU  -2   ;qType field isn't vType
```

Structure of Vertical Retrace Queue Entry

qLink	Pointer to next queue entry
qType	Queue type (word)
vblAddr	Address of task
vblCount	Task frequency (word)
vblPhase	Task phase (word)

Routines

Trap macro	On entry	On exit
_VInstall	A0: vblTaskPtr (ptr)	D0: result code (word)
_VRemove	A0: vblTaskPtr (ptr)	D0: result code (word)

Variables

VBLQueue   Vertical retrace queue header (10 bytes)

12 THE SYSTEM ERROR HANDLER

ABOUT THIS CHAPTER

The System Error Handler is the part of the Operating System that assumes control when a fatal system error occurs. This chapter introduces you to the System Error Handler and describes how your application can recover from system errors.

You'll already need to be somewhat familiar with most of the User Interface Toolbox and the rest of the Operating System.

ABOUT THE SYSTEM ERROR HANDLER

The System Error Handler assumes control when a fatal system error occurs. Its main function is to display an alert box with an error message (called a **system error alert**) and provide a mechanism for the application to resume execution.

> **Note:** The system error alerts simply identify the type of problem encountered and, in some cases, the part of the Toolbox or Operating System involved. They don't, however, tell you where in your application code the failure occurred.

Because a system error usually indicates that a very low-level part of the system has failed, the System Error Handler performs its duties by using as little of the system as possible. It requires only the following:

- The trap dispatcher is operative.

- The Font Manager procedure InitFonts has been called (it's called when the system starts up).

- Register A7 points to a reasonable place in memory (for example, not to the main screen buffer).

- A few important system data structures aren't too badly damaged.

The System Error Handler doesn't require the Memory Manager to be operative.

The content of the alert box displayed is determined by a **system error alert table**, a resource stored in the system resource file. There are two different system error alert tables: a system startup alert table used when the system starts up, and a user alert table for informing the user of system errors.

The system startup alerts are used to display messages at system startup such as the "Welcome to Macintosh" message (Figure 1). They're displayed by the System Error Handler instead of the Dialog Manager because the System Error Handler needs very little of the system to operate.

The user alerts (Figure 2) notify the user of system errors. The bottom right corner of a user alert contains a **system error ID** that identifies the error. Usually the message "Sorry, a system error occurred", a Restart button, and a Resume button are also shown. If the Finder can't be found on a disk, the message "Can't load the finder" and a Restart button will be shown. The Macintosh will attempt to restart if the user clicks the Restart button, and the application will attempt to resume execution if the user clicks the Resume button.

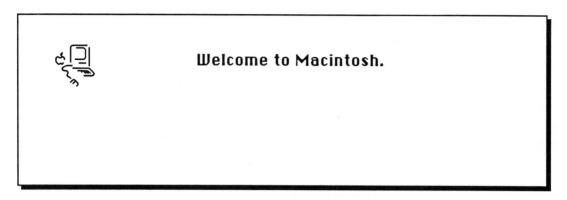

Figure 1. System Startup Alert

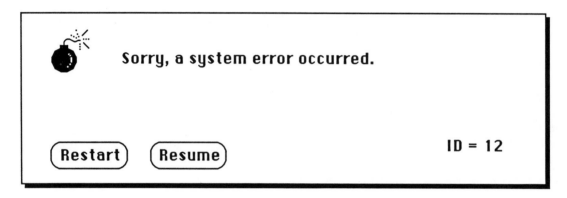

Figure 2. User Alert

The "Please insert the disk:" message displayed by the File Manager is also a user alert; however, unlike the other alerts, it's displayed in a dialog box.

The summary at the end of this chapter lists the system error IDs for the various user alerts, as well as the system startup alert messages.

RECOVERING FROM SYSTEM ERRORS

An application recovers from a system error by means of a **resume procedure**. You pass a pointer to your resume procedure when you call the Dialog Manager procedure InitDialogs. When the user clicks the Resume button in a system error alert, the System Error Handler attempts to restore the state of the system and then calls your resume procedure.

Assembly-language note: The System Error Handler actually restores the value of register A5 to what it was before the system error occurred, sets the stack pointer to the address stored in the global variable CurStackBase (throwing away the stack), and then jumps to your resume procedure.

If you don't have a resume procedure, you'll pass NIL to InitDialogs (and the Resume button in the system error alert will be dimmed).

SYSTEM ERROR ALERT TABLES

This section describes the data structures that define the alert boxes displayed by the System Error Handler; this information is provided mainly to allow you to edit and translate the messages displayed in the alerts. Rearranging the alert tables or creating new ones is discouraged because the Operating System depends on having the alert information stored in a very specific and constant way.

In the system resource file, the system error alerts have the following resource types and IDs:

Table	Resource type	Resource ID
System startup alert table	'DSAT'	0
User alert table	'INIT'	2

Assembly-language note: The global variable DSAlertTab contains a pointer to the current system error alert table. DSAlertTab points to the system startup alert table when the system is starting up; then it's changed to point to the user alert table.

A system error alert table consists of a word indicating the number of entries in the table, followed by alert, text, icon, button, and procedure definitions, all of which are explained below. The first definition in a system error alert table is an alert definition that applies to *all* system errors that don't have their own alert definition. The rest of the definitions within the alert table needn't be in any particular order, nor do the definitions of one type need to be grouped together. The first two words in every definition are used for the same purpose: The first word contains an ID number identifying the definition, and the second specifies the length of the rest of the definition in bytes.

An alert definition specifies the IDs of the text, icon, button, and procedure definitions that together determine the appearance and operation of the alert box that will be drawn (Figure 3). The ID of an alert definition is the system error ID that the alert pertains to. The System Error Handler uses the system error ID to locate the alert definition. The alert definition specifies the IDs of the other definitions needed to create the alert; 0 is specified if the alert doesn't include any items of that type.

A text definition specifies the text that will be drawn in the system error alert (Figure 4). Each alert definition refers to two text definitions; the secondary text definition allows a second line of text to be added to the alert message. (No more than two lines of text may be displayed.) The pen location at which QuickDraw will begin drawing the text is given as a point in global coordinates. The actual characters that comprise the text are suffixed by one NUL character (ASCII code 0).

Warning: The slash character (/) can't be used in the text.

system error ID (word)
length of rest of definition (word)
primary text definition ID (word)
secondary text definition ID (word)
icon definition ID (word)
procedure definition ID (word)
button definition ID (word)

Figure 3. Alert Definition

text definition ID (word)
length of rest of definition (word)
location (point)
text (ASCII characters)
NUL character (byte)

Figure 4. Text Definition

An icon definition specifies the icon that will be drawn in the system error alert (Figure 5). The location of the icon is given as a rectangle in global coordinates. The 128 bytes that comprise the icon complete the definition.

icon definition ID (word)
length of rest of definition (word)
location (rectangle)
icon data (128 bytes)

Figure 5. Icon Definition

A procedure definition specifies a procedure that will be executed whenever the system error alert is drawn (Figure 6). Procedure definitions are also used to specify the action to be taken when a particular button is pressed, as described below. Most of a procedure definition is simply the code comprising the procedure.

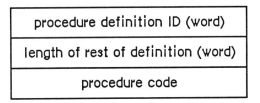

Figure 6. Procedure Definition

A button definition specifies the button(s) that will be drawn in the system error alert (Figure 7). It indicates the number of buttons that will be drawn, followed by that many six-word groups, each specifying the text, location, and operation of a button.

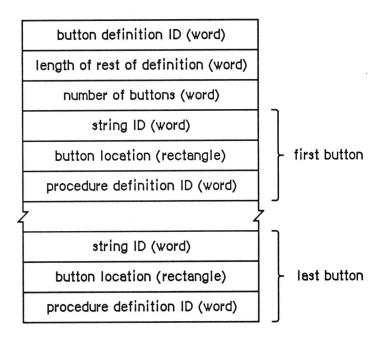

Figure 7. Button Definition

The first word of each six-word group contains a string ID (explained below) specifying the text that will be drawn inside the button. The button's location is given as a rectangle in global coordinates. The last word contains a procedure definition ID identifying the code to be executed when the button is clicked.

The text that will be drawn inside each button is specified by the data structure shown in Figure 8. The first word contains a string ID identifying the string and the second indicates the length of the string in bytes. The actual characters of the string follow.

Each alert has two button definitions; these definitions have sequential button definition IDs (such as 60 and 61). The button definition ID of the first definition is placed in the alert definition. This definition is used if no resume procedure has been specified (with a call to the Dialog Manager's InitDialogs procedure). If a resume procedure has been specified, the System Error Handler adds 1 to the button definition ID specified in the alert definition and so uses the second

```
┌─────────────────────────────┐
│      string ID (word)        │
├─────────────────────────────┤
│    length of string (word)   │
├─────────────────────────────┤
│   text (ASCII characters)    │
└─────────────────────────────┘
```

Figure 8. Strings Drawn in Buttons

button definition. In this definition, the procedure for the Resume button attempts to restore the state of the system and calls the resume procedure that was specified with InitDialogs.

SYSTEM ERROR HANDLER ROUTINE

The System Error Handler has only one routine, SysError, described below. Most application programs won't have any reason to call it. The system itself calls SysError whenever a system error occurs, and most applications need only be concerned with recovering from the error and resuming execution.

```
PROCEDURE SysError (errorCode: INTEGER);
```

Trap macro	_SysError
On entry	D0: errorCode (word)
On exit	All registers changed

SysError generates a system error with the ID specified by the errorCode parameter.

It takes the following precise steps:

1. It saves all registers and the stack pointer.

2. It stores the system error ID in a global variable (named DSErrCode).

3. It checks to see whether there's a system error alert table in memory (by testing whether the global variable DSAlertTab is 0); if there isn't, it draws the "sad Macintosh" icon.

4. It allocates memory for QuickDraw globals on the stack, initializes QuickDraw, and initializes a grafPort in which the alert box will be drawn.

5. It checks the system error ID. If the system error ID is negative, the alert box isn't redrawn (this is used for system startup alerts, which can display a sequence of consecutive messages in the same box). If the system error ID doesn't correspond to an entry in the system error alert table, the default alert definition at the start of the table will be used, displaying the message "Sorry, a system error occurred".

6. It draws an alert box (in the rectangle specified by the global variable DSAlertRect).

7. If the text definition IDs in the alert definition for this alert aren't 0, it draws both strings.

8. If the icon definition ID in the alert definition isn't 0, it draws the icon.

9. If the procedure definition ID in the alert definition isn't 0, it invokes the procedure with the specified ID.

10. If the button definition ID in the alert definition is 0, it returns control to the procedure that called it (this is used during the disk-switch alert to return control to the File Manager after the "Please insert the disk:" message has been displayed).

11. If there's a resume procedure, it increments the button definition ID by 1.

12. It draws the buttons.

13. It hit-tests the buttons and calls the corresponding procedure code when a button is pressed. If there's no procedure code, it returns to the procedure that called it.

SUMMARY OF THE SYSTEM ERROR HANDLER

Routines

```
PROCEDURE SysError (errorCode: INTEGER);
```

User Alerts

ID	Explanation
1	Bus error: Invalid memory reference; happens only on a Macintosh XL
2	Address error: Word or long-word reference made to an odd address
3	Illegal instruction: The MC68000 received an instruction it didn't recognize.
4	Zero divide: Signed Divide (DIVS) or Unsigned Divide (DIVU) instruction with a divisor of 0 was executed.
5	Check exception: Check Register Against Bounds (CHK) instruction was executed and failed. Pascal "value out of range" errors are usually reported in this way.
6	TrapV exception: Trap On Overflow (TRAPV) instruction was executed and failed.
7	Privilege violation: Macintosh always runs in supervisor mode; perhaps an erroneous Return From Execution (RTE) instruction was executed.
8	Trace exception: The trace bit in the status register is set.
9	Line 1010 exception: The 1010 trap dispatcher has failed.
10	Line 1111 exception: Unimplemented instruction
11	Miscellaneous exception: All other MC68000 exceptions
12	Unimplemented core routine: An unimplemented trap number was encountered.
13	Spurious interrupt: The interrupt vector table entry for a particular level of interrupt is NIL; usually occurs with level 4, 5, 6, or 7 interrupts.
14	I/O system error: The File Manager is attempting to dequeue an entry from an I/O request queue that has a bad queue type field; perhaps the queue entry is unlocked. Or, the dCtlQHead field was NIL during a Fetch or Stash call. Or, a needed device control entry has been purged.
15	Segment Loader error: A GetResource call to read a segment into memory failed.
16	Floating point error: The halt bit in the floating-point environment word was set.
17-24	Can't load package: A GetResource call to read a package into memory failed.
25	Can't allocate requested memory block in the heap
26	Segment Loader error: A GetResource call to read 'CODE' resource 0 into memory failed; usually indicates a nonexecutable file.

27 File map destroyed: A logical block number was found that's greater than the number of the last logical block on the volume or less than the logical block number of the first allocation block on the volume.

28 Stack overflow error: The stack has expanded into the heap.

30 "Please insert the disk:" File Manager alert

41 The file named "Finder" can't be found on the disk.

100 Can't mount system startup volume. The system couldn't read the system resource file into memory.

32767 "Sorry, a system error occurred": Default alert message

System Startup Alerts

"Welcome to Macintosh"
"Disassembler installed"
"MacsBug installed"
"Warning—this startup disk is not usable"

Assembly-Language Information

Constants

```
; System error IDs

dsBusError      .EQU    1       ;bus error
dsAddressErr    .EQU    2       ;address error
dsIllInstErr    .EQU    3       ;illegal instruction
dsZeroDivErr    .EQU    4       ;zero divide
dsChkErr        .EQU    5       ;check exception
dsOvflowErr     .EQU    6       ;trapV exception
dsPrivErr       .EQU    7       ;privilege violation
dsTraceErr      .EQU    8       ;trace exception
dsLineAErr      .EQU    9       ;line 1010 exception
dsLineFErr      .EQU    10      ;line 1111 exception
dsMiscErr       .EQU    11      ;miscellaneous exception
dsCoreErr       .EQU    12      ;unimplemented core routine
dsIrqErr        .EQU    13      ;spurious interrupt
dsIOCoreErr     .EQU    14      ;I/O system error
dsLoadErr       .EQU    15      ;Segment Loader error
dsFPErr         .EQU    16      ;floating point error
dsNoPackErr     .EQU    17      ;can't load package 0
dsNoPk1         .EQU    18      ;can't load package 1
dsNoPk2         .EQU    19      ;can't load package 2
dsNoPk3         .EQU    20      ;can't load package 3
dsNoPk4         .EQU    21      ;can't load package 4
dsNoPk5         .EQU    22      ;can't load package 5
dsNoPk6         .EQU    23      ;can't load package 6
```

```
dsNoPk7          .EQU    24        ;can't load package 7
dsMemFullErr     .EQU    25        ;can't allocate requested block
dsBadLaunch      .EQU    26        ;Segment Loader error
dsFSErr          .EQU    27        ;file map destroyed
dsStkNHeap       .EQU    28        ;stack overflow error
dsReinsert       .EQU    30        ;"Please insert the disk:"
dsSysErr         .EQU    32767     ;undifferentiated system error
```

Routines

Trap macro	On entry	On exit
_SysError	D0: errorCode (word)	All registers changed

Variables

DSErrCode	Current system error ID (word)
DSAlertTab	Pointer to system error alert table in use
DSAlertRect	Rectangle enclosing system error alert (8 bytes)

13 THE OPERATING SYSTEM UTILITIES

ABOUT THIS CHAPTER

This chapter describes the Operating System Utilities, a set of routines and data types in the Operating System that perform generally useful operations such as manipulating pointers and handles, comparing strings, and reading the date and time.

Depending on which Operating System Utilities you're interested in using, you may need to be familiar with other parts of the Toolbox or Operating System; where that's necessary, you're referred to the appropriate chapters.

PARAMETER RAM

Various settings, such as those specified by the user by means of the Control Panel desk accessory, need to be preserved when the Macintosh is off so they will still be present at the next system startup. This information is kept in **parameter RAM**, 20 bytes that are stored in the **clock chip** together with the current date and time setting. The clock chip is powered by a battery when the system is off, thereby preserving all the settings stored in it.

You may find it necessary to read the values in parameter RAM or even change them (for example, if you create a desk accessory like the Control Panel). Since the clock chip itself is difficult to access, its contents are copied into low memory at system startup. You read and change parameter RAM through this low-memory copy.

> **Note:** Certain values from parameter RAM are used so frequently that special routines have been designed to return them (for example, the Toolbox Event Manager function GetDblTime). These routines are discussed in other chapters where appropriate.

> **Assembly-language note:** The low-memory copy of parameter RAM begins at the address SysParam; the various portions of the copy can be accessed through individual global variables, listed in the summary at the end of this chapter. Some of these are copied into other global variables at system startup for even easier access; for example, the auto-key threshold and rate, which are contained in the variable SPKbd in the copy of parameter RAM, are copied into the variables KeyThresh and KeyRepThresh. Each such variable is discussed in the appropriate chapter.

The date and time setting is also copied at system startup from the clock chip into its own low-memory location. It's stored as a number of seconds since midnight, January 1, 1904, and is updated every second. The maximum value, $FFFFFFFF, corresponds to 6:28:15 AM, February 6, 2040; after that, it wraps around to midnight, January 1, 1904.

> **Assembly-language note:** The low-memory location containing the date and time is the global variable Time.

The structure of parameter RAM is represented by the following data type:

```
TYPE SysParmType =
     RECORD
         valid:    Byte;      {validity status}
         aTalkA:   Byte;      {AppleTalk node ID hint for modem port}
         aTalkB:   Byte;      {AppleTalk node ID hint for printer port}
         config:   Byte;      {use types for serial ports}
         portA:    INTEGER;   {modem port configuration}
         portB:    INTEGER;   {printer port configuration}
         alarm:    LONGINT;   {alarm setting}
         font:     INTEGER;   {application font number minus 1}
         kbdPrint: INTEGER;   {auto-key settings, printer connection}
         volClik:  INTEGER;   {speaker volume, double-click, caret blink}
         misc:     INTEGER    {mouse scaling, startup disk, menu blink}
     END;

     SysPPtr = ^SysParmType;
```

The valid field contains the **validity status** of the clock chip: Whenever you successfully write to the clock chip, $A8 is stored in this byte. The validity status is examined when the clock chip is read at system startup. It won't be $A8 if a hardware problem prevented the values from being written; in this case, the low-memory copy of parameter RAM is set to the default values shown in the table below, and these values are then written to the clock chip itself. (The meanings of the parameters are explained below in the descriptions of the various fields.)

Parameter	Default value
Validity status	$A8
Node ID hint for modem port	0
Node ID hint for printer port	0
Use types for serial ports	0 (both ports)
Modem port configuration	9600 baud, 8 data bits, 2 stop bits, no parity
Printer port configuration	Same as for modem port
Alarm setting	0 (midnight, January 1, 1904)
Application font number minus 1	2 (Geneva)
Auto-key threshold	6 (24 ticks)
Auto-key rate	3 (6 ticks)
Printer connection	0 (printer port)
Speaker volume	3 (medium)
Double-click time	8 (32 ticks)
Caret-blink time	8 (32 ticks)
Mouse scaling	1 (on)
Preferred system startup disk	0 (internal drive)
Menu blink	3

Warning: Your program must not use bits indicated below as "reserved for future use" in parameter RAM, since future Macintosh software features will use them.

The aTalkA and aTalkB fields are used by the AppleTalk Manager; they're described in the manual *Inside AppleTalk*.

The config field indicates which device or devices may use each of the serial ports; for details, see the section "Calling the AppleTalk Manager from Assembly Language" in chapter 10.

The portA and portB fields contain the baud rates, data bits, stop bits, and parity for the device drivers using the modem port ("port A") and printer port ("port B"). An explanation of these terms and the exact format of the information are given in chapter 9.

The alarm field contains the alarm setting in seconds since midnight, January 1, 1904.

The font field contains 1 less than the number of the application font. See chapter 7 of Volume I for a list of font numbers.

Bit 0 of the kbdPrint field (Figure 1) designates whether the printer (if any) is connected to the printer port (0) or the modem port (1). Bits 8-11 of this field contain the **auto-key rate**, the rate of the repeat when a character key is held down; this value is stored in two-tick units. Bits 12-15 contain the **auto-key threshold**, the length of time the key must be held down before it begins to repeat; it's stored in four-tick units.

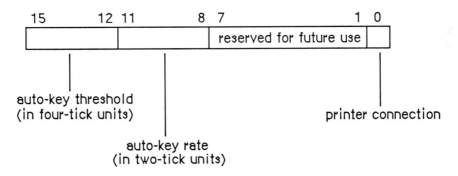

Figure 1. The KbdPrint Field

Bits 0-3 of the volClik field (Figure 2) contain the **caret-blink time**, and bits 4-7 contain the **double-click time**; both values are stored in four-tick units. The caret-blink time is the interval between blinks of the caret that marks the insertion point in text. The double-click time is the greatest interval between a mouse-up and mouse-down event that would qualify two mouse clicks as a double-click. Bits 8-10 of the volClik field contain the speaker volume setting, which ranges from silent (0) to loud (7).

Note: The Sound Driver procedure SetSoundVol changes the speaker volume without changing the setting in parameter RAM, so it's possible for the actual volume to be different from this setting.

Bits 2 and 3 of the misc field (Figure 3) contain a value from 0 to 3 designating how many times a menu item will blink when it's chosen. Bit 4 of this field indicates whether the preferred disk to use to start up the system is in the internal (0) or the external (1) drive; if there's any problem using the disk in the specified drive, the other drive will be used.

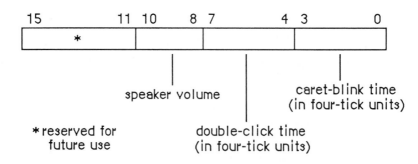

Figure 2. The VolClik Field

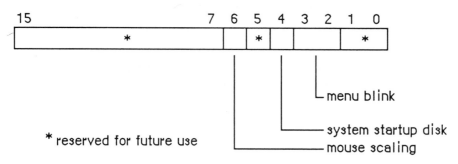

Figure 3. The Misc Field

Finally, bit 6 of the misc field designates whether **mouse scaling** is on (1) or off (0). If mouse scaling is on, the system looks every sixtieth of a second at whether the mouse has moved; if in that time the sum of the mouse's horizontal and vertical changes in position is greater than the **mouse-scaling threshold** (normally six pixels), then the cursor will move twice as far horizontally and vertically as it would if mouse scaling were off.

Assembly-language note: The mouse-scaling threshold is contained in the global variable CrsrThresh.

OPERATING SYSTEM QUEUES

Some of the information used by the Operating System is stored in data structures called **queues**. A queue is a list of identically structured entries linked together by pointers. Queues are used to keep track of VBL tasks, I/O requests, events, mounted volumes, and disk drives (or other block-formatted devices).

A standard Operating System queue has a header with the following structure:

```
TYPE QHdr  = RECORD
             qFlags: INTEGER;     {queue flags}
             qHead: QElemPtr;     {first queue entry}
             qTail: QElemPtr      {last queue entry}
           END;
```

```
QHdrPtr  =  ^QHdr;
```

QFlags contains information (usually flags) that's different for each queue type. QHead points to the first entry in the queue, and qTail points to the last entry in the queue. The entries within each type of queue are different; the Operating System uses the following variant record to access them:

```
TYPE QTypes   = (dummyType,
                 vType,       {vertical retrace queue type}
                 ioQType,     {file I/O or driver I/O queue type}
                 drvQType,    {drive queue type}
                 evType,      {event queue type}
                 fsQType);    {volume-control-block queue type}

     QElem    = RECORD
                  CASE QTypes OF
                    vType:     (vblQElem: VBLTask);
                    ioQType:   (ioQElem:  ParamBlockRec);
                    drvQType:  (drvQElem: DrvQEl);
                    evType:    (evQElem:  EvQEl);
                    fsQType:   (vcbQElem: VCB)
                END;

     QElemPtr = ^QElem;
```

All entries in queues, regardless of the queue type, begin with four bytes of flags followed by a pointer to the next queue entry. The entries are linked through these pointers; each one points to the pointer field in the next entry. In Pascal, the data type of the pointer is QElemPtr, and the data type of the entry begins with the pointer field. Consequently, the flag bytes are inaccessible from Pascal.

Following the pointer to the next entry, each entry contains an integer designating the queue type (for example, ORD(evType) for the event queue). The exact structure of the rest of the entry depends on the type of queue; for more information, see the chapter that discusses that queue in detail.

GENERAL OPERATING SYSTEM DATA TYPES

This section describes two data types of general interest to users of the Operating System.

There are several places in the Operating System where you specify a four-character sequence for something, such as for file types and application signatures (described in chapter 1 of Volume III). The Pascal data type for such sequences is

```
TYPE OSType = PACKED ARRAY[1..4] OF CHAR;
```

Another data type that's used frequently in the Operating System is

```
TYPE OSErr = INTEGER;
```

This is the data type for a **result code**, which many Operating System routines (including those described in this chapter) return in addition to their normal results. A result code is an integer indicating whether the routine completed its task successfully or was prevented by some error condition (or other special condition, such as reaching the end of a file). In the normal case that no error is detected, the result code is

```
CONST noErr = 0;   {no error}
```

A nonzero result code (usually negative) signals an error. A list of all result codes is provided in Appendix A (Volume III).

OPERATING SYSTEM UTILITY ROUTINES

Pointer and Handle Manipulation

These functions would be easy to duplicate with Memory Manager calls; they're included in the Operating System Utilities as a convenience because the operations they perform are so common.

```
FUNCTION HandToHand (VAR theHndl: Handle) : OSErr;
```

Trap macro	_HandToHand
On entry	A0: theHndl (handle)
On exit	A0: theHndl (handle)
	D0: result code (word)

HandToHand copies the information to which theHndl is a handle and returns a new handle to the copy in theHndl. Since HandToHand replaces the input parameter with a new handle, you should retain the original value of the input parameter somewhere else, or you won't be able to access it. For example:

```
VAR  x,y: Handle;
     err: OSErr;

y := x;
err := HandToHand(y)
```

The original handle remains in x while y becomes a different handle to an identical copy of the data.

Result codes	noErr	No error
	memFullErr	Not enough room in heap zone
	nilHandleErr	NIL master pointer
	memWZErr	Attempt to operate on a free block

```
FUNCTION PtrToHand (srcPtr: Ptr; VAR dstHndl: Handle; size:
          LONGINT) : OSErr;
```

Trap macro	_PtrToHand
On entry	A0: srcPtr (pointer)
	D0: size (long word)
On exit	A0: dstHndl (handle)
	D0: result code (word)

PtrToHand returns in dstHndl a newly created handle to a copy of the number of bytes specified by the size parameter, beginning at the location specified by srcPtr.

Result codes	noErr	No error
	memFullErr	Not enough room in heap zone

```
FUNCTION PtrToXHand (srcPtr: Ptr; dstHndl: Handle; size: LONGINT)
          : OSErr;
```

Trap macro	_PtrToXHand
On entry	A0: srcPtr (pointer)
	A1: dstHndl (handle)
	D0: size (long word)
On exit	A0: dstHndl (handle)
	D0: result code (word)

PtrToXHand takes the existing handle specified by dstHndl and makes it a handle to a copy of the number of bytes specified by the size parameter, beginning at the location specified by srcPtr.

Result codes	noErr	No error
	memFullErr	Not enough room in heap zone
	nilHandleErr	NIL master pointer
	memWZErr	Attempt to operate on a free block

```
FUNCTION HandAndHand (aHndl,bHndl: Handle) : OSErr;
```

Trap macro	_HandAndHand
On entry	A0: aHndl (handle)
	A1: bHndl (handle)
On exit	A0: bHndl (handle)
	D0: result code (word)

HandAndHand concatenates the information to which aHndl is a handle onto the end of the information to which bHndl is a handle.

Warning: HandAndHand dereferences aHndl, so be sure to call the Memory Manager procedure HLock to lock the block before calling HandAndHand.

Result codes   noErr   No error
                memFullErr   Not enough room in heap zone
                nilHandleErr   NIL master pointer
                memWZErr   Attempt to operate on a free block

```
FUNCTION PtrAndHand (pntr: Ptr; hndl: Handle; size: LONGINT) :
        OSErr;
```

Trap macro	_PtrAndHand
On entry	A0: pntr (pointer)
	A1: hndl (handle)
	D0: size (long word)
On exit	A0: hndl (handle)
	D0: result code (word)

PtrAndHand takes the number of bytes specified by the size parameter, beginning at the location specified by pntr, and concatenates them onto the end of the information to which hndl is a handle.

Result codes   noErr   No error
                memFullErr   Not enough room in heap zone
                nilHandleErr   NIL master pointer
                memWZErr   Attempt to operate on a free block

String Comparison

Assembly-language note: The trap macros for these utility routines have optional arguments corresponding to the Pascal flags passed to the routines. When present, such an argument sets a certain bit of the routine trap word; this is equivalent to setting the corresponding Pascal flag to either TRUE or FALSE, depending on the flag. The trap macros for these routines are listed with all the possible permutations of arguments. Whichever permutation you use, you must type it exactly as shown. (The syntax shown applies to the Lisa Workshop Assembler; programmers using another development system should consult its documentation for the proper syntax.)

```
FUNCTION EqualString (aStr,bStr: Str255; caseSens,diacSens:
        BOOLEAN) :  BOOLEAN;
```

Trap macro	_CmpString	
	_CmpString ,MARKS	(sets bit 9, for diacSens=FALSE)
	_CmpString ,CASE	(sets bit 10, for caseSens=TRUE)
	_CmpString ,MARKS,CASE	(sets bits 9 and 10)
On entry	A0: pointer to first character of first string	
	A1: pointer to first character of second string	
	D0: high-order word: length of first string	
	low-order word: length of second string	
On exit	D0: 0 if strings equal, 1 if strings not equal (long word)	

EqualString compares the two given strings for equality on the basis of their ASCII values. If caseSens is TRUE, uppercase characters are distinguished from the corresponding lowercase characters. If diacSens is FALSE, diacritical marks are ignored during the comparison. The function returns TRUE if the strings are equal.

Note: See also the International Utilities Package function IUEqualString.

```
PROCEDURE UprString (VAR theString: Str255; diacSens: BOOLEAN);
```

Trap macro	_UprString	
	_UprString ,MARKS	(sets bit 9, for diacSens=FALSE)
On entry	A0: pointer to first character of string	
	D0: length of string (word)	
On exit	A0: pointer to first character of string	

UprString converts any lowercase letters in the given string to uppercase, returning the converted string in theString. In addition, diacritical marks are stripped from the string if diacSens is FALSE.

Date and Time Operations

The following utilities are for reading and setting the date and time stored in the clock chip. Reading the date and time is a fairly common operation; setting it is somewhat rarer, but could be necessary for implementing a desk accessory like the Control Panel.

The date and time setting is stored as an unsigned number of seconds since midnight, January 1, 1904; you can use a utility routine to convert this to a **date/time record**. Date/time records are defined as follows:

```
TYPE DateTimeRec =
            RECORD
                year:       INTEGER;   {1904 to 2040}
                month:      INTEGER;   {1 to 12 for January to December}
                day:        INTEGER;   {1 to 31}
                hour:       INTEGER;   {0 to 23}
                minute:     INTEGER;   {0 to 59}
                second:     INTEGER;   {0 to 59}
                dayOfWeek:  INTEGER    {1 to 7 for Sunday to Saturday}
            END;
```

```
FUNCTION ReadDateTime (VAR secs: LONGINT) : OSErr;
```

Trap macro	_ReadDateTime
On entry	A0: pointer to long word secs
On exit	A0: pointer to long word secs
	D0: result code (word)

ReadDateTime copies the date and time stored in the clock chip to a low-memory location and returns it in the secs parameter. This routine is called at system startup; you'll probably never need to call it yourself. Instead you'll call GetDateTime (see below).

Assembly-language note: The low-memory location to which ReadDateTime copies the date and time is the global variable Time.

Result codes	noErr	No error
	clkRdErr	Unable to read clock

```
PROCEDURE GetDateTime (VAR secs: LONGINT);   [Not in ROM]
```

GetDateTime returns in the secs parameter the contents of the low-memory location in which the date and time setting is stored; if this setting reflects the actual current date and time, secs will contain the number of seconds between midnight, January 1, 1904 and the time that the function was called.

Note: If your application disables interrupts for longer than a second, the number of seconds returned will not be exact.

Assembly-language note: Assembly-language programmers can just access the global variable Time.

If you wish, you can convert the value returned by GetDateTime to a date/time record by calling the Secs2Date procedure.

Note: Passing the value returned by GetDateTime to the International Utilities Package procedure IUDateString or IUTimeString will yield a string representing the corresponding date or time of day, respectively.

```
FUNCTION SetDateTime (secs: LONGINT) : OSErr;
```

Trap macro	_SetDateTime
On entry	D0: secs (long word)
On exit	D0: result code (word)

SetDateTime takes a number of seconds since midnight, January 1, 1904, as specified by the secs parameter, and writes it to the clock chip as the current date and time. It then attempts to read the value just written and verify it by comparing it to the secs parameter.

Assembly-language note: SetDateTime updates the global variable Time to the value of the secs parameter.

Result codes	noErr	No error
	clkWrErr	Time written did not verify
	clkRdErr	Unable to read clock

```
PROCEDURE Date2Secs (date: DateTimeRec; VAR secs: LONGINT);
```

Trap macro	_Date2Secs
On entry	A0: pointer to date/time record
On exit	D0: secs (long word)

Date2Secs takes the given date/time record, converts it to the corresponding number of seconds elapsed since midnight, January 1, 1904, and returns the result in the secs parameter. The dayOfWeek field of the date/time record is ignored. The values passed in the year and month fields should be within their allowable ranges, or unpredictable results will occur. The remaining four fields of the date/time record may contain any value. For example, September 34 will be interpreted as October 4, and you could specify the 300th day of the year as January 300.

```
PROCEDURE Secs2Date (secs: LONGINT; VAR date: DateTimeRec);
```

Trap macro	_Secs2Date
On entry	D0: secs (long word)
On exit	A0: pointer to date/time record

Secs2Date takes a number of seconds elapsed since midnight, January 1, 1904 as specified by the secs parameter, converts it to the corresponding date and time, and returns the corresponding date/time record in the date parameter.

```
PROCEDURE GetTime (VAR date: DateTimeRec);   [Not in ROM]
```

GetTime takes the number of seconds elapsed since midnight, January 1, 1904 (obtained by calling GetDateTime), converts that value into a date and time (by calling Secs2Date), and returns the result in the date parameter.

Assembly-language note: From assembly language, you can pass the value of the global variable Time to Secs2Date.

```
PROCEDURE SetTime (date: DateTimeRec);   [Not in ROM]
```

SetTime takes the date and time specified by the date parameter, converts it into the corresponding number of seconds elapsed since midnight, January 1, 1904 (by calling Date2Secs), and then writes that value to the clock chip as the current date and time (by calling SetDateTime).

Assembly-language note: From assembly language, you can just call Date2Secs and SetDateTime directly.

Parameter RAM Operations

The following three utilities are used for reading from and writing to parameter RAM. Figure 4 illustrates the function of these three utilities; further details are given below and in the "Parameter RAM" section.

```
FUNCTION InitUtil : OSErr;
```

Trap macro	_InitUtil
On exit	D0: result code (word)

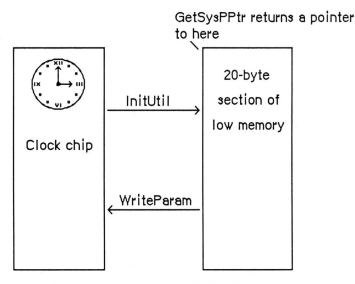

Figure 4. Parameter RAM Routines

InitUtil copies the contents of parameter RAM into 20 bytes of low memory and copies the date and time from the clock chip into its own low-memory location. This routine is called at system startup; you'll probably never need to call it yourself.

Assembly-language note: InitUtil copies parameter RAM into 20 bytes starting at the address SysParam and copies the date and time into the global variable Time.

If the validity status in parameter RAM is not $A8 when InitUtil is called, an error is returned as the result code, and the default values (given in the "Parameter RAM" section) are read into the low-memory copy of parameter RAM; these values are then written to the clock chip itself.

Result codes   noErr   No error
                      prInitErr   Validity status not $A8

```
FUNCTION GetSysPPtr : SysPPtr;    [Not in ROM]
```

GetSysPPtr returns a pointer to the low-memory copy of parameter RAM. You can examine the values stored in its various fields, or change them before calling WriteParam (below).

Assembly-language note: Assembly-language programmers can simply access the global variables corresponding to the low-memory copy of parameter RAM. These variables, which begin at the address SysParam, are listed in the summary.

```
FUNCTION WriteParam : OSErr;
```

Trap macro	_WriteParam
On entry	A0: SysParam (pointer)
	D0: MinusOne (long word)
	(You have to pass the values of these global variables for historical reasons.)
On exit	D0: result code (word)

WriteParam writes the low-memory copy of parameter RAM to the clock chip. You should previously have called GetSysPPtr and changed selected values as desired.

WriteParam also attempts to verify the values written by reading them back in and comparing them to the values in the low-memory copy.

Note: If you've accidentally written incorrect values into parameter RAM, the system may not be able to start up. If this happens, you can reset parameter RAM by removing the battery, letting the Macintosh sit turned off for about five minutes, and then putting the battery back in.

Result codes	noErr	No error
	prWrErr	Parameter RAM written did not verify

Queue Manipulation

This section describes utilities that advanced programmers may want to use for adding entries to or deleting entries from an Operating System queue. Normally you won't need to use these utilities, since queues are manipulated for you as necessary by routines that need to deal with them.

```
PROCEDURE Enqueue (qEntry: QElemPtr; theQueue: QHdrPtr);
```

Trap macro	_Enqueue
On entry	A0: qEntry (pointer)
	A1: theQueue (pointer)
On exit	A1: theQueue (pointer)

Enqueue adds the queue entry pointed to by qEntry to the end of the queue specified by theQueue.

Note: Interrupts are disabled for a short time while the queue is updated.

```
FUNCTION Dequeue (qEntry: QElemPtr; theQueue: QHdrPtr) : OSErr;
```

Trap macro	_Dequeue
On entry	A0: qEntry (pointer)
	A1: theQueue (pointer)
On exit	A1: theQueue (pointer)
	D0: result code (word)

Dequeue removes the queue entry pointed to by qEntry from the queue specified by theQueue (without deallocating the entry) and adjusts other entries in the queue accordingly.

Note: The note under Enqueue above also applies here. In this case, the amount of time interrupts are disabled depends on the length of the queue and the position of the entry in the queue.

Note: To remove all entries from a queue, you can just clear all the fields of the queue's header.

Result codes	noErr	No error
	qErr	Entry not in specified queue

Trap Dispatch Table Utilities

The Operating System Utilities include two routines for manipulating the trap dispatch table, which is described in detail in chapter 4 of Volume I. Using these routines, you can intercept calls to an Operating System or Toolbox routine and do some pre- or post-processing of your own: Call GetTrapAddress to get the address of the original routine, save that address for later use, and call SetTrapAddress to install your own version of the routine in the dispatch table. Before or after its own processing, the new version of the routine can use the saved address to call the original version.

Warning: You can replace as well as intercept existing routines; in any case, you should be absolutely sure you know what you're doing. Remember that some calls that aren't in ROM do some processing of their own before invoking a trap macro (for example, FSOpen eventually invokes _Open, and IUCompString invokes the macro for IUMagString). Also, a number of ROM routines have been patched with corrected versions in RAM; if you intercept a patched routine, you must not do any processing *after* the existing patch, and you must be sure to preserve the registers and the stack (or the system won't work properly).

Assembly-language note: You can tell whether a routine is patched by comparing its address to the global variable ROMBase; if the address is less than ROMBase, the routine is patched.

In addition, you can use GetTrapAddress to save time in critical sections of your program by calling an Operating System or Toolbox routine directly, avoiding the overhead of a normal trap dispatch.

```
FUNCTION GetTrapAddress (trapNum: INTEGER) : LONGINT;
```

Trap macro	_GetTrapAddress
On entry	D0: trapNum (word)
On exit	A0: address of routine

GetTrapAddress returns the address of a routine currently installed in the trap dispatch table under the trap number designated by trapNum. To find out the trap number for a particular routine, see Appendix C (Volume III).

Assembly-language note: When you use this technique to bypass the trap dispatcher, you don't get the extra level of register saving. The routine itself will preserve A2-A6 and D3-D7, but if you want any other registers preserved across the call you have to save and restore them yourself.

```
PROCEDURE SetTrapAddress (trapAddr: LONGINT; trapNum: INTEGER);
```

Trap macro	_SetTrapAddress
On entry	A0: trapAddr (address) D0: trapNum (word)

SetTrapAddress installs in the trap dispatch table a routine whose address is trapAddr; this routine is installed under the trap number designated by trapNum.

Warning: Since the trap dispatch table can address locations within a range of only 64K bytes from the beginning of the system heap, the routine you install should be in the system heap.

Miscellaneous Utilities

```
PROCEDURE Delay (numTicks: LONGINT; VAR finalTicks: LONGINT);
```

Trap macro	_Delay
On entry	A0: numTicks (long word)
On exit	D0: finalTicks (long word)

Delay causes the system to wait for the number of ticks (sixtieths of a second) specified by numTicks, and returns in finalTicks the total number of ticks from system startup to the end of the delay.

> **Warning:** Don't rely on the duration of the delay being exact; it will usually be accurate to within one tick, but may be off by more than that. The Delay procedure enables all interrupts and checks the tick count that's incremented during the vertical retrace interrupt; however, it's possible for this interrupt to be disabled by other interrupts, in which case the duration of the delay will not be exactly what you requested.

> **Assembly-language note:** On exit from this procedure, register D0 contains the value of the global variable Ticks as measured at the end of the delay.

```
PROCEDURE SysBeep (duration: INTEGER);
```

SysBeep causes the system to beep for approximately the number of ticks specified by the duration parameter. The sound decays from loud to soft; after about five seconds it's inaudible. The initial volume of the beep depends on the current speaker volume setting, which the user can adjust with the Control Panel desk accessory. If the speaker volume has been set to 0 (silent), SysBeep instead causes the menu bar to blink once.

> **Assembly-language note:** Unlike all other Operating System Utilities, this procedure is stack-based.

```
PROCEDURE Environs (VAR rom,machine: INTEGER);   [Not in ROM]
```

In the rom parameter, Environs returns the current ROM version number (for a Macintosh XL, the version number of the ROM image installed by MacWorks). In the machine parameter, it returns an indication of which machine is in use, as follows:

```
CONST macXLMachine = 0;   {Macintosh XL}
      macMachine   = 1;   {Macintosh 128K or 512K}
```

> **Assembly-language note:** From assembly language, you can get this information from the word that's at an offset of 8 from the beginning of ROM (which is stored in the global variable ROMBase). The format of this word is $00xx for the Macintosh 128K or 512K and $xxFF for the Macintosh XL, where xx is the ROM version number. (The ROM version number will always be between 1 and $FE.)

```
PROCEDURE Restart;   [Not in ROM]
```

This procedure restarts the system.

Assembly-language note: From assembly language, you can give the following instructions to restart the system:

```
MOVE  ROMBase,A0
JMP   $0A(A0)
```

PROCEDURE SetUpA5;   [Not in ROM]

SetUpA5 saves the current value of register A5 (for restoring later with RestoreA5, described below) and then resets A5 to point to the boundary between the application globals and the application parameters. This procedure is useful only within the interrupt environment, where the state of A5 is unpredictable; for instance, in a completion routine or a VBL task, calling SetUpA5 will ensure that A5 contains the proper value, allowing the routine or task to access the application globals.

Assembly-language note: You can get the boundary between the application globals and the application parameters from the global variable CurrentA5.

PROCEDURE RestoreA5;   [Not in ROM]

Call RestoreA5 at the conclusion of a routine or task that required a call to SetUpA5 (above); it restores register A5 to whatever its value was when SetUpA5 was called.

SUMMARY OF THE OPERATING SYSTEM UTILITIES

Constants

```
CONST { Values returned by Environs procedure }

    macXLMachine  = 0;       {Macintosh XL}
    macMachine    = 1;       {Macintosh 128K or 512K}

    { Result codes }

    clkRdErr      = -85;     {unable to read clock}
    clkWrErr      = -86;     {time written did not verify}
    memFullErr    = -108;    {not enough room in heap zone}
    memWZErr      = -111;    {attempt to operate on a free block}
    nilHandleErr  = -109;    {NIL master pointer}
    noErr         =  0;      {no error}
    prInitErr     = -88;     {validity status is not $A8}
    prWrErr       = -87;     {parameter RAM written did not verify}
    qErr          = -1;      {entry not in specified queue}
```

Data Types

```
TYPE OSType = PACKED ARRAY[1..4] OF CHAR;

    OSErr = INTEGER;

    SysPPtr     = ^SysParmType;
    SysParmType =
      RECORD
          valid:    Byte;      {validity status}
          aTalkA:   Byte;      {AppleTalk node ID hint for modem port}
          aTalkB:   Byte;      {AppleTalk node ID hint for printer port}
          config:   Byte;      {use types for serial ports}
          portA:    INTEGER;   {modem port configuration}
          portB:    INTEGER;   {printer port configuration}
          alarm:    LONGINT;   {alarm setting}
          font:     INTEGER;   {application font number minus 1}
          kbdPrint: INTEGER;   {auto-key settings, printer connection}
          volClik:  INTEGER;   {speaker volume, double-click, caret blink}
          misc:     INTEGER    {mouse scaling, startup disk, menu blink}
      END;

    QHdrPtr  = ^QHdr;
    QHdr     = RECORD
                  qFlags: INTEGER;    {queue flags}
                  qHead:  QElemPtr;   {first queue entry}
                  qTail:  QElemPtr    {last queue entry}
               END;
```

```
QTypes = (dummyType,
          vType,         {vertical retrace queue type}
          ioQType,       {file I/O or driver I/O queue type}
          drvQType,      {drive queue type}
          evType,        {event queue type}
          fsQType);      {volume-control-block queue type}

QElemPtr = ^QElem;
QElem    = RECORD
              CASE QTypes OF
                vType:    (vblQElem: VBLTask);
                ioQType:  (ioQElem:  ParamBlockRec);
                drvQType: (drvQElem: DrvQEl);
                evType:   (evQElem:  EvQEl);
                fsQType:  (vcbQElem: VCB)
              END;

DateTimeRec =
           RECORD
              year:      INTEGER;  {1904 to 2040}
              month:     INTEGER;  {1 to 12 for January to December}
              day:       INTEGER;  {1 to 31}
              hour:      INTEGER;  {0 to 23}
              minute:    INTEGER;  {0 to 59}
              second:    INTEGER;  {0 to 59}
              dayOfWeek: INTEGER   {1 to 7 for Sunday to Saturday}
           END;
```

Routines

Pointer and Handle Manipulation

```
FUNCTION HandToHand  (VAR theHndl: Handle) : OSErr;
FUNCTION PtrToHand   (srcPtr: Ptr; VAR dstHndl: Handle; size: LONGINT) :
                      OSErr;
FUNCTION PtrToXHand  (srcPtr: Ptr; dstHndl: Handle; size: LONGINT) :
                      OSErr;
FUNCTION HandAndHand (aHndl,bHndl: Handle) : OSErr;
FUNCTION PtrAndHand  (pntr: Ptr; hndl: Handle; size: LONGINT) : OSErr;
```

String Comparison

```
FUNCTION  EqualString (aStr,bStr: Str255; caseSens,diacSens: BOOLEAN) :
                       BOOLEAN;
PROCEDURE UprString   (VAR theString: Str255; diacSens: BOOLEAN);
```

Date and Time Operations

```
FUNCTION   ReadDateTime  (VAR secs: LONGINT) : OSErr;
PROCEDURE  GetDateTime   (VAR secs: LONGINT);   [Not in ROM]
FUNCTION   SetDateTime   (secs: LONGINT) : OSErr;
PROCEDURE  Date2Secs     (date: DateTimeRec; VAR secs: LONGINT);
PROCEDURE  Secs2Date     (secs: LONGINT; VAR date: DateTimeRec);
PROCEDURE  GetTime       (VAR date: DateTimeRec);   [Not in ROM]
PROCEDURE  SetTime       (date: DateTimeRec);   [Not in ROM]
```

Parameter RAM Operations

```
FUNCTION   InitUtil :    OSErr;
FUNCTION   GetSysPPtr :  SysPPtr;   [Not in ROM]
FUNCTION   WriteParam :  OSErr;
```

Queue Manipulation

```
PROCEDURE  Enqueue (qEntry: QElemPtr; theQueue: QHdrPtr);
FUNCTION   Dequeue (qEntry: QElemPtr; theQueue: QHdrPtr) : OSErr;
```

Trap Dispatch Table Utilities

```
PROCEDURE  SetTrapAddress (trapAddr: LONGINT; trapNum: INTEGER);
FUNCTION   GetTrapAddress (trapNum: INTEGER) : LONGINT;
```

Miscellaneous Utilities

```
PROCEDURE  Delay       (numTicks: LONGINT; VAR finalTicks: LONGINT);
PROCEDURE  SysBeep     (duration: INTEGER);
PROCEDURE  Environs    (VAR rom,machine: INTEGER);   [Not in ROM]
PROCEDURE  Restart;      [Not in ROM]
PROCEDURE  SetUpA5;      [Not in ROM]
PROCEDURE  RestoreA5;    [Not in ROM]
```

Default Parameter RAM Values

Parameter	Default value
Validity status	$A8
Node ID hint for modem port	0
Node ID hint for printer port	0
Use types for serial ports	0 (both ports)
Modem port configuration	9600 baud, 8 data bits, 2 stop bits, no parity

Parameter	Default value
Printer port configuration	Same as for modem port
Alarm setting	0 (midnight, January 1, 1904)
Application font number minus 1	2 (Geneva)
Auto-key threshold	6 (24 ticks)
Auto-key rate	3 (6 ticks)
Printer connection	0 (printer port)
Speaker volume	3 (medium)
Double-click time	8 (32 ticks)
Caret-blink time	8 (32 ticks)
Mouse scaling	1 (on)
Preferred system startup disk	0 (internal drive)
Menu blink	3

Assembly-Language Information

Constants

```
; Result codes

clkRdErr        .EQU    -85     ;unable to read clock
clkWrErr        .EQU    -86     ;time written did not verify
memFullErr      .EQU    -108    ;not enough room in heap zone
memWZErr        .EQU    -111    ;attempt to operate on a free block
nilHandleErr    .EQU    -109    ;NIL master pointer
noErr           .EQU     0      ;no error
prInitErr       .EQU    -88     ;validity status is not $A8
prWrErr         .EQU    -87     ;parameter RAM written did not verify
qErr            .EQU    -1      ;entry not in specified queue

; Queue types

vType           .EQU     1      ;vertical retrace queue type
ioQType         .EQU     2      ;file I/O or driver I/O queue type
drvQType        .EQU     3      ;drive queue type
evType          .EQU     4      ;event queue type
fsQType         .EQU     5      ;volume-control-block queue type
```

Queue Data Structure

qFlags	Queue flags (word)
qHead	Pointer to first queue entry
qTail	Pointer to last queue entry

Date/Time Record Data Structure

dtYear	1904 to 2040 (word)
dtMonth	1 to 12 for January to December (word)
dtDay	1 to 31 (word)
dtHour	0 to 23 (word)
dtMinute	0 to 59 (word)
dtSecond	0 to 59 (word)
dtDayOfWeek	1 to 7 for Sunday to Saturday (word)

Routines

Trap macro	On entry	On exit
_HandToHand	A0: theHndl (handle)	A0: theHndl (handle)
		D0: result code(word)
_PtrToHand	A0: srcPtr (ptr)	A0: dstHndl (handle)
	D0: size (long)	D0: result code (word)
_PtrToXHand	A0: srcPtr (ptr)	A0: dstHndl (handle)
	A1: dstHndl (handle)	D0: result code (word)
	D0: size (long)	
_HandAndHand	A0: aHndl (handle)	A0: bHndl (handle)
	A1: bHndl (handle)	D0: result code (word)
_PtrAndHand	A0: pntr (ptr)	A0: hndl (handle)
	A1: hndl (handle)	D0: result code (word)
	D0: size (long)	
_CmpString	_CmpString ,MARKS sets bit 9, for diacSens=FALSE	
	_CmpString ,CASE sets bit 10, for caseSens=TRUE	
	_CmpString ,MARKS,CASE sets bits 9 and 10	
	A0: ptr to first string	D0: 0 if equal, 1 if
	A1: ptr to second string	not equal (long)
	D0: high word: length of	
	first string	
	low word: length of	
	second string	
_UprString	_UprString ,MARKS sets bit 9, for diacSens=FALSE	
	A0: ptr to string	A0: ptr to string
	D0: length of string (word)	
_ReadDateTime	A0: ptr to long word secs	A0: ptr to long word secs
		D0: result code (word)
_SetDateTime	D0: secs (long)	D0: result code (word)
_Date2Secs	A0: ptr to date/time record	D0: secs (long)
_Secs2Date	D0: secs (long)	A0: ptr to date/time record
_InitUtil		D0: result code (word)
_WriteParam	A0: SysParam (ptr)	D0: result code (word)
	D0: MinusOne (long)	

Trap macro	On entry	On exit
_Enqueue	A0: qEntry (ptr) A1: theQueue (ptr)	A1: theQueue (ptr)
_Dequeue	A0: qEntry (ptr) A1: theQueue (ptr)	A1: theQueue (ptr) D0: result code (word)
_GetTrapAddress	D0: trapNum (word)	A0: address of routine
_SetTrapAddress	A0: trapAddr (address) D0: trapNum (word)	
_Delay	A0: numTicks (long)	D0: finalTicks (long)
_SysBeep	stack: duration (word)	

Variables

SysParam	Low-memory copy of parameter RAM (20 bytes)
SPValid	Validity status (byte)
SPATalkA	AppleTalk node ID hint for modem port (byte)
SPATalkB	AppleTalk node ID hint for printer port (byte)
SPConfig	Use types for serial ports (byte)
SPPortA	Modem port configuration (word)
SPPortB	Printer port configuration (word)
SPAlarm	Alarm setting (long)
SPFont	Application font number minus 1 (word)
SPKbd	Auto-key threshold and rate (byte)
SPPrint	Printer connection (byte)
SPVolCtl	Speaker volume (byte)
SPClikCaret	Double-click and caret-blink times (byte)
SPMisc2	Mouse scaling, system startup disk, menu blink (byte)
CrsrThresh	Mouse-scaling threshold (word)
Time	Seconds since midnight, January 1, 1904 (long)

14 THE DISK INITIALIZATION PACKAGE

14 Disk Initialization

ABOUT THIS CHAPTER

This chapter describes the Disk Initialization Package, which provides routines for initializing disks to be accessed with the File Manager and Disk Driver. A single routine lets you easily present the standard user interface for initializing and naming a disk; the Standard File Package calls this routine when the user inserts an uninitialized disk. You can also use the Disk Initialization Package to perform each of the three steps of initializing a disk separately if desired.

You should already be familiar with:

- the basic concepts and structures behind QuickDraw, particularly points
- the Toolbox Event Manager
- the File Manager
- packages in general, as discussed in chapter 17 of Volume I

USING THE DISK INITIALIZATION PACKAGE

The Disk Initialization Package and the resources it uses are automatically read into memory from the system resource file when one of the routines in the package is called. Together, the package and its resources occupy about 2.5K bytes. If the disk containing the system resource file isn't currently in a Macintosh disk drive, the user will be asked to switch disks and so may have to remove the one to be initialized. To avoid this, you can use the DILoad procedure, which explicitly reads the necessary resources into memory and makes them unpurgeable. You would need to call DILoad before explicitly ejecting the system disk or before any situations where it may be switched with another disk (except for situations handled by the Standard File Package, which calls DILoad itself).

> **Note:** The resources used by the Disk Initialization Package consist of a single dialog and its associated items, even though the package may present what seem to be a number of different dialogs. A special technique is used to allow the single dialog to contain all possible dialog items with only some of them visible at one time.

When you no longer need to have the Disk Initialization Package in memory, call DIUnload. The Standard File Package calls DIUnload before returning.

When a disk-inserted event occurs, the system attempts to mount the volume (by calling the File Manager function MountVol) and returns MountVol's result code in the high-order word of the event message. In response to such an event, your application can examine the result code in the event message and call DIBadMount if an error occurred (that is, if the volume could not be mounted). If the error is one that can be corrected by initializing the disk, DIBadMount presents the standard user interface for initializing and naming the disk, and then mounts the volume itself. For other errors, it justs ejects the disk; these errors are rare, and may reflect a problem in your program.

> **Note:** Disk-inserted events during standard file saving and opening are handled by the Standard File Package. You'll call DIBadMount only in other, less common situations (for

example, if your program explicitly ejects disks, or if you want to respond to the user's inserting an uninitialized disk when not expected).

Disk initialization consists of three steps, each of which can be performed separately by the functions DIFormat, DIVerify, and DIZero. Normally you won't call these in a standard application, but they may be useful in special utility programs that have a nonstandard interface.

DISK INITIALIZATION PACKAGE ROUTINES

Assembly-language note: The trap macro for the Disk Initialization Package is _Pack2. The routine selectors are as follows:

```
diBadMount  .EQU   0
diLoad      .EQU   2
diUnload    .EQU   4
diFormat    .EQU   6
diVerify    .EQU   8
diZero      .EQU   10
```

```
PROCEDURE DILoad;
```

DILoad reads the Disk Initialization Package, and its associated dialog and dialog items, from the system resource file into memory and makes them unpurgeable.

Note: DIFormat, DIVerify, and DIZero don't need the dialog, so if you use only these routines you can call the Resource Manager function GetResource to read just the package resource into memory (and the Memory Manager procedure HNoPurge to make it unpurgeable).

```
PROCEDURE DIUnload;
```

DIUnload makes the Disk Initialization Package (and its associated dialog and dialog items) purgeable.

```
FUNCTION DIBadMount (where: Point; evtMessage: LONGINT) :
          INTEGER;
```

Call DIBadMount when a disk-inserted event occurs if the result code in the high-order word of the associated event message indicates an error (that is, the result code is other than noErr). Given the event message in evtMessage, DIBadMount evaluates the result code and either ejects the disk or lets the user initialize and name it. The low-order word of the event message contains the drive number. The where parameter specifies the location (in global coordinates) of the top left corner of the dialog box displayed by DIBadMount.

If the result code passed is extFSErr, memFullErr, nsDrvErr, paramErr, or volOnLinErr, DIBadMount simply ejects the disk from the drive and returns the result code. If the result code ioErr, badMDBErr, or noMacDskErr is passed, the error can be corrected by initializing the disk; DIBadMount displays a dialog box that describes the problem and asks whether the user wants to initialize the disk. For the result code ioErr, the dialog box shown in Figure 1 is displayed. (This happens if the disk is brand new.) For badMDBErr and noMacDskErr, DIBadMount displays a similar dialog box in which the description of the problem is "This disk is damaged" and "This is not a Macintosh disk", respectively.

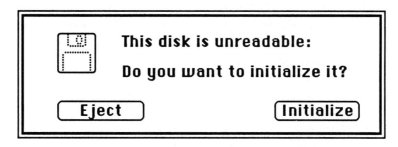

Figure 1. Disk Initialization Dialog for IOErr

Note: Before presenting the disk initialization dialog, DIBadMount checks whether the drive contains an already mounted volume; if so, it ejects the disk and returns 2 as its result. This will happen rarely and may reflect an error in your program (for example, you forgot to call DILoad and the user had to switch to the disk containing the system resource file).

If the user responds to the disk initialization dialog by clicking the Eject button, DIBadMount ejects the disk and returns 1 as its result. If the Initialize button is clicked, a box displaying the message "Initializing disk..." appears, and DIBadMount attempts to initialize the disk. If initialization fails, the disk is ejected and the user is informed as shown in Figure 2; after the user clicks OK, DIBadMount returns a negative result code ranging from firstDskErr to lastDskErr, indicating that a low-level disk error occurred.

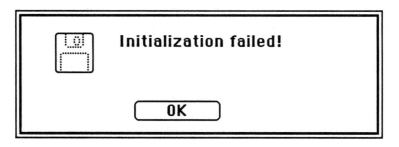

Figure 2. Initialization Failure Dialog

If the disk is successfully initialized, the dialog box in Figure 3 appears. After the user names the disk and clicks OK, DIBadMount mounts the volume by calling the File Manager function MountVol and returns MountVol's result code (noErr if no error occurs).

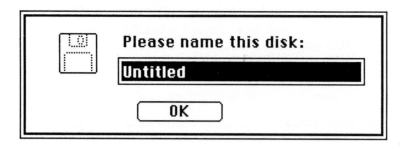

Figure 3. Dialog for Naming a Disk

Result codes   noErr   No error
                 extFSErr   External file system
                 memFullErr   Not enough room in heap zone
                 nsDrvErr   No such drive
                 paramErr   Bad drive number
                 volOnLinErr   Volume already on-line
                 firstDskErr   Low-level disk error
                 through lastDskErr

Other results   1   User clicked Eject
                 2   Mounted volume in drive


```
FUNCTION DIFormat (drvNum: INTEGER) : OSErr;
```

DIFormat formats the disk in the drive specified by the given drive number and returns a result code indicating whether the formatting was completed successfully or failed. Formatting a disk consists of writing special information onto it so that the Disk Driver can read from and write to the disk.

Result codes   noErr   No error
                 firstDskErr   Low-level disk error
                 through lastDskErr


```
FUNCTION DIVerify (drvNum: INTEGER) : OSErr;
```

DIVerify verifies the format of the disk in the drive specified by the given drive number; it reads each bit from the disk and returns a result code indicating whether all bits were read successfully or not. DIVerify doesn't affect the contents of the disk itself.

Result codes   noErr   No error
                 firstDskErr   Low-level disk error
                 through lastDskErr

```
FUNCTION DIZero (drvNum: INTEGER; volName: Str255) : OSErr;
```

On the unmounted volume in the drive specified by the given drive number, DIZero writes the volume information, a block map, and a file directory as for a volume with no files; the volName parameter specifies the volume name to be included in the volume information. This is the last step in initialization (after formatting and verifying) and makes any files that are already on the volume permanently inaccessible. If the operation fails, DIZero returns a result code indicating that a low-level disk error occurred; otherwise, it mounts the volume by calling the File Manager function MountVol and returns MountVol's result code (noErr if no error occurs).

Result codes		
	noErr	No error
	badMDBErr	Bad master directory block
	extFSErr	External file system
	ioErr	I/O error
	memFullErr	Not enough room in heap zone
	noMacDskErr	Not a Macintosh disk
	nsDrvErr	No such drive
	paramErr	Bad drive number
	volOnLinErr	Volume already on-line
	firstDskErr	Low-level disk error
	through lastDskErr	

14 Disk Initialization

SUMMARY OF THE DISK INITIALIZATION PACKAGE

Routines

```
PROCEDURE DILoad;
PROCEDURE DIUnload;
FUNCTION  DIBadMount (where: Point; evtMessage: LONGINT) : INTEGER;
FUNCTION  DIFormat   (drvNum: INTEGER) : OSErr;
FUNCTION  DIVerify   (drvNum: INTEGER) : OSErr;
FUNCTION  DIZero     (drvNum: INTEGER; volName: Str255) : OSErr;
```

Result Codes

Name	Value	Meaning
badMDBErr	−60	Bad master directory block
extFSErr	−58	External file system
firstDskErr	−84	First of the range of low-level disk errors
ioErr	−36	I/O error
lastDskErr	−64	Last of the range of low-level disk errors
memFullErr	−108	Not enough room in heap zone
noErr	0	No error
noMacDskErr	−57	Not a Macintosh disk
nsDrvErr	−56	No such drive
paramErr	−50	Bad drive number
volOnLinErr	−55	Volume already on-line

Assembly-Language Information

Constants

```
; Routine selectors

diBadMount    .EQU    0
diLoad        .EQU    2
diUnload      .EQU    4
diFormat      .EQU    6
diVerify      .EQU    8
diZero        .EQU    10
```

Trap Macro Name

_Pack2

15 THE FLOATING-POINT ARITHMETIC AND TRANSCENDENTAL FUNCTIONS PACKAGES

15 Floating Point

ABOUT THIS CHAPTER

This chapter discusses the Floating-Point Arithmetic Package and the Transcendental Functions Package, which provide facilities for extended-precision floating-point arithmetic and advanced numerical applications programming. These two packages support the Standard Apple Numeric Environment (SANE), which is designed in strict accordance with IEEE Standard 754 for Binary Floating-Point Arithmetic.

You should already be familiar with packages in general, as discussed in chapter 17 of Volume I.

ABOUT THE PACKAGES

Pascal programmers will rarely, if ever, need to call the Floating-Point Arithmetic or Transcendental Functions packages explicitly. These facilities are built into post-3.0 versions of Lisa Pascal (as well as most Macintosh high-level languages); that is, the compiler recognizes SANE data types, and automatically calls the packages to perform the standard arithmetic operations (+, -, *, /) as well as data type conversion. Mathematical functions that aren't built in are accessible through a run-time library—see your language manual for details.

If you're using assembly language or a language without built-in support for SANE, you'll need to be familiar with the *Apple Numerics Manual*. This is the standard reference guide to SANE, and describes in detail how to call the Floating-Point Arithmetic and Transcendental Functions routines from assembly language. Some general information about the packages is given below.

THE FLOATING-POINT ARITHMETIC PACKAGE

The Floating-Point Arithmetic Package contains routines for performing the following operations:

Arithmetic and Auxiliary Routines

Add
Subtract
Multiply
Divide
Square Root
Round to Integral Value
Truncate to Integral Value
Remainder
Binary Log
Binary Scale
Negate
Absolute Value
Copy Sign
Next-After

Converting Between Data Types
Binary to Binary
Binary to Decimal Record (see note below)
Decimal Record to Binary

Comparing and Classifying
Compare
Compare, Signaling Invalid if Unordered
Classify

Controlling the Floating-Point Environment
Get Environment
Set Environment
Test Exception
Set Exception
Procedure Entry Protocol
Procedure Exit Protocol

Halt Control
Set Halt Vector
Get Halt Vector

Note: Don't confuse the floating-point binary-decimal conversions with the integer routines provided by the Binary-Decimal Conversion Package.

The following data types are provided:

- Single (32-bit floating-point format)

- Double (64-bit floating-point format)

- Comp (64-bit integer format for accounting-type applications)

- Extended (80-bit floating-point format)

The Floating-Point Arithmetic Package is automatically read into memory from the system resource file when one of its routines is called. It occupies about 4.4K bytes.

Assembly-language note: The macros for calling the Floating-Point routines push a two-byte opword onto the stack and then invoke _FP68K (same as _Pack4). These macros are fully documented in the *Apple Numerics Manual*.

The package uses at most 200 bytes of stack space. It preserves all MC68000 registers across invocations (except that the remainder operation modifies D0), but modifies the MC68000 CCR flags.

THE TRANSCENDENTAL FUNCTIONS PACKAGE

The Transcendental Functions Package contains the following mathematical functions:

Logarithmic Functions

Base-e logarithm	ln(x)
Base-2 logarithm	log(x) base 2
Base-e logarithm of 1 plus argument	ln(1+x)
Base-2 logarithm of 1 plus argument	log(1+x) base 2

Exponential Functions

Base-e exponential	e^x
Base-2 exponential	2^x
Base-e exponential minus 1	(e^x)–1
Base-2 exponential minus 1	(2^x)–1
Integer exponential	x^i
General exponential	x^y

Financial Functions

Compound Interest	(1+x)^y
Annuity Factor	(1–(1+x)^–y)/y

Trigonometric Functions

Sine
Cosine
Tangent
Arctangent

Random Number Generator

Note: The functions in this package are also called elementary functions.

The Transcendental Functions Package is automatically read into memory when one of its routines is called. It in turn calls the Floating-Point Arithmetic Package to perform the basic arithmetic. Together they occupy about 8.5K bytes.

Assembly-language note: The macros for calling the transcendental functions push a two-byte opword onto the stack and then invoke _Elems68K (same as _Pack5). These macros are fully documented in the *Apple Numerics Manual*.

The package uses at most 200 bytes of stack space. It preserves all MC68000 registers across invocations, but modifies the CCR flags.

Note: Early versions of the Transcendental Functions Package lock themselves when read into memory and remain locked unless explicitly unlocked. Apple high-level languages that access the package through a SANE library avoid this problem by preserving the state of the lock bit across calls to the package. However, pre-3.1 versions of Lisa Pascal

15 Floating Point

require that you explicitly unlock the package with the Memory Manager function
HUnlock, as follows:

```
HUnlock(GetResource('PACK',5))
```

Assembly-language note: In assembly language, you can unlock the package as
follows:

```
        CLR.L           -(SP)           ;slot for handle
        MOVE.L          #'PACK',-(SP)   ;resource type
        MOVE.W          #5,-(SP)        ;resource ID
        _GetResource
        MOVE.L          (SP)+,A0        ;store handle in A0
        _HUnlock
```

INDEX

Index

Index

R

Index